Transactions
of the
American Philosophical Society
Held at Philadelphia
For Promoting Useful Knowledge
Vol. 88, Pt. 5

ARMENIAN MERCHANTS

of the

SEVENTEENTH AND EARLY EIGHTEENTH CENTURIES:

ENGLISH EAST INDIA COMPANY SOURCES

EDITED BY

Vahé Baladouni
University of New Orleans

and

Margaret Makepeace
formerly Head of Reader Services
at the India Office Library and Records

American Philosophical Society
Independence Square • Philadelphia
1998

Documents in Crown copyright are published by permission of Her Majesty's Stationery Office.

Cover: Seventeenth-century Armenian merchant. (Illustration by Jan Grevenbroch, Civico Museo Correr, Venice, Italy.

Library of Congress Cataloging-in-Publication Data

Armenian merchants of the seventeenth and early eighteenth centuries :
  English East India Company sources / edited by Vahé Baladouni and
  Margaret Makepeace.
       p.   cm. -- (Transactions of the American Philosophical Society
  ; v. 88, pt. 5)
    A collection of 270 documents extracted from the archive of the
  East India Company.
    Includes bibliographical references and index.
    ISBN 0-87169-885-4 (paperbound)
    1. India--Commerce--History--Sources. 2. Merchants, Foreign-
  -India--History--Sources. 3. Armenians--Economic conditions-
  -Sources. 4. East India Company--History--Sources.   I. Baladouni,
  Vahé, 1925-   . II. Makepeace, Margaret. III. East India Company.
  IV. Series.
  HF3785.A76 1998
  382'.0954--dc21   98-43975
                                                             CIP

To my wife, Billie,
daughter, Janig, and son, Vahan
and to my parents, Haigouhie and Souren
for their love.

Vahé Baladouni

To John, Philip, and Frances
and to my parents, Jean and George

Margaret Makepeace

ABOUT THE VOLUME

As an organic whole, the present collection of documents—gathered together from a variety of original sources—tells a fascinating story about the trade relationship between the English East India Company and the powerful Armenian merchant community of New Julfa that lasted over one hundred years (17th and early 18th centuries). Multifarious and complex, this relationship revolved around the Company's continuous efforts to break into the Armenian-held silk and cloth markets. Perhaps more than any other single event, this trade relationship epitomizes the economic climate of the period, an age of competitive partnership.

With the publication of this volume, Professor Baladouni and Mrs. Makepeace place for the first time at the disposal of historians a substantive body of documents that tell how this intricate Anglo-Armenian trade relationship started and evolved. Beyond that, these documents also reveal to the astute historian the human experiences that lie behind the participants' actions. The extensive topical indexes provided in the volume will be of great assistance to researchers.

Finally, in the Introduction, Professor Baladouni addresses the question "What was the key to the Armenian merchants' fabulous success during the pre-modern period?" and submits a hypothesis for consideration. He proposes that their "fabulous success" may be attributed to the rare atmosphere of trust that prevailed among the Armenian merchant community which, in turn, led to two significant benefits: (1) organizational cost savings; and (2) organizational innovations.

CONTENTS

ACKNOWLEDGMENTS

There are a number of persons and institutions who deserve special recognition and thanks for their help with this project.

In the first instance, we are indebted to the American Philosophical Society for awarding two grants to Dr. Vahé Baladouni thereby enabling him to initiate and pursue this project. Our greatest debt, however, is to Anthony Farrington, deputy director of the Oriental and India Office Collections, and his staff, who greatly facilitated the compilation of the documents.

We also thank the following people for their contribution at various points along the way: Dr. John R. Perry, professor of Persian language and civilization at the University of Chicago; Dr. Levon Avdoyan, Armenian and Georgian area specialist at the Library of Congress; Aram Arkun, historian and assistant director of the Krikor and Clara Zohrab Information Center of the Diocese of the Armenian Church of America; and Dr. Krikor Maksoudian, specialist in Armenian medieval history.

Special thanks to Dr. Janet F. Speyrer, director of the Division of Business and Economic Research at the University of New Orleans, for making possible the production of the text. In this regard, we express our gratitude to Jeannie H. Shapley who word-processed many versions of this text with a great deal of expertise, patience and conscientiousness. We also owe a debt of gratitude to Dr. Wayne Patterson, professor of computer science, for his technical assistance.

Finally, we express our thanks to the anonymous reviewers for their valuable suggestions; to John Gery, professor of English at the University of New Orleans, for giving the Introduction of the volume a critical reading; and to Carole LeFaivre-Rochester, Editor at the American Philosophical Society, for her constant encouragement and assistance through all phases of the publication.

PREFACE

Publication of documents from the English East India Company's archive has a long but somewhat unsatisfactory history. Beginning in 1862, summaries drawn from the two series *Court Minutes* and *Original Correspondence*, were included in the Public Record Office's *Calendar of State Papers, Colonial Series, East Indies ...1513-1634* (ed W. Noel Sainsbury, 5 vols, London 1862-92). Fired by imperial pride, the India Office began two series of its own in the mid-1890s: modernized transcripts of the *Original Correspondence* series from 1602 to 1617 (ed Frederick Charles Danvers & William Foster, 5 vols, London, 1896-1902), continued in transcript and then in summary form as *The English Factories in India 1618-1684* (ed William Foster & Charles Fawcett, 17 vols, London 1906-36 & 1952-55); and summary calendars of the *Court Minutes etc of the East India Company 1635-1679* (ed Ethel Bruce Sainsbury, 11 vols, London, 1907-38).

These enterprises became old-fashioned long before they each ground to a halt. The sheer scale of the archive proved too much—the *Court Minutes* series for instance covered only 35 volumes out of a total of 236—increasing selection in the *English Factories* series came to concentrate upon those territories which formed the British Raj whereas the East India Company's interests were Asia-wide, a decent critical apparatus was present only in the later publications, and the whole emphasis was Eurocentric.

Beginning in the 1960s, after the appointment of the first professional archivists, work on the Company's archive concentrated upon gaining intellectual control by such basic housekeeping tasks as imposing an overall referencing system on the collection. Meanwhile the perceived needs of historians were changing, with greater emphasis on setting European activities in their Asian context, on economic data (almost invariably omitted from the earlier publications), and on using European documentation as a primary source for *Asian* history. Current publications are based on a geographical area or a subject theme and range throughout the archive for relevant material, which is presented in its original form, properly sourced and with full annotation. A welcome part of this development is a growing number of partnerships between archivists and historians of Asia, each bringing their particular strengths to the editorial task.

The present book by Professor Baladouni and my former colleague Mrs Makepeace is one such fruitful collaboration. Taking a very special group of Asian merchants, the Armenians of New Julfa, they have revealed in some two hundred and seventy extracts from the Company's archive a complex and long-lasting relationship, previously 'known' but almost undocumented. Their work will prove an invaluable source for historians of inter-Asian trade.

Anthony Farrington
Deputy-Director
India Office Collections

OBSERVATIONS ON ARMENIAN MERCHANTS

ARMENIANS, nations who inhabit Armenia. But that name is also given to those who were transported into several parts of Persia by Shah Abas; and more particularly to that celebrated colony of Armenians who dwell at Zulfa [New Julfa], one of the suburbs of Ispahan [Isfahan].

The Armenians are civil and polite, and have a great deal of good sense and honesty: they apply themselves very much to trade, which they make their chief business. . . . They are not only masters of the whole trade of the Levant, but have also a great share in that of the most considerable towns in Europe; for it is very common to meet with some Armenians at Leghorn, at Venice, in England, and in Holland; whilst on the other side they travel into the dominions of the Grand Mogul, Siam, Java, the Philippine islands, and over all the east. . . .

> Malachy Postlethwayt, *The Universal Dictionary of Trade and Commerce*, London, 1751. [Translated from the French entry in the *Dictionnaire Universel de Commerce* by Jacques Savary des Bruslons (1657-1716) and published posthumously in Paris, 1730.]

They [the Armenian traders] were a group of highly skilled arbitrage dealers who were forced through historical circumstances to develop very flexible and geographically mobile forms of commerce. They were prepared to deal in whichever commodity that offered the prospect of making a profit, and their uncertain political and national status made it indifferent whether they resided in Isfahan, Madras, Surat, or Hugli. An ability to measure the risks of overland trade and a readiness to vary the size of commercial transactions were the special services which the Armenians brought to the trading world of the Middle East, India, and even Europe. . . . [T]here were. . .among them merchants whose wealth and position would have compared favourably with the most successful merchant of London and Amsterdam.

> K.N. Chaudhuri, *The Trading World of Asia and the English East India Company, 1660-1760*, Cambridge, 1978, pp. 137-138.

INTRODUCTION

Vahé Baladouni

G rowing interest in the history of Armenian trade and commerce during the early modern period, particularly the seventeenth and early eighteenth centuries, has prompted Margaret Makepeace and me to compile documents from the archive of the English East India Company bearing on the subject. Ranging in length from a one-sentence memorandum to an elaborate, eight-page letter, these documents provide a rich repository of information waiting to be mined by historians.

I first entertained the idea of embarking upon this task as early as the summer of 1980. Over the next few years I collected and transcribed a good number of documents. Then in 1987, by a happy turn of events, Margaret Makepeace, then Head of Reader Services at the India Office Library and Records, expressed an interest in collaborating on the project. From that time, the number of documents grew steadily to its present size.

In a work of this magnitude and scope, no claim can be made for completeness. The sheer abundance of archival material has made it necessary that we exclude from the present collection a large number of the lesser documents. It must also be noted that other documents may well remain inaccessible to us, for one reason or another.

To put this volume in its proper contextual perspective, I provide here both an historical background and a survey of historiographic sources and literature. I then discuss briefly the general theme of the documents and conclude with some comments as well as a hypothesis for consideration.

Historical Background

Occupying an area of approximately two hundred thirty-eight thousand square miles in the eastern part of Asia Minor, historical Armenia[1] was

---

[1] Robert H. Hewsen, "The Geography of Armenia," in Richard G. Hovannisian (ed.), *The Armenian People*, 2 vols. (New York, 1997), vol. I, p. 5. For a general survey of Armenian history, see David Marshall Lang, *Armenia: Cradle of Civilization* (London, 1980); *Idem, The Armenians: A People in Exile* (London, 1988); George A. Bournoutian, *A History of the Armenian People*, 2 vols. (Costa Mesa, CA, 1994). For a general bibliography of works relating to Armenia, see A. Salmaslian, *Bibliographie de l'Arménie* (Erevan, 1969); Vrej Nerses Nersessian, *Armenia* (Oxford, 1993). This publication is the first selective multi-disciplinary bibliography on Armenia in a major European language (English). It contains 879 entries covering all aspects of Armenian history and culture. The entries, with emphasis on recently published material, have been selected from the literature in English, French, German and Armenian. *Idem, An Index of Articles on Armenian Studies in Western Journals* (London, 1976).

strategically located for overland trade between Europe and Asia. This characteristic of the Armenian homeland was, no doubt, one of the major reasons why, from the earliest times to the close of the early modern period, international trade had assumed a central place in the economic life of the Armenian people. Studies of ancient, medieval, and early modern trade[2] testify to the thriving commercial relations that Armenians have enjoyed with many world civilizations.

During the early modern period (16th to 18th centuries) trade originating in Europe reached the ports of the Mediterranean and Black seas, moved eastward through or near Armenia and extended to the southern border of the Caspian Sea. From this juncture, one route continued in a northeasterly direction through Central Asia to China, while another took a southeasterly course to reach the Indian sub-continent and Southeast Asia. Yet another route ran from the Caspian region northward to Russia. However, Armenian merchants were active not only on the transit route that cut across Armenia but also on the many other routes that traversed the Eurasian continent. In addition to the overland trade, Armenian merchants were also engaged in maritime trade which extended from the east coast of Africa through the Indian Ocean to the Philippine Islands in the Pacific.[3]

Venturing abroad and establishing trade communities in key cities[4] in

---

[2] H.A. Manandian, *The Trade and Cities of Armenia in Relation to Ancient World Trade*, trans. N.G. Garsoian (Lisbon, 1965). This text examines the international trade routes crossing Armenia at various periods of history (6th c. B.C. to 15th c. A.D.) and includes fifteen maps. V.H. P'ap'azyan, *Hayastani arevtrakan ughineroe mijazgayin arevtri olortum, XVI-XVII darerum* (Erevan, 1990). Written in Armenian, the text includes three maps, some Persian documents, and a six-page summary of the text in Russian. Jack Lewis Vartoogian, "The Image of Armenia in European Travel Accounts of the Seventeenth Century," unpublished Ph.D. dissertation, Columbia University, 1974. This text contains the accounts of thirty-two travelers to Armenia between 1581 and 1725 and the accounts of an additional thirty-eight travelers to New Julfa in Persia. All seventy travelers are identified by nationality (French, British, German, Italian, Portuguese, Dutch, Spanish, Flemish, Polish, Swedish) and profession (missionaries, diplomats, merchants, tourists, scientists-scholars). The routes taken by them through Armenia are also given.

[3] The Armenian merchants moved large quantities of goods on foreign as well as Armenian-owned ships. One well-known Armenian shipowner was Khwaja Minas. See Ronald Ferrier, "Trade from the Mid-14th Century to the End of the Safavid Period," in Peter Jackson and Laurence Lockhart (eds.), *The Cambridge History of Iran* (Cambridge, 1986), Vol. 6, p. 469. Serafin D. Quiason, *English Country Trade with the Philippines, 1644-1765* (Quezon City, 1966), chapters 3 and 4. P.J. Marshall, *East Indian Fortunes* (Oxford, 1976), chapters 3 and 4. Sinnappah Arasaratnam, *Merchants, Companies and Commerce on the Coromandel Coast, 1650-1740* (Delhi, 1986), pp. 158, 169, 200, 208, 221, 289.

[4] Fernand Braudel, *Civilization and Capitalism: 15th-18th Century*, trans. Siân Reynolds (New York, 1984), Vol. 2, pp. 122-124, 154-159; Vol. 3, p. 55. Kéram Kévonian, "Marchands arméniens au XVIIᵉ siècle: A propos d'un livre arménien publié à Amsterdam en 1699," *Cahiers du monde russe et soviétique*, 16:199-244 (1975). Michel Aghassian and Kéram Kévonian, "Le commerce arménien dans l'Océan Indien aux 17ᵉ et 18ᵉ siècles," in D. Lombard and J. Aubin (eds.), *Marchands et hommes d'affaires asiatiques dans l'Océan Indien et la Mer de Chine XIII-XXᵉ siècles* (Paris, 1988).

Europe and Asia, the Armenian merchants[5] created the infrastructure for a successful long-distance trade. Among other things, the resulting commercial network served as a medium for the regular exchange of business information, the maintenance of trust and credit, and the organization of a system of arbitration and adjudication in business disputes. Together with the merchants of the homeland, these widely dispersed but highly interrelated Armenian trade communities constituted what is known as a "trading diaspora."[6]

* * *

The emergence of the seventeenth-century Armenian trading network or diaspora is intimately bound up with historical events of the preceding century. In the sixteenth century, Armenia had fallen prey to the geopolitical ambitions of two rival states: the Ottoman Empire and Persia. As a result of this rivalry the Armenian homeland was divided between them, the larger part falling to the Ottoman Turks, the smaller part to the Persians. Throughout the century Armenia served as a military borderland between these hostile powers, often turning into a theater of savage wars. The incalculable misery and suffering that these wars brought to the Armenian people are well documented by historians.[7] Tragic as the plight of the Armenians was, the Ottomans allowed them, as well as other minority communities such as Greeks and Jews, to live by their own ethnic laws and administrative arrangements, requiring them only to pay taxes and supply men for the Ottoman army and administration. On their part, the Persians, too, allowed the Armenians to live according to their ethnic traditions.

While the Ottoman and Persian conquests of the Armenian homeland delayed considerably the development of social, economic, and political aspects of Armenian life, it did not greatly disturb Armenian commercial

---

[5] The Civico Museo Correr in Venice holds two illustrations of a 17th-century Armenian merchant by Jan Grevenbroch. Photographic reproductions of the illustrations appear in Edward C. Bursk, Donald T. Clark, and Ralph W. Hidy (eds.), *The World of Business* (New York, 1962), Vol. 1, p. 244.

[6] We follow here the precedent of Abner Cohen, who writes: "The use of the term 'diaspora' in this context has been criticized on the ground that it is applicable only to a specific historical case. This issue is similar to the controversy about the applicability of the term 'caste' to systems of stratification outside India. The term 'network', which has been suggested as a substitute for 'diaspora' has in recent years been used to cover different sociological phenomena and its use in this context is likely to be confusing. I think that the term 'diaspora' can be relatively more easily understood to be referring to 'an ethnic group in dispersal' than the term 'network'." Abner Cohen, "Cultural Strategies in the Organization of Trading Diasporas," in Claude Meillasseaux (ed.), *The Development of Indigenous Trade and Markets in West Africa* (Oxford, 1971), p. 267n. Some scholars refer to "an ethnic group in dispersal" as "transnational group." See *Diaspora: A Journal of Transnational Studies* (Oxford, 1991—).

[7] Vartan Gregorian, "Minorities of Isfahan: The Armenian Community of Isfahan, 1587-1722," *Journal of the Society for Iranian Studies*, 7:652-680 (1974), pp. 658-665.

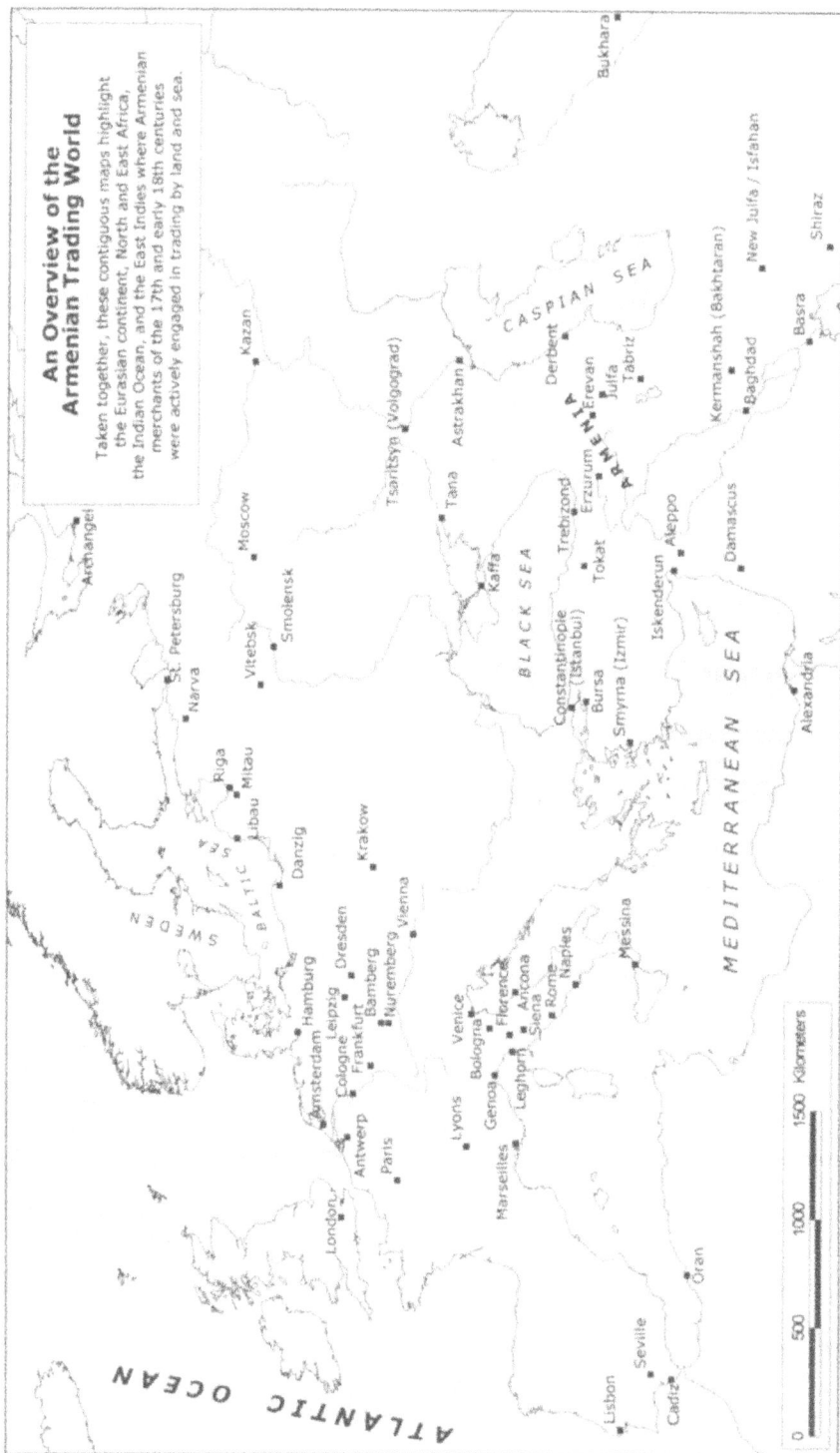

An Overview of the Armenian Trading World

Taken together, these contiguous maps highlight the Eurasian continent, North and East Africa, the Indian Ocean, and the East Indies where Armenian merchants of the 17th and early 18th centuries were actively engaged in trading by land and sea.

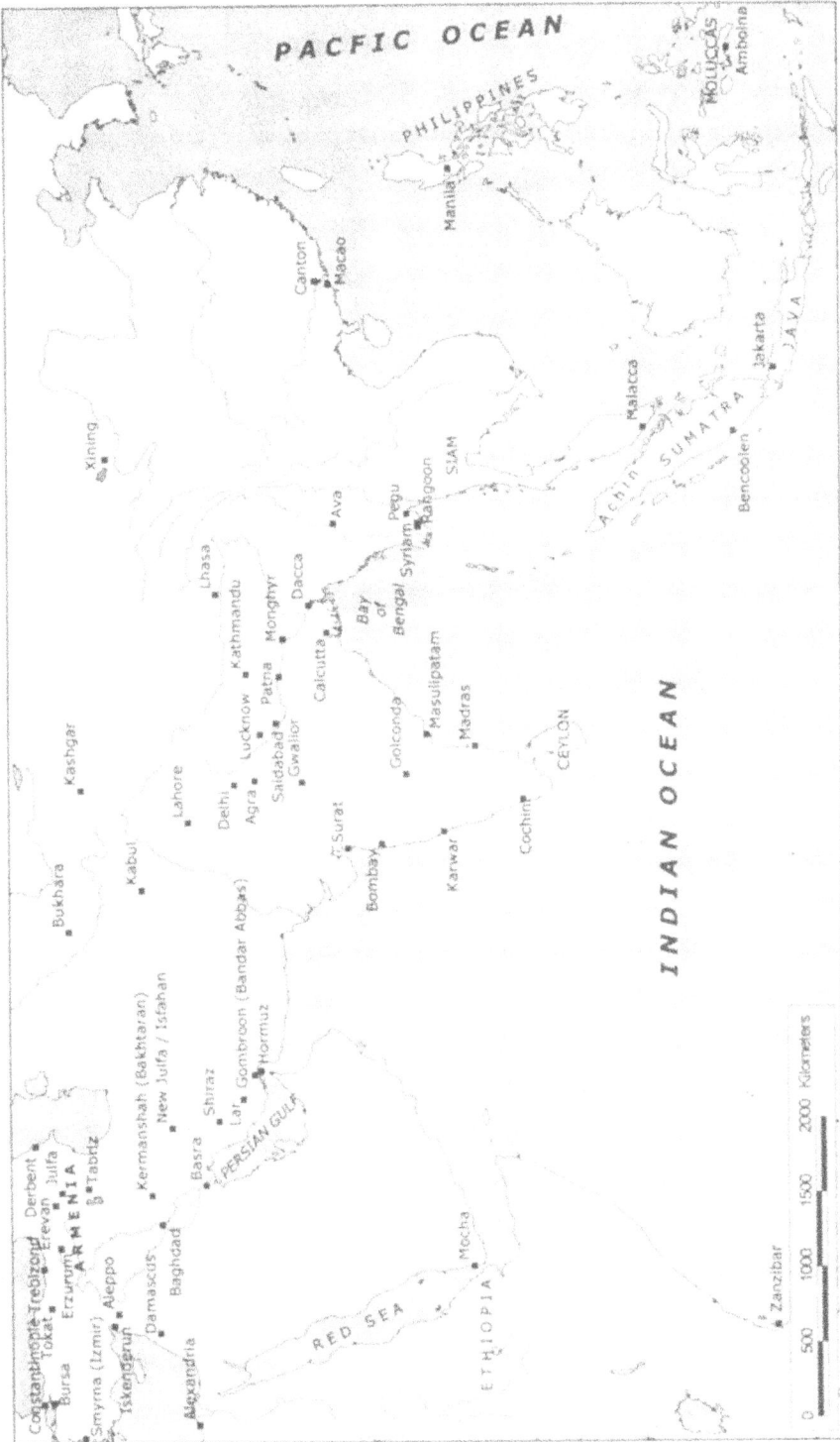

activities.   International trade, which was vigorous in the Black and Mediterranean seas, continued to remain largely in the hands of Armenian merchants. By the second half of the sixteenth century Armenian merchants, particularly those of the city of Julfa on the Araxes River, enjoyed a reputation as brokers and representatives of European commercial firms and interests in the silk and cloth trades.[8]

* * *

Armenian commercial success had not gone unnoticed by Shah Abbas I (ruled 1587-1629) of Persia. With full knowledge of the important role the Armenian merchants could play in the advancement of Persian trade and commerce, the Shah had long wanted to move them from their homeland to his newly established capital of Isfahan. In 1604, violating the 1590 treaty with the Ottoman empire, Shah Abbas invaded the Ottoman domains in Transcaucasia. During this protracted campaign the Shah forcibly moved the Armenian population from Caucasian Armenia to Persia proper, leaving behind scorched cities and villages. The Armenian peasantry was taken primarily to the silk-growing provinces of Ghilan and Mazandaran, while the professional merchants and artisans were settled directly outside the city of Isfahan in a new suburb. This Armenian suburb, which was named after the old home town, New Julfa (in Armenian, *Nor Jugha*), grew to become a self-governing township and the center of world-wide Armenian commercial activities.[9]

With their ready capital and commercial contacts in Asia and Europe, the Armenian merchants of New Julfa were well placed to help Shah Abbas with his economic objective: the transformation of his newly-founded capital city of Isfahan into a major trade center. Armenian entrepreneurial expertise soon helped the Shah to realize his ambition.[10] The Armenian merchants were able to dramatically develop Persia's foreign trade in raw silk, create new markets

---

[8] Gregorian, "Minorities of Isfahan," p. 661.

[9] Gregorian, "Minorities of Isfahan," pp. 665-672. R.W. Ferrier, "The Armenians and the East India Company in Persia in the Seventeenth and Early Eighteenth Centuries," *Economic History Review*, 26:38-62 (1973). John Carswell, "The Armenians and East-West Trade through Persia in the XVIIth Century," in Michel Mollat (ed.), *Sociétés et Compagnies de Commerce en Orient et dans l'Océan Indien* (Paris, 1970), pp. 481-486.

[10] John Fryer, an official of the English East India Company, had discovered in 1677 on a visit to Isfahan that the market there dealt with a more varied selection of English broadcloth than could be found even in Blackwell Hall, a spacious building in London where a weekly market for woollen cloths was held: "For beholding the Sack-cloth *Buzzar*, for so they call English Cloth, I thought it exceeded *Blackwell*-Hall, or an Cloth-Fair in England, being piled in huge Quantities both in their Shops around the *Buzzar*, and Heaps amidst thereof, of all Sorts, Colours, and Conditions . . . ." John Fryer, *A New Account of East India and Persia, being Nine Years' Travels 1672-81*, W. Crooke (ed.), 3 vols (London, 1909-15), Vol. 2, pp. 249-250.

and products, and expand the scope of trade routes.[11] This economic prosperity continued under the succeeding shahs until the invasion of Persia by the Afghans in 1722. The Afghan invasion caused great casualties and losses to the general population as well as to the Armenian community of New Julfa, forcing many of the notable Armenian merchants to emigrate to India, Russia, and various parts of Europe.

* * *

Even as the frontiers of Eurasian overland trade were expanding during the early modern period, a new form of long-distance transportation was gaining momentum. With the fifteenth-century improvements in ship design and navigation, oceanic sailing had now become practical. Northern and western European nations who, unlike the Italian city-states, profited little from the growing Mediterranean trade with the East, began to seek new routes to the Orient. At the turn of the sixteenth century Portugal spearheaded the drive by rounding the Cape of Good Hope and sailing into the waters of the Indian Ocean. In this vast region, specifically in the Persian Gulf, the west coast of India, and the Malay Peninsula and Archipelago, Portugal established a rich commercial empire. A century or so later, it was the turn of the Dutch and the English East India Companies[12] to make inroads into the region and eventually to dominate the eastern trade. Somewhat later, there appeared the French East India Company. Aside from these, there were a number of minor East India Companies, such as the Prussian, Russian, Scottish, Spanish, and Swedish ones operating in the area.[13]

Despite the rich and profitable commerce generated by the European companies in the Indian Ocean, the traditional overland trade, with its wide variety of goods, never lost its importance. On the contrary, alongside the oceanic trade, it continued to thrive well into the eighteenth century. Among the many and varied goods transported overland was the bulk of the highly-prized Persian raw silk. The Armenian merchants of New Julfa, who over the years had consolidated their hold on Persian commerce, carried the raw silk by land to the Levant on the Mediterranean Sea.[14] There they sold it to European

---

[11] Ferrier, "Trade from the Mid-14th Century...," pp. 453-456. Roger Savory, *Iran Under the Safavids* (Cambridge, 1980), pp. 177-202.

[12] English East India Company, formally (1600-1709) Governor and Company of Merchants of London Trading into the East Indies, or (1709-1858) United Company of Merchants of England Trading to the East Indies. Started as a monopolistic trading body, the Company acted as an agent of British imperialism in India from the early 18th century on.

[13] Holden Furber, *Rival Empires of Trade in the Orient, 1600-1800* (Minneapolis, 1976). J.H. Parry, *The Age of Reconnaissance* (New York, 1964), pp. 207-224; *Idem, The Establishment of the European Hegemony, 1415-1715: Trade and Exploration in the Age of the Renaissance* (New York, 1961), pp. 90-104.

[14] "The Armenians had permanent warehouses in Aleppo, and while some did sell to Aleppo merchants (particularly in the last days of Persia trade) the greater Armenian merchants bartered

and English merchants[15] partly for cash and partly in exchange for cloth. It was this silk and cloth trade that both the English and the Dutch East India Companies tried hard, but without success, to divert from the Levant to the Persian Gulf and into their own hands.

* * *

When all other efforts to shift the silk and cloth trade from the Levant to Persia failed, the English East India Company sought Armenian cooperation. On June 22, 1688, the Company negotiated an agreement with a leading Armenian merchant of New Julfa, Khwaja P'anos K'alant'ar who then resided in London. The Agreement[16] extended a variety of privileges to Armenian merchants and Armenians in general living in Persia and India in return for conducting the bulk of their silk and cloth trades with the Company in Isfahan in order "to alter and invert the ancient course of their [the Armenians'] trade to and from Europe."[17] With this agreement, the English East India Company took the unprecedented step of conferring upon the Armenian merchants all of the privileges enjoyed by English merchants:

> . . . That the Armenian nacion [nation] shall now and at all times hereafter have equal share and benefit of all indulgences this Company have or shall at any time hereafter grant to any of their own adventurers or other English merchants whatsoever.[18]

Furthermore, the Armenians were to

> . . . have liberty to live in any of the Company's cities garisons or towns in India, and to buy sell and purchase land or houses, and be capable of all civil offices and preferments in the same manner as if they were Englishmen born; and shall always have the free and undisturbed liberty

---

directly with the English and took cloth back with them to Eerzerum and Persia. Thus the English were not foreign traders using economic power to exploit a poor and backward people; they were tolerated foreigners living in a highly civilised community and dealing with local merchants, as rich, as well-informed, and as sharp as themselves." Ralph Davis, *Aleppo and Devonshire Square, English Traders in the Levant in the Eighteenth Century* (London, 1967).

[15] The English merchants trading in the eastern Mediterranean were members of the Levant Company, formally known as The Governor and Company of Merchants of England trading into the Levant Seas. Unlike the English East India Company which was a *joint-stock* company, the Levant Company was not itself a trading organization. The members of the Levant Company traded individually as independent merchants.

[16] See document 112. The Trade Agreement appearing in this volume is a complete transcription of the archival record. An earlier transcription published in *Revue des études arméniennes*, 7 (n.s.), 1970, omitted the names of many of the goods traded and their stipulated terms of trade.

[17] Ibid.

[18] Ibid.

of the exercise of their own religion.[19]

While the 1688 Agreement generated some business for the Company through private contracts, it never took root. The Armenian merchant community as a whole was not inclined to cooperate with the Company. Nonetheless, some six years later, the English East India Company gave the matter another try by inviting five of the most prominent Armenian merchants to a close trading partnership.[20] The Armenian response to this invitation was at once clear and to the point. It said: "A merchant who has been long used to one sort of trade will not give over to fall into another unless they [sic] can see some extraordinary profit in the new trade."[21] As Chaudhuri correctly observes, "[This] was not merely a blind obedience to customs or traditions that claimed the loyalty of merchants to a trading emporium, but also the certainty that stocks would find a buyer at prices satisfactory to both sides of the bargain."[22] This was indeed the very concern of the Armenian merchants. They said:

> ... as for bringing silk to Ispahan ... that is but wind, for no body will be so mad, when we carry it to Aleppo. We have more ways then one to dispose it; for there are English [the merchants of the Levant Company], French, Venetians and Dutch, and if we can't sell it them for ready money, part money, cloth, cocheneal, amber, coral, or false pearl, then we can carry it to Europe our selves, but if we bring it to Ispahan there is only you to buy it, and if you won't give us a price, then we must let you have it, as you will, and take cloth at what price you will, for you won't let us put it on board your ships for England.[23]

* * *

Despite the determined efforts, the English East India Company never wrested the silk and cloth trades from the powerful Armenian merchants of New Julfa. And only upon hindsight did the Company come to recognize the reason for its failure:

> But some may think it improbable they [the Armenians] should ever depart so much from their own interest, as to advise us how to deprive themselves of the Aleppo cloth trade. To which we reply, its true, that it is not reasonable to expect it, it is against nature and reason to expect that such wise men should further our trade to the ruine of their own,

---

[19] Ibid.

[20] See document 166.

[21] See document 187.

[22] K.N. Chaudhuri, *Trade and Civilization in the Indian Ocean* (Cambridge, 1985), p. 106.

[23] See document 244.

which per adventure, they have been possessed of ever since any cloth
was made in the world, for most certainly they are the most ancient
merchants of the world . . . .[24]

An Historiographic Survey

The twentieth century witnessed a marked change in the historiography
of pre-modern Asia. Before World War I, the history of this period was
narrowly political. It was confined to narratives of European colonization or
empire building that reflected national pride and superiority. After World War
I, the Eurocentric stance gradually gave way to a new and broader vista: the
dynamics of the social and economic phenomena of Asian cultures. This shift
has since helped Western as well as non-Western scholars to understand better
and appreciate the immense variety of Asian cultures and their high degree of
commercial sophistication.

* * *

One of the earliest and most influential scholars who broke away from
the narrow colonial approach to history was, paradoxically, a young Dutch civil
servant, J.C. Van Leur (1908-1942). To this scholar, it was self-evident that
the proper approach to the study of Asian history was the systematic
examination of the social and economic dynamics of the Asian cultures
themselves. His studies, later published in English under the title *Indonesian
Trade and Society* (The Hague, 1955), opened up promising new vistas.
However, some of his more important conclusions were to come under attack
by later historians, such as his claim that "the international trade of southeast
Asia was a small-scale peddling trade" [p. 133]. The term "peddling" has
frequently been used to connote an archaic form of commercial activity and,
by extension, an ineffective means of trading. This view of the Asian trading
world has since been criticized for displaying a form of Eurocentric bias.[25]

Some twenty years after the publication of Van Leur's essays, there
appeared another notable work on Asian trade: *The Asian Trade Revolution of the
Seventeenth Century* (Chicago, 1974). In this meticulously researched study, Niels
Steensgaard upholds Van Leur's characterization of Asian trade, though he
admits that the peddling trade could make use of fairly sophisticated
commercial methods, such as "commenda, bottomry, partnerships and
combined credit and transfer transactions by means of bills of exchange"
(p.30). Then, in a comparative analysis of the two prevailing institutions of

---

[24] See document 245.

[25] For a criticism of Van Leur's view, see M.A.P. Meilink-Roelofsz, *Asian Trade and European
Influence in the Indonesian Archipelago between 1500 and about 1630* (The Hague, 1962), pp.1-12; K.N.
Chaudhuri, *The Trading World of Asia and the English East India Company, 1660-1760* (Cambridge,
1978), pp. 136-7, 138-9; and Braudel, Vol. 2, pp. 120-122.

trade—the caravan, or the so-called peddler trade,[26] and the companies (English, Dutch)—Steensgaard demonstrates the organizational superiority of the companies over the caravans. He also argues that the Companies succeeded in breaking the caravans' hold over the trade of Asia at the start of the seventeenth century. While there can be no doubt that the advanced organizational form of the trading companies eventually brought about a global trade revolution, Steensgaard incorrectly dates the demise of the caravan trade from the early decades of the seventeenth century. In fact, the caravan trade competed successfully against the English and Dutch East India Companies throughout the seventeenth century and well into the eighteenth.

By the 1970s, there was a widening circle of scholars researching trading practices in Asia. One of the most prominent representatives of this period was K. N. Chaudhuri, whose monumental work titled *The Trading World of Asia and the English East India Company, 1660-1760* (Cambridge, 1978) opened up new perspectives and provided fresh interpretations for the study of the commercial economy of Asian countries. In this volume Chaudhuri takes Steensgaard to task for espousing Van Leur's characterization of Asian trade[27] and for concluding that "there is nothing in the sources to indicate the existence of comprehensive coordinated organizations—of an Armenian, Turkish or Persian version of a Fugger, Cranfield or Tripp" [Steensgaard, p. 30]. Studies of other scholars had, in the meantime, provided adequate evidence of the existence of well-organized Armenian trading enterprises. Chaudhuri's own investigations had led him to assert that the Armenian merchants "were in quite a different category." He saw them as "a group of highly skilled arbitrage dealers" who brought their special services "to the trading world of the Middle East, India, and even Europe." Furthermore, he confirmed that among the Armenians there were "merchants whose wealth and position would have compared favourably with the most successful merchant of London and Amsterdam" [pp. 137-8].

* * *

Unlike other trade communities, the Armenian merchant community was comprised of several classes of traders. "In general," writes Mauro, "Armenian merchants in Asia practiced all forms of commerce—caravans,

---

[26] In the strictest sense, the peddler was a very small trader with or without a camel, a pack bullock or ox to carry his wares which he bought from the producer and sold directly to the consumer or, perhaps, to another merchant. He earned just enough to make a subsistence living. Steensgaard [pp. 22-31] derives the portrait of the typical peddler from a unique document which was brought to light by Levon Khachikian [Khach'ikyan], "The Ledger of the Merchant Hovhannes Joughayetsi," *Journal of the Asiatic Society*, 8:153-86 (1966). A French translation of this paper appeared under the title "Le registre d'un marchand arménien en Perse, en Inde et au Tibet (1682-1693)," trans. Nina Godneff, *Annales: économies, sociétés, civilisations*, 22:231-78 (1967).

[27] Today few, if any, historians would subscribe to either Van Leur's or Steensgaard's "peddler" theory.

peddling, large-scale retailing, large-scale trading. They even entered into maritime trade when they realized that it was the only way to fight European competition."[28] Thus, if at the one end of this spectrum stood the peddlers or itinerant merchants, at the other stood the very wealthy and powerful class of merchants who headed the well organized trading houses in New Julfa (Persia) and elsewhere. They conducted their trade on the intercontinental/ international level. These merchants commanded immense economic resources and had considerable political and financial influence. Often they took on diplomatic assignments for their host government. Along with the clergy of the Armenian Church, these merchants represented the Armenian community of New Julfa and the "Armenian Nation" at large.

These notable Armenian merchants were addressed by the salutatory title *coja* (today, commonly spelled *khoja*).[29] This appellation was used as a sign of respect in Islamic countries for a select group of people, such as scholars, teachers, writers, and very wealthy merchants. Historical documents[30] and contemporaneous travel accounts[31] provide ample evidence of the use of this title for Armenian merchants. The Armenian Khojas[32] were at once business financiers and entrepreneurs: not only did they furnish the necessary capital for commercial ventures, but they also stood at the steering helm of their respective trading houses. Aside from their professional activities, they played a major role in Armenian political and public life.[33] So great was their influence on the destiny of the Armenian people that Armenian historians often refer to the pre-modern period as "the Age of Khojas."

---

[28] Frederic Mauro, "Merchant Communities, 1350-1750," in James D. Tracy (ed.), *The Rise of Merchant Empires* (Cambridge, 1990), p. 273, 273n. The Armenian ships bore a red-yellow-red flag marked with the Lamb of God.

[29] See under "khwadja," *Encyclopaedia of Islam*, Vol. IV, p. 907.

[30] For example, see documents 134, 166, and 180 in this volume.

[31] For a bibliography of travel accounts, see Vartoogian, pp. 313-365.

[32] In his *A New Account of East India and Persia, in Eight Letters, Being Nine Years Travels, Begun 1672 and Finished 1681* (London, 1698), John Fryer observes: "The most Honourable of [wealthy merchants] are the *Armenians*, and therefore styled *Cogee* [khoja], or Rich, by the *Persians*, though even among the *Persians* many covet to be so reputed, but care not to measure the wide World, like them [Armenians], venturing no farther than over to *India*, which is their *ne plus ultra*, while the diligent *Armenian, Per Mare per Terras, per quod tegit omnia, Coelum* (By Sea and Land does search for Store, / And all Heaven's Covering ransacks o're)" [p.388]. Elsewhere, he writes: "They [the Armenian merchants] improved the Glory of *Spahaun* [Isfahan] by their unwearied Industry, there being many of them Credible Merchants at this time . . .; so mightily do they increase under this Umbrage, in Riches and Freedom; for whilst they sit lazily at Home, their Factors abroad in all parts of the Earth return to their Hives laden with Honey; to which Exercise, after they themselves have been brought up, they train their Children under the safe Conduct of Experienced Tutors, who instruct them first to Labour for a Livelihood, before they are permitted to Expend" [p. 268].

[33] For a discussion of the influence of Armenian merchant capital on the political and public life of Armenians, see Leo, *Khojayakan kapitale yev nra k'aghak'akan-hasarakakan dere hayeri mej* (Erevan, 1934).

* * *

Despite the significant role played by the khojas in the overall history of the Armenian people, their trade network and commercial activities have not yet been studied in sufficient depth. The reason for this omission clearly lies in the Armenian historians' own preoccupation with the sociopolitical events of the times. This preoccupation is not, however, surprising when we bear in mind the tragic events that befell the Armenian people between the end of the fourteenth century when Armenia lost its independence and the creation of the first independent Armenian Republic (1918-1921). For over five centuries, Armenians heroically resisted the forces of assimilation and struggled to regain their national independence.[34] Under those circumstances, Armenian historians could have scarcely concentrated on such a seemingly esoteric subject as the trading world of the khojas. The scholarly study of this aspect of Armenian economic history had to wait for the appropriate academic climate.

This is not to suggest, however, that the subject was altogether ignored. Several works produced in the nineteenth and first half of the twentieth centuries have, in varying degrees, described the Armenian khojas and their activities.[35] Since then, and particularly in the last four decades, the number of scholars in the field has grown significantly. In part, this increase is due to the broadening interest among Western and non-Western historians in the trading world of pre-modern Asia. Accompanying the increase in the number of scholars has been an expansion of topics. At one extreme, studies deal with individual merchants,[36] and at the other, with entire merchant communities.[37]

---

[34] During those long centuries, Armenia had become a theater of barbaric Turco-Mongol invasions followed by incessant wars raging between the Ottoman Empire and Persia. These tragic events led to several waves of emigration and, at times, forced deportations, leaving only small enclaves of Armenian people in the homeland. Thus reduced to a minority status in their own country, they later were to become the target of three more massacres perpetrated by Ottoman Turkey: the first in 1895-96, the second in 1909, and the third in 1915-22. The last one has come to be regarded as the first genocide of the twentieth century. Following the first short-lived independent statehood (1918-1921), Armenia continued for the next seven decades to exist as a political entity under Soviet protection and rule. Since the dissolution of the Soviet Union in 1991, Armenia has become once again an independent Republic. See Bournoutian, Vol. II. On the Armenian genocide, see Vahakn N. Dadrian, *The History of the Armenian Genocide: Ethnic Conflict from the Balkans to Anatolia to the Caucasus* (Providence, RI, 1995, rev. ed. 1997). A French version of this work appeared under the title *Histoire du génocide arménien: conflits nationaux dès Balkans au Caucase*, trans. Marc Nichanian (Paris, 1996).

[35] Y. T. Ter-Yovhaneants , *Patmut'iwn Nor Jughayu vor y Aspahan*, 2 vols. (New Julfa, 1880-1881); Gh. M. Alishan, *Sisakan* (Venice, 1893).

[36] R. Gulbenkian, "Philippe de Zagly, marchand arménien de Julfa, et l'établissement du commerce persan en Courlande en 1696," *Revue des études arméniennes*, 7(n.s.):361-399 (1970). M.J. Seth, *Armenians in India* (Calcutta, 1983).

[37] Gregorian, "Minorities of Isfahan." R.A. Bekius, "The Armenian Community in Amsterdam in the 17th and 18th Centuries: Integration and Disintegration," paper presented at the First Conference of the Association Internationale des Etudes Arméniennes held at Wasenaar,

Within these extremes can be found a variety of special topics.[38]   For the sake of brevity, only a few are cited here.

* * *

Recent progress in the study of pre-modern Armenian trade communities has resulted in a considerable variety of historical works which, in general, fall into two categories: narrative and comparative. In the narrative or literary mode of structuring, research findings are woven into the larger fabric of national history. Notable works in this category include Roger Savory's *Iran Under the Safavids* (Cambridge, 1980) and R. W. Ferrier's "Trade from the Mid-14th Century to the End of the Safavid Period" in Peter Jackson and Laurence Lockhart (eds.), *The Cambridge History of Iran*, Vol. 6 (Cambridge, 1986).

While the narrative form of historical construction highlights personages and events, it does little, if anything, to illuminate the social and economic institutions of a period. To be able, for example, to portray the distinct character of an historical period, it is necessary to select some constituent parts of an occurrence in a given period and set them against their counterparts at another time or place. This comparative approach to history yields fresh insights. Research findings on pre-modern Armenian trade communities have been taken up by several comparative historians, including, notably, Niels Steensgaard, in *The Asian Trade Revolution of the Seventeenth Century* (commented on above); Fernand Braudel, in *Civilization and Capitalism* (New York, 1984); and Philip D. Curtin, in *Cross-Cultural Trade in World History* (Cambridge, 1984).

In his engaging style, Braudel portrays a vivid picture of the world-wide network of the Armenian trading enterprises, frequently raising questions for further investigation. Here are a few: What were the commercial techniques in use? How did the Armenian merchants tackle the problem of bookkeeping? What was "the compelling commercial or capitalist motive behind [their] trading network?" What was "the key to their fabulous success?" (Vol. 2, pp.

Netherlands Institute for Advanced Studies, August 30-31, 1983.

[38] S. Van Rooy, "Armenian Merchant Habits as Mirrored in 17th-18th Century Amsterdam Documents," *Revue des études arméniennes*, 3(n.s.):347-357 (1966). John Carswell, *New Julfa: The Armenian Churches and Other Buildings* (Oxford, 1968). Kévonian, "Marchands arméniens." Aghassian and Kévonian, "Le commerce arménien." R.W. Ferrier, "The Agreement of the East India Company with the Armenian Nation 22nd June 1688," *Revue des études arméniennes*, 7(n.s.):427-443 (1970). Sh. L. Khach'ikyan, "1667 t'. Hay-rusakan arewtrakan paymanagire ew Nor Jughayi ink'navar marminnere," *Haykazean Hayagitakan Handes*, 8:259-288 (Beirut, 1980). *Idem.*, "Shahvelu vordi Sarhadi hashvematyane vorpes hay-rusakan tntesakan kaperi skzbnaghbyur," *Patma-Banasirakan Handes* (Erevan, 1978), no. 2, 93-108. E.J. van Donzel, *Foreign Relations of Ethiopia, 1642-1700: Documents Relating to the Journeys of Khodja Murad* (Leiden, 1979). R. Pankhurst, "The History of Ethiopian-Armenian Relations," *Revue des études arméniennes*, 12(n.s.):273-345 (1977); continued in 13(n.s.):259-311 (1978-1979).

156-157.) Nor does he fail to offer his own ideas on the issues. Looking at the big picture, he asks: "How were these long-distance connections set up and related to each other? Were they linked by the huge headquarters at [New] Julfa and by this alone? Or were there, *as I believe*, subsidiary centers?" (Italics added.)

In quite a different vein, Curtin examines several cross-cultural trading patterns, including that of the Armenians (chapter 9), in order to determine what, if any, organizational pattern was common to them all. He concludes that before the dawn of the modern era long-distance commerce was carried on by trade diasporas or networks of trading settlements. This trading institution required the migration of kinsmen and trusted fellow-countrymen to those regions where the home merchants intended to sell or buy particular commodities.

* * *

Among scholars of pre-modern Armenian trade and commerce, one, Levon Khach'ikyan, has been pivotal in generating renewed interest on the subject. Of his many valuable studies, the best known is that of the manuscript of the account book of Hovhannes Ter-Davt'yan, more commonly known as Hovhannes Joughayetsi (Hovhannes of Julfa). While Khach'ikyan's article on this account book[39] laid the groundwork for later studies, following its publication he undertook a fuller study of this important document with the collaboration of H. D. P'ap'azyan. The product of this joint effort[40] includes the edited text of the account book, a considerably expanded glossary of terms, and an introduction which penetrates deeply into the commercial practices of the New Julfan trade community.

A study of Vanandets'i's commercial handbook[41] by Kéram Kévonian[42] and a joint study of Armenian trade in the Indian Ocean by Aghassian and Kévonian[43] have also been valuable contributions to the general scholarship. The first of these works includes a translation of the handbook's table of contents, sample pages, and facsimiles. The second work attempts to answer such basic questions on pre-modern Armenian trade as: What were the characteristic features of this trade? Is this trade merely the continuation of a much older commercial activity? And why did it decline in the 18th century? In an appendix, the authors provide facsimiles and translated extracts from the works of Kostand Jughayets'i (1685) and Ghukas Vanandets'i (1699).

---

[39] See note 2.

[40] L. S. Khach'ikyan and H. D. P'ap'azyan (eds.), *Hovhannes Ter-Davt'yan Jughayetsu hashvetumare* (Erevan, 1984).

[41] Ghukas Nurijanean Vanandets'i, *Gandz ch'ap'oy, k'shroy, t'woy ew dramits* . . . (Amsterdam, 1699).

[42] "Marchands arméniens."

[43] "Le commerce arménien."

Another scholar, Levon Khach'ikyan's own daughter, Shushanik L. Khach'ikyan, has also made a significant contribution to the study of Julfan trade. Perhaps more than anyone else she has delved into an examination of the full range of information available in order to depict as comprehensively as possible the commercial and financial features of the Armenian trading enterprises. Under her purview fall the organization of the Armenian community of New Julfa as well as its trading houses; commercial contracts and investments; markets, merchants, merchandise, and means of exchange; the activities of the khojas in other economic realms, such as agriculture; and, finally, the role of the khojas in the early stages of industrial development. Of her many scholarly accomplishments, mention must be made of her study of the 1667 trade agreement between the Armenian merchants and the Russian government[44]; the account book of Shahvelu Son of Sarhad (1711-1718)[45]; and her monograph[46] which incorporates many of her past works along with a considerable amount of new material on the various types of commercial instruments, the role of khojas in the early stages of industrial development, and other issues.

Finally, mention must be made of Edmund Herzig whose unpublished dissertation, "The Armenian Merchants of New Julfa, Isfahan: A Study in Pre-Modern Asian Trade" (Oxford, 1991), continues the line of research opened up by the Khach'ikyans. Herzig offers crucial new data on the mercantile operations of the Julfan community, thereby illuminating further some of the aspects of the Armenian merchant organizations and practices. He also locates the Armenian trade within the broader context of Eurasian economic history.

* * *

In addition to these studies and primary documents, there are, today, several European and Armenian archives that contain material pertinent to pre-modern Armenian trade and commerce. A rich depository of sources is the Matenadaran in Erevan, Armenia. L. Khach'ikyan has brought a wide spectrum of documents held in the Matenadaran to the attention of scholars. For example, his article, "Tntesakan gortsark' neri masin grarumnere hayeren dzeragreri mej ev nrants'aghbyuragitakan n'shanakut'yune," *Banber Matenadarani* (Erevan, 1960), No. 5, pp. 21-41, deals with a variety of commercial instruments used both in the agrarian and trading segments of the economy (14th to 18th centuries). Large numbers of commercial sources, however, still remain uncatalogued and, therefore, unutilized.

Central to the study of New Julfan trading houses and practices are the archives at the Armenian Cathedral in New Julfa—Amenap'rkich Vank (All

---

[44] "1667 t'. Hay-rusakan arewtrakan paymanagire."

[45] *Shahvelu vordi Sarhadi hashvematyane* (Erevan, 1994).

[46] *Nor Jughayi hay vacharakanut'yune ev nra arevtratntesakan kapere Rusastani het XVII-XVIII darerum* (Erevan, 1988).

Savior's Cathedral). In his two-volume work, *Patmut'iwn Nor Jughayu vor yAspahan* (New Julfa, 1880-1881), Y. T. Ter-Yovhaneants provides numerous examples of the documents and letters held in the Cathedral's archives. This work was recently published in modern Eastern Armenian by P. Petrosean, *Patmut'iwn Nor Jughayi*, 2 vols. (New Julfa, 1980-1981), with notes by L. G. Minasean, published separately under the title *Tsanot'agrut'iwnner Nor Jughayi Patmut'iwn A. ew B. Hatorneri* (New Julfa, 1983).[47]

Among the documents in the archives of the Armenian Cathedral in New Julfa is the original of Kostand Jughayets'i's trade handbook,[48] which contains information on measures, weights, moneys, imported and exported goods and their prices. Written for aspiring merchants, the book was used as a text in the Armenian commercial school there. Another trade handbook, this one compiled by Ghukas Vanandets'i, was published in Amsterdam in 1699.[49] In many respects similar to Kostand Jughayets'i's volume, it is intended for Armenian merchants with an interest in worldwide commerce.

Still among other valuable resources are the diaries of Zak'aria Agulets'i,[50] the private papers of Eghia Karnets'i,[51] and the Law Book of the Armenian community of Astrakhan (Russia).[52] As acknowledged by the authors of the Law Book , the commercial section of this work is based on the customary law of the Armenian community of Persia.

Several European libraries also house archival material relevant to the study of pre-modern Armenian merchant communities. The British Library's Lansdowne Collection, for example, contains a few hundred documents concerning Armenian trade in Surat, Basra, Calcutta, and Madras. Aside from this, the India Office Records of the British Library has a variety of documents relating to the trade relationship between the Armenian khojas and the East India Company. This archive also holds letters written in the vernacular by Armenian merchants of New Julfa to the directors of the English East India Company in London. A particularly important source for Armenian trade in Russia is the Lazarian Family Collection (1741-1759) in Moscow which has been quite extensively explored by Sh. L. Khach'ikyan. In Venice is the Shahrimanian Family Collection. The orginal of the well-known account book of Hovhannes Jughayets'i is to be found in the Portuguese National Archive in Lisbon. Source materials are also found in French and Dutch archives.

---

[47] For guide-books to the Cathedral's collections, see S. Ter-Awetisean, *Tsutsak hayeren dzeragrats' Nor Jughayi Amenap'rkich Vank'i*, vol. 1 (Vienna 1970); L.G. Minasean, *ibid.*, vol. 2 (Vienna 1972); L.G. Minasean, *Divan S. Amenap'rkich Vank'i 1606-1960: Arkhivi ughets'oyts grkoyk* (New Julfa, 1983).

[48] Kostand Jughayets'i, *Vas'n norahas mankants ew eritasardats kh'rat* (New Julfa, 1685), See also Sh. L. Khach ikyan, *Nor Jughayi hay vacharanut yune. . .*, p. 11.

[49] See Kévonian, "Marchands arméniens."

[50] Zak'aria Agulets'i, *Oragrut'yun* (Erevan, 1938).

[51] A.G. Abrahamyan (ed.), *Eghia Karnets'i: Divan* (Erevan, 1968).

[52] F. G. Poghosyan (ed.), *Datastanagirk Astrakhani Hayots* (Erevan, 1967).

* * *

With the closing years of the twentieth century, a majority of historians now entertain the global, as opposed to the Eurocentric, view of historical investigation. This newly-found intellectual sensitivity promises a more diversified approach to the study of pre-modern history. Along with this changing perspective, scholars have uncovered increasing amounts of new source material to work with even though much more needs to be documented and analyzed, especially in Middle Eastern and Asian archives. Be that as it may, Armenian and European sources have already set the stage for a productive exploration of the foundations of the economic institutions of pre-modern Asia. This trend can be accelerated by translating the scholarly works of modern Armenian historians[53] into French or English, preferably both, thereby making them available to Western and non-Western historians alike.

The Documents: Some Highlights

In a source book it is neither proper nor indeed possible to discuss the contents of documents at great length. While it is evident that these documents provide a rich repository of information, they will undoubtedly reveal a great deal more in the hands of practicing historians. Indeed, as an organic whole, they have a central theme and unveil a most interesting array of human experiences.

The central theme of this collection concerns the long, multifarious, evolving and complex relationship between the English East India Company and the Armenian merchant community during the seventeenth and early eighteenth centuries. This relationship revolved around the Company's relentless efforts to wrest the silk and cloth trades from the powerful Armenian merchants of New Julfa into their own hands. The players in this drama, however, included more than these two. The Company's side consisted of two distinct groups: the board of directors in London and the Company's factors in Asia. Paradoxically, more often than not the professional interests of the two were in direct conflict. Meanwhile, the Armenian side provided as many players as there were participating trading houses. Indeed, the Armenian merchant community was far from being a homogeneous group; the khojas were united only in their opposition to the Company's efforts to break into the Armenian-held markets.

Throughout the period represented by these documents, relations between the Company's factors and the Armenian merchants continued to be rather uneasy, to say the least. Expected to cooperate with the Armenian

---

[53] The following works would be of great interest to a wide circle of historians: L. S. Khach'ikyan and H. D. P'ap'azyan (eds.), *Hovhannes Ter-Davt'yan Jughayets'u Hash-vetumaré* (Erevan, 1984); Sh. L. Khach'ikyan, *Shahvelu vordi Sarhadi hashvematyané* (Erevan, 1994); *Idem., Nor Jughayi hay vacharakanut'yune ev nra arevtratntesakan kapere Rusastani het XVII-XVIII darerum* (Erevan, 1988).

merchants, the factors, in most instances, maintained hostility towards them. Often this attitude was openly expressed in angry and derogatory comments in their letters to the Company and others.[54] The Company directors, however, did not share the view of the factors; to the contrary, they saw the Armenian merchants as "conscientious honest men and of great prudence and experience,"[55] while they considered the Armenian people themselves "a wise honest and great trading nation."[56] Ironically, the Company directors, even as they held the Armenian merchants in high esteem, were often suspicious and distrustful of their own factors. From very early on, the English East India Company had received reports about their factors' selfishness and negligence towards the affairs of the Company.[57] Another early report read: "There is a great deale of knavery and dishonesty used by the Company's factors in buying silke for themselves and selling it to the Dutch."[58] This distrust the Company held towards its factors continued to the end. As late as 1696, Company directors wrote to the factors in Isfahan, "We cannot but entertaine a suspicion of your integrity to our service or your friendship to them [the Armenians]."[59] And by way of conclusion, the Company stated:

> Tis true, that we had a great relyance on the ability and inclination of the Armenians to serve us, and possibly had they been fairly treated by you, they might herein have given you and us such an assistance in this affair, as might have inabled us to have diverted the course of their former way of trade. . .[60]

* * *

Concluding Comments

As the historiographic survey in this introduction suggests, the dichotomization of pre-modern commercial life into two distinct and separate modes—European and Asian—is not only misleading, but it also invites willful and unsuspected biases. To guard ourselves against such cardinal violations of history, we must, at all times, bear in mind a crucial metaphysical tenet: in all realms of existence things are partly similar and partly different. In other words, "sameness" and "difference" co-exist in all things. There can be no "difference" if there is no "sameness"; no "diversity" if there is no

---

[54] See documents 23, 54, 246.

[55] See document 136.

[56] See document 184.

[57] See document 1.

[58] See document 24.

[59] See document 230.

[60] Ibid.

"identity"; no "otherness" if there is no "likeness."[61] We must thus be equally on the lookout for similarities as well as differences.

Aside from this metaphysical issue, there looms a substantive historical question: What was "the key to [the Armenians'] fabulous success" during the pre-modern period? The question, which is so clearly and succinctly formulated by Fernand Braudel, may, by some, be viewed as rhetorical, for can there be only a single reason for this phenomenon? Be that as it may, the question is so seductive that it cannot be easily ignored or dismissed. I, for one, propose the following hypothesis for consideration: the "fabulous success" of the pre-modern Armenian merchant community was primarily due to its organizational form or arrangements.

As opposed to the single, large, hierarchically organized joint-stock company, such as the English East India Company, the Armenian trading house was a network or alliance of organizations centered around a notable merchant, the khoja, who was at once business financier and entrepreneur. These widely spread but highly interrelated individual enterprises operated under the ethos of trust.[62] Trust, and the shared moral and ethical norms underlying it, helped the Armenian trading houses to avoid the relatively rigid and costly operation of the hierarchic system of organization practiced by the English. Seen in this light, trust served as a human capital, but one that could not be acquired through a rational investment decision. It accrued to the Armenian merchant community as a result of their collective sociopolitical experiences over many generations. Based on family kinship and trusted fellow countrymen, the Armenian trading house did, indeed, rely on trust as its principal means of organization and control.

This economically efficient way of structuring business life permitted the Armenian merchants to reap significant benefits, which can be categorized under two major headings: (1) organizational cost savings; and (2) organizational innovations. The first of these represents a broad spectrum of institutional costs, known in economics as "transaction costs," including those of information, negotiation, drawing up and enforcing contracts, monitoring performance, policing property rights, and changing institutional arrangements.[63] The benefits accrued to the trading houses under the second heading included flexibility—that is, the capability to adapt to new, different, or changing requirements— and creative capacity, or the potential to rise up to

---

[61] To quote Peirce, "Otherness . . . is the inseparable spouse of identity; wherever there is identity there is necessarily otherness; and in whatever field there is true otherness there is necessarily identity." Charles Hartshorne and Paul Weiss (eds.), *Collected Papers of Charles Sanders Peirce* (Cambridge, 1965), 1.566.

[62] For an excellent discussion of the subject, see: Francis Fukuyama, *Trust: The Social Virtues and the Creation of Prosperity* (New York, 1995).

[63] See Oliver E. Williamson, "Transaction Cost Economics," in Richard Schmalensee and Robert Willig (eds.), *Handbook of Industrial Organization*, Vol. 1 (Amsterdam, 1989). Douglass C. North, *Institutions, Institutional Change, and Economic Performance* (New York, 1990).

new and radically different challenges. The Armenian trading houses enjoyed these advantages while at the same time achieving economies of scale and scope.

These comments are, at best, preliminary and suggestive. But it is hoped that they will provoke discussion and arouse interest leading to further research.

EDITORIAL METHOD

In preparing this volume, careful attention has been given to the following editorial matters.

Document Identification

Each document has been identified by (i) a descriptive heading, (ii) date, and (iii) source reference.

Double Dating

Until 1752, the new year officially began on March 25 in England. For documents created in the period between January 1 and March 24, a double indication of the year has been given, for example, 1697/98, a form commonly found in seventeenth century documents.

Transcription

The documents in this volume have been transcribed with some alterations intended to make the text easier for the modern reader.

(i)   The profusion of capital letters has been reduced.
(ii)   Abbreviations have been expanded where possible, including tailed p's and "th"s. Exceptions are monetary, weight, and other measures which have been retained.
(iii)   Some punctuation has been changed.
(iv)   In certain cases, *u* has been transcribed as *v*, e.g., *haue* appears as *have*.
(v)   In certain cases, *i* has been transcribed as *j*, e.g., *iudgement* appears as *judgement*.
(vi)   Interpolations in the text are shown in square brackets.
(vii)   Omissions are indicated by suspension points.
(viii) Very strange spelling or mistake indicated by [*sic*].
(ix)   Blank space indicated by [*blank*].
(x)   Superior letters brought down to the line of text.
(xi)   Ampersand in all its forms is printed *and*.

Abbreviations

The following abbreviations have been used throughout the text: Ar. (Arabic); Chin. (Chinese); Hind. (Hindustani); It. (Italian); Malay. (Malayalam); Pers. (Persian); Turk. (Turkish).

Transliteration

The transliteration system used for Armenian publications is that of the Library of Congress (*Cataloging Service Bulletin*, No. 38, Fall 1987, pp. 73-74). It is based on the phonetic values of Classical and East Armenian.

CHRONOLOGICAL TABLE
OF DOCUMENTS

*The modern convention has been followed in writing the years,
that is, the new year begins on January 1 and not on March 25.*

The numbers refer to the documents.

1708

1709

DOCUMENTS

1

WILLIAM LESK ON BOARD THE GLOBE AT PLYMOUTH TO COMPANY IN LONDON
AUGUST 1617[1]
E/3/5 EXTRACT FROM F. 5

The Armenians dryve a rich trade betweene India and Persia for in regard of the great warrs betweene the great Turke and the king of Persia the inhabitaunts of the cuntrey not able to make the most of there sale buy at deere rates many commodities of India so that severall commodities from thence carryed thither by land, all charges deducted afford two, three and foure for one if then they by land make so great gaine, what might you doe transporting the same by water and yet such and so great was the selfish negligence of your factours that notwithstanding of the plentie they had both of money and meanes what in this bussines was performed you shall from others more perfecktlie learne.

[1] The original document has been annotated with the date March 1617. William Foster gives the date as August 1617 and the location of the Globe as Plymouth in *Letters Received by the East India Company*, volume V (London 1901) no. 462 pp. 175-187.

2

FRANCIS FETIPLACE AND ROBERT HUGHES AT AGRA TO COMPANY IN LONDON
20 DECEMBER 1617
E/3/5 EXTRACT FROM F. 218V

The 23 ditto [February] came safe therwith to Agra wheare we found Joseph Salbanke and the goods remayninge here left in his charge all in good safety, whome presently after our comminge hither, we dispeeded to a place 14 dayes jorny hence, to receave a debt then dew unto us from an Armenian, for cloth sould him in Agemere 5 monthes before, where, after his comminge thither, he found the party, shortly after, torned out of his livinge (rented by him of the Queene) and thereby unable to satisfy us. Yet after much trouble, and 3 monthes abode there, he came to composition with the said party (whose debt was 7500 rupees) and receaved of him $^{1}/_{2}$ of the cloth sould him backe agayne amountinge unto 3500 rupees. 2800 rupees he receaved of him in ready mony, and his bill for the rest, beinge 1200 rupees payable at 3 monthes, which remayner is yet unsatisfyed, but we have great hopes of his speedy payment. We were deceaved in this bargayne by our broker's misinterpretacion in takinge a suerty bound with him, (as we made accompt) for the mony, whereas he was only suerty for his body and forth comminge, and this was the reason of the aforesaid composition but the best is the cloth was sould him at soe good a rate, as that there can be noe losse by the bargayne.

3

COURT MINUTES
23 FEBRUARY 1618/19
B/6 EXTRACT FROM P. 300

Mr Ellam was appointed to wright a letter to Mr Monox and the rest of the factors[1] to let them knowe, that theire care in sending by sundrye conveyances, is well accepted of, but the charge by sending messengers over land, directly with letters, is to greate. And therefore to advise them to continew still their sending, but by the opportunitye of some merchants Georgians or Armenians, whoe doe travill saufley and freely without suspition betwixt Persia and Turkey. And to wishe them to make use of the caracter that is sent, that noe thing may be discovered, although some letters should be intercepted.

[1] at Isfahan

4

THOMAS BARKER, EDWARD MONOX, WILLIAM BELL AND THOMAS
BARKER JUNIOR
AT ISFAHAN TO COMPANY IN LONDON
16 OCTOBER 1619
E/3/7 EXTRACT FROM FF. 46V-48

The Armenians and others the king's subjects who have in precedent tymes exported the Persian sylkes and other comodityes by the waye of Turkie and have thereby purchased unto themselves greate wealth, perceiving that by the divert of theire said traffique they should not onely be impoverished but allsoe manye of them utterlye undone and not have means to maintayne themselves and famylies. Wherefore they use all endeavours to give impedyment to our proceedings and have made offer of great sommes of monye unto the kinge to tollerate theire former free commerce by land viz eyther to give 150 thousand pounds starling as a present or ells to paye 5 tomands[1] custome for every loade of silke they shall exporte which wilbe about 12d starling the pound of 16 ounces. Besides this our auncient opposites the

Portingalls had caussed a false fame to be bruted abroad by the fryars heere rezident, that the kinge of Spayne had sett forthe a fleete of shipps for these partes furnishing them with 3 millions of crownes to buy the silkes of Persia. To these maye be added that ill precedent made by Edward Connock who gave for parte of the silkes he bought the first yeare more then the kinge nowe demandeth for the same sorte for though in his accompt he expresses the payment but of 270 shahees[2] per mand[3] yet it appeareth by accompt since made upp with Lalabeagge that he accorded for 280 shahees whereuppon the kinge observeing such a generall desyre for the trade of his sylkes tooke occasion thereby to improve the price thereof and that he might bring the intyre and totall benefitt of the said improvement to his owne coffers hath caused it to be published that all sylkes made throughout his whole domynions shalbe brought into his treasurye and thence to receive monye for the same. By which meanes haveing made a monopolye thereof and engrossed all into his owne possession, he caused us, the fryars and Armenians to be convented before certaine comissioners by him appointed where we were perticulerlye demanded what we would give for the kings sylkes. The fryars answered that theire comission extended not to make any accorde for the pryce thereof, soe that the contention rested onely betweene us and the Armenyans. Wherefore being severall tymes severallye demanded what we would give, the Armenyans (though unwilling to make the first proffer) yet at length determined to give the kinge 50 tomands for each load of silke poze[4] 36 mandes shaee which will be $1^3/_4$ ryalls of eight[5] the pound of 16 ounces its pryme cost and then demanding what we would give it was replyed that since they had esteemed it at a dearer rate then we did resolve it to be worth it were to noe purpose for us to sett a pryce thereon. Yet after much importunitie we tould them that we could not exceed 240 shahees per maen which was the uttmost we would give and wilbe somewhat more then your Honnors' lymitted pryce which is $1^1/_2$ ryall of 8 per pound but after they had spent much vaine laboure in endeavouring to perswade us to give the Armenyans' profferred pryce, we were lycensed to departe and to expect the king's further resolution upon the delivery of our severall answeres unto him which not long after wee received from his owne mouth and was in effect as followeth: that if we would give that pryce for his sylkes which other marchants had profferred we should first be served and take what quantetye our selves pleased eyther little, much or all, but we signified unto his Majestie that we had allready delivered our fynall resolution concerning the pryce objecting (as we had beene informed) that the Armenyans gave that pryce to pay his Majestie at theire retourne from Aleppo but he vowed the contrarye. We further alleadged the improbabilytie or rather impossibilytie of theire performance since we were assured they would be great loosers thereby and we much more if we should give that pryce in as much as the charge of yts export by sea, (besydes the many inevitable dangers) would much exceede theires by land, giveing his Majestie further to understand that rather then the marchants who transporte the silkes from Aleppo would would

[sic] give a pryce soe much exceeding its accustomed rate they would endeavour to be furnished with that comoditie from other partes soe that in tract of tyme his sylkes would be whollye brought out of use but nothing would prevaile to remove him from his settled resolution, nor were we less constant in our determination, for haveing convocated a councell of all the English marchants here resident we generally concluded for sondry reasons expressed in the said consultation beareing date the 26th of September 1619 rather not to make any retourne in that comoditie this yeare then to give the kinge his pryce wherefore we intended to make somme investments in carpetts but those being likewise in the king's officers' custodie they were soe well tutered that they would neither shew us those which were good nor sell them but at unreasonable rates hopeing thereby to compell us to take sylkes at the specyfyed pryzes but we made frustrate theire hopes and tooke neyther chooseing rather to lett the smalle capitall we have here lye unemployed for one yeare then to make soe ill a president wherefore we have onely shipped you some musters[6] of divers sortes of Persian stuffs.

It is not credible that the Armenians will give his Majestie the mentioned pryzes but it rather seemeth probable by that collection we can make of the sondrye informations and reportes we have had even from some of themselves that they were brought (coulorablye) to offer this pryce hopeing thereby, that we would be induced to give the lyke but when the kinge shall perceive that his project hath fayled we hope he wilbe content to stoope in his pryce the ensuinge yeare, yf not we shall then be forced to yeild unto him whereby to make you retornes of that great cappitall nowe expected.

The Armenyans are not yet come to any agreement for the king's silkes neyther (as I am crediblye informed) doe they resolve to take any at the specifyed rates except the king's tyrannie be such as to force them thereto, soe that it is reported he intendeth to send his silkes to Aleppo with his owne merchants but others saye that he sendeth onely 100 loade to Venice to have his retournes in some toyes of Christendome which he desyreth.

---

[1] *tumān* (Pers.): a sum of 10,000 dinars

[2] *shāhī* (Pers.): a small silver coin

[3] *mān* (Pers.): weight used in India and Western Asia, varying in value; in Safavid Iran, the Tabriz *mān* weighed about $6\frac{1}{2}$ lbs., the Royal *mān* twice as much, i.e., about 13 lbs.

[4] weighing

[5] silver coin, piece of eight

[6] muster: samples

5

WILLIAM BIDDULPH AND JOHN WILLOUGHBY AT THE MOGUL EMPEROR'S CAMP
BETWEEN AGRA AND LAHORE TO COMPANY IN LONDON
25 DECEMBER 1619
E/3/7 EXTRACT FROM FF. 98-99

Now maye it please youre worshipps to understand what hath passed since the departure of the Royall Ann who at hir dispeede with Sir Thomas Roe notwithstandinge his firmaens[1] and presence, left all youre fine and most parte of the grosse goods in the costome house att Suratt not then cleared and there remayned (all labouringe what wee could to release them) untill it was the 18th of March after the cheife time for sale beinge past for sale att court and then were forced to suffer the officers of the costome house to seale upp all what goods they liked for the prince theire master which was all the principall goods there was, and soe were dispeeded from Suratt the 21th same month in companye of John Willoughbye, John Parker, John Yonge, Thomas Hawkeridge attendant and myselfe per the waye of Bramport for Agra or where the kinge should bee. Wee had not bin 6 dayes upon our jornye but received a letter from John Banggam directed to Mr Thomas Keridge and company in Surat and beinge a generall letter I opened itt and found per the contents that himselfe with 200 camells ladinge of goods, as indico, samanaes[2] and goods for Persia were all stayed in Bramport by the governor of that place occasioned per one Condye Suffer Armenian whom Francisco Swaryes Portingall lefte there att his departure for Decann as his procurador to follow this busynes to stay the English goods, pretendinge for 20/000 rupees which the said Swarres did affirme before his departure thence that hee had delivered Nicholas Banggam in Chenyesware and other comodities in Bramport before the said Banggam's departure for England. Uppon receipt of this letter, myselfe with Thomas Hawkeridge lefte the rest of our company with the goods brought with us from Suratt and posted before with what speede wee could to Bramport to endevour the release of the goods as alsoe that yonge man who at my arivall ther found at libertye, Swarres and Musquito another Portingall beinge departed before my cominge thether in company of one of the prince's servaunts for Decan, and found there onlye the Condye Armenian and Thomas Sprage in his possession where wee cold doe nothinge in dayes after our arivall per reason of the governor's eldest sonn's death few dayes before wee came thether and greate heavynesse in all the cittye, soe in that vacant time I informed myselfe the best I could of that busynes of John Banggam and others and afterwards caused a petition to be drawne to the governor concerninge our greivances as detention of our goods, force in his sonne's progenye takinge our indico per force from our people, Conudye Suffer Armenian keepinge an Englishman one Thomas Sprage prisoner in his

house with other things needfull, after 4 or 5 dayes though the governor were
sad for his sonn's death I had admittance who used mee kindlye with promise
of justice for all what I desired. 2 dayes after I visited him againe acquaintinge
him with my busynes, who presentlye sent for the Armenian that stayed our
goods and demaunded of him wherefore hee caused our goods to be detayned.
Hee answered as afore spetified that was that Swaryes had delivered to the said
Banggam 20/ rupees in Chenye ware etc. I tould the governor the partye to
whom hee delivered itt must answere itt, the Armenian replyed itt was our
costome that what one of us did here the rest were liable to answere etc it was
true would bringe 20 wittnesses Christians. Then I said they were none but
Portin-galls and Armenians which were both our enimies and knew not our
costomes, the governor at that time would here noe more but appoynted
another meetinge, the next daye after I received letters from Suratt with theire
petition to the governor the effect beinge as formerlye had given him and with
them the kinge and prince's firmaens all which after the receipt I presented to
the governor and againe urged our busynes and that I was goinge to the kinge
with presents and stayed onlye to know his pleasure what hee would doe with
our goods and that hee might perceave per those firmaens it was the kinge and
prince's pleasures wee should have all right and that the Portingalls being our
enimyes had raysed this untruth against us, who both hard and read all what
I delivered unto him, and presently sent for the justice of the towne to have
forced the Armenian to deliver Sprage unto mee, with promise our other
busynes should bee ended presentlye, but before hee came or anye thinge elce
don hee rose without effectinge anythinge that daye, Swaryes notwithstandinge
his absence what with his liberalitye or rather prodigalitye hath to frend
generallye the whole towne both governor, cheifes, and merchants soe when
I perceaved and understood soe much I expected smale justice to be don on
our partes, yett to prove the uttmost, I stayed some dayes longer then I might
well have don, and dayes after the justice of the towne sent for mee to whom
I went and found that cheetinge Armenian Suffer havinge with him 20 or 25
wittnesses Armenians Moores and Banians, where wee were all carried before
the governor where the busynes was againe handled, the said Suffer
producinge Hackim Eushall's letter beinge the prince's man that went with
Swaryes and Swaryes' owne letter with a role of all the fore said wittnesses,
affirminge that Swaryes delivered into the hands of Nicholas Banggam in
Bramport the fore said some spetified in goods and withall that it was our
costome to answere all debts goods and monyes one for another in these
partes, to which I answered as formerlye deniinge the knowledge of anye such
goods or costomes yf hee had delivered anye such goods to anye perticuler
Englishman hee must answere for them and that other English were not lyable
to paye it nor theire goods, to which the governor and all the mares said that
was theire justice here indeede, but the governor said because that wee were
all Christians that the differance was betweene wee should have justice
accordinge to our owne costomes, I tould him there was greate difference

betweene the Portingalls, Armenians and us both in religeon and justice and
that here were none but Armenians and such as were never in England and
knew not our costomes and more that they were the Portingalls' frends and
our enimies, with that an old Armenian tould the governor that hee had bin in
Turkye in all places where the English did trade there and that theire costome
was that whatsoeever anye English did the consull in that place was lyable to
paye and answere for them and soe in all places and to end his false speach
said yf it were not true cutt of his head, I said itt was false and yf there were
anye such costome in England or here amoungst our nation then I did refer
myselfe to him to be disposed of att's pleasure desiringe him to doe us the
justice of this countrye for that hee did nott understand the Christians' justice
in this busynes and that these men with bribes and hope of gayne of the
Portingalls did beare falce wittnesse, notwithstandinge the governor
demaunded of all the Armenians as the were Christians, whether that were our
costomes as they had affirmed, they all answered that what one English did
owe in these parts the rest with theire goods were lyable to pay itt, uppon
which the governor without heringe more disputes resolved to detayne the
goods for that present, and yf in one or 2 months the English in Surat could
send testimonye thether to the contrarye hee would doe us right, when I saw
noe hope of present release of the goods I tould him that everye yeare our
shipps did guard the prince's and merchants' shipps to and from the redd sea
againe to Suratt and therefore doubted not but wee should finde justice one
waye or other, hee answered he had noe shipps now, yf mett with anye of his
bid us take them, yf tooke the kinge or prince's must give answere to them
who would stricktlye require it of us and what justice hee had herein was as hee
said for god's sake and soe with this reply was forced to lett this busynes rest
urginge him againe for Sprage, who was sent for and att his cominge asked him
what hee knew of this busynes beinge the[re] in Bramport charginge him to tell
the truth, who confessed there was 13 cestas or basketts of Chenye dishes
delivered Nicholas Banggam per Swaryes in Bramport whereof 2 cestas the
said Banggam caried awaye with him and 11 hee lefte behind him in Bramport
whereof some sould some emptye some retorned some broaken, 500 dishes
Sprage confessed to have sould himselfe which Swaryes forgave him beinge
poore as the Armenian wittnessed and some Howard imbesselled this was the
accompt hee gave, soe the governor againe wished me to rest satisfied and lett
the goods remayne in his power untill the busynes were ended and delivered
Sprage into my hands which I was not a little glad of, that hee should beare
noe wittnesse against mee, and att my cominge home with him I demaunded
of him bills of 1400 rupees which were delivered him (beinge imployed per Sir
Thomas Roe for Decan to recover the monye beinge a debte made per Francis
Fetiplace and company in Agra), which bills hee said the Armenian had taken
from him, which brought mee a new trouble to procure them out of his hands,
beinge noe other meanes but by force, soe the next day went to the governor
and acquainted him what force the Armenian had used to Sprage in takinge

bills of debte from him, who presentlye before hee departed caused the bills to be delivered mee which was better then I expected, and for feare of more troubles with Sprage and this busynes the 22th Aprill last I despeeded him and the bills for Surat who I have hard are safe arived, soe you may please to perceave noe hope of the lease of the goods without the kinge or prince's firmaen, Swaryes haveinge per reporte given to the Armenians 3000 rupees, 1000 rupees to the justice of the towne, besides greate guiffs to the governor, soe I resolved to departe the cittye and leave John Banggam there to looke after the goods untill other order from Suratt writinge them at large of all passages before my departure I ended with the camell men that were hired in Agra to carrye the goods to Suratt and goinge little farther then Bramport and detayned there 20 dayes and more in hope of release of the goods and after per indifferent men, itt was soe ordered that they retorned 470 and a[ ] ho[ ] which was more then ever was expected. The Armenian reported to the governor that Sir Thomas Roe att his departure had taken order with the merchants in Suratt that they should content Swaryes for his Chenye which yf were true, was the cause of your Worshipps extraordnary expence with noe smale toyle and trouble to your servaunts, soe the 22th Aprill last att night after despeed of Sprage our goods beinge 10 courses out of towne I departed Bramport after them, and with noe smale trouble (beinge then the heate of the yeare) wee with the goods God be praysed saflye arived in Agra where the kinge was the 23th of Maye past where wee found Francis Fetiplace and Roberte Huges, a daye or 2 after our arivall I presented the kinge and prince, and within 8 dayes after I procured a firmaen for the release of our goods in Bramport and for restitution for the indico forced from John Yonge uppon the waye to Suratt, which I presently dispeeded for Bramport havinge notice they in Suratt had sent Giles James thether to follow that busynes, but that firmaen with James' endevours could not prevayle with the governor there to release the one nor give us remidye for the other which uppon his advice thereof I procured a second firmaen with other meanes and thanks be to God more effectuall then the former for uppon sight thereof all the goods were released without payment of anythinge and the governor alsoe gave his writinge to Giles James to the towne where the indico was forced from John Yonge that wee should have satisfaction, soe how the indico busynes tis followed per them in Suratt I here not as yett beinge good hopes for recoverye which God send effected, I maye saye those goods in Bramport were happylye and in good time released both for this shipp's lading for England, but principallye for the furnishinge Persia with a good quantitie of goods all cominge in good time to Suratt, soe your Worshipps maye please to perceave it hath pleased God after some trouble this busynes is ended for the present, yf the Portingall Swaryes att his retorne out of Decann doe not againe renew our troubles, how soe ever you may be confident for my owne parte I will never consent to the payinge him a pennye unless forced, which yf have anye writinge of Nicholas Banggam's hand for the goods delivered him I feare in the end shalbee constrayned to paye what hee can shew anye writinge for, yf in the meanetime the said Banggam give him not content per writinge of the disposure of the goods, which I doubte not but your worshipps will cause him to doe after the Ann's ariveall per which conveance you will here of his busynes per Sir Thomas Roe who was most acquainted with that busynes the Padrye have often spoake to him about itt.

---

[1] *farmān* (Pers.): royal decree, grant, licence, permit
[2] shamiana; *shāmiyāna* (Pers.): striped calico, possibly used for awning or canopy

6
COURT MINUTES
25 JULY 1623
B/8 EXTRACT FROM PP. 34-35

This meeting beeing appointed principally for conference with Mr Monnox lately retourned out of Persia in the Companie's shipp the Lyon, he was calld in.

Beeing demaunded what become of the goodes which the English took there, he answeared that the sea commaunders and pursers took uppon them the sale but sould much underfoot, for their were none suffered to buy but Persians. The Armenians came downe to Gom-broone[1] thincking to have bought but were not suffered to come neere them. And for that sale (such as it was) they had accompted with the Companie's factors att Suratt.

---

[1] also known as Bandar Abbas, a port on the Persian Gulf

7
WILLIAM BELL, THOMAS BARKER, JOHN PUREFEY AND JOHN HAYWARD AT ISFAHAN TO COMPANY IN LONDON
15 OCTOBER 1623, WITH POSTSCRIPT 9 JANUARY 1623/24
E/3/10 EXTRACT FROM FF. 21, 24

[Conversation with 'Aga Emeere', secretary to the King of Persia]

Concerning losse of waight in silke. We shall what sorts we desire brought to Spahan[1] free of charges and delivered us heere at the full waight at fifty tomans per load. Which price we replied was more then others did give, charges deducted, for that the charges from thence hither would not amount so much as to raise 5 tomans in a load, at which rate we understood he had sold to some Armenians. His reply was it was not so for this was all the king would doe, which with much difficulty he had procured of his majestie.

It hath beene averred unto the king, that the Armenians themselves the last 2 yeares lost much by their silke in Aleppo. Insomuch that we have hope, now they denie the export of the king's silke but on better tearmes, to find farre better price. But however it is manifest that they are forct to doe what they doe.

Postscript

Understanding from Cogiah[2] Nazir Governor of the Armenians this present evening he meant to dispeede a shatir[3] for Aleppo we adventure the hazard of sending, and shall by God's helpe, send you another copie so soone as Bagdate will affoard passage with relation of the state of your affaires in these parts.

[1] also spelled Spahaune, Spahawn, Aspahaune, Ispahaune, Ispahan; modern spelling, Isfahan: the then capital of Persia

[2] also spelled coja and cojah: *khwāja* or *khvāja* (Pers.): a title of respect given in Muslim lands to wealthy merchants

[3] also spelled shoter and shotter; *shāter* (Ar. / Pers.): a running footman, courier, runner

8

THOMAS RASTELL, GILES JAMES AND RICHARD LANCASTER ABOARD
THE WILLIAM IN SWALLY ROAD TO COMPANY IN LONDON 14
FEBRUARY 1624/25
E/3/10 EXTRACT FROM FF. 218-218V

Broad clothes. . . .is a comodity of tedious and most chargeable dispatch to shift of in quantities namely at court, where their speediest vend is expected, fortie or fiftie peeces yeerely is the most wee would wish you to send, seing that their abatement in price will noe way further the sale of quantities for as in all things else in this countrie, soe in that one comodity especially, tis necessitye and not cheapenes that gives life to unusual quicker dispatches. Those apointed for Mocha and Persia, wee have sent along on the fleete for Ormoos, the rest wee have here landed, where they continue at their wonted vallewes, but above in Lahore etc are greatly abased of former esteeme by reason of quantities brought thether by Armenians, though wee supose them clothes of other countries.

9
COURT MINUTES
1 MARCH 1625/26
B/10 EXTRACT FROM P. 297

Mr Abbdy made knowne unto the Court, that in the Lowe Countries are 4 or 5 Armenians who brought silke over to sell, and are desirous to transporte themselves and 50000 Rs for Surratt in the Englishe Companie's shipping, and offer to give content for the same, and that himselfe had given answeare that if they would give warrant to any to treate and conclude with the Companie the motion would be imbraced, which answeare was approved of, and thoughe the Court conceaved it fitt to demaund 10 li per cent for theire monneys, and [?100] per man for theire passages, yet not to declare theire opinion heerein, till some authorized to treate and conclude shall presente themselves to the Company.

10
THOMAS BARKER, JOHN PUREFEY, ROBERT LOFTUS AND GEORGE
SMITH AT ISFAHAN TO COMPANY IN LONDON
14 JUNE 1626
E/3/11 EXTRACT FROM FF. 115V, 117

Wee have received yours of the 15th of March 1623, of the 12th of November 1624, of the 16/18 March ditto anno, and of the 29th Aprill anno 1625, all which came to hands the 27th Maye passed by an Armenian from Aleppo.

For Sir Robert Sherly whoe pretendeth himeselfe to bee an ambassador from the kinge of Persia your Worshipps have truly related howe that his Majestie of Persia did never soe much as to us make mention of hime, much lesse of his ambassadge. This wee knowe that hee hath correspondence with the fryers resident in this place, whoe have advertized the kinge of his intended returne hither, and wee suppose that would bee more welcome newse to his Majestie that hee remayned in Christendom, his proposicions beeinge two are but futilous and unlikely ever to bee accomplished. The first beinge the providinge of a galley manifesteth the truth of his ambassadge for for what cause should the kinge of Persia instance that when there is soe maney 20 at least good friggotts or galliots lye as unprofitable at the port a drye, which yf well maned would bee able to resist the ordinarie number of Portugall friggotts courseringe about Ormuz and other virine[1] partes to the noe small dammadge of the poore inhabitants. For the other beinge the transport of marchants from hence into England and hither againe, that is to bee understood that noe Persian nor Moore will adventure themselves uppon our shipps soe longe voyadges per adventure. Some Armenians or Chulfalines whoe once haveing tasted of the necessitie (oftymes) and the teadiousnes of them will have small encouradgment to undertake them especiallie beinge men timorous of their estates and for the most [document damaged] to travill by land, but wee will leave Sir Robert to his owne inventions.

[1] probably riverine

11

COURT MINUTES
29 DECEMBER 1626
B/11 EXTRACT FROM P. 295

Mr Mun put the Court in mind that although they have resolved to abandon the Persian trade yett it would be good advantage for the Companie to send 100 or 200 clothes to Gombroone by this fleete for that they are advertized that divers Armenians came downe the last yeare to the waterside in great number expecting cloth and that both then and now, they have brought thether great quantities of gold to traffique with us whereby it is very probable the Companie will make a good markett of their cloth there which would not be neglected.

12

COURT MINUTES
5 JANUARY 1626/27
B/11 EXTRACT FROM P. 309

It was this day ordred by erection of hands to send in this fleete 200 cloths to be vented at Gombroone, and other places at the waterside, where it is reported many Armenians, Jewes, and Persians are come downe with great quantites of gould to buy commodities.

13
[SURAT TO COMPANY IN LONDON]
[DECEMBER 1628]
E/3/12 EXTRACT FROM F. 56V

Wee gave presente order to your servants in Amadavad to goe through for the whole parcell of old indico of the last yere's groweth which wee weare ascertained to be extraordinary good and in opinion of some of our people and brokers is little inferiour to that made in Agra. This also gave noe hopes of itts falling in price, neither doe wee conceive it will if all hereafter except the Armenian and Moore marchants doe forbeare their buying for Persia etc where it is in much request and this yere not so little [] 1500 bales laden upon your and Dutch shipps.

14
WILLIAM BURT, ROBERT WODDER, WILLIAM GIBSON, ROBERT
LOFTUS AND JOHN BORIMAN
AT GOMBROON TO SURAT
20 FEBRUARY 1628/29
E/3/12 EXTRACT FROM FF. 64-64V

Concerning our holding frindshipp with the Armen[ians] it must bee referred to our discrecions, wee let not to know them well enough and their base proceeds, yet the cheife of them are many times usefull to us, in our masters' busines, with whome wee shall hold noe more correspondency then needs must.

15
RICHARD BARBER, RICHARD PREDYS, ARTHUR SUFFEY, RICHARD
PYKE, JOHN SKIBBOWE, NATHANIEL MOUNTENEY, AND JOHN
NORRIS AT SWALLY TO COMPANY IN LONDON
13 APRIL 1630
E/3/12 EXTRACT FROM F. 123

One thing bee pleased for the future to provide for a more faire correspondency from the factors of each stock or your accion, both there and here, will suffer, and why the two shippes of the new stock made noe more freight from hence, Mr Heines will or can give a reason, as also why somany of your rialls of eight are come back from thence, aswell by English as Moores and Armenians. sterling upward of 50˘000 ryalls all new and the greater part in your owne baggs. number and seales as from England, as our brokers and sheraffs[1] doe informe us, to have seene past in custome house. Your worships may therefore spare the charge of strengthing the chests with iron hoopes for there more safe transport to Spahan, whether by generall report doe verry few of your rialls arrive in the same kinde you doe send them.

---

[1] *sarrāf* (Ar. / Pers.): money-changer, moneylender, or expert employed to detect bad coins

16

THOMAS RASTELL, JOSEPH HOPKINSON, JAMES BICKFORD AND ARTHUR SUFFEY AT SURAT TO COMPANY IN LONDON
31 DECEMBER 1630
E/3/12 EXTRACT FROM F. 204

And for callicoe lawnes, or shashes, namely sallowes, guldares, surfalles and cuscosees etc, wee will desist in the buying of any more untill you may be better confirmed in the sale of those already sent home, which if transferd for Turkey, wee are confident would yeeld good proffit, and vend in infinite quantities, for evidence whereof you may please to observe that they are the cheifest comodities wherein the Persians and Armenians (who takes yearely passage on your shipps) doe invest great summes of mony here in India, some of them makeing instant sale thereof att Gumbroone, from whence they are dispersed and sould againe to second marchants in Spahan, Balzar, Bagdat etc, who transport them yet further for a third markett at Constantynople, and other places at extraordinary charge of camell hier, customes, and other exactions on the way, and yet every of these at the first, second and third hand doe become great gainers, and make it their constant trade of liveing. Now the premises considered, wee see noe reason why their should not be a divertion of this great traffique thus expensive by land by your less chargeable conveyance by sea (at least for a good partt thereof) as hath ben brought to passe allready for those great quantityes of indicoe and callicoes, wherewith you now dayly furnish those forraigne parts yourselves, which in the selfe same kinde by land hath been formerly performed by others.

Your commission injoyning a large investment this yeare in both sorts of indicoe that wee might the better make choyce of the fewer quantities of callicoes required, is greatly crost by the great want of raines in these partts, espetially about Amadavad, where their this yeare's whole cropp on the ground is not likly to produce above two or three hundred fardles[1], which in former tymes hath not been soe little as 4 or 5000. And for that of the passed yeares growth, the many buyers as well Dutch as Persians, Armenians etc having furnished themselves with the choycest ware at excessive high rates, there is left but a poore remaines of refuse stuff behinde enough only for this countrye's service and yet that not to be purchast under 18 rupes the maund, which therefore wee determine not to meddle with though at farr lesse rates in respect of its badd condition.

¹ fardel: bundle or small pack

17

EDWARD HEYNES AND WILLIAM GIBSON ON BOARD THE DISCOVERY AT GOMBROON TO COMPANY IN LONDON
17 MARCH 1630/31
E/3/12 EXTRACT FROM F. 244V

The Augustine and Carmalite friars att Spahan solicite the kinge and chon for Ormous againe, and the Frenche Capochine friars are peticioners to contract with the kinge for all his silkes for ready mony for the Frenche Company to be past by the way of Alleppo, in both theis they have little hope, being strongely oposed by ourselves, Dutch, and Armenian Jullfareyns, who are in joynt faction with us. There shall want no meanes by us to prevent their designes there.

18

EDWARD HEYNES AND WILLIAM GIBSON AT ISFAHAN TO COMPANY IN LONDON
26 SEPTEMBER 1631
E/3/13 EXTRACT FROM FF. 69-73

You shall not have cause to doubt of the securitie of your estate in theis partts, if this kinge should breake contract with you, which wee have byn very fearefull of as on a succeedinge claws, wee shall express unto your Worships more at large. The worst that could have happend would a byn butt forbarrance a year or two in tyme, such a cargazon of cloth and tynn cannot be expected to be vended in many years, if the kinge leaves us, espetially where the country is as completly supplied with the like commodity from Turke and Russia by the Armenian and Alleppo merchants, at the like price, and by which trade they live, our advices overland will satisfie you in that doubt, and per adventure give you more incouradgment to this trade then indeed att present wee should wish or desier. Butt to direct your fleete to make Persia their first portt in such a seazon as August or September, the tyme of heats, in expectacion of your servants' readines to receive your goods, transportt downe silks (if soe tymely procured) and goods from portt to Spahan, out of danger of your fleet's absence, is a project delivered unto your Worships by one that was either ignorant of the quallitye of the country, or did not well digest the probabillite thereof, Gombroone in that seazon of heats is unpeopled, either of Governor, shabandar[1] or merchants, all fleed in feare of contagion, poore fishermen natural of the place remanyninge, cammells for transportt of goods downe or upp not to be procured one any tearmes, watter nor feedinge found in ther travells to sustayne liefe for man or beast.

The ould Emperor Shaw Abbas. . .prohibited all men what nation soever to buy any silks unless from his hands, and to the ende all should bee collected and brought into his magazenes[2], hee sent his servants with ready money to all places where silks grewe to buy from the countrey people. . .hee complied yearlie with the English and Dutch nacions, sould partt unto the Jullfaleyne Armenians att 10 tomands the loade proffitt, which was transportted by the way of Alleppo, some hee adventured with them one his proper accompt and the rest hee hoorded in his magazenes, providentlie doubtinge silks in some yeares might faile, and then such thus reserved would both satisfie his contractts and sell to his greater profitt.

After the death of the ould Emperor, this his successor. . .ignorant of such provident courses of his grandfather gave content to all, continued contract with us, and gave lycence to buy silks in all partts of his kingdome without restriccion which brought him into want, and now doth inable him to complie with us and the Dutch as his father did. . . Why then doth hee not prohibitt the buyeinge of silks, as his grandfather did? It is answered that the faccion of the Julfelynes Armenians and other merchants of Guyland and Sherwan, whoe have there trade to Alleppo by their extreame bribes to his ducks nobles and ministers prevents him where have alsoe there factors in those partts, to buy and sell yearly to there most advantage, regardinge more there one perticular proffitt then there king's honour, or benifitt of there common weale.

The Julfaylene Armenians and other merchants that yearely trade with silke to Alleppo and those partts, had the greatest partt of the nobles in faccion with them to oppose stronglie our proceedings.

The Emperor. . .hath prohibbited all transportt of silks by way of Turkie, and not any man to buy a baile butt from his hands the better to performe with us, makeinge Spahan his martt and Gombroon his portt for all silks in his empire. He will offer to your consideracion certaine propositions for a further contract when this off 3 years is expired.

Itt is not to bee doubted but silks will be more plenty, and at reasonable rates, then in former tymes itt hath byn, when not any is to bee transportted butt by our selves and the Dutch, and that from the hands of the Armenians and other merchants that usuall trade with itt for Alleppo, espetially if the

Russian trade for silks that way proceede not, which is nowe in agitacion with the Emperor.

Wee hope our service in divertinge the streams of silks from the currant of Turkie will not bee displeaseinge to your worships. Wee have had stronge oppositions therein by the Armenians Jullfaleyns and others.

The Dutch. . .are now fallen one contract with the Armenians, to receive silks from them at portt Gombroone att 50 tomandes the loade in halfe mony halfe broadcloth, and India commodities at rates of the martt in that place.

[1] *shāh-bandar* (Pers.): literally, harbor-king; port officer, often also head of customs

[2] magazine: warehouse, depot

19

EDWARD HEYNES AND WILLIAM GIBSON AT ISFAHAN TO COMPANY IN LONDON
10 OCTOBER 1631
E/3/13 EXTRACT FROM F. 97V

This yeare silke is like to be scarce and very deare the Armenians have given for silke in Quyland 43 tomands the loade first peny in hope to transportt itt to Alleppo where by advice wee understand itt is worth 13 and $13^1/_2$ royalls de ratle[1], wherein faylinge by reason the Emperor's crook or prohibition hath overtaken them, that they may not vend their silks that way, they are forced to bringe all to Spahan, and will rather keepe itt by them then sell itt unto us at reasonable profitt to pay them at Gombroone, soe spightfull they are against us, because wee have soe farr prevayled with the kinge, as to forbidd the transportt of all silks by the way of Turkie. Wee doubt not butt under hand some will bee transportted, but the currant of their generall trade will be greatly hindred. Wee have indeavored to buy silk uppon creditt, but cannot prevaile with these people, which are doubtfull of our complie with them in case our shipps should faile us, as the last yeare they did the Dutch, but if you please to invest us yearly with ready monys, more then will com-plie with the kinge, wee shall not doubt to make you a more profittable returne then formerly.

[1] sic - unidentified [?royalls = currency; de ratle = per *ratl* (measure of weight)]

20

EDWARD HEYNES, WILLIAM GIBSON AND RICHARD COOPER AT GOMBROON TO SURAT
26 FEBRUARY 1631/32
E/3/13 EXTRACT FROM FF. 176-176v

The Dutch notwithstandinge the kinge oweth them neare uppon the amount of 12000 tomands one former accompts, and have not this yeare delivered them one baile of sylke towards satisfaction, yett have they landed in money and goods to the amount of 300000 li starlinge of which 150000 li ready money, whoe beinge refused contract with the kinge and distracted in their bussines, yett with this cavidall[1] intend to f[ ] this trade at portt, and this yeare beinge not silks brought downe by merchants as was expected, wherby to invest ther ready moneys and put of goods in barter theroff, indeavors to make sale of ther goods for ready money in this place, with which and other ther speties, they resolve to deale with the Julfaline Armenians by way of contract for sylks, and soe leave the kinge altogeather. This is a project secyable, and greatlie desiered one both sides, which if not crosed by the kinge, will produce a certayne proffitable trayde unto them, if our abillities could answer thers, our experience is as much, and our reputacons with these Armenians more, wee asure you if they runn therin a thriveinge course, wee will share with them as farr as our small meanes will give leave, or elce spoyle ther marketts.

[1] possibly distortion of caveat: warning, admonition

21

WILLIAM GIBSON, JOHN SHERLAND, RICHARD COOPER AND WILLIAM FALL AT GOMBROON
TO COMPANY IN LONDON
22 MARCH 1631/32
E/3/13 EXTRACT FROM FF. 182v-183

Mr Wild who homewards bownd meetinge with President Rastell, our unfortunate freind, att St Lawrense, itt should seeme faling in discourse aboute Mr Burtt, tould him the better parte of royalls sent on your fleete by Captain Weddall for accompt of the first voyadge, was disburst att portt for his and our owne privat uses as appeared by the greate quantitie of India commoditys wee bought that yeare and the greate quantitie of royalls many Armenians which tooke theire passage one our shipps weer possest withall from us, which is a most falce tayle, as I shall make itt appeare unto your Worships in these following lynes. That wee disburst royalls and bought India comoditys is trew, butt howe Mr Burtt being in Spahan wrote downe to us att portt that if any quantitie of India comoditys should arive, and to bee hadd att resonable rates, wee should invest therin to the vallew of 800 or 1000 tomands for your accompts and bringe itt upp to Spahan for sale there, for that hee thought hee could putt them off to the treasurer with advantage, and to bee accepted of as readie money, which accordinglie wee did, and as by the bookes for accompt of the first voyage will appeare. And for the quantitie of royals the Armenians hadd from us, was thus, Mr Burtt att our departure Spahan by consultacion resolved towards the courte, and what monies hee thought fitting for expences or otherwise, was agreed hee should take upp in Spahan and charge us by bills of exchange downe to portt which he did, and these whome hee tooke itt of weere Armenians, who receaving them from us, sent them for India, and this was the bussines, and the truth as your bookes of accompts of this factorie will wittnes.

22

EDWARD KIRKHAM, THOMAS ROSSE, JOHN SHERLAND AND WILLIAM FALL AT GOMBROON TO COMPANY IN LONDON 21 OCTOBER 1632 E/3/14 EXTRACT FROM F. 62V

There hath byn an overture made unto us by the grand Armenians in Spahan that they if wee shall like off that wilbee come our contractours for whatsoever quantitie of silke wee shall have occasion to transporte from Persia, and that with a free approbacion off the kinge. Wherefore wee only now give your Worships a touch, but shall more at large advise yow at our comeing up to Spahan. Wee confesse that if ther be a meanes that wee may deale in a more merchant like way then wee can do with the kinge, that is worthy to bee embraced provided the condicions bee as good. Neither is that unlikely but it may bee done in regard they are great monyed men that proffer it, besides that will bee a meanes to extenuate the excessive charges wee are at in presents.

23

WILLIAM GIBSON, RICHARD COOPER AND WILLIAM FALL AT
ISFAHAN
TO COMPANY IN LONDON
26 JUNE 1633
E/3/14 EXTRACT FROM FF. 167V-168

Wheras yow would have us to deale with the Armenians, knew your worships the bassenes of the nation in all manner of degrees yow would never wish us therto, for experience in small matters wee have had occation to use them hath made all of us (that knowe them) vowe never to have to doe with them againe, soe unfaithfull in word and deede soe ungratefull for curtesies when their owne turnes are served soe griping and deceiptfull in their dealings and soe slowe in performing of theire promises are they even from the meanest to the very best of them all. That there hath beene such an overture made unto us by them we must confesse is truth, but knowing them to be as aforesaid how thinke your worships tis to be imbraced besids will not this Emperour wonder thinke yow when our king's majestie (whose bussines both himselfe and people takes it to be) shall leave him to deale with such as they are whom wee alsoe knowe should we accept of the proffer they are not able to performe it, but only as we conceave a meere trick to bring us first in disgrace with the king and soe by a little and a little to worke us cleane out of all which wee are perswaded is both their desire and the end of their purpose, and to deale plainely, they have reason for it for our trade heere hath taken the very bread out of their mouthes, which before our coming they frely enjoyed and were this king's only merchants for most of his silkes that was transported out of his country, but since ours and the Duches' arivall they have been glad to content themselves with what by much labour and travayle they can gett and not to be attained to any vallew but by some of the best of them nether as by our advises formerly seing the king's soe long denyall of contract to the Hollanders (as aforesaid) we thought, perceaving some extraordinary familliaritye and by some of the Armenians themselves confessed thinking therby to drawe us in, they had made one with them but since wee have found it to be noe such matter. This is a bussines wee find yow are much wisht unto by Mr Kirkham in his letter by the James whom we are perswaded had it beene his fortune to have lived to have tryed the fedility of the nation would have repented him of the project. It may be notwithstanding all these reasons, your worships, seeing the great charge yow are att and the king's soe badd performance, will wish rather one of theise two courses to be imbraced vizt ether the leberty of the marketts or contract with the Armenians, which if yow doe we must tell yow we shalbe loath it should be in our tymes in that we knowe whatt wilbe the issue, and as we have given yow our reasons and opinions as aforesaid soe doe we still conforme it, yow cannot drive any trade heere to any purpose except yow deale with the king whom although hee hath much fayled us at his first entrance wee have hopes that by his good comply in the future he will give us content. God willing within this 5 or 6 dayes at furthest wee are to take our journey towards court, where we shall by all meanes possible indeavour to settle our bussines wholy upon one as formerly.

24
COURT MINUTES
2 AUGUST 1633
B/16 EXTRACT FROM PP. 33-34

Edward Oakely peticioned the Court shewing that hee being taken into the East Indies by Captain Greene deceased was after his death taken a shoare by Mr Heynes the Companie's Agent in Persia where and ever since untill his arrivall in the Blessing hee did the Company service in which respect his humble suyte was that being destitute of freinds, and having noe meanes of livelyhood the Court wold bee pleased to take him into their consideracion and to bestow something upon him. The Court observed hee went without the Companie's order, and therefore that hee rather deserved to bee punished and to pay for his dyett then to expect any recompence from them. But understanding that the said Oakely was one of them that came along with the Companie's silke in company of Walter Mountford from Spahan to Gombroone, and that hee was able to give the Company a perticuler relation of the 2 bales of silke which are missing hee was demaunded his knowledge therein. Hee confessed hee came in company with Mountford, that they travayled togeather all night, that hee was at the baling of the silke, and for ought hee knowes all was delivered into the Companie's warehouse as it came from Spahan, remembers that after their coming to Gombroone 2 bales were missing which were stolne by an Armenian, but Gove by causing a figure to bee cast for them hee found them againe under a pile of wood, acknowledged that there is a great deale of knavery and dishonesty used by the Companie's factors in buying of silke for themselves and selling it to the Dutch, that there came from Spahan 50 camells laden with silke for the Company which brought above 100 bales, whereof 4 of them was Mr Gibson's. The Court having discovered thus much from him wished him to sett downe what hee knew in writing, and thereupon referred him to Mr Ellam to take an exact accompt from him both concerning the said 2 bales of silke, or any other abuse done the Company wishing him if hee expect to receive any favour at their hands to deale truly and faithfully with them which hee promised to doe.

25

WILLIAM FREMLIN, WILLIAM METHWOLD, ANDREW COGAN,
FRANCIS BRETON, BENJAMIN ROBINSON AND JOHN WYLDE ON
BOARD THE ROYAL MARY OFF SURAT TO COMPANY IN LONDON 4
JANUARY 1638/39
E/3/16 EXTRACT FROM FF. 198-198v

You may please to remember that the Swann arriving from Gombroone
the 26th of Aprill rode at the river's mouth and from thence by boates of this
towne, your silke with such passengers and theire goods as came uppon her
were landed at Suratt which occationed her 8 dayes stay, and then she sett saile
for Mesulapatam but before shee departed two Armenians pretended unto
Francis Breton then aboord that theire goods were embeazeled, one whearof
had lost his buckshaw[1] whearin hee named severall thinges amounting to the
value of 146 m[aund]. The other produced his sapetto[2] which beeing filled
with amber beades a hole was cutt open uppon the cover and theare appeared
some want which was apparant to the master of the shippe and all his
company, but then was no time to make search, soe that theare was litle other
remedy but that these men must have sattisfaction which the shippe's company
without all scruple were to make good, and heere wee hoped that this
businesse would have had an end. But much contrary to our expectation it
beeing now the 8th of May and the shippe some dayes since departed, her
passingers beeing now in action to cleare theire goods in custome house
proofferred diverse complaints against us for severall sorts of goods stolne out
of theire sapettoes some of which were cutt upp and sowen againe, others had
the lockes broken off and new lockes hung on which theire keyes would not
open and zerbasses[3], taffataes, amber beades, saffron, ready money etc taken
out by the English, for which they required sattisfaction from us heere because
it befell them in our shippe and was done by our people, and now againe in all
posthast wee must appeare before the governor who noe sooner saw us, but
by his invective and contumelious speeches hee declared with what
praejudicary hee stood affected to our praejudice, wee answered that the
shippe was now departed and that during the 8 dayes time which shee
continued heere no man found himself aggreived the two Armenians excepted
which wee formerly mentioned. Wee produced besides an accompt of fraught
made in Gombroone which mencioned no such goods to have bine shipt
aboord as they now praetended to have lost for theare appeared onley
rosewater, fruite and provisions for which they paid fraught accordingly, and
wee tooke care of the goods according to the fraught. Wee urged also the
knowne abuses of the cammell men in Persia and of the boatmen both theare
and heere which steale all which they can carry away unseene experiencd often
on our parts, especially the former yeare in this place.
    These goods had bine also certaine dayes in the custome house during

which time theeves had broken in and stolne certaine parcells which were found againe about 2 dayes after cast into an obscure corner. In all which places theare was more probability theire goods might have bine stolne then aboord the shippe wheare they lay in hold whither our people seldome resorted. . .All which with whatsoever else wee could add would not serve our turnes. . .and wee must pay the money.

¹ probably some kind of container
² *sabad* (Ar. / Pers.): basket
³ also spelled zerboff; *zarbāf* (Pers.): gold weave, i.e., brocade silk or gold brocade

26

HENRY BORNFORD'S REPORT ON TRADE ROUTES IN INDIA
[MARCH 1638/39]
E/3/16 EXTRACT FROM F. 256

From Agra to Lahoare are counted 300 course, 22 mounzells¹ or ordinary dayes journies, places of noate bettweene them are divers, first Dillie some 80 course from Agra, formerly the seate and title of these kings, now less famous, and little frequented unless by Armenian and Persian merchants, the comodity that invites them thither being only chints, which are heere made in good quantities, well cullored in appearance little inferiour to those of Mesulapatam, different sorts and goodnes and soe diversly prized.

¹ *manzel* (Ar. / Pers.): a halting place, stage of a journey, a day's ride

27

ANDREW COGAN NEAR GOLCONDA TO MASULIPATAM
9 AUGUST 1639
E/3/17 EXTRACT FROM F. 35V

I am heartily glad your usage in Mesulapatam is soe good and that you injoy such priveledges as were graunted Mr Joice, tis not your kind useage of them hath occasioned it for since my being heere severall complaintes have bine made insoemuch that I have bine tould you have made forffett the king's firmand graunted Mr Joice, for in that firmand wee are injoyned not to farther any strangers' goodes and yett very lately a horse which was brought upon the Thomas belonging to an Armenian must be taken into the Company's howse as the Company's.

28
COURT MINUTES
19 FEBRUARY 1639/40
B/19 EXTRACT FROM P. 138

At this Court Yeldowes an Armenian servant to Cojah Suffras cheife of the Armenians in Persia presented a peticion recomended and subscribed by the Lord Maior, wherein hee desired liberty for himselfe and Carrabett another Armenian with their 2 servants to take passage on their shipp bound for Suratt paying such fraight as the Court shold thinck meete, and though the Court held it just in the first place to provide for the stowage of their owne goods, yett did they direct Mr Thomas Steevens to view the Armenians' goods being as they say putt upp in 8 chests, and to see what stowage the said chests will require, and then the Courte will give further answere.

29
COURT MINUTES
10 MARCH 1639/40
B/19 EXTRACT FROM P. 150

The Court was pleased upon the peticion of Cojah Pedroffe an Armenian to permitt him passage in their shipp Crispian with his 2 chests payeing for his passage and fraight 100 ryalls of 8 which ryalls are to bee paid to the Company's President at Suratt before his said chest bee delivered out of the shippe.

30
WILLIAM THURSTON AND EDWARD PEARCE AT BUSSORA TO COMPANY IN LONDON 22 JUNE 1640
E/3/17 EXTRACT FROM FF. 279-279v

The next thinge . . .is the traffique of this place, the which is occassioned and cheifly consists by the caphilas[1] which doth annally come hither from Alleppo in Aprill, and about the fine[2] of July with the more frequent caphilas from Bagdat, or supposed Babilon as more nearer adjoyned, as alsoe from other adjacent parts, and for the furnishment thereof, it hath hitherto received its supply (ever since the re-uniteinge of the Isle of Ormus to the Persian Empire) by barkes from Goombrone and Congo, within the Gulph, but principally from the Portugasses' Muscatt fleet, which usually setts fourth in June for Congo, and arives here sometyme in July, where they have 2 Romish covents, and secular padres residentiaries therein. . .As for the inhabitants themselves, being a Messaline nation, consistinge of Arabs in cheife, Turks, Persians, Armenians, Moores and Banians, who are generally in gesture grave, but in discourse facetious, what other good properties they possess wee must leave it to an after tryall, onely this much beleeve, inconstant, and soe consequently not much trustable, of which wee are very cautious.

[1] qāfela (Ar. / Pers.): caravan
[2] end

31
WILLIAM FREMLIN, FRANCIS BRETON, BENJAMIN ROBINSON AND JOHN WYLDE AT SWALLY TO COMPANY IN LONDON
29 DECEMBER 1640
E/3/17 EXTRACT FROM FF. 314V-315

What you are pleased to prescribe touching non admission of strangers to passe to England on your home bound ships shall God willing be punctually observed and your Worships farther desired hereby never hereafter to grant license to any as you did on this your ship Crispiana to those Armenians (in name only) for here the greater part of them doe call themselves Mussulmen and have adferd no small trouble to your ship's company in theire voiage, wherof Mr Steevens will more largely informe you, from whom (though with some wrangling) we have received what they covenanted to pay you, they pretending we know not what damage was befallen theire looking glasses, which they might better have looked unto, and so they were answered. Theire chests were on the greatest part stuffed with broad cloth and corall beads sold by them at very meane prizes to this Governor, who we beleive will make them dance attendance for theire monies, in which predicament we leave them.

32
COURT MINUTES
4 APRIL 1645
B/21 EXTRACT FROM P. 287

Mr Deputy acquainted the Court that there was 3 Armenians now in London, which came from Persia to the king of Poland, desired that they might have passage on the Mary for Bantam, whereupon the Court willed them to bee called in, and they declaring that they would give a reasonable fraight for their goods, and pay for their diett, the Court was pleased to order that they should goe on the Mary paying 200 ryalls of eight for themselves and their goods, and to have the shipp's dyett.

33
COURT MINUTES
2 MAY 1645
B/21 EXTRACT FROM P. 291

The Court was this day pleased to bestowe upon a poore Armenians preist 10s in charity out of the poores box.

34
WILLIAM PITT, PHILIP WYLDE AND THOMAS CODRINGTON AT
ISFAHAN TO SURAT
7 SEPTEMBER 1645
E/3/19 EXTRACT FROM FF. 232V-233

William Pitt. . .tooke his journey for Spahan where he arrived the 17 June and found that Thomas Codrington had disposed of all butt 5 peices of our Honourable imployers' broadcloth. . .and pretends that if he had not made sale of itt as he did it would have laine by us a yeare longer, we must confesse that tradinge here at present is very dead in soe much that the report of all men never knowne to bee worse yett since not any but our Honourable Company hath any quantity of broadcloth here, wee cannot conceave but the smale quantity we had here might find vend in all this time, had it been diligently looked after, beside we thinke it had beene noe more than fittinge that since it was not sould off in the 9 months time of our absence from hence, Thomas Codrington (well knoweinge by the latenesse of the yeare that we could but arrive with him in 3 or 4 dayes as we did) might have aweighted soe longe time which will of necessity enforce us to leave one here upon noe small expences to recover the debt (which might have been prevented it may bee had he aweighted for long time to take our advices about the sale of itt rather then to put it of as he did, of his owne head without order at soe long time) and yett could the mony be receaved when it falls due and speedily sent downe unto us that soe we might send it unto you the next monzoone the busines would not be soe bad, but it is much to be doubted, since the cloth is sould off to Carra Kaun etc Armenians experienced bad paymasters such as (if William Pitt had arrived time enough) should not have binne trusted in the least butt since they have it already in their possession it is now to late to recall whatt is done. If you should send more cloth the next moonzone (as we hope you will nott) we must resolve to putt it off in Bundar for what itt will yeild for to transport up to Shiraz or hither in hope of better marketts for itt we cannot expect to make salle of itt in a yeare's time, soe little is it esteemed here att present nor is it likely to find better or more ready vend here till such time we have tradinge againe with the King then peradventure it may as formerly be put of in trucke for silke but till then wee cannot advise you to send any quantity of that specie hither.

35

Edward Knipe and William Jesson at Agra to Surat
12 November 1645
E/3/19 Extract from ff. 279-279v

By reporte of all men that have bynn uppon the indico imployment, thoes that are the owners therof will not bee brought to anie reasonable price for their commodity till necessety forceth them to sell, and have heard itt by English and Dutch spoken they have not uppon their comeing to Byana bought one seare[1] of indico in a moneth after, the sellers beeing soe extraordnary unreasonable in their demands. Then how is itt possible wee showld advise of the rates therof before wee have beate a bargaine, for allthough about Corja and other partes where English and Dutch useth not to goe, to make their owne investments, the price is comonly broken by Mogulls and Armenians, but in Byana, Hendowne, and thoes partes adjacent no Mogull or Armenian can breake price there, because their whole dependance is uppon our 2 nacions, and in tyme when they have bynn att varience with ech other, striveing whoe showld give most for the comodity, then hath bynn the sellers' harvest. Wee to prevent this inconveinencie, findeing Signor Van Burgh a rationall honnest man, have soe accorded as not one to out vie the others, conceiveing a sufficient proporcion for both parties. Now soe long as the Hollanders shall walke with us upprightly wee intend our correspondencie shall admitt of noe exception. But if once wee finde them fallter will use them according. Three daies since wee had musters sent from Corja, from such wee imployed there to buy, giveing us intelligence that there bee abonndance of buyers both Mogulls and Armenians, whoe have brought the price to 33 rupees per maund not fully dry. These men by us sent have bought a small parcell, wee intend to suffer them buyeing till wee are certeine of haveing our quantity compleated att Byana and Hendowne, of which so soone as wee shall have notice intend to forbidd them att Corja proceede any further in that investment, allthough wee finde the indico without exception.

[1] also spelled seer; *sir* (Pers.): weight varying in different parts of India or a measure of capacity

36

FRANCIS BRETON, THOMAS MERRY, WILLIAM THURSTON, GEORGE TASH AND RICHARD FITCH AT SWALLY TO COMPANY IN LONDON
3 JANUARY 1645/46
E/3/19 EXTRACT FROM FF. 305v-306

Since Agra was so aboundantly supplied with broadcloth overland by Armenians, and the King plentifully furnished with that specie. . .it hath been much disrequested, but we hope will in few yeares recover its pristine esteem and price, which we shall endeavour to procure by continuing some last year's practice, in sending all to Persia, rather submitting thare to take for it what may be procured (in regard we cannot hope to rule those markets, which are constantly supplyed by way of Aleppo) then to vend it here for what it will yield, and so keep it from rising, to which purpose, it hath until lately been continued on the Marine, and reported to be all intended to Persia, which this Governor and Duan perceiving have upon view of 2 peeces contracted with us for 150 covets[1] of stamel[2], and 400 of green, the former at $8^1/_2$ rupees and the latter at 9 rupees.

[1] covid: measure of length; its length varied at different places and times, from 36 to 14 inches
[2] stammel: coarse woollen cloth, usually dyed red

37

WILLIAM PITT, ROBERT HEYNS AND SAMUEL WILTON AT GOMBROON TO COMPANY IN LONDON 9 MAY 1646 E/3/20 EXTRACT FROM FF. 20-20v, 22

In our last wee advised you of a greate difference here betweene the king of Persia and the Hollanders. . .since when as about the beginning of June last the Hollanders with 7 ships beleagured the Castle of Kishmee. . .The king. . .being more afrighted than hurt, presently sent for Signor Bastian second of the Dutch in Spahaun, and told him if his Comaundor Block would cease from his warre and come unto him, hee should have what justice and content himselfe should desire. . .which accordingly was effected. . .Comaundor Block. . .presently resolved to goe up to Spahaun, where hee arrived the 27th July and by order of Ettamen Dowlett[1] was brought into the citty and to his house by the Governour there Meir Cassom Beage. Three daies after (not withstanding hee was somewhat indisposed to health with a cold hee tooke before hee arrived) hee visited Ettamendowlett who received him very courteously and after hee had feasted him 3 houres gave him leave to retourne to his house without conferreing about any busines. This was the first and last meeteing hee had with Ettamen Dowlett, for his cold turneing to a burneing feavor and that encreaseing every day more and more upon him the 10th August died, and the next day by order of Ettamen Dowlett was accompanied to his grave by all the Armenians in Jelpha.

Two daies after the aforesaid Ettamen Dowlett was slaine the king established one Cullafa Sultan in his place, a man that in this king's father reigne had the place once before, and as wee heare carried himselfe very well, especially to our nation. What hee will doe now time onely must demonstrate. About 8 daies after hee was confirmed in his place William Pitt visited him, when hee promised to doe us what courtesy lay in him, also said our busines should goe better than in the time of his deceased predecessour. This hee promised when William Pitt was with him, but since wee understand hee is an inveterate enemy to all Christians and soe hath already shewed himselfe unto the poore Armenians about in Spahaun endeavouring what hee can to make them turne Moores which (if true) is to bee feared hee will proove as bad as his predecessour, and yett wee hope the best till wee find to the contrary.

[1] *E'temādu'd-dawleh* (Pers.): chief minister

38

FRANCIS BRETON, THOMAS MERRY AND WILLIAM PITT AT SWALLY
TO COMPANY IN LONDON
25 JANUARY 1646/47
E/3/20 EXTRACT FROM F. 94

The Armenians, unto whom you graunted passage upon the Dolphin, were at her arivall with their goods permitted to land, who have since expressed much thankfulnes, as did one which came by way of Bantam, for the favour you were pleased therin to do them, and so they have left us very well content.

39

FRANCIS BRETON AT SURAT TO COMPANY IN LONDON
DECEMBER 1647
E/3/20 EXTRACT FROM FF. 172-172v

In your adces lately received by the Eagle you are pleased to enorder the provision of Persian silke, but such returnes (under favour) I conceive suite not with your later letters overland, nor would itt (had there been noe other impediment) have been possible to comply with your directions therein this yeare in regard itt must bee bought in Spahan, or att a farther distance, and by consequence bee enordered a yeare beforehand, which specie not being of long tyme desired by you, I conceived might continue still unrequested. Allso the conveniency of transport favouring mee therein, but cheifly a desire that you might have exact notice of its value (hopeing thereby you will againe bee encouraged to renew that trade) animateing mee thereunto, I gave directions in March last to provide 10 loads of that specie for my accompt, and entrusted the busyness unto one Coja Arabett an Armenian merchant, with order to pay customes att Gombroone on his owne name that I might bee noe way injurious to your port priviledges, nor could itt bee otherwise continued, in regard the Persian King will not yett consent that either you or the Dutch owne that commodity custome free, to the payment whereof I beleeve neither of you will submitt. Which said silke conteyned in 29 bundles or buckshaws being the whole import and entyre hopes of my future subsistance is shipped upon the Eagle, Antelop, and Greyhound, which returning full laden for that stock whereunto I have been soe ancient a servant I hope itt will neither bee thought burthensome to the ships, nor any way prejudiciall to you. I am therefore emboldned herewith to present unto you the cost and charges, humbly entreating you that itt may by your appointment bee disposed of, and haveing experimented its worth it is my farther suit that the product thereof (the charges being discompted) may bee delivered unto my brother Mr William

Breton minister att Clapton in Northampton shire for my use.

40

JOHN LEWYS AND THOMAS BEST AT GOMBROON TO SURAT
4 DECEMBER 1648
E/3/21 EXTRACT FROM FF. 42V-43

This Kinge sendinge an embassadour for Russia few monthes since made silke soe scarce, hee carriinge great quantities with him, besides beareinge soe greate price in Turkie as was said induced Armenians to buy all up they could light on.

The passed day wee received a letter from our linguist, who adviseth us of the death of Cogee Suffras the cheife of the Armenians and that another of good quality Meggardone[1] is turned Moore.

[1] possibly distortion of *moqaddam* (Ar.): a headman, leader and, by extension, representative of a community

41

FRANCIS BRETON, THOMAS MERRY, JEREMY BLACKMAN, EDWARD
PEARCE AND GEORGE OXINDEN AT SWALLY TO COMPANY IN
LONDON 31 JANUARY 1648/49
E/3/21 EXTRACT FROM F. 111V

What unhappy fate interposes our endeavours of furnishing you with such Agra indico as you desire wee know not. . .The time of its making being in August and September the principall season for its vend is October and November. Although it would bee much more advantagious to the buyers if they would desist untill the fine of December or January that the commodity might bee dry and merchandable, but such Mores Armenians and Banian merchants as buy it to transport for Persia Bussora and Mocha cannot protract time soe long, and if wee should not buy with the first, it would bee impossible to procure any good as wee experiment as often as wee have occation in February March or Aprill or afterward to make any addition to what formerly bought, and from this early buying, whilst the commodity is greene, proceeds the greate want of weight, whereof you soe often soe much complaine, which befalls you not only in England but in these parts in such as wee revend in Persia, Bussora etc.

42

THOMAS CODRINGTON AT ISFAHAN TO COMPANY IN LONDON
18 AUGUST 1650
E/3/22 EXTRACT FROM F. 23

I betooke myselfe to the writeing a few lines, thereby to give you notice of the base abuses offended unto you by your owne servants. . .viz

1th The fathering of goods inwards belonging to Moores and Armenian merchants which ought to pay custome to you and the King of Persia, this they tooke to themselves.

2 The bribs taken of the shawbander by the cheife here to make up the moitie of customes as hee pleaseth himselfe.

3 The collouring of other men's goods outwards wherein you are noe sharers with this King, I say for which great bribs are taken by them and their servants.

4 The disposeing of your goods etc busines, without the councell or knowledge of others your servants in this factorie, contrarie to your orders.

43

RICHARD DAVID AT DELHI TO SURAT
14 DECEMBER 1650
E/3/22 EXTRACT FROM F. 83

In the said accompt of quick stocke you will find what proffitt hath beene made on sales of broadcloth, which consideringe the greate quantety of that spetie in the hands of Armenien and Persian merchants is noe small proffitt, soe that the charge that the honourable Company hath beene at in presents and other things is countervailed by the sale in broadcloth which hath beene for the most part sold into the king's dullbarre[1], I refuseing otherwayes of disposure for feare of makeinge of bad debts which become very quickly unrecoverable.

---

[1] dalbehera: officer in charge of subordinate collectors of revenue

44
RICHARD DAVID AT DELHI TO SURAT
4 JANUARY 1650/51
E/3/22 EXTRACT FROM F. 102V

For broadcloth allthough heere be noe hope of sales more then formerly advised of yett you desire noe more to be truckt which order of yours I shall punctually follow untill it be contradicted and indeed there is small hopes of trucke soe that if you can dispose of that vast quantety you advise is come out on the Europe shippeinge some other waye I suppose it better then to send it upe hither where I see noe hope of sales the kinge beinge allready furnished and none elce demandinge, besides within this 2 months the Court is likely to remove to Kishmeerre at which remote distance cloth will be out of request espetially since the Armenians have clogd the markett but with badd cloth which they brought from Alleppo. Neverthelesse affter all this if you thinke it fittinge to send upe any to awaite some faire oppertunity my endeavours as becomes my dutye shall be noe wayes wantinge for disposure thereof.

45
THOMAS MERRY, EDWARD PEARCE AND GEORGE OXINDEN AT
SWALLY TO COMPANY IN LONDON
31 JANUARY 1650/51
E/3/22 EXTRACT FROM F. 141V

Wee take notice of what you write touching the fained and false pretence of certaine Aremenian merchants in the Courte of France, and as it is likely that they may preferr their complaints unto the King of Persia, seing they had noe releife in France, but found their suite there rejected, soe wee have advised your Persian factors thereof, and sent them transcribed that sexion of your letter to prepare them for your indempnity if any such thing shall happen.

46
JOHN LEWYS, THOMAS BEST AND MATHEW ANDREWES AT
GOMBROON TO COMPANY IN LONDON
8 MAY 1651
E/3/22 EXTRACT FROM F. 199V

What marketts wee shall finde aloft for the broadcloth wee cannot well advize you, since great quantities arrived there from Alleppo and those parts brought by Armenians and other merchants, besides these which wee have now received beinge all redds (wantinge divers sortments) will not give soe good contentment.

47

JOHN LEWYS, THOMAS BEST AND MATHEW ANDREWES AT ISFAHAN
TO SURAT
15 SEPTEMBER 1651
E/3/22 EXTRACT FROM F. 211

Of those Armenians which lost theire goods on our nacion's shippinge wee heare nothinge more then complaints of theire bad fortune. But few dayes since was with us 2 Jelpaleenes whose vackelles[1] had embarqued some silck etc on a French vessell, which in her voyage from Smirna to Livorne was seized on by English shippinge, and they did implore our letters unto you in theire behalves, that theire addresses may be made knowne unto the state of England in such manner as you shall thinck fitt, either from the Companie or otherwise. From this Kinge they are now procuringe a letter, which will be inscribed [Punto] ours (for yett they know not but wee have one) touching on this affaire and will be imediately by a vackeele sent for England per viam Smirna. Indeede theire case is most pitifull, heerein consistinge theire whole livelywhood and substance, beinge men of good repute and quallitie, and indeede if restoracion heerof be not made, peradventure some inconvenience may heereby accrew unto the Companie in theise parts.

Wee will heere perticularize the marchants and theire vackeeles' names, with the import of theire losses soe neere as they can guess.

Suffer vackeele to Cogee Gerragooze had silck mands shaw[2] 427 with one bale silck and 6 bale woormeseede[3].

Jacob vackeelle to Cogee Auga Beague had silck mand 246$^1/_2$

Pedruss for himselfe there aboute 1000 Royalls not knowne in what spetie.

All being laden aboard a French shipp whose Captain's name was Howder.

---

[1] also spelled vukkel, vuckell, vuckeelle; *vakil* (Pers.): an agent or representative especially of a person of political importance; a minister, envoy, or ambassador

[2] sic - unidentified

[3] wormseed: various plants, or their dried flower heads, used to treat intestinal worms

48

WILLIAM NETLAM AT MASULIPATAM TO AARON BAKER, PRESIDENT
AT BANTAM
17 SEPTEMBER 1651
E/3/22 EXTRACT FROM F. 214

Mr Thomas Peneston seles to two brother Armeneans all the tobacco he should send downe in to Bay Bengalla thatt monzon, and with the first parties cam downe one of the sayd brothers, and receaved itt into his custody to pay att the end of fouer monthes att $7^1/_4$ rupes per mand if for mor to be accomptable for halfe thatt proffitt, if for lesse Mr Peneston to bear halfe thatt losse, butt in the intrim fell a greatt deluge of rayne in Piplee whear the tobacco was delivered, which damnified much therof, doubtting and to avoyd candle, broughtt the Armenians to a sett price which was seven rupes per mand. The time being ended I repare to Piplee, for the mony, the two Armenians nott having any coude nott pay, and wantting mony boath for my selfe and Mr Wrightt, for the use of Mr Thomas Peneston, was constraynd to take the tobacco from them, which was don by order of justice, to possese the good tobacco, and the bad tobacco to be left on ther handes, and sould itt with other tobacco of Mr Peneston's for $6^1/_2$ rupes per mand mony. After which the Armen-ians complaynd I had don them much wrong, and did much intreatt thatt I would be favorrable unto them, in thatt bad tobacco I had left on ther hands, and finding they soughtt butt for equitty, on debatt att last I condecended to furgeive them two hundred rupes, which is the som with itts intrest the Duch hath putt on me (verry unjustly) they paying the rest which was due on ther bill befoar I partted Piplee, which they soughtt to doe butt could nott, soe thatt itt was 40 dayes mor or lesse, befoare the full som came to my hands the 200 rupes ecepted, however noe bussines of Mr Peneston's was hindrd for wantt of the sayd mony. After all which mony payd, one of the two brothers goes for Rajamall, his owne cuntrie men raysed a scandall on him, devoulging he was gon to the Prince, for to requier justice, for that greatt quantety of tobacco Mr Pen-eston had sentt down for which they had agreed for, as in the begining herof declard, as lickwise his cuntrymen had reportted, if he could nott have justice with the Prince, he would to the greatt King. These things coming to my heerring, made me doubttfull wheather itt moughtt prove prejudiciall to Mr Peneston or noe, accquaynted Mr Wrightt somwhatt therof and Mr Peneston. Mr Peneston by advise finding the sayd Armenian to be a knave, knew noe reason he oughtt to loose thatt mony, butt in conclution the reportts above sayd provd false, and noe such thing was ever intended by eyther of them the sayd two Armenians.

49
Court Minutes
17 October 1651
B/25 Extract from p. 83

Mr Keeble a merchant came into the Court on the behalfe of some Armenians now in London for their passage into India. The Court told him they had formerly receiped much prejudice by such men therefore they advised him to perswade them to go the same way they came hither.

50
John Spiller at Basra to Company in London
17 July 1652
E/3/23 Extract from f. 33

As yet I doe not heare of that Armenian intended to be sent by the late queene of England to disturbe your affaires in Persia, so opine he hath either let fale the imployment if come, or did not proceed at all, however we are as vigelent as may bee, and take all possible care of your indemnitie.

51
John Lewys, Henry Young, Edward Joscelyne and Thomas Parker at Isfahan to Company in London
15 September 1652
E/3/23 Extract from f. 46v

Wee yett heare nothinge of the Scotts king's agent nor is that Cogee Pedro arrived, though his employer a Jelphalin (whome wee verry well know) dayly expects him.

52
Court Minutes
26 August 1653
B/25 Extract from p. 265

The Court did this day bestowe forty shillings in charity out of the poores box upon John Christian and John Joseph two poore Armenians.

53

JOHN SPILLER AND ANTHONY DANIELL AT ISFAHAN TO SURAT
10 NOVEMBER 1653
E/3/23 EXTRACT FROM F. 218V

Wee have ben lately informed that the Dutch Commissary last yeare when hee was heere, procured a phirmaan of the King, that if they tooke any prizes in the Gulph and landed the goods, the Sultan nor none else should molest or trouble them aboute it, but they have free libertie to dispose of what soe brought ashoare as they pleased.

This certaine is true, for otherwise the King of Persiae's servants at port would never have permitted the Hollanders to doe as they did, by which we gather if we had given away in pishcashes[1] at Gombroon greate summs of money, it would have done little good. Wee know not what the matter is, but yet this we are sure, they carry their business in a very commaunding way, and report that what they doe is for the King, which if true, then they have received such order, as the Company last yeare advised the Queene was sending hither out of France, by an Englishman and an Armenian, for else these two men would have ben heere ere this, and that the Dutch is soe favoured, wee conceive is along of these wrytings which if soe, we must expect to doe our masters at Court but small service, or not soe good as otherwise we should.

[1] *pishkash* (Pers.): present, offering

54

JOHN SPILLER AND HENRY YOUNG AT ISFAHAN TO COMPANY IN
LONDON
8 SEPTEMBER 1654
E/3/24 EXTRACT FROM FF. 86-86V

You cannot but know how much we have from time to time ben inveloped, intangled, and molested with contracts for silke with the Kings of Persia, in so much that we nor the Dutch neither could not buy any quantetie (as this is which you have now wrote for) except we bought it of them or the ministers, in regard of their greate gaines and proffitt they make by it in selling it to us, wherefore we must not expect but that we shalbe hyndered by the Vizeere of Guillan, if we send Englishmen about this imployment, or any other whatsoever, so the business comes but to his knowledg, from which to keepe it, we suppose t'will prove a very difficult and hard matter. And to contract with him or any other of the King's servants for such a parcell you wilbe sure to pay 10 tomands per loade or carwarr[1] more then the currant rate, (besides what it will want in goodnesse) as the Hollanders now doe, which will amount to a greate summe of money, even so much that we finde this way will prove (and so we imagine you will likewise judge of it) to be too incommodious and burthensome.

So we conceive that to imploy an Armenian with some of our trustiest servants about it, wilbe the best way, yet that also if it could be avoyded we should be loath to doe, well knoweing that most of the factors of that nation are become very deceiptfull and dishonest in thier merchandizeing, and will certainely much abuse us doe what we can, except we could be with them our selves, and have an eye to thier actions and crafty dealeings.

[1] *kharvār* (Pers.): ass load, about 700 lbs.

55

JOHN SPILLER AND HENRY YOUNG AT ISFAHAN TO COMPANY IN
LONDON
14 OCTOBER 1654
E/3/24 EXTRACT FROM F. 109

By advices from Tabreeze etc we were informed by Armenians, that their was an English embassador arrived in those parts by way of Turkey, haveing 3 Englishmen more in his company, and was received by all this King's governours with greate respect, which also a letter to the cheife of the Carmalite Order heere in this place confirmes, and sayes the embassador goes by the name of my Lord Belamount and somuch does some Frenchmen's letters averr that were sent from Khazbien.

56

HENRY YOUNG AND DANIEL OTGHER AT SHIRAZ TO WILLIAM
WEALE AT LAR[1]
3 JUNE 1655
G/36/103 EXTRACT FROM PP. 48-49

The Aspahaune and Armenian Governours you will finde are anually piscashed, and would take it very ill if they should this yeare bee neglected, yett I am absolutely resolved not to run my selfe under the hazard of any censures of giveing away the Company's money on these accompts of presents without your positive order though I tould Mr Weale at Bunder that hee would bee forced to bee at such charge as I conceived if hee came up to Spahaune, yett heereby I promise to withstand it what possible I can soe it may stand with the

Company's honour now in these ticklish times, you well knowe wee have one lyeing at courte that will lay hold on all advantages to injure the Company who is the embassadore.

[1] Weale arrived at Lar 17 June to find this letter awaiting him.

57
WILLIAM WEALE AT LAR TO HENRY YOUNG AND DANIEL OTGHER [?AT SHIRAZ][1]
18 JUNE 1655
G/36/103 EXTRACT FROM PP. 57-58

Mr Pitts were 3 yeares in Spahaune and never presented the king all that time and yett though with some trouble hee did his businesse. . .in case any buying of silk bee prepounded by the Etamon Dowlett the old answer must serve that wee want order from our masters but expect it very shortely and soe stop his mouth, or if that will not rather then indanger a greater damage to the Company must contrive a piscash for him to doe the businesse with faire words and promises of strange things till wee shall heare what the Company will say to this theire lost credit in Persia. For presenting the Aspahaune and Armenian Governours I conceive it may easely bee excluded for one yeare except as you say these ticklish times should urge a necessity therefore then it must bee submitted to.

[1] Young was preparing in early June to move to Isfahan.

58
COURT MINUTES
28 NOVEMBER 1660
B/26 EXTRACT FROM P. 321

Upon the petition of Ovanes, a poore Persian, the Court was pleased to permitt him to take passage on the Discoverie, for some part of India, and ordered him a fitt accommodation in her, and the ordinarie allowance of the ship, and that hee shall pay but 10 li for the same, in reguard hee is a stranger.

59

COMMISSION GIVEN BY GEORGE OXINDEN, JOHN GOODIER AND
GERALD AUNGIER AT SURAT TO THOMAS ROLT AND ROBERT
SAINTHILL FOR VOYAGE TO MOCHA
28 FEBRUARY 1662/63
G/36/2 EXTRACT FROM P. 138

Wee require you Mr Thomas Rolt and Mr Robert Sainthill to embarque
your selves upon the St Michaell appertaining to Cojah Minaz an Armenian
merchant of this towne, with whome wee have prevailed to give you passage.

60

COMPANY IN LONDON TO SURAT
10 AUGUST 1663
E/3/86 EXTRACT FROM FF. 150-150v

Wee have received a peticion from one William Bell an Armenian, whoe
hath formerly lived as an interpreter to Mr William Garway and Mr Buckridge
in Persia. Hee hath peticioned to us, to recomend him to you, that hee may
bee imployed as one of those for the making of wine in Persia, to which his
request wee condiscend, and referr him unto you.

Wee haveing given lybertie to our President to imploy his twoe shipps in
India for his owne accompt from port to port, it is our expectation, that for
what goods shall bee sent on the said shipps or any others that shall saile with
English collors for his or any others accompt to Persia or elce where, that our
full due of customes bee made good unto us, and noe part thereof withheld
from us, and also that noe English shall collour the goods of Banians,
Armenians or others, that shall bee carried in any shipps for Persia, but let
them pay their full customes to the Persian, that thereby the former complaints
of the Persians for this too often practized abuse may bee now at length taken
of, and they thereby encouraged to give us a larger proportion of the customes
then formerly.

61

SURAT CONSULTATIONS
10 DECEMBER 1663
G/36/2 EXTRACT FROM P. 176

The next considerable offer was made by Cojah Minaz an able and well
reputed Armenian merchant, who taking advantage by Virge Vorah's

mischeivous plot, was hard to be brought to better tearmes. But after some tyme offered $4^5/_8$ rupees per yard at 6 months time, which being long debated in Councell, and the disadvantages of the season of the yeare, the distracted condition of the country, the designes of Virge Vorah with his complices, and the quantity of cloth exceeding former yeares being duly discussed, it was generally resolved to conclude the bargaine with him.

62

COURT MINUTES
27 JANUARY 1663/64
B/26 EXTRACT FROM P. 728

The Court was pleased to give leave that Jacob Callender and Avetick Armenians might take their passage to Surratt in one of the next shipps paying for the same and that they might carry 2 caske of refuge[1] of amber if on veiw it appeare to be all of the sort which was now shewed to the Court.

[1] variant of refuse: dross; worthless but still saleable

63

GEORGE OXINDEN AND HENRY GARY AT SWALLY TO COMPANY IN LONDON
28 JANUARY 1663/64
E/3/28 EXTRACT FROM FF. 108, 111

[Report of irregular dealings by Mathew Andrewes]

Wee hope you will accompt with Mr Andrewes for these his illegal proceedings, soe dishonest in it selfe and dishonrable to the nation. And yet this is not all in point of indico. That parcell bought of an Armenian Cojah Minaz by name, wherein you are yet more wronged then the attestation makes out, as carrying a just suspition, as first, hee enterred upon it against your positive order and prohibition, which was to send no indico home that yeare, which clause of your letter hee answered but a little before with a promise not to send you any. Secondly he brought it without the consent of his Councell. Thirdly, hee bought it without a broker, a thing never practiced in these countryes, by which you yet further sufferr in his ignorance not to make those due deductions accustomary which hee was not verst in. These three reasons considered, what can any man suggest, but that there must be some sinister ends in this man for his actings in this nature against order, against consent of Councell, and against custome.

Chout layde the charge of the consultation drawne up by Mr Andrewes against him to bee the fictions of his owne braine, and it appears no lesse, for Mr Gray your then Secretary doth avouch they appeared soe unreasonable to Mr Lambton and Mr Forster that they refused to signe it. . .wee finde you have but small pretence against him, Mr Andrewes haveing made Cojah Minaz come in and accuse him wrongfully. Wherefore Chout expectes your answere in favour of him.

64

GEORGE OXINDEN, JOHN GOODIER, HENRY GARY AND GERALD AUNGIER AT SURAT TO FORT ST GEORGE
16 FEBRUARY 1663/64
G/36/86 EXTRACT FROM F. 31

Mr Anthony Smith in the time of troubles was so inconsiderate as to come from Swally hither alone, and was snapt comeing through the towne, and carryed to the said Sevagy, who after hee had threatened him with the losse of his head, caused him to bee bound with his armes behinde him amoungst the rest of the prisoners demaunding 300000 rupees for his ransome, but by the freindship of an Armenian that was of his acquaintance, of whom Sevagy asked his quality and condition, who assured him that hee was a common man, the next day tooke 300 rupees and sett him free, sending him to us upon his peroul, with a message full of threats and menaces, but haveing him in our possession, wee were resolved not to sufferr him to returne but sent our answere per those that came with him, that hee was a rebell and a theife, and therefore valued not his threats, and that Mr Smith was our servant and wee would keepe him.

65

COURT MINUTES
24 FEBRUARY 1663/64
B/26 EXTRACT FROM P. 739

The committee appointed to consider what may be fitt for Callender an Armenian to pay for passage of himself and for freight and permission of 2 fatts[1] of amber on the London for Surratt, reporting that they conceived 15 li for his transport and 25 li for freight and permission of the 2 fatts of amber to be reasonable for him to pay the Company, and that his cockquett for impost of one fatt veiwed by them be allowed for soe much mony as it amounts to, when it is perfected, the other to be landed at Dover on the composition trade, they could not see. The Court approved of their opinions herein.

[1] fat: cask, barrel; measure of capacity

66

COURT MINUTES
2 MARCH 1663/64
B/26 EXTRACT FROM P. 742

Sir Samuel Barnardiston Mr Vandeput Mr Canham
We[r]e desired to veiw some further goods desired to be carryed for Surratt by the Armenians and make a report touching the same.

67

COMPANY IN LONDON TO SURAT
9 MARCH 1663/64
E/3/86 EXTRACT FROM F. 198V

In our overland letter wee gave you notice of John Bell an Armenian, whome we then recomended to you for a wine maker in Persia, this person now taketh his passage on the London, which wee give him gratis.

There also taketh passage on the London one Jacob Callender an Armenian, and bringeth with him twoe fatts amber by our lycense. Hee hath heere paid us 15 li for his passage, and 25 li for fraight and permission of his amber.

68

COURT MINUTES
9 MARCH 1663/64
B/26 EXTRACT FROM P. 746

The Court now gave way for Nazareth an Armenian to take passage to Surratt in the Charles with 800 li of amber paying 25 li for his diett, passage, and fraight and permission of amber.

And likewise for Chiragos an Armenian to take passage for Surratt on the Charles with two fatts of amber each about 1000 li weight, 200 sword blades, 100 li of cocheneele and 150 li of teeth[1], (which lye all at Dover), paying 50 li for his diett, passage and permission, but this to be noe president of shipping goodes from Dover in the future.

¹ (slang) ivory

69
COURT MINUTES
16 DECEMBER 1664
B/26 EXTRACT FROM P. 913

Sir Samuel Barnardiston Mr Bromefeild
Were desired to veiw a parcell of amber belonging to an Armenian who is pooore and report what they thinck fitt to him to pay for transport of that and himselfe to Surratt.

70
GEORGE OXINDEN, JOHN GOODIER AND RICHARD CRADDOCK AT SWALLY TO GERALD AUNGIER AT SURAT
22 FEBRUARY 1664/65
G/36/86 EXTRACT FROM F. 88V

This morning early came yours to hand of yesterday's date, to which we answer that the parcell of Cojah Minasses be either very bad or unreasonable in price, meddle not with it, we would willingly know what the quantity is.

If that Cojah Deylaune yet speakes truth in that his goods are at this side Broack, they may arrive time enough for our occasions, soe that you may proceed to buy them provided they are good in their qualities and reasonable in their price, according to those sortments we have already bought, and this lett be done with all possible expedition.

71
GEORGE OXINDEN, JOHN GOODIER AND GERALD AUNGIER AT SWALLY TO COMPANY IN LONDON
12 MARCH 1664/65
G/36/86 EXTRACT FROM F. 181

Jonne Belly the Armenian is arrivd and gone for Persia, with our letters for settling him in the wine office according to your order.

Jacob Callender the Armenian, whom you advise to have paid you there for his passage and 2 barrells amber, we have dismissed without any further demands.

72

GEORGE OXINDEN, JOHN GOODIER AND GERALD AUNGIER AT
SURAT TO HUMPHREY COOKE AT BOMBAY
13 DECEMBER 1665
E/3/29 EXTRACT FROM F. 142

The King's intelligencer of this towne hath given many informations up
to Court, which hath caused severall letters to be writt downe to this Governor
concerning our King's Majestie settling his souldiery on Bombaim, enordering
a strict inquisition into your actions there, and what new fortifications you
have erected since your taking possession of the island, togeather with many
other perticulars from advices gonne up from hence, which caused this
Governor to give us a greate deale of trouble, and would have commanded us
to write to you to desist from further fortifying, which he backt with menaces
and threats that he would turne us out of his country. Our answer was that we
were strangers, and upon permittance and that it was the King's country he
might doe with us what he pleased, but it lay not in our power to forbidd or
enorder anything there with you being his Majestie's of England, our King's
officers and subjects, and that the government was independent to ours, who
were noe other then merchants and therefore dare not presume to concerne
ourselves in state affairs. Next he told us the King was greatly offended that
we endeavoured to inveigle and draw away the King's subjects and strangers
that frequent his port to goe and inhabit with you which was designed to
destroy and draw away all trade from hence. This we stoutly denyed,
whereupon this Governor proceeded to summon all the merchants in towne
and caused them one by one to signe a paper how that we had not laboured to
draw off any of them, which they confirmed with hand and seale under a
penalty and forfeiture to the King in case hereafter it could be prooved to the
contrary. This went on untill it came to Cojah Minnas the President of the
Armenians to firme and seale, who boggled at it, and fearing least it should in
time be discovered what had pass't between himselfe and you produced an
instrument signed and sealed by you that invited him thither, declaring what
priviledges should be allowed him if he and his nation would remoove thither,
which was noe sooner given into the Governor but we were sent for again, and
charged as before, which we still opposed, whereupon the Governor shewed
the President the writing you had sent to Cojah Minnas, which having read we
told him we were not privy too the writing, and that it was probable he had
invited himselfe first. Whereupon we received very hard language from him,
and as hard usage since, and we had thought all had been pass't over untill a
day or two since we are acquainted that there is both a phirmaund from the
King and an husball huccum[1], which is a writing pass't by the King's immediate
order upon this Governor, that one Sied Mahmud, a factious and troublesome
person, once customer here, is enordred to be sent downe to view your workes
and place, and give an accompt thereof to this King. Whereupon we are again

sent for, and commanded to give him a letter of recommendacions to you to admitt him, which we refused, telling the Governor it was not accustomary to permitt strangers to view fortifications, or suffer them to come into castles, of which there was not anything upon the iland. This our denyall did much offend him that we know not but he may force such a paper from us.

---

[1] *hasbu'l-hukm* (Ar.): literally, "in accordance with the decree"; a phrase used in document issued by officers of state on royal authority

73
Court Minutes
29 November 1667
B/30 Extract from pp. 138-139

This day one Signor Kogea Keriakos a subject of the King of Persia, as appeared by his letters testimoniall, came into Court and by an interpreter acknowledged the favour done to him about 3 yeares since, in permitting the landing of some goods on the Companie's then bound for India, for which the King did by him now give them thanckes, and desired that having bought some looking glasses, and other things for the said King's use, and also 50 clothes in Holland for the said King's household, hee might lade them on some of the Companie's shippes that were bound for Surratt, togeather with a parcell of amber bought for his owne accompt, whereunto hee receaved this answer, that the Court had perused the said King's letters, with all due honor, and shall bee readie to shew their respect to any person that shall come so recomended to them.

That as to the particulars enumerated there appeared some difficulties in the answearing his desires, for that they can permitt no cloth to bee sent for India, much lesse of forraigne make to be laden on board their shippes, and therefore hoped hee would bee very tender in the point of cloth. But for any other accomodacion, they should bee readie to afford it him, and that if hee would give in a noate of the goods hee had to send for transport for India, they would consider thereof, and give him answer on Wednesday next.

74
COURT MINUTES
4 DECEMBER 1667
B/30 EXTRACT FROM P. 142

Signor Kogea Kiriakos this day presenting in Court a particular of such goods as hee desired to transport for Surratt, it was ordered that permission bee granted for his lading on board the Companie's shippes now freighted for the East Indies the particular parcells undermencioned, vizt tenn chests of Venice wares, glasses and looking glasses, 25 whole English clothes, five barrells of amber, one chest of gunnes, one chest of swords, one chest of musicall instruments, one chest of severall rarities, one chest of gilded leather, and that his brother Signor Avedike with 3 servants and 3 mastives have their passage also on the said shippes upon such termes as shall be agreed on.

75
COURT MINUTES
30 DECEMBER 1667
B/30 EXTRACT FROM P. 167

Sir Samuell Barnardiston Peter Vandeputt Esqr Rowland Wynn Esqr were desired to speake with Signor Keriacos about the customes of Persia, and Pattana saltpetre, and Agra indico, and to heare what hee hath to offer concerning the same and to make report.

76
COURT MINUTES
2 JANUARY 1667/68
B/30 EXTRACT FROM P. 171

Sir Samuell Barnardiston reporting unto the Court that the committees having discoursed with Signor Keriacos on the severall particulars to them referred, doe find him very willing to improve his interest with the King of Persia, to serve the Company in the settlement of their customes there, which hee engageth to doe with effect. The Court thereupon were pleased to order that permission bee granted him to transport on their shipping now bound for Surratt 50 whole clothes, so as the same bee consigned to Sir George Oxinden, and to bee sent directly for Persia, and not to bee sold in India.

77

COMPANY IN LONDON TO SURAT
27 MARCH 1668
E/3/87 EXTRACT FROM F. 78

You advise us that the Dutch have sollicited the King of Persia to purchase our halfe of customes, and of the carriage of the Persians relating to that and other perticulers. Here hath byn one Cojah Karic-koes, with a letter of recomendation from the King of Persia to us, the French and Dutch Companies, to assist him as a person imployed by him, with a stock to buy some goods and procure some rarities for him, and hath byn very sollicitous with us for permission to carry out [gap in text] clothes of severall collours that hee bought in Holland as he saith for the King of Persiae's owne court, which wee were very unwilling to graunt, doubting it was but a feigned thing or a writing that might bee easily there procured. Yet least it should bee reall, and that by our refuseall, wee should discontent the said King, and this person seeming to bee very desirous, and promising to use his utmost endeavours to begett a good understanding betweene the King of Persia and us, either in the setling of an equall proportion for our halfe customes, or an agreement for the selling thereof to the said King, wee have condiscended for the shipping of the said cloth, and his brother's passage on the ship Constantinople Merchant, provided that he consignes the goods to you that so you may see them unladen at Surratt, and from thence reshipt for Persia, without making sale of any part of them at Surratt, or parts there-aboutes. And this wee aprehend will bee noe great prejudice to us, if not reall, and will prevent the like sollicitacions for the future, wee having put this our graunt upon the promise of his asistance in the busines of our Persian customes, wherein hee may bee much helpfull if it proves truth, which causeth us againe to put you in mind of setling our said customes, as we have before desired, or selling them to the King of Persia, for the best rate you can. In order to which instruct Mr Thomas Rolt, whome wee have enterteined Cheife for that imployment and such others as you shall imploy in this affaire, that they make use of the endeavours of this Cojah Karickoes, for the begetting of a good agreement. This person himselfe is intended overland, but by his brother, and a writing from him, which wee herewith send you, those which you imploy will be directed how and where to meete with him in Persia.

78

AGENT AND COUNCIL AT SURAT TO COMPANY IN LONDON
15 APRIL 1668
G/40/2 EXTRACT FROM P. 21

The French are fallen all to peeces amongst themselves, and little better then mutinyed against their great Director the Heer Charoon, the Mounsieurs accounting it very dishonourable to be att the dipose and command of a Dutchman and an heretique, as they would have it, which hath raisd their differences to that height, that the Armenian, who was next in Councell to the Director, was clapt up close prisoner and since putt in irons and sent aboard their shipp etc. The French creditt is totally overthrowne in Surratt.

79

AGENT AND COUNCIL AT SURAT TO COMPANY IN LONDON
2 NOVEMBER 1668
G/40/2 EXTRACT FROM PP. 34-35

We particulerly observe what you write by your Bantam pinke touching Persia, which now you again reminde us of, and how that the Armenian Cojah Karickos was with you, and brought the Kinge of Persia's recommendations to you in his favour, it is true that such things are easily obtayned his pretence was plausible, but we finde he hath served himselfe more then the Kinge, and had it bin otherwise, it now ceases, for this younge prince that was soe lately admitted to the throne is since dead alsoe, and we cannot yet heare whom the nobles will make choyce of, for it is much in their wills. This Armenian hath bin often with us, and received what civilityes we could shew him, to heighten the obligacion, since there hath bin soe much done already, although we beleeve he will be able to doe you little good, for the Persians have but a very slender esteeme for the Armenians, and accompt them more their slaves them subjects.

80

STEPHEN FLOWER AT GOMBROON TO COMPANY IN LONDON
2 MARCH 1668/69
G/40/2 EXTRACT FROM P. 48

His sacred Majestie's royall guift his island of Bonbain to your Worships, the government whereof you were pleased to conferr on the worshipfull President who was gone on your shipping to settle affaires and through whose prudent management noe question but in a short time will prove a flowrishing port and of great concerne to your Worships' interest in India, to the improvement whereof as before I want not dayly to to [*sic*] sollicite and incourage both Armenians and Banyans of all sorts to imbarke themselves and goods for said port, where they are promised all cevill usage and favourable treatment in point of customes, which I finde is of little force to draw them theether, neither may it bee expected soe long as the imposicions are equall with those at Surratt, which the polliticke Mogoll hath lately reduced in favour of all nations as well as English and Dutch, cheifely out of designe to hinder the suspected growth of Bonbain, and maintayne their owne greatness, that port as they advise from thence being never in a better condition then at present.   But would your Worships please but for a few yeares to make Bonbain a free port as I have hinted to the President and Councell now doubt you would finde it the readiest and best way for itts establishment as Legorne Genoa etc may at large this day give evidence.

81

SURAT CONSULTATIONS
29 JULY 1669
G/40/2 EXTRACT FROM P. 55

Coja Meenas an able Armenian merchant made some overtures for buying all the cloth expected this yeare and say that he is an able merchant, haveing for severall yeares bought the same bargaine and never fayled in paying the monies in due time, likewise our wonted custome is such that wee deliver out at one time noe more goods then wee receive money in hand for.

Sould and agreed with Coja Meenas for all the Company's broad cloth expected in their this yeares shipping from England reserveing onely soe much as shalbe convenient to be sent downe the coast. The length to be taken off the tillett[1] and to pay 4³/₄ rupes per yard, the Company allowing for all damage (excepting extraordinary) one yard upon every halfe peece, the money to be paid in 10 moneths which time being abated in account to bee at ³/₄ per cent per annum and the said time to comence one moneth after the first cloth delivered and for what comes afterward in any shipp to bee accounted from the said day the first cloth was delivered.

Sold the said Coja Menas all the fine cloath scarlett and greenes to the amount of 100 peeces at 40 per cent advance upon the price in the invoyce at the same time as above.

Also sold to the said Coja Menas all the small perpetuanoes[2] in the warehouse at 20 rupes per peece at 10 moneths time.

---

[1] tillet: coarse cloth used for wrapping textile fabric and garments
[2] perpetuana: durable English woollen cloth

82
RICHARD SMITHSON AT MASULIPATAM TO COMPANY IN LONDON
28 AUGUST 1669
E/3/30 EXTRACT FROM F. 155

Last night came to this towne 6 French men from Golchondah, they at present lodge in the house where Mr Jearsey formerly lived. This day they viewed the house that was the Danes' factory, but rejected it as not having sufficient accommodation, (it was new built this yeare by the owner, and is much better then it was when Mr Sambrooke was here[)]. They have since treated about a stately house built but 2 years since by the shabander. They have not as yet given or received any visit. Only the second called at Goodrah to acquaint the Governour of their being come. The factor and Armenian at Narsapore are not yet come to them. They expect a ship from Achin.

83
PRESIDENT AND COUNCIL AT SURAT TO COMPANY IN LONDON
26 NOVEMBER 1669
G/40/2 EXTRACT FROM P. 59

Sold Coja Meenas 100 peeces of fine cloth scarletts and greenes at 40 per cent advance on the invoice at the time and allowance of last yeare. The contract for the above to begin 30 daies after the deliverey of the primo parcell of cloth course or fine, tenn months after which time the interest on the whole parcells are to bee reckoned, for 250 peeces of small perpetuanoes all damage included at 20 rupees per peece 10 months time per cent rebate to begin from 30 July on which day the contract for the cloth was made.

84
SURAT LETTER TO THOMAS ROLT
24 DECEMBER 1669
G/40/2 EXTRACT FROM P. 110

The Governor of Surratt. . .desires that in case Cojah Minas' vakell shall buy any horses for his account you would grant them transport on the Company's ship paying the usuall freight.

85

AGENT AND COUNCIL AT FORT ST GEORGE TO COMPANY IN
LONDON
19 JULY 1670
G/40/3 EXTRACT FROM PP. 128-129

The Aveldore or governour of St Thoma sent to desire to speake with a chitty of good accompt that then was in this towne, whoe went to him and was there privately murthered. . .Soone after an Armenian servant to the French and sonne to their then cheife at Metchlepatam, who had lived some time in St Thoma, and had traded with and trusted that murthered chitty with considerable sumes of money to buy cloth which hee had accordingly provided, this Armenian departed from St Thoma and comes to this towne and desired leave to stay heere untill hee could heare from his prinsipals haveing been informed that the Aveldore would doe by him as hee did by the chitty, and by the sequell it is probible hee might have such intencion, but for what cause wee cannot say unless posibly hee might aime to swallow up all those goods if both the one and the other were soe made away. This Armenian being heere, hee sent some peones hether to have carried him to St Thoma by force, wherewith your governour being acquainted, it being within this jurisdiccion he sent the peons back and wished them to tell their master, that such a thing ought not to have bin done under his jurisdiccion without leave first asked and obtayned, but desired him to write what hee would have and hee should receive answer, and any reasonable curtesy that he could grant. The next day hee writes a letter to mee desireing me to send this Armenian to him pretending he owed monies to the divan. I presently applyed myselfe to anwer itt, and tould him I had inquired after the Armenian with an intent to speake to him to goe believing their was noe hurt intended him, but if he refused to goe I could not in justice compell him, but upon returne of my inquiry after this Armenian, I was informed that hee had taken boate and was departed for Metchlepatam which alsoe I writt in my letter to him which was given out to bee translated but in the meane time before it was finished, the Aveldore had intelligence that hee was gone from hence, who thinkeing that wee had conveyed him away fell into a rage and sent a mesinger to his peons that waited to carry my answer as soone as the translacion was finished, and comanded them presently to come away and bring noe letters in answer, and soe they did and would not receive it though it was ready seald up by that time. The next newes I had was that the very next morning he caused all places on that side to bee sett and stopt all provisions for coming to the towne, and some few dayes after Chenepella Mirzah comeing with part of his army to St Thoma, haveing been at and about Pollicatt from whence I received a cevill letter from him hee being soe neare and a great person I sent to vissett him, and with the vissett a piscash to the vallue of 200 pagodas, but the Aveldore perswaded him not to accept of itt, for if hee would stop provisons from the towne, hee might force us to give him what more hee would desire. Upon which hee refused the present and turned it back. Wee considered that hee was a great poerson and of power were willing by all faire meanes to keepe his frindshipp, and therefore was resolved to make an addicion of 100 pagodas to itt and send it to him, which wee did accordingly, and presently after hee sent a messenger whose errant was to perswade hee being a great man to give him content and hee would bee our friend and the content was to give him 1500 pagodas, to which unreasonable demand wee answered that there was nothing due but of volentary curtesy, and soe wee had bin forward to shew respect to him but hee had refused itt, and the English doe not like to bee compelled to doe that from which they free but of curtesy.

The next morning hee besetts the towne on all sides, and hinders all provisions into the towne, which putt us upon our posture of defence, without offering any offence, and some debates passing betweene him and your Governour,. . .hee continued his seige untill upon complaint of the Governour to the Nabob, hee was comanded to depart, and to have nothing to doe to give us any trouble.

86
THOMAS ROLT AT ISFAHAN TO COMPANY IN LONDON
21 AUGUST 1670
E/3/31 EXTRACT FROM FF. 73V-74

Att my arivall at Spawhawne there presented him selfe to me an English gentleman whose name is Palmer who hath formerly been a collonell in the King's armey in the time of the late troubles but when that party was forced to disband and shift for them selves, his lot fell to go for Russia where he hath served the Empiror severall yearrs, considerable comands, but Abass, the late King of Persia (a generous Prince) haveing by his embassodors often requested a Fringgee officer (as these people call all European Christians) to discipline his people in the millitary art, this gentleman was chose by the Empiror from amongst the severall English, French and Dutch officers in his servis to this imployment, and sent for Persia in the company of one Mr Bryon an English merchant that had long lived in Russia whom the Empiror sent as his envoy extreordenary to the King of Persia to treate about the trade of raw silke, which envoy unhappely dyed and the greatest part of his retinue before they arived Spawhawne, and which was a second misfortune Abass, King of Persia was dead, and his sonn that now raignes being younge and wholly ruled and governed by his Attomondowlett a grimme and seveare man espetially to Christians whom he greatly hates, this gentleman therfore was not taken notice off with due respect, for when he presented him selfe to the Attomondowlett he told him if he would turne Moore he should have a handsome pention settled uppon him and put into an honorable comand, and his sonne which is now with him (a lad about twenty yeares old) should waite uppon the King's person if he would doe the like, at which he was so much disturbed espetially some threats accompaning them that he removed from the place where he did reside (which they had apointed him) to your house for protection, but before my arivall was removed to Jellfa amongst the Armenian Christians with his wife and sonne who are now with him, he hath another sonne somewhat elder who accompanied Mr Flower to Suratt hopeing to be received there in to your servis by your President and Councell, as is now his father's ernest request both for him selfe and other sonne desireing verry importunately that I would further him in his passage to Suratt, where he resolves to offer him selfe to your President and councell to serve you as a souldier uppon your island Bombay where if hee likes his entertainement he will settle with his famely, for his life. And truly, he appeares to me to be a grave and sober man and one whom I thinke may doe you good servis.

87

GERALD AUNGIER, MATTHEW GRAY, STREYNSHAM MASTER, CHARLES JAMES AND ALEXANDER GRIGBY AT SWALLY TO COMPANY IN LONDON
20 NOVEMBER 1670
E/3/31 EXTRACT FROM FF. 150-152V, 155V-156, 161

After severall treatys (having taken the advice and concurrence of Mr Matthew Gray etc of Councell at Bombay) wee concluded a bargaine with Cojah Menas the 14th June for all your course cloath, fine cloath and cloath rashes[1] expected by your shipping at the prizes and conditions following

For the course cloath 4 rupees per yard, 1 yard per each halfe peece allowance for short measure etc dammage, except what shall be extraordinary which is to be refferred to our selfes.

For all the cloath rashes $3^1/_2$ rupees per yard, 1 yard per halfe peece allowance as above.

For the fine cloath 20 per cento proffitt on the invoyce from England. The time to beginn 20 dayes after delivery of the parcell by the first shipp, from which day tenn monthes after the money is to be due, for which your old friend Virgee Vorah stands engaged being equally concerned with Minas in the bargaine, and what he shall pay in before due to be rebated at $^3/_4$ per cento per month.

In your journall letter K folio 49 there is an indentall error committed by a mistake both in Sir George Oxinden and Gerald Aungier to wit, an old charge of rupees 2595 in Cojah Minas's debt transferred from severall bookes, the true state whereof they not well understanding by reason of Mr John Goodier and Mr Streynsham Master's absence, and looking on it as a dead charge, in regard that Cojah Minas absolutely refused to allow anything on accompt of the goodes bought of him in anno 1664 thought good to write it off to proffitt and losse, but since finding our mistake wee have renewed our demand, and with much adoe have ended sayd accompt with Cojah Meenas as you will finde in this yeare's bookes, of which we intreat your auditor may be advised.

Some monthes after wee had deliverd your broad cloath sould last yeare to Cojah Meenas and made up the accompt he surprized us with a demand of rupees 800 for allowance of a strange and extraordinary dammage on about 70 peeces of course cloath, which he sent into our house, exceedingly full of holes and spotted by wett received whereof most were greens. Wee were not a little startled at this unmercantile way of proceeding and expostulated the matter sharply with him, Mr James being present offerred to declare that when he received the bales from on board shipp and sent them for Surratt they were all outwardly well conditioned except what had been opened and allowed for. Mr Smeaton being sent for declared that Cojah Minas's servant coming to receive the cloath desired it might for dispatch sake be delivered to him in bales as they were, which accordingly was done, and that the bales were all outwardly well conditioned and not the least signe of dammage, this allsoe Minas's servant and broker could not deny, nay he affirmed that they appeared so when they were opened soe many moneths after delivery, but that the severall peeces when taken out prooved so much dammaged, which being soe extraordinary Cojah Meenas earnestly demanded reparation for, according to the contract. Wee answered that no reparation was due, nor none wee would allow, that the goodes were delivered him well conditioned which if he had questioned he might have opened them and what he had since done with them or where they received this dammage wee knew not nor would conceme our selfes for, in regard noe law or reason could demand any allowance from us, after so long delivery. Minas replyed that for severall yeares he had been the Companie's merchant for their cloath, and as he had never found any such occassion, soe he never made any such complaint before, that on the credditt of our dealing he had received our goodes in bales without opening, that he verily beleeved the goodes came so dammaged out of England, otherwise had they received wett on board it would have appeared by the bales, and that if wee did not doe him right, but putt falsified goodes on him, he must be more wary in dealing with us hereafter. In fine after many hott words on both sides, the brokers interposed and prevayled at last with us to allow him 200 rupees towards his losse which wee were more willingly perswaded to, in respect to the reputation of your house which wee thought not fitt should be any way censured, but wee shall take all due care to prevent the like disputes hereafter.

A yet greater advantage have wee made and are in hopes to perfect for you by this overture in refferrence to your island Bombay for the care which wee tooke of the Banians, Cuttarees and Armenians and allsoe Moore merchants which flede to us for protection hath for ever obliged them. The misery and danger they sufferr in Surratt doth make them consider of changing their abode and Bombay is the onely place whither they thinke of retiring whereunto they have so great encouragments as freedome in matters of religion, kind usage and small customes that there is nothing that checks them therein but the feare of not being secure for they have made a very dilligent enquiry into the strength of the place and nomber of English menn to defend it, they have examined how many menn you have sent out this yeare, seeming much concerned that you have no greater regard to that hopefull island. Wee have used the best of our arguments to satisfy them, assuring them of the effectuall care you have taken to render the place secure to the inhabitants, the great privilledges you have granted, the ammunition you have this yeare sent out, that with the present strength that is there, wee doe not feare any enemy, promising to defend them to the last dropp of bloud, but wee find it difficult to perswade them that one hundred Englishmen with some Portugalls are able to secure that island. Had it pleased God that the fort had now been finished and sufficiently manned with Englishmen there would need no arguments to invite inhabitants to dwell there, their owne intrest would convince them and till then t'would be in vayne to expect them for menn of estates are wary whither they remoove, and of the poorer sort, the island is even burthened with them allready. Hodgy Zayed Beague's sonne the richest merchant in Surratt declared his resolution with an oath in the presence of Gerald Aungier and Matthew Gray that he would goe with his family to Bombay. Wee hope you will beleive wee did not discourage him therein.

A Dutch shipp lately arrived from Batavia hath brought a letter from the Manilas written by Cojah Carikoos to Cojah Meenas, wherein is advised that by reason of the Governour of Manila's death the shipp Hopewell was kept foure moneths in port without breaking bulke till a new Governour arrived who was very inquisitive whether the ship's goodes did not belong to Dutch or English, and being satisfied it did belong to the Armenians gave Cojah Carikoos freedome of trade with considerable privilledges. He writes further that the marketts are very goode that he hath sold most of his commoditys to reasonable proffitt and that about the beginning of November he intends to sett sayle for Surratt so that in January at furthest the shipp is expected.

---

[1] rash: a smooth textile fabric made of silk or wool

88
SURAT CONSULTATIONS
5 FEBRUARY AND 23 MARCH 1670/71
G/40/2 EXTRACT FROM P. 113

[5 February 1670/71]

The Armenians in Jelpha envited to come to Bombay and a letter writt to them in the Itallian language to that purpose.

[23 March 1670/71]

Cojah Menas sent to for 47000 rupees owing by him for broad cloth.

89
GERALD AUNGIER, MATTHEW GRAY, STREYNSHAM MASTER AND
CHARLES JAMES AT SURAT
TO COMPANY IN LONDON
7 APRIL 1671
E/3/32 EXTRACT FROM F. 9V

The Manila shipp belonging to Cojah Meenas is not yet returned. The newes is she hath made a trading voyadge to Siam and Timor and thence sayled to Manila againe. What the issue will be wee cannott yet certainly declare unto you.

90
GERALD AUNGIER, MATTHEW GRAY, STREYNSHAM MASTER AND
CHARLES JAMES AT SURAT TO COMPANY IN LONDON
1 JUNE 1671
E/3/32 EXTRACT FROM FF. 12-14

Your approbation of our services in the sale of your woollen manufactures, as also copper, tynn, quicksilver etc gives us great encouragement to proceed in the same nature. You will find we tooke the same course last year, which had we not done, you would have suffered about 10000 li sterling in your cloth, a great part whereof though sold 11 months since to Cojah Meenas lyes still in your warehouse, and he sells it now dayly in retaile under the price he paid you for the whole, whereas had we not put it of before the arrivall of the last ships, we should never have procured more then 3 rupees per yard for it. We take notice and worthily esteeme your order, touching the consumption of your woollen manufactures of all sorts, and that you will not be discouraged at what the Dutch and French bring, so that we have great hopes you will soon weary them out, especially the latter, who are already suffitiently discouraged, having two years' cloth still remaining on their hands. We have already given your broker Bingee Parrack order to endeavour the sale of the cloth etc goods expected in your next year's shipping, and if we can advance above 3 rupees per yard, we shall thinke we make a very good bargaine for you considering that Cojah Meenas hath now on his hands neer 2000 peeces unsold, most whereof lyes in your warehouse, which we keep for your security, till he pays us in more money, for we dare not trust out too much at a time. The last month Cojah Meenas finding the great loss he was like to sustaine by this bargaine of broadcloth, tooke an occasion to renounce it and fling all the remaining cloth on our hands, which put us on very sollicitous thoughts how we should dispose of it, (considering the distraction of the times caused by these intestine warrs) and also how we should recover your dammages from Meenas, but wee so roundly dealt with him, declaring our resolution to seise all his shipping and estate, wherever we could find it, that we at last made him stand to his bargaine, and hitherto he promiseth us very faire, and hath of late paid us considerable summs of money thereon, this we thought worthy your notice that you may see what streights we are put to in these troublesome times, to secure your interest and manage your trade.

As to the Manilla trade we have no certaine accompt as yet, the ship which Cojah Meenas sent thither being not yet returnd, but expected in January next when we hope she will bring such news as may encourage your further attempts.

Our thoughts are often employed in contriving all meanes possible for the planting and peopling your colony at Bombay, in pursuance whereof your President hath begun a private correspondence with the Armenians, and hath reason to hope that the next year will produce some happy effects of our endeavors for now that the castle is neer finished and become formidable to our neighbours and somewhat secure to our inhabitants, we doe not question but by the blessing of God, trade will encrease. One hundred weavers more are of late come into the island and more are coming. For the better management and encouraging your cloth investment there, we have sent downe Mr Henry Chowne, who having gaind some experience at Broach in the making of callicoes during his service to you there, we hope will be very instrumentall to that worke, we have for his encouragement given him the charge of all your warehouses, and made him one of your Councell on the island, and we promise our selves that he will deserve encouragement from you.

91

GERALD AUNGIER, MATTHEW GRAY, STREYNSHAM MASTER,
CHARLES JAMES, HENRY YOUNG AND ALEXANDER GRIGBY AT
SWALLY TO COMPANY IN LONDON
7 NOVEMBER 1671
E/3/32 EXTRACT FROM FF. 87V, 94-94V

We have employed the utmost of our industry to make a gennerall sale of all your woolen manufactures before the shipps' arrivall, as wee have practised these two yeares passt to your great advantadge, but could not effect it though severall overtures passt about it as you will finde in our consultation booke, the great losse which Cojah Meenas hath sustained in the sale of your last yeare's cloath (wherein he suffers above 4000 li sterling) together with the unsettled posture of the times made all other merchants wary, and the more in regard there were 2000 peeces of cloath remaining in the towne unsold belonging to Meenas, the Dutch, French and other menn, insomuch that it was retailed in towne at $3^1/_2$ rupees per yard, notwithstanding which wee have had such good success through God's providence over your intrest.

Wee shall attende your orders about the Manila trade from whence the last advices give no great encouragement, as to marketts the shipp sent thither from hence is not yet returned, Cojah Carikoos having spent his time in trading voyages and hath hitherto given but a slender accompt of his proceedings 'tis given out the shipp is expected here in January next. If she comes wee shall give you a full accompt of all things.

In our last yeare's advices wee desired you to send out some small parte of your stocke in amber, the reason which prompted us thereunto was for that wee understood that vast parcell which you had permitted to be brought out by Cojah Carikoos was neer disposed of and therefore wee judged if you would please to make it your owne commodity and strictly forbidd all others dealing therein that it would turne well to accompt by that time, but this yeare to our trouble wee find there are brought out 32 very large chests to witt 14 on ship Falcon and 18 on shipp Antelop shipped by and consigned to Armenians of which you please to give us no notice but the commanders say they are laden by your order. Wee cannott disproove it, but the bussiness was so subtely contrived here that all the goodes were cleared out of the custome house before ever wee were aware of them. Wee beseech you hereafter to forbidd such proceedings unlesse the advantage you reape thereby be greater then wee apprehend.

92

SURAT CONSULTATIONS
23 NOVEMBER 1671
G/40/2 EXTRACT FROM P. 118

There depending a dispute between the President and Councell and Coja Menas concerning some broad cloth that was damaged on the Marine and in the warehouses on which account hee demands 6000 rupees which difference if hee should be pressed to accommodate would possibly take advantage thereof and insist the more on his unreasonable demands, and therefore it is resolved in respect the generall bookes are on ballancing that 2000 rupees be charged unto account of damage hopeing nevertheless to bring him into a better agreement and to accept of less.

93

MATTHEW GRAY, CHARLES JAMES AND ALEXANDER GRIGBY AT
SWALLY TO COMPANY IN LONDON
14 OCTOBER 1672
E/3/33 EXTRACT FROM F. 166V

The Governour of Suratt being the other day att an invitation in the shawbunder's house, together with severall other merchants sent for Coja Meenaz and caused him to bee beaten with slippers and staves untill they had almost killed him. Itt was for writing to the King of injustice done him by said Governour hee threatens Culleanchand and Muza Mosum on the same accompt and two others which hee names not.

94

MATTHEW GRAY, CHARLES JAMES AND PHILIP GIFFARD AT SURAT
TO COMPANY IN LONDON
20 AUGUST 1673
E/3/34 EXTRACT FROM OC 3832 [VOLUME NOT FOLIATED]

On the 18th Cojah Meenaz vissited us, declaring how gladly he would discharge his debt to the Honourable Company and how sencible he was of our forbearance. Hee then gave us a writing to receive his Swakin[1] stock when it arrives from Mocha, upon our promise that wee will take but $1/3$ on accompt of his debt to the Company, and deliver him the other $2/3$ for discharging other debts. He is also about the sale of his shipp Selymone to the Governor when she arrives from Bussora, and gave it under his hand that wee shall have 20000 rupees of that money, and wee will see what may yett further be done without proceeding to extremity and loss of his reputation, which is his livelyhood, upon which wee have trespassed somewhat too much this yeare (contrary to our inclinations) by keeping peons at his doore day and night.

[1] possibly port of Suakin on the Red Sea

95
MATTHEW GRAY, CHARLES JAMES, PHILIP GIFFARD AND CAESAR CHAMBERLAIN AT SURAT TO THOMAS ROLT AT GOMBROON
12 FEBRUARY 1673/74
G/36/87 EXTRACT FROM F. 104v

Wee shall expect more Carmania wooll from you for the next shipping, the Honourable Company write to you for a large quantity and give you caution that you buy none of the white sorte, but if you trust to the next Bussorah shipping to bring it to us, twill not be with us in tyme to lade on the shipps, you may finde conveighance to send it to us, if you have more down at port, upon such Surat ships as shall returne hither this monzoon, under Armenians' marks or Banians', without any such great scruple or feare of the enemy, had wee 10 millions of money there, wee would not question to bring it hither without breaking our braine for contrivance.

96
COMPANY IN LONDON TO PERSIA
7 APRIL 1674
E/3/88 EXTRACT FROM F. 60v

It having pleased God to give us peace with our neighbours soe that we may proceed in our trade we thought fitt to advise you what is come unto our notice of the practise of some residing with you which as we are informed if not prevented wilbe very much to our prejudice which is the owing Moores Bannians and Armenian merchants' goods for to be English, and bringing such goods into our house at Gombroom, to the defrauding both the King of Persia and us of our due of customs. The consequence of such accions must of necessity produce bad effects, for although the Persian doth not give unto us our moiety of the customs of all goods imported in the port of Gombroom according unto their agreement with us, yet such practizes may not only be a pretence for them to give us soe little of our due as they doe, (but when known) to deprive us altogether of our right, and wee doe beleive that none in our factory can carry on such designes without the knowledg of our Chief. Therfore it will concerne him and all our other servants also to endeavour the discovery of such unjust dealings and to hinder them that noe prejudice befall us in obtaining of what share of the customs is due unto us, and also that we suffer not in our reputacion.

And that we may prevent for the future such ill practises as we now complaine of that Moores and Bannians' goods are owned as English, we have appointed our President and Council to register all goods sent on any ship or junck that shalbe sent to the port of Gombroom and a list on each ship sent unto our Chief and factors in Gombroom of all such goods that are on each ship belonging unto the English, and that they be for the proper account and the reall estate of the English and noe others, and that noe other goods be received into our house or owned by our Chief and factors in Persia, but what are soe registered and sent in a list as premencioned, that soe we may make appear to the Persian, our just and true dealings, which may be a good argument, when well urged to perswade them to the allowing of us a larger proportion of our dues of customes than ever they have done.

97

MATTHEW GRAY, CHARLES JAMES, PHILIP GIFFARD AND CAESAR CHAMBERLAIN AT SURAT TO BOMBAY
29 APRIL 1674
G/36/87 EXTRACT FROM F. 127

Meenaz his Harry boate is arrived from Mallacca, shee hath been 4 months on her voyage the winds are soe high that shee had like to have foundred at an anchor at the river's mouth, haveing 7 foote water in hold, shee runn in at a venture into the river, and is safe with her carga, which chiefly consists in: 200 chests of copper, a small quantity of tynn, soe much as they could steale the custome of, it being prohibited to be shipt off, the rest of her carga consists in sapan wood[1], some sandall wood and what elce they could scrape up they not haveing sold ½ their carga have taken up a great part of this stock at interest at extravagant rates to be paid when the goods are there sold. About 15 dayes since Mr James and the rest of the Councell were with him to demmand his debt when hee promised us at the arrivall of this vessell to pay us 5000 rupees which wee shall now endeavour to secure.

---

[1] wood yielding a red dye; also known as brazilwood

98
MATTHEW GRAY AT SWALLY TO CHARLES JAMES AND PHILIP
GIFFARD AT SURAT
26 SEPTEMBER 1674
G/36/87 EXTRACT FROM F. 154

You write us alsoe that Meenas hath sold his Ormoos Merchant for 60000 rupees but you mistake when you write that hee promised us some moneys on the sale of this shipp. It was on the sale of the Selimony when shee should returne the last January from Bussorah but instead of makeing sale of that ship I alwaies understood that hee had taken in another share of her, and soe discharged noe part of that which wee expected. And I hope Byingee Parrack hath been soe wise for himself as well as to secure the Company's debt, that hee will have a due proportion out of this ship's sale towards the discharge of said Meenas his debt, and have a provident care and inspection how the said Meenas disposes of his other vessells that he doth not make them over to other of his creditors as wee too justly may feare for his ship's being gone wee finde noe other meanes to recover soe great a debt.

99
SURAT CONSULTATIONS
12 AND 15 OCTOBER 1674
G/36/3 EXTRACT FROM PART 4, P. 40

Surat 12 October 1674

The Councell having notice that Cojah Meenas had sold his ship the Ormous Merchant to a Turk for upwards of 60000 rupees and taking no care to pay us any part thereof on account of his debt, although he had promised so to doe, they thought fitt to send 2 English men with the broker to Sied Mahmud the customer and cheife minister of the towne under the Governor to acquaint him therewith, and that hee will call upon the said Meenas and apoint him to give satisfaction, otherwise to put a stop to that mony that was yet remayning from the Turke to be paid him, and in case that the said Sied Mahmud should refuse to doe us justice in this affaire, then wee desired the liberty to help our selves the best wee can for the recovery of his debt.

Surat 15 October 1674

The Councell having received an answer the other day from Sied Mahmud about Cojah Meenas his business, that he would assist us therein what he could, and did then send for Meenas before the persons wee sent to examine

there about the said debt. The said Meenas declaring that he owed the
Company mony, but the greatest part of it was for interest (thinking thereby
because the laws of Moors allow not of interest) to baffle us by the assistance
that he might receive by corrupting this King's ministers, yet notwithstanding
the said Sied Mahmud did then severely check him and strictly charge him to
goe to the English and make an end of his business within 1 day at furthest.
But the said Meenas hath neither come nor sent to us, and wee beleive hath
bribed the said Sied Mahmud, for our broker visiting the said Sied Mahmud
yesterday, he told him that Meenas had not bin with him upon which hee sent
for the said Meenas, who coming before him in presence of our broker,
absolutely denyed that he owed us any thing, wherefore the Councell hath
concluded that one or more of them shall goe to Sied Mahmud, and signify
unto him, how much wee doe resent the disgrace this Meenas doth put upon
us, by denying his debt, since wee are persons so well knowne never to
demand that which is not our due, and to produce his bills of debt before the
said Sied Mahmud. Moreover to lett him know that the said Meenas never
disputed the paying of his debt with interest before wee brought him to him,
and that wee doe wonder that he did not reprehend the said Meenas when he
found him so egregious a lier, having confessed before him the other day that
he owed us 30000 rupees, that wee have already troubled him about this
business 3 times, and doe make this our last address unto him wherein if wee
find wee have not speedy reparation, wee will apply our selves to the Governor
and if we cannot have justice from him, wee shall take such course as shall
seeme best for the recovering of this debt.

100
SURAT CONSULTATIONS
23 OCTOBER 1674
G/36/3 EXTRACT FROM PART 4, P. 42

In our preceeding consultations of the 12 and 15 currant our applications
to Sied Mahmud about Meenas his debt are discoursed, to whome wee then
sent Mr Giffard and Mr Oxinden to lett him understand what the councell had
resolved on, that if he did not doe us justice we should appeale to the
Governor. Hee then exprest the great kindness he had for our nation, and the
many services he had done us, and that wee should find the like in this,
presently sending two of his peons to sett at Meenas his door to demand our
mony, but some days being past, he finding that the said Meenas is not able to
make us present satisfaction to any considerable amount, doth perswade us to
accept at present what he is able to make us, which he promises shall be 5000
rupees in ready mony and that Vetchecund his broker shall give us a bill to pay
us 3 in 4000 rupees more in some months time, which offer being brought the

Councell by our broker from Sied Mahmud, they have debated the business and have made choice rather to accept of this at present and bring him to make up accounts with us, which hitherto wee could not doe then to refuse it, and take other courses which must be by seisure of his shipping, which may bring such inconveniencys upon us, that wee shall not dare to adventure on without further consideration and deliberate councells with the advice of our President therein.

101

CERTIFICATE SIGNED BY MATTHEW GRAY, CHARLES JAMES, PHILIP GIFFARD AND CAESAR CHAMBERLAIN AT SURAT
26 OCTOBER 1674
G/36/3 EXTRACT FROM PART 4, P. 48

These are to certify whome it may concerne that whereas Vedjecrun Shipputt the broker of Cojah Meenas the Armenian for and in consideration of the summ of 32000 rupees the said Vedjecrun hath lent unto the said Meenas, hee hath made over to him the fraights of his two ships the Hopewell and Surat Merchant now bound on a voyage for Mallacca and Siam, and whereas the said Vedjecrun by his endeavor and perswasion hath brought the said Meenas to pay us at this time in parte of his debt to the Honnourable 8000 rupees, that is to say 2000 rupees in ready mony, and the said Vedjecrun given us his owne bills to pay the rest at certeine times, vizt 3000 rupees at 2 months and 3000 rupees at 5 months from date hereof, by which his service wee have obligd our selves not to molest or make seisure of the said 2 vessells of Cojah Meenas for his debt during this their voyage, in regard to the satisfaction, Vedjecrun is to receive out of their freights and the further services he may doe us in the recovery of this desperate debt, provided the said Vedjecrun Shipputt doe faithfully comply with us in the payments of the moneys he hath engaged to us for at the prefixed times.

102

MATTHEW GRAY, CHARLES JAMES, PHILIP GIFFARD AND CAESAR CHAMBERLAIN AT SURAT TO BOMBAY
28 OCTOBER 1674
G/36/87 EXTRACT FROM F. 170

Cojah Meenaz hath sold his Ormooz for 63000 rupees to a Turke but tooke noe care to pay us any part of the money, which gave us occation to apply our selves to Sied Mahmud, and make knowne his debt to the Honourable Company which Meenaz had the impudence to deny before him, although wee had severall bills under his hand for the same, which were produced before him, who thereupon sent for Meenaz, strictly chargeing him to satisfie the English, employing the Governor's broker to moderate him, and bring him to some termes that might content us for the present. The issue of all is this that hee hath paid us 2000 rupees downe, and his broker Vedcherun hath given us his bills for 6000 more, 3000 to be paid in two months, the rest at 5 monthes, for which wee are obliged not to medle with Meenaz vessells the Hopewell or Surat Merchant untill their freights have satisfyed to the said Vetcherunn 3200 rupees that hee lent said Meenaz to sett them to sea etc and now hee is to make up accounts with us and give us a bill for what hee owes us from this tyme, which will be about 40000 rupees. Hee hath yet his part in the Selymone, and his Harry is gone to Siam and hath some ground in this towne to sell, wee shall take all opportunities to gett what wee cann from him, but his debt is desperate.

103

WILLIAM THOMSON, GOVERNOR OF COMPANY IN LONDON,
TO EPHRAIM SKINNER AND COMPANY IN LEGHORN
9 MAY 1676
E/3/88 EXTRACT FROM F. 152

Suposeing that corrall may be at reasonable rates with you the next fishing, and hopeing you will use your utmost endeavors to procure as cheape as may be, wee doe order you to buy for our account twenty chests of the best well coullored and largest Grezzio corral, each chest to weigh about three hundred weight, and not more, provided you can buy it at 3 dollars the Legorne pound, or as much under that price as you can possibly gett it. Also five chests of Recadutti corrall of the best sort, and at the cheapest rate procurable.

And in regard our giving comission for a greater or lesser quantity of this comoditye depends much upon the deareness or cheapeness and goodness of it, and the many comissions there may [be] for the buying of it, wee desire you upon receipt hereof to advize us what the goodness and markett is like to bee. For though it cannot bee fully knowne before the retorne of the boates, yet there may be some probable conjectures from what the new banke or place of fishing doth affoard, the nomber of boates sett forth, the seasonableness of the weather, and the more or less comissions that are given for buying. For though we would have you private as to what wee order, and not prye into the secretts of others, yet what is publique, advize us. For know, that wee stand in competition in trade with the Dutch Portingalls Armenians etc. And if it be deare, and they buy much, wee would buy the less, and if it be good and cheape, and they buy little, wee would buy the more.

104

GERALD AUNGIER, MATTHEW GRAY, CHARLES JAMES AND CAESAR CHAMBERLAIN AT SURAT TO BOMBAY
27 MAY 1676
G/36/89 EXTRACT FROM F. 20V

The 23 currant we received yours of the 5th ditto. It was well contrived to send a letter that required speedy advice of the Armenians' shipe's arrivall by the peon whome you ordered to attend Savajee's vackeele, who was 18 dayes in the way.

You have done well to spare the merchants the Company's warehouse, and to treate them civilly, they tell us they are to pay 400 rupees for hire of the warehouse, which wee would have charged to the creditt of the East India house, and in regard we have here some dispute with Cojah Meenaz touching his debt to the Company, and the owners of the ship are at difference at present which will require some time to be decided, wee would have you put a stop to all buisnesse there belonging to the ship, and to forbid them carpenters or calkers or any other assistance what soever till you heare further from us, and not to suffer the ship to goe out of porte, or any goods to be laden upon her, and you may signifie to the necquedah[1] that the reason of this prohibition is, because Cojah Menaz doth not comply with his contract here.

[1] *nākhudā* (Pers.): ship's master

105

GERALD AUNGIER, MATTHEW GRAY, CHARLES JAMES AND CAESAR CHAMBERLAIN AT SURAT TO BOMBAY
17 JULY 1676
G/36/89 EXTRACT FROM F. 27

Wee wrote you lately a letter of recommendation in the behalfe of Cojah Menas and Cojah Delaune desiring your assistance to them in the fitting up of their shipp since which they have againe earnestly importuned us to bespeake your kindnesse to them, and perticularly in reference to the carpenters, for which they say they are in very great want, wherefore these are to desire you that you use your best endeavours to supply them with said carpenters, and if they are not procurable on the island that you use your interst to send for them from Basseen, Tannah, or Bandora, wherein see you faile not, and if they desire any further assistance, or want any of the Company's stores, or any thing the island can furnish them with lett them be supplyed for their money. Cojah Meenas and Cojah Delaune was with us this day, and complained of the [?rouble] they received from your customer's demand of anchorage, and though they were very importunate yett wee would give them noe possitive answere till wee heard further from you. They have alsoe laid a very severe charge against Captain Francis Birkin, and desire leave to prosecute him at law, and to have justice of him which wee cannot deny, but hope Captain Birkin will not deserve soe ill from them as they represent wee would have you write us how the case stands between them. In the meane time lett their business be soe dispatched there that the shipp may proceed timely on her voyage.

106
SURAT CONSULTATIONS
2 MARCH 1676/77
G/36/4 EXTRACT FROM FF. 16-16V

On Swally Marine the 2d March 1676/77

Mr James Adames etc having caused the two nocquedahs of the shipp Sellymony to be detained prisoners on board the Returne, by reason they would not deliver up the shipp's freight money unto them.

Ordered that Mr Isaac Lawrence and the moody[1] be sent on board to treate with them concerning the delivery of the said money.

Ditto die

Mr Lawrence and the moody returning from on board, and declaring that the two said nocquedahs were willing to come to any agreement, and very desirous of coming on shore to speake with the President and Councill.

Ordered that Captain Smith send them on shore soe soone as can conveniently may be.

John Penning Secretary

Captain William Smith

These are to desire you to send on shore the two Armenian nocquedahs belonging to shipp Sellymony, who have entreated us that they might have liberty to come on shore to have a hearing before us, and are willing to come to any just and reasonable termes. We remaine

Your loving freinds

Gerald Aungier
Cesar Chambrelan

Swally Marine the 2d March 1676/77

[1] modi: steward, chandler

107

CHARLES JAMES AND CAESAR CHAMBERLAIN AT SURAT TO
COMPANY IN LONDON
10 MARCH 1676/77, 7 APRIL AND 31 AUGUST 1677
E/3/37 EXTRACT FROM OC 4270 [VOLUME NOT FOLIATED]

[10 March 1676/77]

When Mr Adames departed in the Returne for Bussorah, the shipp
Sellymony belonging to Cojah Meenas went in company with her, on whom
at said Meenas' request, wee putt an English commander with some other
officers, and wee made him to consigne her to Mr Adames, to whome wee
gave instructions accordingly, being in good hopes by this meanes to hedge in
his debt unto you, but it seemes Cojah Meenas designed to put a cheate upon
us, for unknowne to us he put two Armenian nocquedahs on board her, who
both at Bussora and Gombroone have given Mr Adames a great deale of
trouble about said freight money, and defeated him wholy of it, which seemes
hath soe offended Mr Adames that he sent the said two nocquedahs prisoners
on the Returne to Bombay, and alsoe ordered the Sellymony thither, wherein
wee can by noe meanes approve of his proceedings, having never had such
order from us, for it hath given great offence to the Governor and cheife
customer, and to all the merchants in generall, who threaten to demand
satisfaction from the English Company for all dammages they shall sustaine
thereby, which hath put us to no meane perplexity, the Sellymony being not
yet arrived, who though she hath made as wee heare but a very meane freight,
yet she hath a great treasure of silver and gold on board her, wee trust in God
by her safe arrivall wee shall be eased of further molestation. But as to
Meenas' debt, wee must now looke upon it as wholly lost, for he in prison and
in a manner quite broke, soe that wee have little hopes of recovering anything,
notwithstanding wee shall not be wanting to use our best endeavours therein.
Wee send your Honours herewith such papers as wee have received from
Persia relating to this affaire, and what elce requiring your notice.

[7 April 1677]

The same day the Persia Merchant departed, the shipp Seelymony arrived
after a very teadious expectation, when having summoned all the merchants,
who cast out ill and scandalous reports of us, wee made them ashamed of their
unworthy ingratitide, and the injurys they cast upon our reputation, and that
of the nation, and having strictly examined the whole affaire, wee doe not find
Mr Adames soe blame worthy as the malicious nocquedahs and other
merchants have represented him, but rather that he hath acted with care and
much zeale in your concernes, wee wish indeed that he had not consigned the
shipp to Bombay, for that only gave occation of offence, but when wee

consider the gross provocations which were given him by those ungratefull and ill natured Armenians, wee doe the less wonder at what hath past. Wee thanke God all things are now well accommodated, and wee doubt not but wee shall keepe them soe. But Cojah Meenas continues still in prison, but wee have made publique demands of his debt to you of the Governor and cozzy[1], who promise us all faire assistance, and when they come to make a valuation of his estate, they assure us your interest shall not be forgotten.

[31 August 1677]

Mr Anthony Smith your old servant deceased here the 13 February last. Cojah Meenas by old Bennidas' meanes having gott the better part of his estate into his hands, that its recovery is some what desperate.

---

[1] *khāss* (Pers.): select, eminent, noble; applied to chief officers of state and the nobles of the court

108
Surat Consultations
4 April 1677
G/36/4 extract from ff. 23-23v

The seamen who were ordered to voyage to Bussorah on the Sellymony the last yeare, at Cojah Meenaze earnest request, being now returned, and making their addresses to the President and Councill to assist them in recovering their wages from the said Cojah Meenaze, wherein they have not been wanting. But he being ruyned totally by meanes of some of his Banian creditors who have maliciously cast him into prison, there is very little hopes of recovering anything of their wages for them, wherefore in regard the men have formerly served as souldiers and that they may have some reasonable subsistance whereby to maintaine themselves.

Ordered that they be enlisted as souldiers and monthly receive souldiers' pay.

109

COMPANY IN LONDON TO PERSIA
4 APRIL 1684
E/3/90 EXTRACT FROM F. 172V

We shall consider of the proposicion you make us of employing an Armenian to buy silk Quilone after we hear what Sir Thomas Grantham hath done for the recovery of the arreres of our customs, which we intend not to loose.

110

COMPANY IN LONDON TO BOMBAY
11 APRIL 1688
E/3/91 EXTRACT FROM FF. 262-262V

We have enclosed in our packet a note of what goods we have permitted the Armenians to ship on board our ships, for which they have paid us for cloth ten per cent permission for sword blades and amber twelve per cent these and all other permitted goods are upon landing to pay us our sea custome of 5 per cent and the cloth if it be sold at Bombay or in India is to pay us 5 per cent more for permission, which you are to collect, and bring to our account there. But if it be shipt of for Bussorah, you are to take nothing but our sea custome once, that is to say inwards only, for whatever hath once paid us custome, may afterwards be shipt off gratis to any place, neither are you for the amber sword blades or hydes to exact any thing more from the Armenians besides what they have paid here, but only our sea custome whether those commodities be sold at Bombay or in India or elsewhere, the reason of which differences in the commodities is, because we have cloth of our own to sell, but have none of the other commodities.

By this indulgence we hope to encrease the trade of your place, and in consequence our own revenue, and the numbers of our subjects under his Majestie, for which reason and many others to the like consequence we could heartily wish you had three good rich Jewes houses settled with you at Bombay, as we have now to the Company's great advantage at Fort St George, and we should be glad if you could invent such encourageing invitations to the Armenians that some good rich houses of them might settle with you att Bombay, and bring all their silke this way according to what was formerly writ you on this subject, towards the effecting whereof we know the principle inducement must be that they shall have libertie to transport their returnes back in cloth upon the termes of our present indulgence to these men, and if you promise them any thing else, they shall find here most punctuall performance.

111
COURT MINUTES
22 JUNE 1688
B/39 EXTRACT FROM P. 132A

The Deputy Governour acquainting the Court, that he hath had severall discourses with an Armenian about matters of trade, to and from the East Indies, which may in time prove very beneficiall to this Company it is ordered that the Committees for the Treasury be desired to affix the Companie's seal to such agreement with Coja Panous Kalendar, as shalbe made and attested by the Governour Deputy and any two more of the said Committees for Secrecy.

112
COURT MINUTES
22 JUNE 1688
B/39 PP. 133B-135A

[Trade Agreement]

The Governour and Company of Merchants of London trading to the East Indies, To all to whom these presents shall come send greeting. Whereas representacion hath been made to us, by Sir Josia Child baronet our Deputy Governour, that upon long conferences by him had with Coja Panous Calendar an Armenian merchant of eminency and an inhabitant of Ispahan in Persia, as also with Sir John Chardin of London knight, they had on behalf of the Armenian nation proposed to him several particulars for carrying on a great part of the Armenians' trade to India and Persia, and from thence to Europe by the way of England, which will redound greatly to his Majesty's advantage in his customs, and to the encrease of the English navigation, if the Armenian nation might obtain such licences from this Company as will give them encouragement so to alter and invert the ancient course of their trade to and from Europe: And we being allways willing to encrease and encourage the publick trade and navigation of this kingdom, after a serious debate of all the proposicions relating to this affayr, have thought fit to agree and resolve as follows, vizt.

First, That the Armenian nacion shall now and at all times hereafter have equal share and benefit of all indulgences this Company have or shall at any time hereafter grant to any of their own adventurers or other English merchants whatsoever.

Secondly, That they shall have free liberty at all times hereafter to pass and repass to and from India on any of the Company's ships, on as advantageous terms as any freeman whatsoever.

Thirdly, That they shall have liberty to live in any of the Company's cities garisons or towns in India, and to buy sell and purchase land or houses, and be capable of all civil offices and perferments in the same manner as if they were Englishmen born, and shall allways have the free and undisturbed liberty of the exercise of their own religion. And we hereby declare, that we will not continue any Governour in our service that shall in any kind disturb or discountenance them in the full enjoyment of all the privileges hereby granted to them. Neither shall they pay any other or greater duty in India than the Company's factors or any other Englishman born doe or ought to doe.

Fourthly, That they may voyage from any of the Company's garisons to any other ports or places in India the South Seas China or the Manillas, in any of the Company's ships or any permissive free ships allowed by the Company, and may have liberty to trade to China the Manillas or any other ports or places within the limits of the Company's charter, upon equal terms duties and freights with any free Englishmen whatsoever.

But whereas all persons in England doe pay for bullion outwards two per cent for freight and permission, and three per cent homewards for diamonds and other precious stones, it is hereby declared and agreed, that the Armenians shall pay three per cent outwards for bullion and two per cent homeward for diamonds, for corral and amber beads they shall pay six per cent for freight and permission, and for corral and amber raw, cochineil, quicksilver, sword blades, fire arms of all sorts, haberdashery wares, iron of all sorts wrought or unwrought, paper, all sorts of stationary wares, English looking or drinking glasses, and for all sorts of Norimbergh wares and merchandizes, ten per cent for permission and six pounds per ton freight. That all sorts of leather Venetian wares and merchandizes may be shipt out permission free, paying only six pounds per ton freight. For all cloth or woollen manufactures of what kind or sort soever they shall pay $12^1/_2$ per cent in lieu of all charges whatsoever, excepting only the freight and the Company's customs in India. For lead ten per cent permission and 3 li per ton freight. For provisions of all sorts for eating and drinking £6 per ton freight, but no permission. And for all sorts of goods homeward bound they shall pay in manner and form following, vizt. For diamonds pearls rubies all sorts of precious stones and ambergreice two per cent freight and permission as aforesaid. For musk of any kind six per cent for freight and permission. For pepper one penny per pound, and for coffee ten per cent permission besides freight. For all raw silk of Persia £21 per ton freight, but no permission custom or any other charges whatsoever; excepting only $2^1/_2$ per cent towards demorages[1] of our ships. For all goods whatsoever of the growth and manufacture of Persia, (red Carmania wool excepted, which is hereby totally prohibited) ten per cent permission, and the same freights as the Company themselves pay, without any other charges whatsoever. For all sorts of China and Bengal goods, during the Company's indulgence for those kinds of goods and no longer, in what place soever loaden, thirteen per cent for permission, and all other charges whatsoever over and above the same freight as the Company pays, and the custom hereafter mencioned, vizt, all goods outward and homeward bound are to pay the Company in East India five per cent custom on the first cost as per invoice of the said goods, whether they be laden from or delivered into any of the Company's ports or places, or into any other ports or places whatsoever, excepting only from this article all bullion diamonds and other precious stones ambergriece musk and raw Persian silk. And it is agreed, that the permission mony and freight for all goods outward bound to be paid in India as aforesaid shalbe accounted for at $8^1/_2$ rupees per £ sterling upon hypothecation[2] of the goods to the Company in London. And we doe declare, that for the ease of accounts, the custom due to the Company in East India, is to be included together with the other charges, vizt. freight, and permission according to the premisses, and all inserted in one summ upon the respective bils of loading, which summ is allways to be paid before the delivery of the goods to the persons mencioned in the said bils of loading, which is the true intent of the hypothecation before expressed. That all goods which have once paid custom, are not to pay any again either upon importacion or exportacion of the said goods to the place where they first paid it, or to any other port or place belonging to us in the East Indies. That every person that shall take passage on any of the Company's ships shall pay in East India twelve pounds sterling for his permission outward, at the rate of 8 rupees and $^1/_2$ per £ sterling; and the like sum to be paid here for every person that shall take passage homeward, besides 8£ per head for sea provisions, which it is hereby agreed shall always be paid in London. And for such persons as shall board at the Captain's table, they shall pay ten guinies each to the Captain for the same. But the servants shall be messed apart by themselves and allways have the same allowances of ship provisions as the officers and seamen of the ship have or ought to have. And it is also granted to the said Armenians, that the passingers shalbe allowed both out and home to carry with them their wearing clothes furniture and provisions not exceeding one quarter of a tonn for each man freight free. And whereas the said Armenians have used to drive a great trade from India to Turkey overland by the way of Persia and Arabia, and are now desirous to drive that whole trade by the way of England, it is hereby declared and agreed, that the said Armenians have liberty to send upon any of the Company's ships for England any sorts of goods of East India, consigning them to the Company by true invoices and bils of loading and not otherwise, paying ten per cent permission on the value of the said goods in London, besides the same freight as we ourselves pay. And it is hereby declared, that the Company have liberty to detain and keep in their possession all such goods as shalbe consigned unto them as aforesaid, until they have shipped them off upon English shipping bound for Turkey Venice or Leghorn and taken security that they shall not be landed in any other ports or places of Europe except the places to which they shalbe consigned, according as they shalbe directed by the said Armenians proprietors or their agents. And lastly, it is declared and agreed, that notwithstanding anything aforesaid, it shall and may be lawfull for the said Company to reserve and keep for their own use any of the said goods so intended for Turkey as aforesaid, paying the proprietors one third part cleer profit on the first cost of the goods as aforesaid, all freight charges and disbursments whatsoever being first deducted and foreprized, eight rupees in India being in this case to be accompted for one pound sterling. In witness whereof the Governour Deputy- Governour and three of the Committees of the said Company have hereunto sett their hands and caused the larger seal of the said Company to be affixed this two and twentith day of June Anno Domini 1688 and in the fourth year of the reign of our Sovereign Lord James the Second by the grace of God King of England Scotland France and Ireland Defender of the Faith et cetera.

Signed

Benjamin Bathurst, Governour
Josia Child, Deputy Governour
Worcester
John Moore
George Boun

The Governour and Company of Merchants of London trading into the East Indies, To all whom it may concern send greeting. Whereas Coja Panous Kalendar an Armenian merchant of eminency and an inhabitant of Ispahan in Persia hath taken great pains in making an agreement with the said Company for a great trade to be carried on in English shipping by himself and others of the Armenian nation, the said Governour and Company, in consideracion thereof, doe by these presents (at the request of said Coja Panous Kalendar) freely grant unto him and his family the sole trade of garnats, he paying ten per cent custom for the same and the usual freights paid by the Company. And the said Company doe hereby declare that they will neither trade in the said commodity themselves, nor suffer any other persons English or strangers for the future to trade or traffique in that commodity. Given under the Company's larger seal, as also under the hands of the Governour Deputy-Governour and three of the Committees of the said Company this two and twentith day of June Anno Domini 1688. And in the fourth year of the reign of our Sovereign Lord James the Second by the grace of God King of England Scotland France and Ireland Defender of the Fayth et cetera.

Signed

Benjamin Bathurst, Governour
Josia Child, Deputy-Governour
Worcester

John Moore
George Boun

The Governour and Company of Merchants of London trading into the East Indies, To all whom it may concern send greeting. Whereas it hath been represented unto us that the Armenian nation have a great desire to carry on a trade and commerce with our people in the East Indies, we doe for the better encouragement of that nation to settle and cohabit in the several garisons cities and towns in the East Indies under our jurisdicion, by these presents declare grant and agree, that whenever fourty or more of the Armenian nation shall become inhabitants in any of the garisons cities or towns belonging to the Company in the East Indies, the said Armenians shall not only have and enjoy the free use and exercise of their religion, but theire shalbe also allotted to them a parcel of ground to erect a church thereon for the worship and service of God in their own way. And that we will also at our own charge, cause a convenient church to be built of tymber, which afterwards the said Armenians may alter and build with stone or other solid materials to their own good liking. And the said Governour and Company will also allow fifty pounds per annum during the space of seaven years for the maintenance of such priest or minister as they shall choose to officiate therein. Given under the Company's larger seal, as also under the hands of the Governour Deputy-Governour and three of the Committees of the said Company this two and twentieth day of June Anno Domini 1688. And in the fourth year of the reign of our Sovereign Lord James the Second King of England Scotland France and Ireland Defender of the Faith et cetera.

Signed

Benjamin Bathurst, Governour
Josia Child, Deputy-Governour
Worcester
John Moore
George Boun

[1] demurrage: a charge for detaining a ship beyond the agreed period of time
[2] pledging as security

113

COMPANY IN LONDON TO PERSIA
25 JULY 1688
E/3/91 EXTRACT FROM F. 268v

We have made a contract with the Armenians to bring all the trade they used to drive for Turky overland by sea in our English shipping, and to carry their returnes in cloth or any other thing in our outward bound ships for India or Persia of which you shall hear further and have copies of our contracts with them sent you by the next conveyance.

114

COMPANY IN LONDON TO BOMBAY
26 JULY 1688
E/3/91 EXTRACT FROM F. 269v

Besides advising you of the arrivall of the Success the 21th instant for which God be praised, the most materiall thing we have is to acquaint you with a contract we have made with the Armenians (copies whereof you will have inclosed) and by our ships which depart in September we shall further explain them to you, and the publick advantage we hope to acquire to this kingdom and the Company by this agreement. In the mean time before goods rise too much and since you have stock enough, we would have you proceed to buy all the usuall sorts of callicoes as well white as coloured, concluding you may now have them 20 per cent cheaper than before the war begun with the Mogull, which war we now conclude is honourably and happily ended, your main care must be in sorting well, for although you should agree upon very cheap terms, if your sorters do not discharge their duty justly and faithfully, we shall find little fruit of your carefull and prudent contractions for us.

115

COMPANY IN LONDON TO BOMBAY
27 AUGUST 1688
E/3/91 EXTRACT FROM FF. 272-272v, 273v, 274v, 275

Now we have made such a contract with the Armenians as you shall hereafter understand, we think it is not for our advantage to continue an English factory at Bussora but since this Armenian contract will create an employment for more of our ships to sail for Bussora than formerly, we leave it to your discretion to do what you shall think best for us in this matter.

Copies of our contracts with the Armenians we send you enclosed and desire and strictly injoin you to perform every part and article thereof, that they may have no cause to complain of the least discountenance or discouragement from you in any respect.

Mr Calendar aforesaid having been the good instrument of makeing this agreement for his nation, we have granted to him on the terms of the inclosed contract the sole trade of garnets which you are duely to observe.

We have no mind to a war with the Arabs in the King of Persia's quarrel. They owe us no money neither is any thing to be got of them if they did and for obtaining more of the Persia trade by pleasing that King in such a conjunction it is not worth while besides that we have done that business a hundred times better allready by our contract with the Armenians who will certainly comply therewith being greatly for their own interest as well as for ours especially while the Turks' dominions are all of a flame with civil wars intestine broiles and multitude of bold and powerfull robbers.

116

COMPANY IN LONDON TO FORT ST GEORGE
27 AUGUST 1688
E/3/91 EXTRACT FROM FF. 281-281V

Copies of our contracts with the Armenians we send you inclosed and desire and strictly enjoyn you to perform every part and article thereof that they may have no cause to complain of the least discountenance or discouragement from you in any respect. It may be if we had not been in a war when we made that agreement we should have made it somewhat more streight, and a little harder upon them in a few particulars, but since it is done we would inviolably keep our faith and promise to them, and hereafter when your wars are quite over and peace and our trade not onely restored but well setled, and also this new course of their trade for Europe et cetera wee may with their own consent make some alterations for the better or at least restrain part of the Bengall trade wholly to the Company but for the present and untill you have other orders from us we would have you deprive them of nothing they can fairly claim by our contracts, but on the contrary cherish and countenance them all that possibly you can, for we shall esteem those who are kindest to them to be our best servants, because undoubtedly if they be not discouraged this foundation which we have happily laid may grow to a famous superstructure and much augment the English navigation as well as his Majestie's customs and discover a multitude of new goods that will turn to a great advantage, and hereafter we may oblige that whole nation to load no goods in India et cetera but upon English shiping. They are an innocent harmless people that will not be apt to contend or plead law with us and are certainly sober frugal and very wise in all the commodities and places of India and when they cohabit with you and you are well acquainted with them, you may make great use of them for the Company and for yourselves in some places where we have no factories.

Let them allways have tonnage for their goods on our homeward bound ships on the terms we have agreed, and give a strict charge to all commanders to use them kindly in their passages for Europe or elsewhere, and always know of them as soon as you can what tonnage each year they design for Europe, that you may appoint such a proportionable number of shipps to return as may be sufficient to bring home yearly all their goods as well as our own.

We have considered of the fruitless charge of imploying a paultry inconsiderable vakeel at the Mogull's Court who spent us more money than would have obliged the mufti or high Priest and five or six potent courtiers that always attend near the Mogull's person where ever he is, which we understand is always the Armenians' way of doing their business at Court with small expence and much more effect than hireing a poor vakeel that dare not speak to such great men as you may correspond with by letters, and in them write what you think and send your letters by Armenians or your own peons, concerning which we desire you to confer with Coja Panous Calendar when he arrives with you or with his son in the mean time, and with some others of the most substantiall knowing and experienced of the Armenian nation.

If you find this designed imbarcation of the Armenians for Europe should prove bulky and considerable, there will be a necessity you should build more convenient warehouses for containing their goods in security as well before they are shipped for England, as for such as shall be landed from England, before they are taken away or shipt for any other place, and for such warehouse you must impose some duty by the bale or tun lying in our warehouses by the week as will in a few years reimburse us our charge of building them and the charge of collecting the money we having as you will observe in our contracts made no provision concern-ing this duty because wee could not compute what it might amount to.

Mr Calendar the Armenian before mentioned having been the good instrument of makeing this agreement for his nation, we have granted to him on the terms of the inclosed contract the sole trade of garnetts which you are duly to observe.

It's the 6th August, and we have yours of the 21th January by the French ships, which we are sorry to tell you gives us little satisfaction, for you have been very weak and unhappy in the management of all our political affaires. The force you sent to Mergee was too little, as you may see we feared before by the foregoing paragraphs of this letter. But that which almost astonisheth us to see, is that you should have so little sense and understanding of the Armenians' letter, as not to observe that the Mogull and all his great Princes were in paine to have peace with us, and that it was not your complements, nor our money, which you vainly wasted in sending up your vakeel and Mounsieur Charden, nor theirs, or either of their sollicitation nor your letters, but our successe on the other side of India, the want of trade, and the misery and cry

of the Mogull's poor subjects, occasioned by our war, that were the potent
advocates and procurers of our peace, and therefore you might have spared
our purse in that unnecessary message, or rather have spent it in makeing
another strong bastion at our Fort; for 'its onely strength that must preserve
and better our peace.

117

COMPANY IN LONDON TO BENGAL
27 AUGUST 1688
E/3/91 EXTRACT FROM FF. 287-288V

You have with this packet the copies of three contracts made with the
Armenian contracts when we thought our war with the Mogull would have
continued a great while longer than it did, and if we had thought otherwise we
should have made some variation in it, however since it is done and many
nationall advantages may accrue to this kingdom thereby especially to the
English navigation. We resolve for this year at least to keep our bargain
inviolably with them, and although we have a liberty by the contract hereafter
to restrain Bay goods intirely to the Company, we will for this year make no
alteration but require you to suffer them fully to enjoy all the priviledges
granted to them by the contracts aforesaid untill you receive our orders to the
contrary.

We are apt to think you might with a little pains and correspondency
procure yearly quantities of the best sort of sticklack[1] and bees wax, and it may
be the right sort of shellack[2] from Raccan, pray try your skill therein, and at
every other place where those commodities are like to be had but this likewise
must be done by degrees and with industry, for you must never expect that any
new thing will fall into your hands of itself, or that you can easily meet with a
great parcell very good at once.

Possibly some of the Armenian poor merchants which can travell further
for 2d than you can or will with the charge of ten shillings may be fittest to
employ to provide those commodities for you, or for themselves being
encouraged by you to that purpose, especially since by our contract if they
desire it they may bring those commodities for Europe by our shipping for
their own accompts, and the more they do so bring especially of kintlage[3]
goods the better it is for the English navigation and for the Company.

Though we have wrote for a great quantity of indico from Surrat of
severall sorts yet considering your want of kintlage goods, and that Agra is
within 3 days journey of Pattana, from whence you have all water carriage,
which is much cheaper than land carriage, we are apt to think if you were in the
way of it, you might buy indico cheaper in the Bay than we can buy it in Surrat,
where the land carriage from Agra is somuch further and dearer. We would
therefore for an experiment desire you to buy carefully and send us 50 tons of

indico vizt.: 20 tons of the best sort, 10 tons of the 2d sort, 10 tons of the 3d sort and 10 tons of the 4th or cheapest sort of all. But we shall like it altogether as well or better if you can perswade the thrifty experienced Armenians to break the ice first in buying and bringing this commodity by the way of Bengall on our ships for Europe for their proper accompts, and for the following reasons first.

1st Because if they so bring it, it serves as well to kintlage our ships as if we brought it ourselves.

2d If you employ not our stock in indico you may employ it in other commodities that may turn to as good or a better accompt.

3d When the Armenians' indico comes hither it is ours if we like it without being at any disbursement or hazard of the sea paying then only 30 per cent advance on the prime cost.

4th If we take it not to ourselves on those terms, we shall send it for them to Turkey, or far enough out of the way for spoiling our own marketts at home.

5th Whether we take it to ourselves or send it abroad, it must certainly pay the King and us the custome and duties reserved by our contract before we part with it, so that every way we have reason to conclude this Armenian contract will prove in time of great advantage to the English nation in general as well to the Company in particular if you do your parts in being kind and courteous to them.

[1] sticklac: crude form of resin, a substance secreted by a scale insect and used chiefly in the form of shellac

[2] shellac: purified lac resin with dye extracted, chiefly used in varnishes, polishing and sealing waxes

[3] kentledge: pig-iron used as permanent ballast

118
COMPANY IN LONDON TO ISFAHAN
5 NOVEMBER 1688
E/3/91 EXTRACT FROM F. 296V

Wee have formerly given you intimation of our severall contracts made with the Armenian nation by the administration of Coja Panous Calendar, which contracts, we desire you to favour and further all that in you lyes, having a well grounded assurance, that they may in time prove of great advantage to this kingdom in generall, and to this Company more particularly as well as to the Armenians themselves. And in regard the family of the Calendars are desired to provide some particular musters of goods of that country and some presents for our King and Queen, we would have you receive such chests of presents and musters, which they shall deliver unto your care at Spahaun, and cause them to be safely conveyed to our Generall and Council at Bombay, and from thence to be sent upon our ships, consigned to us. But the whole you are to do at the charge and risque of the Calendars, they paying us the dues and dutyes reserved and adjusted by our contracts made with them, besides the charges you are at for them, and in all other respects you are to shew favour to the family of the Kalendars, as being the first instruments of that good agreement we have made with the Armenians which our ancestors did attempt seaventy years past, and many times since but never could bring to so good effect.

119

COMPANY IN LONDON TO PERSIA
10 DECEMBER 1688
E/3/91 EXTRACT FROM F. 297V

This serves to give cover to copy of our letter written to Spahaun on behalf of the Armenians, the originall whereof was left to their care to send forward. We are greatly troubled that we have no account of late overland, how our affairs stand in India with reference to war or peace, and do again require you to be more frequent in sending us what intelligence comes to your knowledge.

120

COMPANY IN LONDON TO BOMBAY
15 FEBRUARY 1688/89
E/3/92 EXTRACT FROM F. 10V

We have formerly given you many methods for the improvement of our revenue and we believe our Generall establisht some new rules for that purpose, before he went to Madrass. Now to the intent we may see your care and diligence in that respect, we would have you once in every year to send us a particular account that we may the easilier understand the annuall increase of our revenue, which must of necessity augment exceedingly now that we have made that place the center of our trade, and the constant road of our shipping, and brought the Armenians to have such occasion of frequent resort to that place.

Now we have mentioned the Armenians, we must remind you to use them kindly, abate them nothing of our customes, and other duties according to contract, but in all other respects treat them with the greatest humanity. It will be a great thing to England, if we can turn the course of the silk trade that used to passe through Turkey to come for Europe this way. The freight and custom thereof will be all clear profit to the kingdome, besides something gained to the poor labouring men of England, such as lightermen, watermen, porters et cetera which will be imployed about it.

121
COMPANY IN LONDON TO BENGAL
15 FEBRUARY 1688/89
E/3/92 EXTRACT FROM F. 13

Some supply we hope likewise to have from the Armenians by vertue of a contract we have made with them, of which contract we hereby desire our Generall President and Councill of Fort St George to send you a copy. Those people are a thrifty close prudent sort of men that travell all India over and know almost every village in the Mogoll's dominions and every sort of goods with such a perfect skill and judgment as exceeds the antientest of our linen drapers. We would have you give them all imaginable incouragement to invest their own stocks, especially in such fine goods as you know or suppose we may be in most want of, and which are most difficult for you to provide or not to be had, but in places most remote from you. The finer the goods are which they so purchase, the better it wilbe for themselves and us. They are all to be consigned to the Company and when they arrive here, we are to have them for our own accounts if we please, allowing them 30 per cent profitt on the first cost and charges which we think is little less than our own charges have amounted to upon all Bengall goods viis et modis ever since we traded thither, and therefore we say again let those men have all the favour you can show them and your utmost assistance in shipping their goods upon the first ships that are likelyest to arrive in England.

122
JOHN CHILD, JOHN VAUX AND GEORGE COOKE AT BOMBAY TO
COMPANY IN LONDON
7 JUNE 1689
E/3/48 EXTRACT FROM FF. 20-21

Wee have received severall copies of your Honours' contracts with the Armenians, and shall punctually comply with every part and article thereof, that they may have no cause to complain in the least, we give them all the encouragement that we can suitable to your orders and our duties. They are really a very cunning sort of people and very hard dealers, and will truly cavill and contend for a penny, but are really as frugall people as any in the whole world and very knowing in all manner of commodities and traffick, and we hope the nation and your Honours may reap a benefit by them. We shall on our parts not fail your Honours may rest assured to pleasure you what in us lyes. We have not any of them come to us, nor received any advices from any of them. As soon as any appears to us wee shall endeavour to learn what tonage they design yearly for England, and accordingly provide as your Honours are pleased to direct.

We take notice of your Honours' pleasures in ordering that Mr Callendar have the sole trade of garnets. What that commodity is we cannot well tell, neither can we inform ourselves from any about us what it is, but a due obedience to your orders in this and all other things we shall punctually obey.

123
FORT ST GEORGE CONSULTATIONS
3 JULY 1689
H/634 PP. 599-600

Amongst the newspapers received from Persia was sent a copy of the Honourable Governor's et cetera agreement with some Armenian merchants in England, about inhabiting and trading at the Right Honourable Company's several settlements of Bombay, Madras, et cetera, as also to freight upon their ships according to the conditions therein specified, which probably may be now of greater benefit to the Right Honourable Company than hereafter, by helping to lade the great tonnage we are charged with, and little possibility of procuring goods, for half of it in these parts. The Governor therefore sent for Senor Gregorio, and some other of the chiefest of the Armenian merchants, and acquainted them of the favorable agreement the Right Honourable Company had made with their nation for their settlement and trade, and several kind privileges under their governments, which they seemed greatly satisfied and pleased with, desiring a translate thereof, to communicate to their friends at Bengal et cetera and to invite them hither, which is accordingly ordered to be given, with all other due encouragements so great and advantageous a design requires.

124

COMPANY IN LONDON TO BOMBAY
11 SEPTEMBER 1689
E/3/92 EXTRACT FROM F. 33

All our advices from the Fort and Bay are so late and uncertain, that we know not what to think of affairs in the Bay, but whether there be peace or war, we would have you give all the encouragement you can to the Armenians to make considerable investments in Bengall, and send them hither by our returning ships, upon the termes of their contract especially in taffaties, raw silk of Bengall, and the finest white goods of all sorts far up in the river of Ganges, from Cassimbuzar upwards to Dacca Maulda and Benharris, in all which places, many of that nation are as well acquainted as they are at their own homes in Julpha, and can buy any goods that are wanted, such as we cannot procure for money at Hughly or Chutanutte, such goods will turn the Armenians to a very great accompt, which we shall be glad of, being satisfyed with that participation of their profits, for the countenance and liberty we give them, which we have provided for in our contract.

125

ELIHU YALE, JOHN LITTLETON, THOMAS WAVELL, JOHN CHENEY,
WILLIAM CAWLEY AND THOMAS GRAY AT FORT ST GEORGE TO
COMPANY IN LONDON
1 FEBRUARY 1689/90
E/3/48 EXTRACT FROM FF. 134v-135

The Armenians in all these parts have been advised of your Honours' contract with their nation, but they and their concernes are so disperst that there is little encrease to those were formerly here, but we doubt not the tearmes and encouragement are so good and well approved by them, that those here give us great hopes of a numerous encrease to the enriching and advantageing the place with all other benefitts proposed therein.

126
FORT ST GEORGE CONSULTATIONS
14 APRIL 1690
H/634 PP. 601-602

A confirmation of the contract with the Armenian merchants in London.

To all persons whom these presents may concern We the President and Council of Fort St George and city of Madras for account of the Right Honorable English East India Company have and do for ourselves and successors engage to observe the contract and agreement made between the said Right Honorable Company and Cojee Panure Callendar et cetera Armenian merchants in England for themselves and all others of their country and nation as per copy of said agreement sent us hither, and also delivered to Senor Gregorio Paroan, and several other Armenian merchants of this city, whereby they are not only invited to settle and trade here and live and be as free therein, as any English whatever paying only 5 per cent custom to the said Right Honorable Company, and nothing to Peddanague Town, Coimacaply Muskeet pagoda or any other petty custom or duty whatever, nor any other taxes or customs, than what all English inhabitants do or shall for the future pay, besides which we hereby also promise and confirm all other liberties and privileges specified in their said contract with the Honorable Company and to assist and encourage them by our power both in their trade religion and liberties to induce as many as possible of their nation to come and settle here with their families and estates for the good and comfort of themselves and improvement of the place, hereby engaging constantly to give them all due and friendly respect and civility.

Dated at Fort St George in the city of Madras this 10th of April Anno 1690.

127
COMPANY IN LONDON TO BOMBAY
3 OCTOBER 1690
E/3/92 EXTRACT FROM FF. 57-57V

Our President and Council of the Fort write us that the Armenian nation at the Mogull's Court have been very forward and industrious in inclining the courtiers and all persons concerned to make a pacification with the English and the truth is, our advantage here by that contract has been very great allready, and would have been much greater if the seas had been open as at other times. The freight permission et cetera that you will receive from them before they can receive their goods from you that are to go per the King

William will amount to about 20000 li for that ship and by their East India goods return'd hither we shall be greater gainers abundantly if we accept them for our own accounts on the terms you will observe which we may do if we please by their contract, and the King and kingdome's advantage by turning the course of their trade this way will be exceedingly more than ours to the King by the encrease of his customes, and to the kingdom by the encrease of the navigation by such warlike ships as we send for India and the vent of the woollen manufacture, which they by reason of their excessive diligence and thrift can do more and better and transport it further even to Usbeck Tartaria and the backside northward of India and China than any Europe people whatsoever there being scarce a market towne or great village in those countries but some of them know very well by their pedling and peregrinations and therefore we must inculcate to you our desires to have them treated with the utmost kindness and encouraged in their negotiations according to the terms of our contract with them. Especially encourage them to bring any sorts of new goods they can procure in their travells within the land superfine goods such as superfine baftas[1] (of which we have seen two peices inclosed in a pacquet of letters from Mr Charnock at Patana to Mr Shelden) and other superfine muslins a little of a sort will do extreamly well for them to our great ladys who will give any rates for such fine things that other people cannot have and no men in India can buy such fine things so well because none know them better nor yourselves or our brokers that have greater affairs to mind can intend to looke after the getting of such small quantities of severall sorts of unusual goods from the makers as they will do and attend the workmen de die in diem at the expence of about an halfpeny a day.

---

[1] *bāfta* (Pers.): woven; coarse to fine quality calico

128
COMPANY IN LONDON TO FORT ST GEORGE
3 OCTOBER 1690
E/3/92 EXTRACT FROM FF. 58, 59

Wee must highly applaud our President's accute judgement in his apprehending so suddenly the nationall advantage to this kingdom as well as our own by that Armenian contract and we do give him our hearty thanks for the encouragement he hath given to it and for the increase he hath made of our revenue in Madrass and the good designs he had in his mind of a further increase thereof in imitation of the Dutch wisdom as time and opportunity should give him leave for which and other his good services we shall make him an acceptable present by the Dorothy. Wee cannot apprehend whatever hath been said that a settlement at Pegu can ever be of service to the Company, there being nothing in that country besides sticklack to do any thing towards the loading of our ships, but rather a pocket trade for private persons in gold rubies et cetera.

Wee cannot doubt but now you will have occasion to be so well acquainted with the Armenians you may by them procure much better sorts of indico to be brought to you from some bordering countreys not far distant from Madrass cheap enough by land carriage to the Fort of which we would have you make experiment, as also of some superfine goods from Benharris and those parts above Patana or between that and Agra, in which charge of fine goods the land carriage is very triviall if the roads be safe which the Armenians can thoroughly inform you, and so we must leave this matter to your discretion.

129

JOHN GLADMAN AT GOMBROON TO COMPANY IN LONDON
27 OCTOBER 1690
E/3/48 EXTRACT FROM F. 222

Your honours are sencible that the Dutch will endeavour what they can to raise all scandolous reports they can contrive or invent, whereby to deminish the creditt of the English nation at court. And to this purpose they have imployed I suppose an Armenian fellow, who came from Suratt in their ship, haveing procured of the Vockenaviss the coppy of the Mogull's phirmaund, by bribeing him with twenty or thirty rupees, which he read publickly at severall carravanseroys[1], in a derideing, scornfull manner, and likewise made use of others to shew it to the great men. And at last it arrived the King's hands, who onely said, had the Mogull done somuch for the English, and granted them their former privilidges again, soe that it was understood by him otherwise then was expected by your honours' enemys, and your honours have severall friends at court, to stop the mouths of prejudiced persons, who feign would bite but cannot.

[1] caravansary: an inn in eastern countries where caravans rest at night

130
COMPANY IN LONDON TO SURAT
18 FEBRUARY 1690/91
E/3/92 EXTRACT FROM FF. 64V-65, 66-66V

The owners of the great new ship at Blackwall (which we hoped to send out to you about this time) had killed some part of their provisions and fitted some part of her rigging, when the ship was taken up for their Majesties' service in the narrow seas, and is since bought outright for that purpose, by which means we are disappointed of loading that great quantity of cloth, which the Armenians had provided here, and was ready embaled, there being about 14 or 16 of that nation here and more are comeing from other parts of Europe. But to make them as much requitall for that disappointment as we can at this time, we have ordered the Dorothy to proceed directly for Bombay, and there will goe upon her only 2 or 3 Armenian vaqueels for fear of the present hazard of the sea, but we and they must submitt to the fate of war, which is such at this time, that neither any great ship or such a number of men as are fit to navigate such a ship can this spring be permitted to go to sea in merchants affairs, but by this little we have done for them we have demonstrated our willingness to accommodate them.

It falls out happily in one respect, that you have at this time so many good ships in India, for although they may be a little burdensome to you in respect of their loading home their great tonnage, they may be very beneficiall to us and the Armenians, if you and they can procure goods enough to ship upon them, which would now come to a greater market here then hath been in Europe for 30 years past, and to much the better market by an accident that hath befallen the Dutch, four of their last years fleet, that we heard of safe on the backside of Ireland (in which were the greatest part of their piece goods) having miscarryed as it is thought in Holland and here, there being no newes of them. We mention this to you as a further argument to encourage the Armenians to take the opportunity of the great tonnage for Europe which you are now in a condition to spare them. There is nothing they can buy at Surratt or on that side of India, but will now turn to a great account, so as the commodityes be good in their kinds.

The Armenian contract is of so great advantage to the nation and this Company, that we would have you indulge them by all means whatsoever and in no case to hinder them from loading baftaes or any sort of goods of India, consigning them to ourselves according to their contract, because when they come hither they are our's upon the termes of their contract which you need not doubt, but at this extraordinary market we shall gladly accept of, and punctually pay them for according to our contract, though they should amount to above 100000 li sterling for the profit upon them by the Company, wilbe little less (if not altogether as much) as the profit of their own goods, upon which they run the adventure of the sea, besides the growing charge of their fort and factoryes.

The Armenians in London petition and press us hard to send out 3 or 4 great ships on which they designe considerable adventures in cloth and money, and to comply with them as far as in us lies we resolve to lay the case before their Majesties and Councill, setting forth the advantage it is to this nation to have such a quantity of cloth bought and sent abroad, and the poor manufacturers thereby set at work at such a dead time of trade as this is, by which we hope to prevail for a permission to send out four of our great ships the later end of this summer when the fighting of the great fleets wilbe over.

131

COMPANY IN LONDON TO FORT ST GEORGE
18 FEBRUARY 1690/91
E/3/92 EXTRACT FROM FF. 67v, 69v-70

You will in our Surratt letter observe the reason of our sending this small ship Dorothy first to Bombay, and it wilbe your part as soon as she arrives (if it be possible) immediately to send her home to us with bale goods, which are wanted exceedingly, and this is the time, wherein the Armenians may do themselves and us singular service by loading great quantities of bale goods to dispatch those ships you have remaining in the country, it being a most difficult thing to get out any one great ship at this time. We hear the States of Holland would allow their Company but permission for 3 ships this year, and we could not possibly get leave for any more than two small ships vizt. the Tonqueen Captain Knox, and this ship Dorothy Captain Thwaites. The Tonqueen sailed out of Downes without our paquet, which considering the times, we cannot blame the Captain for, because if he had stayed one hour longer, he must have lost his convoy and good company, and probably his Madagascar voyage likewise. He is bound from Madagascar with slaves for Bencoolen, and thince home, if he can have his full loading of pepper, and if but half of his loading he is to go to you to fill up with Coast goods or otherwise as you shall think best to dispose of him for our service. Our intended paquet by him we send you by this to peruse and send forward as you find necessary.

We would have you give the Armenians all possible encouragement to load home quantities of Indian goods upon our returning ships from your place. They can send nothing amiss at this time when everything of India is so much wanted.

You must take notice that the Armenians by their contract may send us any kind of goods of India whatsoever, and we doe not doubt, but we shalbe almost as great gainers by the goods they send us on the termes of their contract, as by the goods we buy our selves after we have twice run the hazard of the sea, and have been so many years out of our money. Wherefore give them all manner of encouragement, and let them load upon our ships in all places whatever East India goods they will (none excepted). They are travelling people, and know almost every city and great town in India critically and what fabricks or sort of goods are made chiefly in every particular place as far as Usbeck Tartaria and many places in Tartaria, and when you can find no goods about your place, or among your merchants or at Coinmere, (where you deal but with the same merchants in masquerade or disguise) they will find goods for their money in other places and from other men and find means to bring them to you for their own accounts.

132

COMPANY IN LONDON TO BENGAL
18 FEBRUARY 1690/91
E/3/92 EXTRACT FROM F. 74V

You must observe that our perpetuall contract made with the Armenians extends to all parts of India and all sorts of goods and therefore you are at all times to permitt them to load what goods they please upon any of our returning ships because their goods arriving here are our own if we please without running any part of the hazard or being in disburse of our money we allowing them only thirty per cent proffitt which will render their goods as cheap and profitable to us as those bought with our own money considering that upon their goods we are at no charge of factorys sloops et cetera and therefore we would have you give them all the countenances and encouragement you can, possible as you value the welfare and prosperity of this Company.

133

COMPANY IN LONDON TO PERSIA
18 FEBRUARY 1690/91
E/3/92 F. 76

Wee have yours of the 21th June last from Gombroon being very glad thereby to hear of the safe arrivall of our honest Mr John Gladman.

Wee have not the same reason to fear your troubles will be soe difficult to compose in Persia as they have been formerly since wee perswade our selves we have a better interest correspondence and advice there than ever we had in past times by the means of our Armenian contract which we would have you cultivate and indulge in all things not being apparently to our prejudice and we have the greatest reason to hope they will be very assistant to you and beneficiall to us if they have understanding enough to know their own interest which we do not see those want whom we have conversed with here and we shall hereafter oblige them so farr now the trade is open that we doubt not but the best of that nation at Julpha will by their united councills so farr as in them lyes corroborate and improve your interest in the Court of Persia. For which purpose some of us have writt to Coja Panous Calendar now at Venice to recommend you to all the chief of their nation at Julpha joyntly to assist and advise you on all occasions and in order thereto you must direct your linguist Doud in the first place to consult and advise with the family of the Calendars at Julpha and you your selves must correspond with them who will bring you into a thorough acquaintance with the rest of the chief of their nation whom we doubt not will be as indulgent to you and our affairs there as we shall be to their nation here.

Wee take due notice of the advice you give us of the proceedings of our ship Royall James and Mary and of the Dutch embassy.

You must insist upon the speedy payment of our arrears of custom and send us all the Carmania wool you can possible and the oppoponga[1] and other druggs formerly writt for in which the Armenians may assist you to encrease the quantity especially of Carmania wool and you must permitt them to load what ever goods they please in Persia to be brought for Europe or otherwise according to the terms of their contract as they think best. The 30th January last arrived the Chandos from Fort St George for which God be praised.

[1] opopanax: fetid gum resin obtained from the root of a yellow flowered plant, formerly of repute in medicine

134
SIR JOHN CHARDIN IN LONDON TO COJA AUGA PERE CALENDAR
20 FEBRUARY 1690/91
E/3/92 F. 76v

I received the letters you did write to your father and to mee in his absence which I did immediately dispatch to him at Venice and I was very glad to hear of your good health and of the safe arrivall of the goods laden on board the Kempthorn which came to a good and convenient markett. I do hope those laden on the Benjamin will meet with the like successe.

I have now propounded to your father a matter of more concern which is if it be convenient for you and your father approves it that you should accomodate the President and Council at Suratt with four lacres[1] rupees for which or somuch thereof as you shall have order from your father to pay to the said President and Council you are to take five receipts of one tenour and date I having received a security from the Company for the whole value in a bond of fifty thousand pounds for your father's account which I take to be a great advantage to your father as you will easily find your self. This agreement I could not have made so advantagiously but for the accident of the present warr in Europe which hath hindred the Company from sending out any great ships this spring but only two small ships for advice one for Sumatra and Choromandell and one small shipp for Suratt by which you will receive this letter. The Company did not think fitt to adventure any money by him though they have many ships to load home from India but thought it safest to make use of that expedient of giving security for the aforesaid summe of four lacres rupees at the rate of eight rupees for a pound sterling with interest from this day at the rate of five per cent per annum and as what you shall so pay is for your father's account so you are to follow this direction because in regard of his absence from this place we cannot here fix the summe certain that you shall pay. But your father with his friends as Aga Mathous and others will doe it better at Venice and from thence give you via Basra the necessary instructions.

The security above mentioned to be given
Sir John Chardin is entered in the Company's
Court Book fol. 49 in the Court of the
24th February 1690/1.

[1] lac: *lākh* (Hind.): one hundred thousand

135
COURT MINUTES
24 FEBRUARY 1690/91
B/40 PP. 49A-49B

Ordered That whereas wee have entered into a bond or obligation to Sir John Chardin of London Knight agent for the Armenian nation in England, a copy whereof is here underwritten: Wee promise notwithstanding that as soon as he the said Sir John Chardin can exhibit to this Court the letters of Coja Perir Calendar Armenian merchant now at Venice, assuring him of what part of the sum mentioned in the aforesaid obligation, wee may depend upon at Surrat, wee will then pay in part thereof, what ever money the said Sir John Chardin shall have occasion to make use of for the accompt of the said Armenians, he securing us by the goods he shall buy with it, and abateing the growing interest of what shall be so paid to him beforehand.

Whereas Sir John Chardin of London Knight agent for the Armenian nation in England hath given unto us the Governour and Company of

Merchant of London trading into the East Indies a letter of credit upon Aga Pirir Calendar an Armenian merchant at Surat in the East Indies for the payment of four hundred thousand rupees unto our President and Councill at Surrat aforesaid after the rate of eight rupees for a pound sterling Now wee the said Governour and Company for us and our successors do hereby oblige and promise that wee will pay unto the said Sir John Chardin fifty thousand pounds sterling for the said four hundred thousand rupees paid in Surrat as aforesaid, or for so much thereof as the said Aga Pirir Calendar or any of his agents or factors shall pay to our President and Councill at Surrat, accounting after the rate aforesaid of eight rupees for a pound sterling, together also with interest for the same from the date thereof at five per cent per annum. In witness whereof wee have affixed our common seal this four and twentyeth day of February Anno Domini one thousand six hundred ninety.

136
COMPANY IN LONDON TO PERSIA
13 MAY 1691
E/3/92 EXTRACT FROM FF. 82-82V

Those knavish linguists and brokers that have been nursed up in the time of the late agents you must cashire and get honester men by the advice of the ablest of the Armenian merchants of Ispahan many of whom are conscientious honest men and of great prudence and experience particularly the family of the Calendars who must be such if they are like Coja Panous Calendar that was here and has been obliged by us and must be again hereafter and therefore is the more likely to endeavour to please us and serve our interest in Persia but of their sincerity in that you will be the best judges upon experience and therefore after this hint we leave it to your discretion to make choice of such instruments as you conclude will serve our interest best.

That affair of the silk which we so earnestly recommended to Captain Shaxton is now better accomplisht to the benefitt of this kingdom and of the company by our general contract made with the Armenian nation which we would have you indulge and cultivate to the utmost of your power not doubting but they will reciprocally be very serviceable to you because it is manifestly their own interest so to be.

After you are better acquainted with them we hope you may make some of their great men good checques or supervisors of what our servants which you imploy at Spahaun do transact in our service and whether they give you just and true accounts of things and affairs or not.

It would be of mighty advantage to this kingdom if the Court of Persia could be perswaded and prevailed with to let the Armenians bring all their silk for Europe by sea in our English shipping such a matter well accomplished would greatly augment their Majesties' revenue here endear the Company to the government and encrease the English navigation and our customs at Bombay. This is a subject deserves your serious contemplation and consultation with the chief Armenian merchants who are rich enough of themselves to make a large purse to deal with that avaritious Court and if the making use of your name or your utmost assistance will do them any service herein you may afford them that liberally but at their own expence.

137

JOHN GLADMAN AT GOMBROON TO COMPANY IN LONDON
16 MAY 1691
E/3/49 EXTRACT FROM FF. 17V-18

I understand which I allwayes feared that the Armenians don't intend to lade their mony on board the Diana, but will keep it in the Dutch house, pretending they have noe orders from the owners thereof that are up at Spahaun, who knew nothing of the King's phirmaund, it being delivered by the King privately to Mahmood Allee Caun's mother who sent it hither to her son without the least intimation to any body, about which I was angry with Attamcaune and ask't him what was the meaning when themselves knew they had noe power to make the proposition to me, when their heart and tongue did not accord.

138

COMPANY IN LONDON TO BOMBAY AND SURAT
25 SEPTEMBER 1691
E/3/92 EXTRACT FROM F. 84V

The main thing you have to do is before our ships arrive to get into your godownes[1] at Swalley (or rather at Bombay if you can do it) great quantities of those goods that wee mentioned in our last, especially such as are bulky and cheap, vizt. olibanum[2], myrrh, coffee and about 100 tons of sal armoniac[3] for kintlage of our three great ships. Indico will not come under the denomination of a cheap and bulky commodity with you, but is of absolute necessity that you should stretch your credit to provide for us against our next ships about 100 tons of indico of all sorts. The sellers of it to you shall have their money paid them before you ship it off from Swally if they desire it, and upon those termes you will be better supplied with it and cheaper by the rich Armenians than by your knavish brokers, from whom you must recover not onely for the new cheats you have detected them in, but for the old debts they owe us, upon the account of Coja Menos and others, with the interest thereof for many years. Mr Harris, and Mr Annesley know the case, and the justice of our demands, and the Generall often writ he would make them pay it to the full before he cleared accounts with them.

Upon some late discourse with Sir John Chardin, wee have some reason to doubt whether the credit of 50000 li: wee sent you by the Dorothy upon the Armenians will be fully complyed with, although in some part wee know it will; and if it be not intirely complyed with by the Armenians wee think it may be a very good and easie way for my Lady Child or any other particular persons that have occasion to return estates for England, to supply you with the rest of that credit, which shall not be supplyed by the Armenians; for which purpose Sir Josia Child intends by this overland conveyance to write to my Lady Child. And wee do hereby give the like liberty to any others that shall desire to make such remittances hither, whose bills wee will punctually pay.

[1] godown: a warehouse or store for goods in Asian countries (perhaps a metathesis of *dukkān* (Ar.), meaning store)

[2] aromatic gum resin in the form of yellowish lumps, formerly used as medicine

[3] sal ammoniac: ammonium chloride

139
ELIHU YALE AT FORT ST GEORGE TO COMPANY IN LONDON
20 NOVEMBER 1691
E/3/49 EXTRACT FROM F. 55V

Some few more Armenians are lately come to settle among us, but many suddainly expected those here haveing publisht Your Honours' libertys to them in all parts, inviteing them to the priviledges and advantages themselves enjoy, so that we hope they will greatly encrease to the benefitt of the place.

140
COMPANY IN LONDON TO BENGAL
22 JANUARY 1691/92
E/3/92 EXTRACT FROM FF. 90-90V

Another proposition we would make you is by imploying some trusty Armenian merchant in buying some part of those goods which you would have from the upper factoryes. Their way is if they make use of their own money untill the goods are delivered into your godownes to have 20 or 25 per cent, and sometimes they wilbe content with 15 per cent profit. If they invest our money, they will never ask above $1^1/_2$ or 2 per cent commission. You must needs observe they are frugall industrious knowing people and will travell further and doe more busyness at the expence of a shilling, than one of our proud vain glorious petty factors will doe at the expense of 5 li. These methods we do not impose upon you, but leave to your discretion to proceed in any manner, that may most enlarge our investment, we being thoroughly satisfyed of your integrity.

The Armenians tell us they paid you in Bengall 5 per cent custome for the Company's use for the goods now brought home of which advise the truth though we do not much doubt it, notwithstanding you have forgott to mention it in your letter.

141

SURAT TO COMPANY IN LONDON
3 FEBRUARY 1691/92
G/40/4 EXTRACT FROM PP. 239-241

[Digest of letter entered in Factory Records]

Armenians did not answer the letter of credit sent by Sir John Chardin this made them to comply with the broker's demands.

Issa Coolley etc Armenians at Court have been serviceable to the Company with whom they correspond. Shall endeavour to find out some superfine cloth, such as Agent Charnock sent to Mr Sheldon.

The Armenians have not assisted them as Sir John Chardin promised, wish had a duplicate his letter overland, they have laden only 25 bales.

The Armenians have and shall be encouraged.

142

INSTRUCTIONS ISSUED BY COMPANY IN LONDON
TO SIR JOHN GOLDSBOROUGH, COMMISSARY GENERAL OF INDIA
29 FEBRUARY 1691/92
E/3/92 EXTRACT FROM F. 94V

We would have no more factoryes setled or continued on the coast of Gingee and Choromandell, but only 3 vizt: Tegnapatam Madrass and Vizagapatam. If you have occasion for the enlargement of your investment or variety of goods to buy any at Coinmere Metchlepatam or Madapollam you may do it cheaper aboundantly by honest dubashes[1] or by Armenians or by sending for the merchants of those places up to the Fort than by that consuming intolerable eating of subordinate factoryes, in which a little English Chief with the vanity of equipage et cetera will wast and spend more money than 20 wise honest experienct Armenian vacqueels or factors.

Give all just encouragement to the Armenians, and let them have in every respect the full enjoyment of their contract and let the Jewes Mr Bartholomew Rodrigues and Mr Peter D'Costa and all other free merchants of what nation soever have the full liberty and freedom of trade which we have allowed them, they paying justly their customs and other dutys to us which is the only way to encrease the people and the Company's revenues and to make the city of Madrass a famous emporium of trade and a mart of nations.

---

[1] *dōbāshī* (Hind.): literally, "man of two languages"; interpreter or commissionaire, employed in transacting business with natives

143
COMPANY IN LONDON TO FORT ST GEORGE
29 FEBRUARY 1691/92
E/3/92 EXTRACT FROM FF. 96V-98

The Armenians by their contract which we resolve inviolably to observe in every article thereof are to pay no commission to you or any of our Councills for any goods they send by our ships but for as much as themselves have voluntarily consented to pay for such goods as they send from hence to such of our chiefs as those goods shalbe consigned to one per cent for their dispatch and encouragement of our chief we do consent thereunto, but require you that nothing more be taken or received from them although they should be willing to pay it upon any pretence whatsoever.

We think we need not tell you, because it is inserted in the contract, that the Armenians have our liberty to send for England all sorts of goods whatsoever none excepted which we mention to you again at their request to prevent any mistakes that may arise by your misconstruction of the said contract. They are to pay you our custom there before shipping of the goods for England, and if they are as we hear a competent number of inhabitants in Fort St George, you are to find them a convenient place for the worship of God according to the rites of their own Church which is our agreement with them, that we will (God assisting) perform in all the particulars of their contract.

We have discoursed Sir John Goldsborough about enlarging our Christian town to a quadrangle so as it may be done without detriment to the Company with handsom stone bridges over the river in which designed new moyety of the city one quarter of that moyety may be set apart for the Armenian Christians to build their new church at their charge with stone and other durable materialls and convenient dwelling houses for their merchants, they paying us such ground rents as will fully defray our charges. And that quarter so set apart for their use you may call Julpha, that being the town from whence Sha Abas the Great brought them when he conquered Armenia and setled them in a suburb of his new made metropolitan city of Ispahan, and called the quarter he allotted there to the Armenians Julpha by the name of the city from whence he brought them, and they are encreased there to be the richest people and most expert merchants that we know in the universe.

If there be any poor people among them that will take arms, we would have you entertain them as soldiers at the same pay you give our English souldiers. And if any of our souldiers desert our service without leave let them be tryed, and if found guilty be proceeded against according to law.

If by such taking into our pay of Armenian souldiers you happen to have any souldiers to spare you may send them to strengthen our garrison of Tevenapatam or Bombay, at which later place they are greatly wanting and you will do us good service therein.

We have been the more inclinable to comply with this request aforesaid, and to give you these orders and directions thereupon, because the Armenians have made such great profitt of their goods that came hither in our last ships, and are a nation of such great stocks and of such interest and knowledge in India, that for ought we know we may want tonnage to bring home the goods they will have provided for the ships we now send, and the two others we designe to send from hence for your coast in May or June next, and we have promised them they shall not want tonnage for any goods they shall provide to send hither upon the terms of their contract which we intend to performe and you must comply with.

The Armenians being justly dealt with and encouraged, as we would have them wilbe able to bring into Madrass to inhabit in a few years double the number of artificers which you have there already, although we know they are now a very great number, concerning which we would have you frequently to consult with them.

144
COMPANY IN LONDON TO BENGAL
29 FEBRUARY 1691/92
E/3/92 EXTRACT FROM F. 99

The Armenians by their contract which we resolve inviolably to observe in every article thereof, are to pay no commission to you or any of our

Councills for any goods they send by our ships, but for as much as themselves have voluntarily consented to pay for such goods as they send from hence to such of our chiefs as those goods shalbe consigned to one per cent for their dispatch and encouragement of our chief we do consent thereunto, but require you that nothing more be taken or received from them, although they should be willing to pay it upon any pretence whatsoever.

We think we need not tell you, because it is inserted in the contract that the Armenians have our liberty to send for England all sorts of goods whatsoever none excepted, which we mention to you again at their request to prevent any mistakes that may arise by your misconstruction of the said contract. They are to pay you our custom there before shipping of the goods for England.

145

COMPANY IN LONDON TO BOMBAY AND SURAT
29 FEBRUARY 1691/92
E/3/92 EXTRACT FROM FF. 104-104v, 106v

The Armenians by their contract which we resolve inviolably to observe in every article thereof are to pay no commission to you or any of our councills for any goods they send by our ships. But for as much as themselves have voluntarily consented to pay for such goods as they send from hence to such of our chiefs as those goods shalbe consigned to one per cent for their dispatch and encouragement of our chief we do consent thereunto but require you that nothing more be taken or received from them although they should be willing to pay it upon any pretence whatsoever. There goes upon this ship one Mr Forbes a man of years and ripe for busyness. We send him as we do all other men at this time under the denomination only of factors, but he is throughly qualify'd to be of our Councill in Bombay, and if he desires it you may put him into that station or in some other of our subordinate Councills where such a man of true honesty and experience in busyness may do us best service. There is likewise one Mr Bruce the son of an honest able minister he goes over a factor he is a very good latine scholar and hath an extraordinary aptitude to the learning of languages. We would have you by the first opportunity to send him with one of your youngest writers that you shall think most fitt to reside for the space of two years in the house and family of Coja Panous Calendar at Julpha near Spahaun Mr Calendar having assured us that he will take great care of them, and to find masters to instruct them in the Persian and Armenian languages, and the Persian and Armenian arithmetick, and see that they shalbe well provided with lodging dyet cloths and all other necessaryes for which we have agreed to allow him his demands which was but the value of twenty pounds sterling for each of them. While are there we would not have them converse with any European whatsoever nor be removed from thence when the 2 years are out, untill we hear from the Calendars that they are as perfect in those languages as if they had been born in the place. This we conceive is the only means to raise good servants to mannage the Companye's affairs in Persia under our Agent for the frugall moderate honest way of living among the Armenians of Julpha wilbe as good an acquisition to those young men themselves and tend to the preservation of their lives and health as the languages will to their future advantage where ever and as long as they shall live in our service or after their finall return to England.

The Armenians have made so great a profit of the goods they brought home by our ships last arrived, that we think they will load very great quantityes homeward upon these ships now goeing out, so that besides these two ships, and the other two we intend you in May or June you may want tonnage for all their goods and ours, and we would not have, if we could help it a bale of theirs left out for that or any other cause, we haveing given them assurance that they shall have shipping enough to send hither what they will and therefore if your case should prove to be such as you may fear a want of tonnage In that case we would have you freight of the free ships remaining in the country sent out by our permission that upon survey shalbe found stanch and fitt to performe a voyage for Europe and load upon such freighted ship some part of the Companye's gruff[1] goods of small value such as salarmoniack olibanum or coffee for weighty goods and for light goods to fill up coton wooll or sticklack, such a loading will cost but little money, and if the commander and officers of such a ship who best know the condition of the ship will adventure their lives home, we may well adventure such a cheap loading of goods. You must make a short charter party for the purpose there and take bills of loading for us to pay the freight here after the rate of 20 or 25s per cent cw[t] of each sort of the goods aforesaid delivered here accompting one with the other, which is a short way of accompting without reference to what we or they may think to be a ton of such or any sort of goods or to any former rule or custome of making up our tonnage in our own great ships.

[1] coarse-grained

146

COMPANY IN LONDON TO PERSIA
29 FEBRUARY 1691/92
E/3/92 EXTRACT FROM FF. 109-110

We are now perusing yours of the 10th and 27th March and 16th May 1691 received overland wherein first we observe the abominable abuses and cheats we have suffered by Mr Snape and Mr Edwardo, David, and the brokers, concerning all which abuses we can add little advice to help your honest endeavours more than that you should consult Coja Panous Calendar's family at Julpha or such of them as shall come downe to Gombroone. We find Coja Panous here a very honest man, and indeed we can see no other by their whole nation, and we could heartily wish that you had one or two of them of the Calendar's proposing to you that could speak Portugueez constantly in the factory with you believing you would find them better assistants than ever our agents of Persia have had. There is now about 40 of them in this city with most of whom some of us have conversed. They seem all to be inspired with principles of honesty, thrift, diligence, and wisdome in their affaires.

We have had such ill success with your last Banyan broker, that we do not greatly care to have another sent you from Surratt, those travelling Banyans are many of them great knaves like the dubashes on the Coast of Choromandell, We had much rather you should take an Armenian as aforesaid of the Calendars' recommendation, because as Coja Panous Calendar the father is now goeing home to Julpha overland his son Aga Pirir Calendar is comeing hither from India, and there wilbe always some one of that family here, with whom we shall have much dealings which wilbe a kind of guarranty for the honesty of those you shall imploy there.

We must now tell you that we have sent by the Modena 1000 cloths of right Persian colours provided by the joynt councill and consent of all the Armenians here. They are the Companye's own goods and for their own proper account and risque, and we would have them sold at Ispahaun with the advice and consent of the Calendars and your broker there not at all to be trusted with them. If our Agent goes up himself and thinks it for our service so to doe we shalbe content therewith. We leave it to his own discretion to do what he thinks best in that case as also what application to make to the Court when he comes there.

We have ordered one Mr Bruce an ingenuous hopefull youth, and such another youth as our President and Councill at Surratt shall think best to be sent up to Coja Panous Calendar's house at Julpha to abide there two or 3 years to learn the Persian and Armenian languages and arithmetick. The termes of their residence we have agreed here and advised our President and Councill at Surratt who will give you an account thereof, and we would have you take care that our agreement be complyed with. Those youths after they are perfected as aforesaid may be very fit to assist our Agent either at Gombroone or at Ispahaun and we expect in a little time the Armenians will send some boys hither to be perfected in the English language and arithmetick.

147

COMPANY IN LONDON TO BOMBAY AND SURAT
29 FEBRUARY 1691/92
E/3/92 FF. 111-111V

This will come to you by the hands of some of our Armenian merchants by whom we have understood that you tooke of them $2^1/_2$ per cent commission for their goods consigned you by the Kempthorne and Benjamin supposing you might lawfully take the same commission of them as you did of others and you did ingenuously and fairly in giving them notes to repay the said commission in case we did not approve thereof. But for as much as there is no such commission mentioned in the generall contract we have made with them, (which we are resolved justly and inviolably to preserve on our parts), we cannot approve of taking or detaining the said commission money, but they have voluntarily condescended to allow you one per cent for dispatch upon all goods (bullion only excepted). It is a free will offering of their own, or else we could not admit it, but since it is so, you are to pay them back upon sight hereof one and $^1/_2$ per cent which is $^3/_5$th parts of what you have received and for the future our President is to have only one per cent of what goods shalbe so consigned to him upon the account of the Armenian merchants' contract of which take due notice.

148

COMPANY IN LONDON TO BOMBAY AND SURAT
1 APRIL 1692
E/3/92 EXTRACT FROM FF. 117V-118

We would not by any means that the Armenians should be disappointed of tonnage for any goods they would load on our shipping, and on the other hand being uncertain what quantity of tonnage they may have occasion of, we can think of no better expedient under such an uncertainty, than to permit you as we do hereby to leave in our godownes at Swalley, or to take out of our ships so much sticklack or cotton wooll being bulkey commodities of small value as may make room in our ships for taking in all the Armenians' bale goods.

We haveing many godownes at Carwar very commodious for the lodging of goods and being likewise desirous by the diligence and thrift of the Armenians to find a trade for such goods, as we know are to be bought very cheap in the country of Decan and other parts adjacent to our fort at Carwar, which by the unacquaintedness of such English as have been of our Councill at Carwar in all former times, we could never arrive at, or at least at any moderate prices, and we being now under a contract with the Armenians, which we suppose is famously known all over India before this time we have therefore given leave to the Armenian nation to make use of any of our godownes for the safe keeping of any sorts of goods they shall think fit to put into any of our said godownes within our fort, to the end that they may be ready to be imbarked upon any of our returning Europe Ships when they shalbe demanded. This order we require you to send to our Chief and Councill at Carwar by the first conveyance and order them expressly to be in all other respects aiding and courteous to the Armenians, and let them have alwayes the custody of the keyes of the godownes so imployed by them, and require our guards to have the same care of the said godownes as they have of those in which our own goods are lodged. The Armenians having agreed to pay us 4 per cent lodge hyre per monsoon for such goods as they shall ship off from that place by monsoons we reckon but one shipping monsoon in one year which duty you are to receive accordingly of them and bring the same to our accompt, advising us by every shipping what you so receive.

In this time of war it is very necessary our ships should as much as is possible keep company in their homeward as well as in their outward voyage, and therefore we shall think it very good service, if you can be so expeditious as to load these 3 ships together vizt. the Modena, the Elizabeth and the Resolution which comeing home together will likewise much encourage the Armenians to load the larger upon them, being a nation inclinable to be not a little timerous.

Our ships in their passage through the Channell stop't at Falmouth from whence we hear that the Armenians are very well treated on board all our ships, except the Modena where Captain Wildey is so far from being kind to them, as we did charge him, that he is scarce civill. Tell him we take it very ill from him, and he is mistaken in his own interest, if he thinks himself or his owners shall thrive ever the better for pinching of them.

149
COMPANY IN LONDON TO PERSIA
1 APRIL 1692
E/3/92 F. 118V

With this you will receive copies of our two last letters unto which we have nothing to add but to advise you, that we have sent as per invoices by our three ships Modena Elizabeth and Resolution about 150000 li stock to Surratt, notwithstanding which we would have you bestirr your selves to send to our President and Councill there what further effects and money you can, because we are more than ordinarily ambitious, to have our said 3 ships richly loaden home to us with all the expedition that is possible while our markets for East India commodities are so extraordinary good here. As to all your just complaints of Doud and the Banian broker, we can apply no present remedy here, if please God Coja Panous Calendar meets you at Ispahaun, you will find a prudent and honest adviser of him. He thinks it wilbe very hard to perswade any worthy Armenian merchant who is fit to be trusted to reside constantly at Gombroone as tokassy[1] and your late broker did by reason of the unhealthiness of that place at some seasons of the year, but we hope our President Mr Harris et cetera hath sent you an honester Banyan for that purpose before this time, but it is next to impossible we should ever be well served or you have very good assistance untill you have bred up some English boys at Ispahan to be perfect in the Armenian and Persian languages.

[1] probably related to *takāzā* (Ar. / Pers.): demand, requisition; process of debt collecting

150
COMPANY IN LONDON TO BOMBAY AND SURAT
27 APRIL 1692
E/3/92 EXTRACT FROM F. 121

We take well Binja Parrak's son's kind assistance to you and shalbe ready to requite it, by imploying and honouring him in our busyness, but you must detain our just debts which his father owed us so many years on the account of Coja Menas and Hagesall Bead et cetera concerning which we wrote you very largely in our former letters.

As we do never intend to leave of Bingee Parrock's son in our busyness, so on the other hand, we resolve not to be tyed to him, nor to any one family or cast, but some times to make use of Armenians, which we know you may in many cases make use of to our great advantage, which we require you to doe, that you may see with both eyes, and not to trust to one only and at all times, advise us particularly what you do in this matter.

151
BARTHOLOMEW HARRIS, SAMUEL ANNESLEY AND STEPHEN COLT
AT SURAT TO COMPANY IN LONDON
11 JANUARY 1692/93
E/3/49 EXTRACT FROM F. 170V

Some time since imported in Bombay, ship President from Persia in which your President is concerned but brought us no further letters from your

Honours then of the 3d May last was twelve moneth and now the 7th instant
arrived a ship from Cong belonging to an Arab merchant Abdell Sheek but
without any letter from your Agent of Persia or your Honours to our very
great astonishment and trouble. On the said ship is come eight Armenians on
which we enquired all the newes we could but can get little satisfaction and
more perticularly wee desired of Aga Pere Calender to acquaint us of what
advices he had about the credit of your Honours expected from the Armenians
upon the 50000 li on which he declared that letter to he nor none of them had
notice of any such thing which seemes very strange that since the 18th of
February last was twelve moneth that they should have no order about such
important affaires and they do to this day refuse to pay any thing to us on the
agreement you have made in England and indeed we must needs say this that
at last we doe realy belive your Honours will find them no wayes or at least
very little complyant to your desires especially in this respect but wish we may
be decieved in this our opinion for your Honours' advantage if we can procure
it at this juncture of time.

152

BARTHOLOMEW HARRIS, SAMUEL ANNESLEY AND STEPHEN COLT
AT SURAT TO COMPANY IN LONDON
11 FEBRUARY 1692/93
E/3/49 EXTRACT FROM FF. 194-200v

What your honours are pleased to write concerning the family of Coja
Fanos Callender about comission for your President and Cheifs shall be
punctually complyed with.

The Armenians wee beleive may have made very great profitt and
advantage on what goods they sent home in your honours' former shipping as
your honours are pleased to advise us. But upon returning of your honours'
ship Benjamin, wee have prest the matter very urgently upon them for ladeing
something considerable upon her, but truely all that wee can be able to
perswade them to [word obscured] only that they have loaded five bales of
Bengall cloth, on which likely they may make very great profitt and advance
being so small a quantity, they being so extraordinary timerous in these warr
times. But if on any occasion wee find cause they shall not want for any
substanciall English bottoms for to carry home what ever comodities they shall
provide if possible procurable, according to what your honours have ordered
us to help out if it so happens for your honours and their tonnage so.

Wee shall proceed to other occurrances, and wee thinke fitt first to begin
with ship Benjamin, and it is very much to our sorrow that he hath not made
a more advantagious freight to your honours then he hath done, it not

amounting to more than [gap in text]. However wee doe declare to your Honours, it was at first cheifly designed and intended for your interest, being promised by our brokers a very considerable stock more then wee amongst us intended to lade upon her, but the merchants flew back from their promises, and fed us continually with hopes of performance till the season of the year was too late for to recall our resolutions from that voyage, all or most of our goods being on board, and as to our ordering her to Siam your honours will see by the Captain's instructions what reasons induced us thereunto. But all things are fell out this voyage mightily unfortunate to us also in exceeding great measure by the Captain's stay on the Mallabarr Coast and Carwarr, when at the same time ship Blessing and other shipping came up in good time hither, and more particularly a small sloop, Captain William Minchin Comander who arrived here a long time after the Blessing, so that what ever pretences he make in a sort of a formall protest when arrived at Carwarr are alltogether invallued and very insignificant. To all which wee should have responded in due forme, but the continuall troubles that we have been involved in, and for the keeping of all things in the peaceablest manner wee could, was the reason wee did not doe it, but wee think yett ere his departure from us to give him a reply, and what wee shall doe herein shall be advised your honours, and you will perceive upon the arrivall of the French ships how wonderfully she escaped them by runing into Swally hole, in the conduct whereof wee must needs say the Captain was highly comendable, and wee imeediately set our selves to work as fast as possible to unload her, which being done and takeing it into consideration for a ladeing for her, wee met with so many disheartening accidents that allmost put us in dispair of effecting it according to our desires. For first of all proposeing it to our brokers, they did declare downright to us that they could not doe anything without mony, assureing us that our creditors were so very clamorous upon them that they could not sturr in anything till they were better sattisfied. Upon this wee sent for Aga Pere Callender etc and most seriously discoursed them about the credit of 50000 li your honours were to have from them, but they protest that they nor none in Suratt knows anything of it, nor could they doe any thing in it. They wee asked what goods they would lade on ship Benjamin, but to this they showed the fearfullness of the whole cast of them, saying it was warr time and they were unwilling to venture anything. After which wee discoursed them about letting us have goods on our bills of interest on which they did bring us some few sorts of Bengall goods and musters of 38 bales indico, which indico being kintledge goods wee imeediately sett a price for it, and we had agreed the price to be 37 rupees per maund, and the writeings were drawn up between your honours' broker and them as usuall, and wee were to give our bills for the same, but on a suddaine the owner of the said indico flew off from his bargain and unless wee gave half ready mony wee should not have his goods. Of which wee largely discoursed Aga Pere telling him if wee our selves had ready mony why should wee give our bills, and sett him to use all the arguements he could to perswade the owner to let us have the goods as wee had agreed, but he came and acquainted us that he could not prevaile with him, so that wee were forced though very unwilling to let the Armenian goe to his house. And for the Bengall goods upon examination wee found them extraordinary dear, and being fine goods would take up but little room to the filling up a ship's hold so wee thought fitt to relinquish them. Would they have any ways assisted us at this juncture of time it would mightily enabled us to contest with your honours' brokers, and after many contests at last they came to this that except wee would supply them with 50000 rupees ready mony to sattisfie in some measure the clamourous creditors they could doe nothing, but if wee would doe that they might be able to doe something and buy some more course goods upon our bills of interest that were in town, to which wee consented to, and wanting 10000 rupees wee ourselves supplyed it in proportion. But just at this juncture also the Governor had orders from court to stop our trade and exportation, and what would it signifie to buy goods if could not send them on board and on this diallemna wee stuck for some time.

Wee much importuned the Armenians to lade on the Benjamin gruss goods on the great priviledge your honours have been pleased to grant them at a juncture of time when wee procured her cargoe with so much difficulty when it might have been highly serviceable to your honours, but notwithstanding all perswations wee found them averse to venture any more then five bales of goods as aforesaid and 300 maunds of pepper which Aga Pere sent on board just at the ship's departure, haveing a dread struck into them of the warrs in Europe by their late loss in the Elizabeth, and formerly wee have found them backward to the same which as to ours must needs be to your honours' disapointment, therefore wee presume to become humble petitioners to your honours for the same liberty, which wee promise to employ in the best manner wee are able to your interest, and doe assure your honours the alone dependance of our fortunes being on your honours' favour wee shall on noe accountt displease you by abuseing so great a kindness in not giveing a faithfull accountt and just invoyce as the Armenians can doe haveing lately had the happy experience of your honours' indulgence to the President and Samuel Annesley, wee have hopes of granting a request you have condescended to give to the Armenians, Sir Stephen Evans and Company and Mr Francis Gosfright etc, however humbly acquiess in what ever your honours shall please to determine about it.

153

JOHN GLADMAN AT GOMBROON TO COMPANY IN LONDON
13 MARCH 1692/93
E/3/49 EXTRACT FROM F. 218

My last most humble addresses to your Honours was the 12th February which I ordered Senor Doud (being only advices from this place) to deliver Coja Lucas and Avadeik Calendar to forward to Aleppo along with some particular letters of President Harris's directed to them.

The Ormuse still remains here, who having a considerable treasure of Armenians and Arrabs on board her, I am not sorry for, because if should fall into the hands of the French I believe they would make no distinction between the English and them, but seize upon all for interest sake which mony if so may do the French King a great peice of service. By Surrat advices I believe they may be gone and she safely in a short time sail for Bombay.

I am much affraid that the reports spread abroad in the Mogull's countrey concerning the English (done by rogues or pyrates) will give occasion for these people to take advantage of your Honours' affairs here pray God they may not, but doubtless it will something lessen your interest except some shipping speedily arrive there, and that King is better satisfyed then at present, which when understood will disperse all clouds of prejudice against the English nation here.

154

COMPANY IN LONDON TO FORT ST GEORGE
10 APRIL 1693
E/3/92 EXTRACT FROM F. 125V

By what we have said before touching our indulgence and permission for Bengall and China goods you are not to understand that we intend to abridge the Armenian merchants of any part of their contracts with us but that notwithstanding you are to give them leave to send hither upon our ships whatever Coast goods they think fitt upon the termes of the particular contract made with their nation for that purpose.

155

COMPANY IN LONDON TO BOMBAY AND SURAT
1 MAY 1693
E/3/92 EXTRACT FROM FF. 140-140v

We do continue to the Armenians the entire benefit of their contract in all respects, and require you to give them all just encouragement for the shipping of what ever goods they will on the termes of their generall contract. We have likewise further granted to them for the space of two years, that is, upon this and the next year's shipping to bring whatever goods they think fit into England of the growth or manufacture of the province of Scindie upon the river Indus for which they are to pay us the same permission as they do for Bengall goods.

156

BARTHOLOMEW HARRIS, SAMUEL ANNESLEY AND STEPHEN COLT
AT SURAT TO COMPANY IN LONDON
12 MAY 1693
E/3/50 EXTRACT FROM FF. 26-26v

Here is come to us on shore here James Bruce, Joseph English, John Robinson and Andrew Top factors and Joseph Harris and John Johnson writers, according to the list enclosed and William Ryves and Stephen Blany kept at Bombay. And so soone as Mr Bruse came to us wee discoursed Aga Pera Callendar about him, who did very readily embrace him, and considering amongst us all about sending him directly on this same ship Modena Aga Pera did assure us that if wee would let him goe home to his house here in Suratt he would take care of him till a ship should goe the beginning of next monsoone as his owne brother. So sending for the young man he being contented wee sent him theither, where he now remaines and this way of traineing up youth wee question not but will redound highly to your Honours' advantage for futurity and he and a[ll] such will ever be bound to pray for your honours for your great goodness and paternall care of them.

157

COMPANY IN LONDON TO PERSIA
24 MAY 1693
E/3/92 EXTRACT FROM FF. 147-147V

Coja Panous some months since informes Sir Josia Child that the Emperor of Persia did formerly offer upon the Dutch difference in their silk contract to deliver or rather indeed to impose upon his subjects the Armenian merchants all his silk that has so long layn by him since the Dutch refused to comply with their contract, and proposed to give them 3 years time for the payment of their money. The price or quality of the silk, we do not know, but the Calendars are well skilled in it, and if they or the generall Armenian merchants with the advice of the Calendars would buy the King's whole parcell of silk and give that time for the payment of it, and send the whole parcell home by the Company's ships according to the termes of the Armenian contract for that purpose we should be content to hold $1/3$ part or share thereof on the Companye's own account and risco. This comes but now into our minds upon answering your letter, and we have not yet communicated anything of it to Coja Panous, and if we find him anything inclinable to this or any other project of the like nature for this commodity you shall hear again from us very speedily, and he will write to his friends at Spahaun.

We the rather think of this matter at this time because the Turky trade is so much interrupted by the French war that raw silk is become an extraordinary commodity here, and further we think if this project takes effect it may render you a favourite in the Court of Persia, facilitate all your other busyness, and disappoint the sinester designs of the Dutch in that Court, and therefore if any thing be done in it, it must be managed with great secrecy, and you must no further move or appear in it, then as you shall be advised by the chief of the Calendars.

We hope there may be with you before this an ingenuous young man we sent by the Modena one Mr Bruce, who going in company of severall Armenians by the said ship learned very much of the Persian language by the way as we hear, and we hope when these ships the Defence and Resolution arrive at Surratt our President and Councill will send you two more young youths to learn the language according to our former orders to that purpose.

158

COMPANY'S INSTRUCTIONS TO SIR JOHN GAYER, LIEUTENANT
GENERAL, GOVERNOR OF BOMBAY AND DIRECTOR IN CHIEF FOR
WESTERN INDIA AND PERSIA
26 MAY 1693
E/3/92 EXTRACT FROM FF. 136, 137-137v

Vitall Parrack and his brother (both brethren of Binjee deceased) we have
found to be errant knaves the honestest man of that family is Binjee's eldest
son and him we would have you chiefly to respect and deal with, but you must
bring him or who else it concerns to make us satisfaction for the old debts he
owes us of Coja Menas and Hogee Zagbig and others of that kind which
amount to above 20000 li sterling, the nature of which debts we have more
particularly explained to you in discourse and Mr Harris, and Mr Annesley can
inform you fully.

In the Companye's generall letter of the first April 1 1692 you will observe
a long paragraph concerning the liberty given the Armenians for making use
of our warehouses at Carwar for good purposes and upon termes therein
mentioned for the Companye's advantage, which designe we would have you
cultivate by all the means you can, many other advantages may in time arise out
of it, if by the Armenians' frugality and assistance you can arrive at a trade
higher up in the country from Carwar in the kingdom of Deccan where many
excellent commodities are extream cheap, and particularly cassia lignum[1] may
be procured high up in the country from Carwar little inferiour to cinamon of
Zeilon, cheaper than we have formerly bought old rotten insipid trash, fitter
for the fire than to be used for cinamon.

---

[1] lignea; cassia lignea: an inferior kind of cinnamon

159

JOHN GLADMAN AT GOMBROON TO COMPANY IN LONDON
6 JUNE 1693
E/3/50 EXTRACT FROM FF. 78v, 80

The Armenians begin to have a very considerable trade from Bengall
hither, your shipp Rebecca is bought by them and now at Congoe, there has
been one at this port, something bigger then she, but the nocqudah repented
his comeing to Gombroone. I heare they are about buying severall other
shipps, which if soe, it will be a great deteriment to your honours, in respect
of freight, because as soone as ever unlivered they are imediately for takeing

in goods for Suratt or any where, likewise it will in many respects dammage your consolage, by discourageing your servants tradeing, they waiere their owne coulers, this last shipp has a Dutchman for her pylott and two or three Englishmen, likewise they take passes from all Europen nations.

I can't informe your Honours what price broad cloth bares here further then that Attam Caune tells me it was very high about 4 or 5 months agoe, but beleives it's now fallen by reason of one Coja Vosseel an Armenian, lately bringing a very considerable quantity to Spahaune overland, which he judges may be at least two thousand peices, from Senor Doud in a little time I expect to know further.

160

BARTHOLOMEW HARRIS AND SAMUEL ANNESLEY AT SURAT TO SIR JOHN GOLDSBOROUGH, CAPTAIN GENERAL AND COMMANDER-IN-CHIEF IN INDIA
22 AUGUST 1693
E/3/50 EXTRACT FROM F. 154

Wee find the Armenians have deceived the Right Honourable Company's expectations at Madrass as well as they have done here, and wee question not but the Right Honourable Company in a short time will better know them and wee can expect noe good from them for the Modena.

161

COMPANY IN LONDON TO PERSIA
27 OCTOBER 1693
E/3/92 F. 149v

Wee have many letters of yours to answer which we shall do punctually and particularly by our shipping, and per adventure by another overland conveyance before the departure of our first ships for the present, we can say no more, then what we have inserted in our generall letter to Surratt, which we send open to you for your perusall wherein you will see what we design for your place, and how well we accept of your services.

We hope the Calendars of Spahaun wilbe faithfull to us and kind and true to you in their advices and assistance against the designs and fraud of your knavish linguist Doud and that abominable rogue your broker last sent from Surratt.

Make all the returns you can in Carmania wooll and money to Surratt and if you can arrive at any certain skill in the commodity your selves or with the advice of some faithfull Armenian we would have you buy and send us for the present 30 or 40 bayles of very good liggee[1] or ardass[2] silk, we must hereafter as you will observe by the inclosed necessarily trade in greater quantityes of that commodity which we hope may be an encouragement to sellers of that commodity in Persia to afford you the better peny worths at first, that they may have the greater dealings with us hereafter.

[1] legee; fine quality Persian silk
[2] Persian silk, coarser in quality and cheaper than legee

162

BARTHOLOMEW HARRIS AND SAMUEL ANNESLEY AT SURAT TO SIR JOHN GOLDSBOROUGH, CAPTAIN GENERAL AND COMMANDER-IN-CHIEF IN INDIA
11 DECEMBER 1693
E/3/50 EXTRACT FROM F. 183V

Wee have often discoursed the Armenians about what they will lade on board the Modena that wee might be at some certainty which they promise suddenly to come to. We expect it will be about 100 tons. Wee shall lade the remainer of the adventure's designed cargoe for England on the Modena which are 140 bales in cotton yarn, quilts, sovaguzzes[1], brawles[2], Guinea stuffs, niccanees[3], tapseils[4], chintz and pautkaes[5] blew. From Persia wee received 390 bales of Carmania wool which wee are steeving at Swally.

[1] medium quality white cotton cloth from Gujarat and Broach
[2] brawl: blue and white striped cloth from Gujarat
[3] niccanee: medium to coarse quality striped cotton cloth from western India
[4] tapsail: medium quality striped cotton cloth from Gujarat
[5] white and dyed coarse cotton cloth from western India

163

COMPANY IN LONDON TO FORT ST GEORGE
3 JANUARY 1693/94
E/3/92 EXTRACT FROM F. 153V

We are glad to hear the Armenians begin to buy small ships, and should be well pleased if they had 20 of them, where they have but one, for then you might at any time freight one or more of their little countrey vessells to serve the Company upon occasion in your short countrey voyages. And we find by woefull and corroding experience, that it is better and cheaper for the Company to make use of in such cases 3 or 4 hired ships than maintain one of their own in India. It is undoubtedly our interest to make our garrisoned ports in India marts for nations, which will in a few years aggrandize our revenue, and with that our strength 200 Armenian Christians living in Madrass by whom we get money in every thing they eat or drink or trade for as well as by the ground rents of the houses they live in, and to whom we pay no wages being as good a security to our garrison and trade as 100 hired English soldiers which we send to India at a vast charge, pay great wages unto and sometimes have had more trouble to govern them, and have been in more danger of them than of the natives, but this we did so largely discourse with our worthy Generall before his leaving England, and he has himself such a stock of wisdom and long experience of India, that we shall need to say no more upon that subject at this time.

164

COMPANY IN LONDON TO BENGAL
3 JANUARY 1693/94
E/3/92 EXTRACT FROM FF. 159, 160

It is your mistake or the writer of our letters to you, that the Armenians said they paid you 5 per cent custome. They never pretended any such payment, but said they offered it to Mr Charnock, who received it not, and therefore they paid it fully to us here.

Since we cannot by reason of a clause in our new charters at the present proceed to permit the Armenians to send home goods on the generall permission in the great contract we made with them formerly, yet if you find they have before the arrivall of these letters or return of these ships provided any quantity of goods proper for England with their own ready money or money given out aforehand you may receive and buy such goods of them paying the Armenians for them 15 per cent profitt above the first cost and imbale such goods so bought of the Armenians by themselves with such distinction that we may know them here, from those you buy of Muttridas or any other way, and by our sales here be the better able to judge which sort of goods, or which manner of buying proves best and turnes best to our account and this you may lett all the sellers know which wilbe some check upon them.

165

COMPANY IN LONDON TO PERSIA
3 JANUARY 1693/94
E/3/92 EXTRACT FROM FF. 165V-166, 167

Our greatest disadvantage is, their factors at Aleppo are bredd to understand cloth and silk here in their apprentice ships, before they are sent abroad, ours going for India have little skill in either of those commodityes. To supply which defect, and that we may not rely upon such great knaves as Doud and your brokers have proved to be, we have thought of an expedient, that is to put our chief trust for skill in the commodityes aforesaid into the hands of great and worthy merchants at Julpha, as you will observe by our inclosed letter to them according to the contents whereof our order to you is, that assoon as the aforesaid ships shall arrive with you at Gombroon, you do immediately send up all our cloth and woollen goods to our house at Ispahan leaving only by the way at Shyrash to be sold there to the same persons 100 bales of our cloth and ten bales of stuffs. But our absolute order is that as well as those left at our house at Shyrash as the greater quantity that you send to Ispahan be sold to the aforesaid merchants Coja Mourat Surhad, Coja Mercara Surhad, Coja Googas Calendar, Coja Gregory Coldarente, and Coja Hoan Coldarente or to such others and at such prices as they shall advise or direct you to in truck for present silk or present money or else one third money and two thirds silk zerboff Burma legee and ardass at 8 or 12 months after the delivery of our cloth, the silk to be rated and apprized by the said 5 merchants or any three of them, whether the silk be their own or the silk of any other merchants, to whom with their advice, you shall sell our goods.

Further in regard our Agent himself hath done all the writing work in Persia for 4 or 5 years past, we are very well satisfyed, that our said Councill of 3 persons in each place aforesaid may be aboundantly sufficient to do more than all the merchants' work we shall have to do in Persia, and the reason we do send more is only for mortality sake. We do therefore think that there wilbe no immediate necessity of keeping the writers we now send in either of our own houses, but that they may be severally sent and confined to some Armenian houses, where they may not talk English one to another as we did Mr Bruce for a year or more untill they are perfect in the Persian language, and the Armenian or Persian way of accompting to qualify them the better hereafter to save the Company instead of linguisters and to rise to preferment in our Councill.

Coja Panous Calendar did since the first writing of this letter advise us to agree for our silk to be paid at 12 months after the delivery of our cloth, for this particular reason, that it could be brought from Giland and Shambace in no less time than 12 months, and that the whole charge of buying it in Giland and Shambace at the coarsest rate, and bringing it to Ispahan would not stand us in above 12 per cent all charges, and we should by so doing save 20 per cent because the buying up of so great a quantity of silk at once in Ispahan would raise the marketts upon us exceedingly, however what ready silk you can meet with at Ispahan be it little or much would be very pleasing to us by this ship the Nassau.

166

COMPANY IN LONDON TO THE FIVE ARMENIAN MERCHANTS COJA
MORATT SURHAD, COJA MARCARA SURHAD, COJA GEOGAS
CALLENDAR, COJA GREGORY COLDARENTE,
COJA HOAN COLDARENTE AT JULFA
3 JANUARY 1693/94
E/3/92 FF. 167V-168V

[Invitation to Trade Partnership]

It is by frequent communication with your countreyman Coja Panous Calendar here, that we come to know that there are such men in the world as you, and that you are great and worthy merchants of Julpha near Ispahaun in Persia, and which is more to our satisfaction that you are Christians not only in name and profession but in your pious and just lives and conversations as becomes the professers of the Gospell of our Lord and Saviour Jesus Christ.

These considerations have encouraged us to make this address to you, and to desire a further correspondence with you, and in the beginning thereof to repose great trust and confidence in your justice in pursuance whereof, we have consigned to our Agent and servants in Persia a considerable cargoe of cloth and other woollen goods of the manufacture of the island, as you will more particularly observe by the invoice thereof inclosed.

Now for as much as our servants which we now send for Persia are some of them raw and unexperienced in the affairs of that country and wanting the language thereof, and that our linguist Doud has not so behaved himself as to give us much assurance of his integrity, we desire you or any three of you, to be a separate Councill to advise and assist our Chief and Councill, which we or our Agent Mr Gladman shall settle as constant residents in our house at Ispahan for which kindness and service in and to our affairs there, we shall as we find the good effects thereof, be always ready to do greater services for your nation here.

This cargo of goods for Persia, we would willingly have sold to your nation in generall or to you our five friends particularly at a certain price upon arrivall of our goods at Ispahan, but Coja Panous wanting your order for so doing, and fearing the arrivall of our Turky fleet which is now gone to sea might cause an abatement of price of such goods in Persia, would not make any certain agreement with us, but instead thereof has given us the assurance of your cordiall and honest assistance in the disposall of this cargo.

By this advice we have ordered one hundred bales of cloth and ten bales of stuffs to be left at Sheras, and all the rest of the cargo to be sent up immediately for Ispahan: he gives us hopes that you may and will allow us for all this cargoe or procure other customers that shall do it twenty two abassees[1] for one pound sterling of the invoice price more or less which we leave to your

selves, relying for the price upon your fidelity and generosity desiring only that
they may all be immediately disposed of, and that our payment for them, if
made in money shalbe one third of the whole in present money, one third at
three months time, and one third at six months time after the sale, or
otherwise, one third in money, and two thirds in silk at eight or 12 months
time after the sale, upon which another question did arise if we should take our
payment in silk, sherebaft, Burma, legee, and ardas who should be judge of the
quality of the silk and price, for which we could not have confidence in the
skill of our young factors, nor in the integrity of Doud. This question brought
us to the conclusion of relying in this matter intirely upon your honour and
justice, and accordingly we have ordered our servants to accept the silk of such
sorts, and at such prices as you or any three of you shall set upon it, whether
it be your own silk or the silk of other men.

Thus you see we have put our selves intirely into your hands upon a
presumption of your real goodness, and that we shall never repent it, and if
this first beginning prove to your advantage and ours, as we would have it be
to both, we shall God willing have much more to do with you of the same kind
hereafter to such a degree that your nation shall not need to travell to Aleppo
to sell their silk or buy their cloth, but may do both better and cheaper in their
own country and at their own doors.

We have desired Coja Panous to send you with this the translate of it in
the Persian and French or Italian languages, and if you have occasion to give
us any answer we shall understand it in French, the Italian language, and would
pray you to direct your letters to the Governour and Company of East India
Merchants in London.

We send you this the sooner to prevent your over hasty sending your silk
to Aleppo hoping our cloth may arrive at Ispahan before or near the time that
our English Turky Companye's cloth shall arrive at Aleppo.

---

[1] *abbāsi* (Pers.): silver coin worth 200 dinars

167

COMPANY IN LONDON TO SURAT
3 JANUARY 1693/94
E/3/92 EXTRACT FROM FF. 171V, 172V

You complain injuriously of Aga Pere Calendar for his not accepting the
creditt of 50000 li for he tells you nothing but the truth in saying that he knew
nothing of the 50000 li credit which he did not, for his father was not in
England when Sir John Chardin gave us that credit upon a presumption that
the Armenians or English might accept thereof in whole or in part upon the
termes he agreed with the Company as Sir John Chardin himself my Lady

Child and many others have done, although Coja Panous Calendar assoon as he heard of it upon his return from Venice hither did utterly dislike and never consent to it.

We desire you to give Coja Panous Calendar or his assignes all the ease and quick dispatch you can in the contract we have made with them. We have given our personall obligation to their Majestyes to export this season to the value of 150000 li in goods of the growth product and manufacture of this kingdom. We do hereby require you to send us 2 certificates under your hands, one by each of our first returning ships of the contents, number and quality of the goods you shall receive from us by this shipping, whereof let there be no failure.

168
COMPANY IN LONDON TO SURAT
5 FEBRUARY 1693/94
E/3/92 FF. 174-174v

We have at length, to our great satisfaction accomplished that bargain hinted in our general letter with Coja Panous Calendar for all our outward bound cargo of goods which go by this ship Thomas, and four other ships, which we are now designing for your place, to depart in March, saving that one of them we propose first to Mocho, that we may stop all holes where any interloper can creep in to make a voyage, as we are sure none can nor ever did when the company had a ship there.

Our agreement, you have inclosed under Coja Panous Calendar's hand, and we shall send you a duplicate of it by our latter ships. It is a matter of so great concernment to us, that we must injoyne you punctually and readily to comply with our said agreement.

If the Parrocks are offended with it, you may tell them, we are not a little sensible of their abuse in the loading the two last ships we had from your place, and that we scorne to be long in their debt.

We have heard that Vittack Parrock has had the confidence to sitt in the chair, while our President hath stood talking with him, which is such a meaness in our President, and such an insolency in Vittack Parrock that we cannot but resent it, and hope our Lieutenant Generall will better maintain the post we have placed him in, for where respect and honour ceases busyness can never be well carryed on.

You see by the inclosed agreement our contrivance and care never again to have our goods lye by the walls a dead stock, or to be destroyed by moths and ants. To the same purpose we desire our Lieutenant Generall to take an exact accompt of all the remain of Europe goods, which you have lyeing by unsold, and dispose of them immediately, altogether either to the Armenians or the Banians, that you may, as we have often hinted, perfectly sweep your warehouse clear of all old remains be then good or bad, concerning which we have discourst Coja Panous, and we hope prepared him to write Aga Pirir and his friends to be your chapmen[1], but we say trye allwayes, and all persons, and take the best chapmen without partiality, but fail not to do the thing.

We understand, we have some broken guns at Swally or Bombay or both. If they will yeild nothing there, let or sell them to some of our own shipping for kintlage iron, which we are apt to think some of them are in great want, such kintlage iron being now here dearer by 50 per cent, then used to be formerly in Sir John Gayer's time.

The goods that Aga Pirir and his countrey mens shall provide for you, we doubt not but will prove much better for their kind and price than any you have or shall buy of the Parrocks. And his father here has assured us, he shall provide what ever you order him in part of the contract as well and as cheap as if you gave him ready money to do it. However, and to make the issue of this matter clearer beyound all ambiguity, we injoyne you that the goods bespoke of Aga Pirir may be the same that you do bespeak of the Parrocks, that is the same sorts, the same numbers, and that Aga Pirir's be markt, imbaled and invoist by themselves by which kind of emulation, we shall hope to have our goods the better from each party and if we did not know our selves, our candle here will certainly discover, which of the partyes have served us with the most fidelity.

If there be any guns, or ankers unbroak or any other thing that you cannot immediately expose to sale, however fail not to send us a list of them as well from Bombay as from your place, that we may be able to have a perfect view of our estate on your side of India.

We think it fitt you should have an idea of the method we intend to carry on in our great affair in Persia, and therefore have sent you copyes inclosed as well of our letters to our Agent and Councill at Gombroone as to our new friends in Espahan without whose assistance we could have no prospect of disposing of such vast quantitys of English manufactures that we have and must yearly send into that empire.

Mr Jacob Uphill our Chief at Carwar having by my Lady Butler his sister made it his desire, that he may returne for England, we have thought fit to consent thereunto, and would have you give order therein accordingly if he desire it.

The concern in the two ships sent out by the interlopers called Edward Captain William Gyfford commander, and the Henry Captain Hudson commander being now by bargain with most of the interessed, become so far our own, we have thought good to give you notice thereof to the end, that what ever remaines of their cargoes or may yet be left ashore, may be carefully looked after befreinded and sent home unto the joynt interessed with whom we have a good understanding here.

We desire you to give Coja Panous Calendar or his assignes all the ease and quick dispatch you can in the contract we have made with them.

¹ chapman: merchant, trader

169

NATHANIEL HIGGINSON, JOHN DOLBEN AND WILLIAM FRASER AT FORT ST GEORGE TO COMPANY IN LONDON
17 FEBRUARY 1693/94
E/3/50 EXTRACT FROM F. 196V

Wee have hithertoe maintained a very fair correspondence with the countrey government Zulphachor Caune the Generall and Nabob upon all occasions very civill and kind but the phirmaund is not yet received which upon the large present of 12000 pagodas made two years agoe he and his father promised to obtain and it does not yet appear certainly whether Assid Cawn the grand Vissier on whom that matter entierly depends be in or out or favour till when there can be noe further applications made and that we may certainly understand the truth we have lately sent letters to Assid Caun by Bramings who have orders to make the strictest enquiry and the Armenians here have wrote to Issa Cooleyan Armenian merchant in the Mogull's court.

170

COMPANY IN LONDON TO PERSIA
30 MARCH 1694
E/3/92 F. 184

We think it needfull by the first opportunity to advise you of the sad disaster which hath happened to the English and Dutch Turkey ships, by which the woollen manufactures designed for Aleppo is lost, but severall of the ships bound for Smirna thanks be to God escaped. This loss hath so disabled the Turkey merchants, and is otherwise accompanyed with such fatall circumstances, that we know not when to advice you any considerable number of ships and goods wilbe gott ready again for the supply of the Turkey markets we think not in twelve months time.

The particular relation of that unfortunate accident, we are not willing to repeat to you, but rather refer you to the inclosed which we received this day from the post house, and which we find but too true by many other private advices as well as the gazett enclosed. The end of our giving you this early intelligence is that you may make the best of our cloth and other English manufactures, which we lately sent you by the ships Nassau and Mary which by reason of this accident must necessarily advance in price at Aleppo and in Persia at least 50 per cent more than what they would have been worth if the Turkey fleet had gone safely, and raw silk in consequence must be much cheaper. This we would have you acquaint our five Armenian friends with at Ispahaun and assure them, that it is a real truth, as we doubt not, but they wilbe advised by Coja Panous Calendar, and we rely upon their fidelity to make the best of this accident which seems to be to the Companye's advantage although to the excessive loss of many of our acquaintance and very good friends, and at another turn of providence the same loss may befall us, and as it is our duty to submit to God's will in all unhappy events, so it must be our care to improve all occasions for the Companye's advantage, that we may be the better able to bear such damages as lately happened to us in the loss of the Orange, Herbert, Samuell and Elizabeth.

171

COMPANY IN LONDON TO THE FIVE ARMENIAN MERCHANTS AT JULFA
30 MARCH 1694
E/3/92 F. 185V

By our letters sent you on the Mary and Nassau, you will see what confidence we have put in you for the disposall of our two cargoes of woollen manufacture, and for the returns thereof, our commission therein we doe still confirm unto you. But upon the fatall loss of the English and Dutch Turkey fleet, of which you wilbe fully advised by our Agent in Persia, and Coja Panous Calendar here, we reasonably suppose all cloth and woollen manufactures must needs advance at least 50 per cent in price, and raw silk in consequence must be much cheaper. We entreat you to improve this accident to our most advantage not only in sales and returnes, but in the quicker dispatch of that whole affair, for that raw silk must needs turn to the better advantage here comeing hither by the long sea, while there wants effects to purchase it at Aleppo and ships to bring it away from Turkey. Upon the whole matter we have trusted you, and we will trust you, hopeing that we shall never repent it, but that our correpondence in this way may continue many years, as well to your advantage as ours.

172

JOHN GLADMAN AND EDWARD OWEN AT GOMBROON TO
COMPANY IN LONDON
5 JUNE 1694
E/3/50 EXTRACT FROM F. 213V

The 30th past Mr James Bruce arrivd in the President's shipp, called the Qudah Merchant who brought the enclosed pacquett from Suratt. His stay here shall be only for an Armenian to accompany him, because he understands not the Persian language soe can't well goe without a linguist.

The broad cloth went all up to Spahaun the 5th of Aprill, that the broker as yitt has not wrote is arrivd, but wee question not it's safe in the house before this. We have orderd its speedy sale, and are in hopes it will come to a good markett. Moola writes fine cloth is much wanted there; but mentions nothing of course.

173

COMPANY IN LONDON TO BOMBAY AND SURAT
6 JUNE 1694
E/3/92 EXTRACT FROM FF. 186-187

You have yeilded too much to that illman Vittal Parrack, and too much slighted the Armenians that are honest men, and it is very impertinent that you write us Coja Minas's and Hodges Zad's Debts are cleared out of our Surratt books as your accompt doth say and inform us, which we know as well as he or you we did many years since upon making up the Companye's clean estate here, order our accomptant to write them off to account of desperate debts, but never did nor will forgive them, and yourselves know they are as just debts to the Company as any they have, and we have too much reason to fear they have been kept so long unpaid by bribery and corruption together with the troubles of the late war in India, during which war our late worthy Generall often wrote us that as soon as the war was over he would compell the Parracks, to pay those debts.

Mr Bruce before this comes to your hands, we hope may be a perfect linguist and would have you send him to Persia as we formerly ordered, and put two more of our youngest writers unto Aga Perer's family to be initiated in the Persian and Armenian languages, and sent from thence to Julpha to be perfected in those tongues in the family of Coja Panous Calendar.

We promise our selves a very great advantage by thus disposing of our manufactures and effects to the Armenians at a certain profitt, as you will observe by the contract made with Coja Panous here of which you will have a copy in this pacquet, this renders all our effects to you upon their arrivall as good as so much ready money prevents vast losses which we have formerly sustained by having guns anchors cordage and stores of all sorts ly 3 or 4 years upon our hands unsold or else so embezled or made away amongst your country ships that the Company scarce ever had half the first cost duely accompted to them, and a great part of the Companye's cloth hath often heretofore layn so long neglected in the Companye's godownes untill it has been destroyed or at least spoyled by moths and white ants. This is one of the reasons, why we have and do indulge the Armenians, and why we have to so often required you to make their busyness easy to them, another is because we hope in time by their means to bring the trade of Persian silk not only for the supply of England, but of other parts of Europe by English ships from Persia which would be so great an advantage to this kingdom in generall, to their Majesties' customes, and to posterity that we must not expect to bring this design to perfection without great application patience and difficulty.

Let Aga Perer and his friends have any of the goods they bought out of our warehouses as they bring in money or goods to answer for what they demand out without obliging them to take all at once, or to pay or deliver all at once, we having no doubt, but they will pay or deliver us goods for the whole time enough to have our returns by the next years shipping or within the limited time of their whole contract, and for the purpose, that they may better know what India goods to provide, give them a note of the sorts writt for in our last list, and receive Indian goods from them in payment at the prices they shall affirm to you, they bought them, we having not the least doubt, but we shall find them here better chose, better bought, better sorted, and better packed, than any you sent us from the Parracks since the death of our late worthy Generall, however we are resolved to make this tryall of their vertue and to trust them therein, and if we find they make an ill use of this our trust we can and shall soon alter our stile to them, as we are forced to do to you.

Our invoices and bills of lading will informe you what cargoe we have on board these three ships, the Benjamin, Mocha Frigott, and Tonqueen, which in regard they are like to arrive late with you, we think wilbe difficult for you to lade presently home to us, and therefore we have resolved to divert the two latter of them for your ease, vizt after the discharge of the Mocha Frigott in Swally hole we would have you put on board of her proper money and effects to provide for a full lading of coffee olibanum and mirrh at Mocha and consign her effects to the commander and some skilfull Armenian, which you may send along with the Captain, the Captain and he joyntly to dispose of our goods and reload the effects aforesaid, taking bills of loading for them, consigned to the Company for their proper accompt and from Mocha, order the Captain to make the best of his way home for England, and to steer such course, and make such ports in Europe as you have been lately advised by the Companye's secret letter.

We would have you allow the Captain and the Armenian joyntly 5 per cent for their commission, but in such case we are not to be at a penny charge of house rent, housekeeping or otherwise, but custome freight and charge of landing and shipping the goods.

174
COMPANY IN LONDON TO PERSIA
6 JUNE 1694
E/3/92 EXTRACT FROM FF. 188-188V

But the Armenians' encrease in shipping in India, we do not so much resent as you seem to do for the reasons following, first, because they pay us a great custome at Fort St George, besides excises coinage and ground rents which amounts to six tons, as much as ever our whole consulage[1] did at Gombroon. 2dly because the Company never gained by Persian freights upon their own ships, seldom saved the demorage they paid. 3dly because we can never hope to deliver you from the cheats of Dowd and Banian broakers, which you have so long and so justly complained of by any councill or orders we can give you from hence, but onely by the aid councill and assistance of the great Armenian merchants of Ispahaun, neither is it possible for you with the assistance we have sent you from hence to be able to turne the course of trade between Persia and Aleppo, which hath continued many hundreds, it may be thousands of years, for the Persians et cetera to buy vast quantities of silk in the province of Guyland, carry it from thence to Aleppo et cetera truck it off there for cloth and other Europe goods, and bring that cloth to Persia where it is finally consumed within the limits of our charter whereas our aim is to turn the great course of this ancient trade by bringing the silks from Guyland to Ispahaun and trucking thereof for English cloth and stuffs sent from hence by this Company by long sea, as they call it, and to bring the silk for Europe by the same way which would wonderfully encrease the English navigation and greatly augment their Majestys' customes here, and this is no new thought or project of the present age, but was long since designed and consulted in the reign of King James the first, when Sir Thomas Row was embassador at the Mogol's, and Sir Robert Shirley at the Persian Court as you may observe by severall ingenuous printed letters yet extant in Purchase Pilgrims the first part. But this design never took effect, and we know it is a matter of great difficulty to bring to perfection, especially considering that the Medes and Persians were alwayes a people most addicted to preserve their ancient customs, but of this we are sure without the aid of the capitall and great Armenian merchants at Julpha, it is impossible ever to be effected, and therefore you must not wonder, if we do in small matters indulg the Armenians and trust them in so great a matter, as the sale and returns of so great a cargo of woollen manufacture, as we did by our last ships without whose assistance we have too much cause to fear a great part of that cargoe must have lain by the walls till it was spoyled, though you were as able and as honest to us as any English man that ever set his foot in that country, as we have reason to think you are, but your under tools such as linguists and broakers you know are false and stark nought, and which is worst of all, neither we nor you know how to procure better, except otherwise than by the help of Armenians.

We have further to informe you upon this head, that we doubt not, if God please to give us success in our great affair aforesaid to perswade the Armenians in a year or two to allow us our Persian consulage for all goods shipt from Bengall, Fort St George, Fort St Davids and other places where we have jurisdiction, but from places where we have no jurisdiction it would be unreasonable to propose it.

When the assistants we sent you by the ships Mary and Nassau are arrived at Ispahaun, consider whether it may not be necessary to complain to the Etamond Dowlet of your being denyed camells or any other obstruction you have or may further meet with in the buying of Carmania wool, and consult our friends the five Armenians of Julpha in what manner you were best to make your necessary applications to the Court to prevent such or any other abuses.

We send this by the Benjamin which ship is now at Gravesend in company with the Mocha Frigot and Tonqueen all bound out for Surratt fully laden with cloth and other proper goods for that place which we have sold upon arrivall at Surratt to Coja Panous Calendar and company upon the termes contained in a paper enclosed but we send no treasure by these ships, because their cargoes will amount to a very considerable sume, and all the goods being already sold by contract as aforesaid their proceed wilbe as usefull to us in Surratt as ready money, but notwithstanding this Surrat being a place as yet, and since the late war in India the meanlyest supplyed with stock of any great place, we trade to in India, we must and we do depend upon your supplying that place as soon as possibly you can out of those very large effects we sent you by the Nassaw and Mary.

---

[1] duties on goods

175

COMPANY IN LONDON TO SIR JOHN GAYER AT SURAT
8 JUNE 1694
E/3/92 FF. 192v-193

The Companye's generall letters, being already sealed and sent away and Coja Panous Calendar now informing us that he cannot accept of the goods on board the three ships, the Mocha Frigott, the Benjamin and Tonqueen, on the terms of his contract for cloth and other goods we sent by the Thomas, because our ships are like to depart so late and unseasonable, and that he alwayes told us, that he would not be obliged except our ships for Surratt departed before the last of Aprill which being truth we cannot constrain him thereunto. But for as much as our said three ships may possibly have a better voyage than we expect and may arrive with you in all the month of December next, we have desired Coja Panous unto whom we give likewise a copy of this letter that he would write to his son Aga Perir to accept of these goods on the former termes if he can without loss to himself.

If he thinks he cannot so accept them, in such case we desire you however that he may assist in the disposall of them, and in providing returnes for them, because we conclude he will do it much more for the Companye's advantage by your direction and encouragement than the Parracks can or will. And if you shall approve of this advice, we conceive it is best to conceal the matter from the Parrocks, but let them think if they will that the goods were so disposed of by contract made in England as the Thomas's goods were, and as Aga Perir brings you in any East India goods let him always have out in like value in cloth or any other Europe goods he desires little more or less not standing nicely or critically with him as Mr Harris did because we have great reason to believe he is a very honest man and disposed to serve the Company faithfully as we are sure his father is.

If he doth this busyness upon the Companye's account and not upon his own and friends we would have you pay and allow him for his truth and pains in the busyness the same commission as you did alwayes allow the Parracks.

In case any of the ships now going out or the Thomas already sent should miscarry (which God forbidd) we believe the goods on the rest would come to the better markett and in such case we must leave it to you, if you should find any great advance thereupon to agree with Aga Perir on such higher terms as you shall think most for the Companye's advantage.

176
AGREEMENT MADE AT SURAT BETWEEN SAMUEL ANNESLEY AND TWO ARMENIAN MERCHANTS
13 JULY 1694
E/3/50 F. 225

Agreed with Coja Augau Peree, and Gregory Armenian merchants for the sixty six pieces of broad cloath course which I sold to them and have received money, to clear it at the custom house of Surat and Gombroon, and that it shall be carried in our name to Shirash, and delivered to their orders there, but they to be at the charges of transporting it, (the danger of the seas and wayes excepted). And in case no Surat vessell is bound for Gombroon, but Cong, then it is agreed a trankey[1] shall be sent for them in the English name, but at the owners' charge: if the goods in Persia are not cleared at the custom house in the English name, and custom shall be paid, then the agreement is to pay the owners the custome back again on the Right Honourable Companie's account.

Samuel Annesley

Surat July 13th 1694

[1] *tränkeh* (Pers.): small vessel used in pearl-fishery in the Persian Gulf

177

JOHN GLADMAN AND EDWARD OWEN AT GOMBROON TO COMPANY IN LONDON
14 DECEMBER 1694
E/3/50 EXTRACT FROM F. 290

On the 26th past one Coja Auvaite formerly Callenter[1] of Julpha an Armenian, but since turned Mahometon by name Mahmoud Osaine, a person who's son marryed Augau Doud's daughter, reported to be a great enemy to the English, but the Dutches' friend, was pleased to write us a line, wherein your honours will find by its coppy how he railes against the broker, and his brother in law Doud, that know not what to make of it, therefore don't intend to answer it.

[The following is the letter described by Gladman and Owen: E/3/50 f. 248.]

Coja Auvaite's letter brought by Auvaite his servant, without date, received in Gombroon the 26 November 1694.

I thought fitt findeing the broker to be a great rouge to the Right Honourable Company in the saile of their broad cloth wherein I myselfe am sufferer, to advise you thereof. Which comodity, when first arrived at Spahaune, after haveing been twice to see it, I tould Moola that after the shopkeepers had viewed, lett them offer what they would, I would give a shahee more, to which the broker replyed he was content, (the man I was to buy it for designeing to pay the money in chequeens[2]), who was not so good as his word, he strikeing up the bargain with them without ever acquainting me thereof. Your linguist since came hither have had some words with, on which account judge he perswaided Moola not to lett me have the cloth, whereby the Right Honourable Company are loosers at least one hundred if not one hundred and twenty tomands. Those who bought it now dispose of it at 46 shahees present payment. I am informed Doud has gott five or six hundred tomands by owneing other people's goods in the Company's name that of necessity must take him of from minding his masters' business. What I writt you is out of kindness being well assured by such pratises the Right Honourable Company have been very great sufferers. My son being att Surratt have sent the bearer hereof to goe to him soe desire he might have his passage on your shippe.

Mahmoud Osaine

[1] *kalāntar* (Pers.): elder or alderman; city official appointed by central government, with functions like those of a mayor in western Europe

[2] also spelled sequins; *zecchini* (It.): gold coin current on the shores of India

178

JOHN GLADMAN AND EDWARD OWEN AT GOMBROON TO
COMPANY IN LONDON
10 JANUARY 1694/95
E/3/50 EXTRACT FROM F. 297

By two Armenians, one Coja Kerrecore, t'other Coja Saubmaul, we are informed the Arabbs landed at Congo near 1200 men, broke open the bancksall[1], and took what they could find, that in all they had as many goods as laded two of their shipps, which with the money amounted to near sixty thousand tomands. Also that off Larack, they took one Coja Ahmud's ship full freighted for Suratt, with another that had nothing but horses for India, and that they have given over all hopes of getting the Bengall shipp, or goods out of their hands. Coja Saubmaul saying that the whole belongs to him and his kindred; which losse being twenty thousand tomands has allmost undone them.

[1] bankshall: warehouse; office of a harbor master or other port authority

179

JOHN GLADMAN AND EDWARD OWEN AT GOMBROON
TO THE FIVE ARMENIAN MERCHANTS AT JULFA
6 FEBRUARY 1694/95
E/3/50 FF. 320-321V

To Coja Moratt Surhad
    Coja Mercara Surhad
    Coja Googas Callendar
    Coja Gregory Coldarente
    Coja Hoan Coldarente

Shipp Nassau arriving here the 29th past with a great cargoe of cloth and stuffs from the Rightt Honourable Company and bringing instructions to us and your selves, we thought fitt by this express to forward their advices, that you may understand how they designe it shall be disposd off, as likewise what returnes they expect, which you'l see by the enclosed list that we desire and intreat you'd be getting in a readyness with all possible speed to send hither. The broad cloth shall send as soon as ever the weather is soe settld as that it may be thought to goe safe. There's a great deale of it damagd allready, and if the raine takes it the loss falls upon the Rightt Honourable Company that will very much trouble us. Here we can't compute what the whole wormeaten and rotten will amount too therefore pray be very exact in overlooking the same when with you, and send us an account to what vallue it comes too, and likewise advise the Rightt Honourable Company your selves. Their orders are one hundred bales with ten bales of stuffs be left at their house in Shyrash, but all to be disposd of or sold to you. Therefore it would be reqisit you make choise of some honest trusty person to send thither in a readyness to receive it, where if he finds any of Doud's servants lett him turne them out. The invoyce we have not time now to coppy over that's the reason it goes not with these before the caphilas arrive you shall be sure to have it. There's in all nine hundred and seventeen bales viz broad cloth 792 bales course and fine perpetuanoes severall sorts 80 bales each 20 peices ratteens[1] 3 bales qtg[2] 10 peices each sayes[3] long 23 bales 20 peices each, sayes short 5 bales qtg 20 peices each cloth rashes 9 bales qtg 5 double peices each shaloones[4] 2 bales swan skinns 3 bales. If some Armenian where here to procure camells possible they might be gott upon cheeper freightes then we can have them. Shipp Mary expect every day to see. She has in her as we are informed about 6 or 7 hundred bales of cloth more whereupon we judg it highly necessary that on recaite hereof you send a man that we may confide in and not rely wholy upon Sychan our banyan, to convey these goods up. Possible he'd be so timely here as to save the Rightt Honourable Company some charges that otherwise will be imposed upon us. It's noe small concerne but what deserves your serious consideration. God be tanked we have not now to deale with such a knave as Doud but men of reputation, honesty and integurity that's a great satisfaction and ease to our minds. Whatever money for the Modena's broad cloth Moola has in his hands gett from him and dispatch hither as directed in our former to Coja Aveatick Callander etc that he may have noe oppertunity of playing the rogue, when sees the sale of this cloth etc is not committed to his mannagement. The Carmania wooll affaire is now carryd on by one Benwalledass who we aprehend is too much Doud's slave then to serve the Rightt Honourable Company. Of late he promises fare however we are very jealous of him therefore are willing he should be displact which we shall doe if you can give us encouragement of finding out a better it being impossible for any of that cast to prove good.

The Rightt Honourable Company are very pressing as you will see by theirs to you, to have the cloth disposd of with all expedition and not to let it lye in the godownes to take further damage as has been formerly practict, this they intimate to us.

What induces them to send soe great a quantity to these parts is to trye whether they can't afford this comodity as cheep as those at Aleppo and have returns in silk at as good a rate as they the Rightt Honourable Company not questioning your skill and judgment in that affaire. Further it is their pleasure that you truck for present silk or present money or els one third money and two thirds zerbaff Berma legee and ardass at 8 or 12 months after the delivery of their cloth the silk to be rated and aprized by you or any three of you.

It's a clear and quick dispatch the Rightt Honourable Company require in the sale of these goods, esteming it the best way to accept of the markett that presents at their first arivall haveing found themselves very great sufferars by the contrary. They hope it will go of at more then twenty-two abasses a pound starling wherein depend much upon your just and fair dealings gentlemen we can't give you more encouragement then our masters have allready. If this cargo goes of well they'l increase their trade and advance your interest.

In the generall letter the Rightt Honourable Company are pleased to order 5 or 6 chests of lapis lutia[5] to be bought but in the list it's said unless very cheep none. In our judgements the aforesaid five chests will be very convenient to send, therefore provide so many at the best rate you can.

Whatever part of silk the buyars are contented to deliver in truck for the woollen goods, presently the Right Honourable Company would have sent downe to be shipt imediately.

If you know of any sorts of haire which the Turkey merchants have carryd from Constantinople or Smirna advise us. In their pacquett to us it's wrote theirs a note of them but we found none when opend it, soe can't say more thereto.

These goods being shipt of in great hast maks our masters jealous the colours of this cloth are not so well sorted as the former but we hope it will prove otherwise.

Coja Panous Callender advises in Englant to agree for the silk to be paid in 12 months after the delivery of the broad cloth alledgein it could be brought from Gelon and Sambase in no less time, and that the whole charge of buying it in Gelon and Sambase at the lowest rate to bring to Spahane would not stand the Rightt Honourable Company in above 12 per cent all charges, adding that to procure soe great a quantity of silk in Spahane would raise the price exceedingly. Nevertheless the Rightt Honourable Company are desirous of having what ready silk can be mett with at Spahane be it little or much to put on board this shipp Nassau.

It will be convenient after your disposeing of this cargoe to send us an account what colour goes off best, and how much of tother will be sufficient to supply the markett.

You must see these goods housd in the Rightt Honourable Company's factory takeing the keys of the godownes your selves, that wee shall order Moola to deliver. It's needless to remind you about opening the bales, you knoweing what's necessary to be done in this particulars, especially, when the goods has been soe long aboard, we begg you to take all the care possible to secure them.

Wee beleive the Rightt Honourable Company expect now a better price for their broad cloth then they lookt for when wrote these advices which was long before they understood the loss the Turkey Company had sustained by a storme in the streights wherein most part of their woollen manufactures designed for Aleppo was lost, which accident they hope you'l make use of to their advantage, as we doubt not but you will.

In complyance to the Rightt Honourable Company's orders had the Agent strength of body would have gone to Spahane with this caplila my selfe but I am not able therefore don't expect me. We have not else to advise you at present soe conclude and remaine Gentlemen

Your very affectionate friends

John Gladman
Edward Owen

Gombroone the 6th February 94/5

[1] ratteen: thick twilled woollen cloth
[2] also spelled qt: containing; amounting to
[3] say: woollen cloth of fine texture
[4] shalloon: closely woven woollen material
[5] also spelled lapistutia: mineral used pharmacologically and for finishing of copper and zinc

180

Yours of the 14th past received the 4th instant. Our orders concerning buying the 30 or 40 bales of legee or ardass silk was not from Sir John Gayer but the Rightt Honourable Company who don't desire it at the price you mention. We wrote if to be procured upon reasonable termes then to send that quantity otherwise not. To be sure at Gelon it must of necessity be much cheaper then in Spahaun. The Rightt Honourable Company who don't desire it at the price you mention. We wrote if to be procured upon reasonable termes then to send that quantity otherwise not. To be sure at Gelon it must of necessity be much cheaper than in Spahaun. The Right Honourable Company have advised the five Armenians in this affaire at large so that we shall not medle further therewith.

Wee approve of the way you designe to send the cheequeens for the cloth. What most we feare is that Doud will betray it. God send wee mayn't be jealous without reason. Our hopes are it will arive soe seasonable as to go to Suratt in the Nassau, who has ten chests of the Rightt Honourable Company treasure on board and the Mary as many, but she appears not as yitt, we dayly expect to see her. She has 6, or seven hundred bales broad cloth, besides other commoditys. These two shipps have sufficient to supply the Rightt Honourable Company to lade the Resolution and Defence without takeing up the 2 thousand tomands formerly ordered Moola who if has gott any part of it that's not upon the way lett be paid back that our masters may not pay interest for what they have noe occasion for.

181

The broad cloth of ship Thomas is extreamly damaged, more then ever wee any car[goe?] before, some of it wholly lost, and rotted away to raggs ... Wee have assisted the Armenians in clearing the cloth in your Honours' name, whereby they have the same favour as you yourselves in the rate of their goods and the Dutch and French have exclusive to others. They are housed in your warehouses, and when they send away any of the cloth up countrey it shall goe as ours. Lead being a drugg[1] here, and Augau Peree unwilling to land it because of paying custome and the trouble of exporting it afterwards, wee have accomodated him with your warehouses at Swalley.

Wee have discoursed with Mr Calender's son to advance some money on his bargain of the Thomas's cargoe about 100000 rupees, which at this time would doe us a great kindness. He tells us he is upon a bargain for the cloth after conclusion of which he can better consider what to doe. Wee replyed wee would discount 2 month's time for a 3d part of it allowing him $1^1/_2$ per cent on immediate payment according to the custome of the place. But wee have had his answer. The roads are much infested by Ram Raja's troops, who have plundred again Dungom, and other adjacent towns in the province of Candess. And great robberies have been committed by them near Orangaband, and the wayes to Agra, Candahar etc to the Tartarian Empire are very hazardous to travailers by the Rashpootes thereabouts. Besides a scarcity of corn little less then a famine is in most parts of this great unweildy kingdome. All which considered it will be difficult carrying up the cloth, and here is no vent for a $^1/_4$ part already in town, soe that wee expect to stay to the utmost time limitted in the contract before wee receive our money from Augau Peree.

The Muscatt Arabs have taken a long ship and sent 5 of their stoutest ships to plunder that place, which has infused such a dread into our merchants that they are timerous to lade on a great Dutch ship laid in on freight for Persia, and the Armenians have proposed to borrow 100000 mammodies[2] of them on bottomaree[3], and to have a writeing likewise that they shall make good all damages the Arabs may doe to them. At present this is in agitation. So wee come to noe agreement for freight and never shall on new and dishonourable terms.

[1] drug: commodity no longer in demand and thus very difficult to sell
[2] also spelled mamuds; *mahmūdi* (Pers.): Persian silver coin (worth 25 tumans) and money of account
[3] bottomry: contract whereby owner or master of a ship borrows money for a voyage at interest or premium, pledging the ship as security (if the ship is lost, the lender loses the money)

182

SIR JOHN GAYER AND GEORGE WELDON AT BOMBAY TO COMPANY IN LONDON
11 FEBRUARY 1694/95
E/3/50 EXTRACT FROM FF. 333, 334V

Your Honours' agreement mencioned in your letter of the 5th February 1693/4 with the Armenians, wee have sent a coppy of to Suratt, requiring the President etc duly to observe your orders concerning them. The Parracks no doubt are offended at this contract, but they seem through what hath been wrote to them to be pretty well satisfied; but wee well know tis because they can't help it. Wee did keep the Thomas here a week to conceale the contract from them, although wee imediately advised of her arrivall and cargo, this wee did to prevent their being coole in the lading the Defence and Resolution.

Your Honours' agreement with the Armenians is certainly a very good and great thing, but wee much fear when the son's advices reach the father, he will not venture on such another contract, for wee really beleive, they will be loosers by it.

Coja Auga Peree Callendar hath wrote us, that he will faithfully comply with his father's contract and wee give him all possible encouragement and assistance.

183

JOHN GLADMAN AND EDWARD OWEN AT GOMBROON TO COMPANY IN LONDON
11 FEBRUARY 1694/95
E/3/50 EXTRACT FROM FF. 338V-340V

Your Honours' letter to the five Armenians with the list of what goods you ordered to be provided is sent them, with a breviate of what we thought convenient to incert out of your generall to Persia, dated the 3d January 1693/4 ... This shipp's[1] broad cloth etc comes out the worst that ever we saw, some of the bales soe eaten and rotten that it will be a hard matter to pick out enough to make a pair of stockings off, a great many whereof loose and without canviss or any thing. We are a sorting the good from the bad, but when have done all that can doe, there will be noe adjusting the damage here, therefore must be refered to the five Armenians, who's best way in our opinions would be to sell those first. That shall signifie to them, but leave to their judgement to act as they shall think fitt, when the account is given in we feare it will amount to some thousand pounds.

The Armenians' goods are all disposed of, some sold there[2], and the remainder sent to Procah.

Had it not been for the imposition on gold, which is $12^1/_2$ wz[3] upon every chequeen, the money for the Modena's broad cloth had been with us before, that Coja Aveatik Callandar would by no means have us to allow saying if we did concent thereto it would be such a bad president as never to be broke. Whereupon desird him to receive the money and send it us pack't up in a caphila of goods. That he directed us too, likewise to lett Mr Bruce come a long with it, purposeing not to lett the broker know of it, but before our letter came to his hands there was brought some ruinass[4] and skinns and other small things to make a caphila of 20, or 30 loads to stow it in that we hope to have here shortly. By these commoditys your Honours can be noe loosers at

Suratt if bought on reasonable terms. It happens out very ill that it could not be effected without Mr Bruce's company because he'l be very much wanted to interpritt your Honours' instructions etc to the five Armenians who writes their carricter, and speaks the language very well. By the account received from him, he's upon the way and may be with us in a few dayes except something unexpected hinders him.

We expect more Carmania wooll but at present have only one hundred seventy two bales. The broker there we think do's not behave himself as becomes him, he's put in by Doud soe are jealous he won't doe right, therefore have desird the five Armenians if can find out a person able and honest to recommend him to us.

Allthough the factors in Aleppo are brought up to understand cloth and silk in their apprenticeships they can never be more skillfull and expert in those commoditys then the Armenians, and these five persons on whose judgements you rely and put confidence in, Mr Bruce writes are very rich and able men, whom we are glad your Honours have made choise of to dispose of the Mary and Nassau's cargoes, which will ease us of those cares discontents and fears which wee lay under whilst Doud and the broker werre in place. The cloth shall goe up with all convenient speed, only one hundred bales of them with ten of stuffs left at Shyrash to be sold there to the same persons with what goes up to Spahaune, or to such others, and at such prices as they shall advise or direct in truck for present silk or present money or else one third money and two thirds silk zerbaff, Burma, legee, and ardass at 8, or 12, months after the delivery of the cloth, the silk to be rated and apprized by them or any three of them, which they will see in your Honours' generall, the same being wrote by us, likewise to make a cleare and quick dispatch of the sale of these goods. There's nothing left out that concerns this cargoe but what they have, whether twenty two abasses for a pound starling upon invoyce price will be given, or more or less cannot now informe your Honours.

Whatever your Honours order or direct we shall observe; and accordingly doe nothing without the advice and councill of the five Armenians, we desireing to act soe in all cases, that we may be blameless.

Your Honours we think have wrote the five Armenians whenever any goods are sold if five or six or more men be in company to take their obligations for payment of the money. They are wise men that know the customes better then we, and will understand your Honours' meaning herein.

By what Aveatik Callandar advises your Honours will see their's noe probability of trucking the cloth for silk to be delivered presently it being att too high a price, and besides, neither can the broad cloth goe up this month or more. We shall slipp noe oppertunity of consigneing the returnes when comes, either to the Lieutenant Generall and Councill at Suratt or Bombay or to your Agent and Councill in Bengall.

What that sort of hair is which your Honours say the Turkey merchants usually bring from Constantinople or Smirna we know not, neither have received by the pacquet a note of them, but have wrote the five Armenians about it.

Possible some damage may come to this cloth by the ill package, but not compareable to what we find. The colour when opened the five Armenians will see whether proper or noe, doubtless they'l give your Honours the full price since you are pleased to rely so much upon their fidelity. They never had the like honour done them before, therefore it being the first time your Honours ever tryed them, they deserve not the name of men if don't strive to serve you herein. Your Agent at present is soe weak in body, that he can very heardly ride a league, nay except once has not bin out of the house for some months, soe hopes your Honours will pardon what he is not able to performe. For these shipps there's noe expectation of getting silk that his being there will be of little importance; besides he'l be dunned continually for pishcashes, haveing not given the Attamondowlett, Vizier of Shyrash nor any of the great men at Spahaune presents since has been here, wherein Doud will not be wanting to spurr them on.

[1] The Nassau

[2] Muscat

[3] sic - unidentified

[4] *rūnās* (Pers.): madder; dyestuff, red root from Ardabīl area

184
COMPANY IN LONDON TO FORT ST GEORGE
6 MARCH 1694/95
E/3/92 EXTRACT FROM FF. 193-193V, 196

The Armenians as you observe are extreamly near and apt to make many words for small matters, but they are a wise honest and great trading nation, and will much augment the customes of that place, if they be encouraged, which we greatly desire, they may be in all respects, and the rather because we have found by experience in other places, that such of our servants of any quality, as were unfriendly to the Armenians, have proved false and treacherous to the Company first or last. And we cannot much blame the Armenians of your place for not sending Coast goods hither upon that covenant of our taking them here to our own advantage at thirty three or forty per cent, which was too streight for a time of war, when twenty per cent was paid here for assurance but you and they must consider that that contract was made in time of peace and not calculated for a time of war, when twenty per cent was paid here for assurance, but you and they must consider.

We are in great want of the fine paintings which used formerly to be made at Metchlepatam, and we did write to Mr Yale et cetera to procure some of those workmen to settle at Madrass what ever it cost us to encourage them, but that opportunity was lost and many others, for his want of a true affection to the Companye's service, and we hear those workmen secured by the Dutch at Tegnapatam, now to retrieve that loss if it may be we would have you, as you will see we have in Bengall to agree with two or three Armenian merchants to travell to Gulconda and other places where they know good paintings are made for the value of 10000 pagodas in coloured goods, according to a small list sent herewith under Mr Ongley's hand, for which disbursing their own money in the countrey, you may give them 15 per cent profit, when the said goods or so many of them as they can procure are delivered you at Fort St George.

A copy of our contract made here with Coja Panous Calendar for Patana goods we send you herewith for your government.

For what stock we shall send to your place or Bengall we refer you to the bills of lading and invoices accompanying this.

Let the Armenians you send into the country, if it be possible perswade some fine painters to come along with them to the Fort upon such hopefull termes of invitation as you shall think fit to propose by allowing them rice for themselves and familyes, the first year gratis, or for half a year, besides good payment for their work or otherwise as you shall think convenient, if some come first, and find good entertainment, we hope that more of their kindred or cast may follow them, possibly the Armenians that speak the country language well, may find some of them yet remaining at Metchlepatam Pettipolee or up in the country there-abouts.

185
COMPANY IN LONDON TO PERSIA
8 MARCH 1694/95
E/3/92 FF. 209V-210

By reason of the present war with France, we have lost our first season for the departure of our Surratt and Persia ships, and least this letter should fall into the enemyes hand by land or by sea, we do not think fit to tell you in this when our said ships shall depart either for Surratt or Persia and therefore we have not much more to say to you, but what you will find in the inclosed copy of our last.

It being sufficient at the present to tell you, that we are making a great provision of the woollen manufactures for your place, which shall go by the first ship of which you must advise our Armenian friends at Ispahaun, that they may with the greatest expedition send to Surratt the returns of our last cargo, according to the contents of our former letters, and we desire you not to fail of sending us all the Carmania wooll oppoponax you can possibly procure 10 or 15 chests, of lapistutia one or two chests, of good lapis lazula the value of about 200 li in the best and freshest wormseeds to be stowed in the great cabin or as near as can be to the air for fear of turning black by the heat of the hold, and the like value in the best and freshest rhubarb.

The obligation laid upon us by our late charter for sending great quantityes of cloth et cetera goods yearly to India and other places within the limits of our trade hath made us to send you last year much more woollen goods, than we were used to doe heretofore, and fall upon that expedient of engaging the Armenians to assist you in the sale thereof, that so we might not suffer by any part of those cargoes remaining unsold, and being spoiled in your warehouses. We hope you have done your part in this great affair and taken the advantage of clearing your godownes when cloth bore so great a price at Aleppo and other parts by reason of the unhappy miscarriage of the Turky fleet 2 years ago and detention last year. But in as much as we must continue to export yearly great quantitys of woollen goods to your parts, we would have you send us by every opportunity patterns of the severall sorts and colours of cloth or stuffs that find the quickest vent and are in best esteem in your markets, and what quantityes of each sort you can sell every year together with such other observations as you shall make, the better to direct us constantly in our exportations to your parts.

186
CORRESPONDENCE BETWEEN CAPTAIN RANDLE PYE AND SURAT COUNCIL
9 MARCH 1694/95 - 22 APRIL 1695
E/3/50 EXTRACT FROM FF. 343-344

To the Honourable President and Councill att Suratt
Sirs

Forasmuch as the last of the cloth was put a shore the 25th January and the adjusting the damages has been delayed till now and I see it will be some time before it will be made an off without some better order be taken about it which I of my self can't do and if it should so happen that a ship from Europe should arrive with more cloth it is most certain that the price would fall so that it will be an exceeding great loss to whomesoever it falls on. Whereof some I suppose may be to the Rightt Honourable Company for as much as there is considerable of said cloth refused by the Armenians, which I suppose will not be esteemed the ship's damage for which reason and the great damage which in probability will fall on the owners of ship Thomas by a longer delay. I therefore desire you the President and Councill will please to consider and take care in this matter which is the needfull att present from Sirs etc

Randle Pye

Suratt March 9th 1694/5

To the Honourable President Samuel Annesley etc Councill

Sirs

Foreasmuch as it is seaven days since the Armenians had the last of the good cloth away, and I see no likelyhood of the damage being adjusted for the rest, nor know whether they will take the damaged (with reasonable allowance) or leave it, although I have desired very often, at least tenn times that you would cause them to deliver one, and you doe know that they say if they take away any of the damaged cloth it shall be what they please of it and no more, so that when it is done so far (which when will be I can't guess at) there will be a great deal of business to doe, I fear more then will be done before I shall be ordered away. Whether it be a designe of the Armenians to delay it I know not he expecting as you know cloth from England which if comes (as probably it may) before this is disposed off (as I suppose it might have been before this) the place will be supplyed with such plenty of cloth that you are not insensible what a loss it will be to the Company as well as more particularly to the gentlemen which are the owners of ship Thomas and I haveing been here at Suratt ever since the 26th February by your order of the 25th ditto which when I came up you told was for the abovesaid business I have feard to goe down on board ship least it should be said the above busyness stayed for me, but now must goe to see how business is on board it being near time to get out of Swalley hole, the winds already blowing hard at south west which with the aforesaid business of the cloth (as in my letter of the 9th instant to which I had no answer). So now I desire you will please to consider that some order may be taken for if it [sic] last it should be turned upon my hands to dispose of I shall not be able not haveing time to do it but shall have busyness as much as one man can manage in such bad weather as will be to lade and to take care of the ship which is the needfullest att present from Sirs etc

Randle Pye

March 21th 1694/5

To the Honourable President Annesley etc Councill att Suratt

Sirs

Foreasmuch as you know I have written severall letters to you about the damaged cloth, to never a one of which I have yet had an answer, so now again I send to desire I may have justice done in behalf of my owners for the cloth has already received great damage by the dirt and dew since the 25th January and in all probability will be quit spoled if it lay till my return from Persia which for ought I see it is like to do except I will allow it half to be quite lost which is so unreasonable thing that my owners will be extreamly abused by such allowance. I therefore as many times before (although you know how little time I have to stay now) still desire I may have liberty to dispose of it for what I can get for it, for although it is now so late yet I doe not doubt but to save for my owners considerably and if could have had liberty which ought to have been above two moneths past could have saved ten thousand rupees. It is in your power either to order the Armenians should take it att reasonable damage, or that I may have it to dispose off for my owners. Therefore pray consider that the Armenians' answer may be had as it ought to have been long since, and as I have many times desired you both by writeing and dayly by speaking, haveing been here at Suratt from my ship near a moneth at a time to attend this business but hitherto to no purpose I have and still doe offer good security for the payment of the money and am etc

Randle Pye

Suratt Aprill 16th 1695

To the Honourable President Samuel Annesley etc att Suratt

Foreasmuch as the damaged cloth etc brought hither on ship Thomas has lain from the 25th day January till now at the Armenians' devotion to know whether they would take it with reasonable damage allowed or leave it on my hands to make the best I could of it. And now there is no likelihood of a conclusion allthough I have ofteen (as will appear) written and much oftner spake, attending here at Suratt near a moneth att a time and severall times a week and more to desire you would to let my owners have justice done, that the Armenians might declare whether they would take it as above or leave it, or if they would not declare that you would let me have the liberty to make what I could of it and this again yesterday I earnestly desired but could by no meanes have it although as you know I have offered to pay the Company considerably more then the Armenians would offer and if I could have been permitted since it came on shore could I doubt not but to have sold it for a thousand pounds sterling more then now it will be sold for and now if had time could have it all taken off at a great deal less damage then as I perceive it is like to be left at. But now my time of stay is so short here (as will appear by when I shall be ordered away) that no man can think I can possibly have time to dispose of such weighty concerns, to know not what will become of it. I therefore in behalf of the owners of said ship Thomas doe hereby protest against you the said president Samuel Annesley etc for not doeing justice nor giveing me liberty to get justice done in the aforesaid business and you are and must be lyable and make satisfaction for all damage or damages whatsoever that shall or may accrew to the abovesaid owners by the abovesaid cloth etc being left behind and the damage not adjusted whilst I am commanded to make voyage to Persia. I have not elce at present but remain etc

Randle Pye

Suratt Aprill the 17th 1695

To the Honourable President Samuel Annesley etc att Suratt

Sirs

Although I received no answer but pish to the protest I gave you yesterday morning for keeping the damaged cloth so long till I did not dare bid for it within a thousand pounds of it vallue because that could not have time to dispose of it. Yet now again seeing how my owners are wronged doe hereby in their behalf protest against you the said President Samuel Annesley etc for delivering that certain parcell of cloth being nine hundred and fourty peices (or thereabouts) into the hands of the Armenians at their own rate of damage and not so much as at any time to send for any other merchants whatsoever to know or enquire whether any more might be gotten for it. You therefore are and must be lyable and make satisfaction for all loss and losses whatsoever that shall or may accrew unto the said owners of ship Thomas by your so irregularly disposeing of the abovesaid parcell of cloth for near a thousand pounds less then it is worth which would easily by proved but that all here are cautious of signing to anything that may cause you to be their enemy. Not elce but that I am etc

Randle Pye

Suratt Aprill 18th 1695

Captain Randle Pye

Wee saw no necessity of answering your letters of the 9th and 21th March in writeing but att leasure times have often discoursed you about the Thomas's cargoe what was requisite.

Wee could not clear it from the custom house till the 5th February when wee were busye in ladeing the Defence and Resolution for England to the 13th and to the 8th March the town was in danger of Sevajee's forces invading it, so that it was difficult to get the merchants and banyas together who where secureing their estates and families as well as the governour, wee, the Dutch and French were preparing for our defence. Yet encompast with such busyness and troubles wee neglected not your owners' interest but after great and dayly disputes with Augau Peree wee cleared 1808 peeces of cloth without any allowance. Wee were to determine of the damages for Augau Peeree by the Right Honourable Companie's contract with them and no wayes obliged to concerne you in it, yet to give all manner of satisfaction, the 27th March Jacob Upphill the warehouse keeper called you to see adjusted the damages with the Armenians of 386 peeces and it was agreed on to allow 300 yards. As soon as ever the rest of the cloth was over lookt and sorted which was about the 8th of this moneth you was wrote for up to see the remaining 932 peeces which was in such a bad condition as wee never saw cloth before, in severall peeces scarce a yard remaining that was not rotted to raggs. The 13th you came up at night, the next day being Sunday nothing was done, the 15th wee told you Augau Peere was by contract to have the refuall of the cloth but if he demanded more then the reall damage came to, you or anyone elce might take it upon good security for the payment of the money. The 16th in Councill where Augau Peere proposed an allowance of half the cloth for damages and att last came $^{15}/_{32}$ wee gave you till the morrow time to consider of it. When wee meet again it was brought to $^{7}/_{16}$ and you declared to us you would not take it att loss so consented in the behalf of your owners he should have it and a firm bargain was made. This short account answers your letters of the 16th, 17, 18th instant. Not an inch of cloth is allowed for the dew and dirt. You write of the Armenians' answer could not be had ere the cloth was sorted, and wee used all possible speed to have that done. Wee employed our peons dayly to call Augau Peere the merchants and brokers together. Your protesting against us for 1000£ damages is vain and idle, for when did we hinder you and that you wanted time is false for you was here by your own confession a moneth together. The cloth allways lay open you or any one elce might have seen it when you pleased. Nay wee have in Councill bid you doe it and ordered you to take your banyan Ininmidas with you and assured you both those that bid most should have it and the warehouse keeper has severall times spoke to you the same. With what face now can you say wee do not doe justice nor give you liberty to have justice done. In your second protest of the 18th instant you say you did not dare to bid within 1000£ of the cloth because you had not time to dispose of it. Could you not from the 25th February when you say you was sent for up to this day get the knowledge of the true value of the cloth and what merchants would give for it, especially when you had recourse to it (as aforesaid) when you pleased and you and your banyan was ordered to enquire into it. All the merchants in town wee beleive have seen the cloth and put their valuation on it, not onely by our permission but order that your owners might not be imposed on and wee might know what ought to be allowed. Wee admire how you can write not one has been sent for when a dozen you have seen looking on it at once and now att last have not eight joyned together and bought it with Augau Peree, and has not your broker Ininmydas brought merchants to see the cloth? Name the persons are affraid to signe 10000£ more might be got for the cloth. 'Tis a bold and false assertion and wee gather nothing from your letters or actions but that you have a mind to be troublesome. Ininmidas will own it to your face, that wee charged him in Councill and severally to bring merchants to examine what the reall dammages of the cloth were and that wee would give him encouragement for to do it. In consideration of the premises, wherein by your own confession you could have got one thousand pounds sterling more for the cloth then it was sold for and least wee should not beleive you you acquaint us you can produce witnesses for it, wee must publickly declare against you for your negligence and avowed unfaithfullness to your owners.

Samuel Annesley
Jacob Upphill

Suratt Aprill 22th 1695

187

ARMENIAN MERCHANTS AT JULFA TO GOMBROON
11 MARCH 1694/95
E/3/50 FF. 357-357V

What wrote on the 6 February wee received the 28 ditto togather with the Right Honourable Company's letters and Sir Josia Child's, all which arived safe to our hands, whereby we understand the arrivall of the ship Nassaw and further wee here by a chuppar[1] from Gomroon that the Mary is likewise safe arrived thither. By the letters wee received from your Worships etc wee understood your will and likewise by the Right Honourable Company's letters wee understand what it is they desier of us.

The Right Honourable Company's first orders are that your Worship shall come to Spahaun that wee in consultation with your Worship may fulfill the Right Honourable Company's desiers but your Worship writes that you cannot come to Spahauen and then how [can] wee act in this business according to the Right Honourable Company's orders without your Worship. Certainly it would be fitt that according to the Right Honourable Company's orders your Worship should come to Spahauen that so wee may be able in consultation with your Worship to fulfill the Right Honourable Company's desiers, it is a great quantity of goods and cannot be turned into money, in so little a time as the Right Honourable Company has sett us but wee think it absolutely necessary your Worship should come hither that togather with your Worship wee might consult the severall methods to be taken in this affair.

In this country at present woolen manufactures are some what less used then formerly. Your Worship has wrote that since the Turkey Company is broken the Right Honourable Company would expect a better price for their goods than formerly but the Turkey Company ships we see are again repaired and come to Allepo and Smirna and their cloath is already come to Tavris and Allepo and more a coming from Smirna. And further the Right Honourable Company's second orders are thus that our people instead of carrying their silk to Allepo shall bring it to Spahauen and their receive broad cloath in exchange for it at theire owne doors but it is a plaine case that a marchant who has been long used to one sort of trade will not give that over to fall into another unless they can see some extraordinary profit in the new trade.

For thes 2 last years silk has grown dearer and dearer here and the marchants at Allepo not understanding how much the price of silke is risen here have undersold theirs and at this time it would be a great loss to the Company to barter their cloath for silk because the silk is very deare. It further appears that the Right Honourable Company's designe is the next year to send more cloath but wee would have your Worship to advise them as wee likewise shall that it would not be fit to send any more so long as this is unsold. Wee desier your Worship would aquaint the Right Honourable Company from us that year by year wee begin to grow old so that wee ourselves are forced to get others to doe our owne business for us and are not able of ourselves to go through with [so] great a business as this is and further your Worship etc have desie[red] that some man may be sent to Carmania and another to Shyr[az] the former to procure Carmania wool and the latter to dispose of the Company's cloath at Shyraz but untill by God's blessing your Worship comes hither wee cannot of ourselves do any such thing. So desiering your Worship prosperity wee remain,

Your Worship's etc asured friends

Googas Calendar son of Petro[o]
Marcara Surhad
Moratt Surhad
Hoan Caldarentes who excus[es]
himselfe as being decrepit and not
fitt for business
Gregory Caldarentes

---

[1] *chāpār* (Turk.): mounted messenger or courier

188
AVATICK CALLENDAR AT JULFA TO GOMBROON
11 MARCH 1694/95
E/3/50 F. 359

To the Rightt Worshipfull Agent etc Councill

Much honoured Sirs

The Rightt Honourable Company's togather with Sir Josia's and your worship's letters for the 5 Armenians which I received was delivered them and their answer your worship etc will receive togather with this whereby you will understand their meaning. They seem very desirous that your worship should come hither and indeed I likewise think it very fitt that your worship should come because until you com there is no likelyhood that these persons will set their hands to the business. The time of silke begins to come neare, 4 months more will be the time to buy it in Geloun. If your worship were here you might take up as much money presently as would buy up a considerable quantity of silke and when the broad cloth is sold pay the money back again. Your worship might be able to do such a business but thes 5 Armenians will not doe it. If your worship comes not who will take charge of the cloath when it comes and when the cloath is turned into cash who will keep it for they will not bring it to their owne houses, if they should buy silk who is their to receive it. For all thes reasons I likewise look upon it as mighty necessary for your worship to come. If you be weak you may come in a paladkeen[1] and when you come hither the good air of this place will (by god's blessing) make you better and so may have my desiered opertunity of serving your worship according to my abillity. As for answering the Rightt Honourable Company's and Sir Josias' letters we shall in a short time send a shoter to Aleppo whereby we shall write to them when by god's blessing your worship comes hither I shall be ready as far as my little power reaches to further the Rightt Honourable Company's business according to your orders. Till then I remain

Your worships etc humble sarvants

Aveatik Calandar

Julpha March the 11th 1695

[1] palanquin: covered litter borne by means of poles resting on men's shoulders

189

INSTRUCTIONS FROM JOHN GLADMAN, EDWARD OWEN AND THOMAS
HARBIN AT GOMBROON TO CAPTAIN BENJAMIN BRANGWIN, THOMAS
MAJOR, JAMES BRUCE AND JAMES RAWLINGS
20 MARCH 1694/95
E/3/50 EXTRACT FROM FF. 373-376V

The Rightt Honourable Company's intent in sening so many of their servants to this place, you have understood by their generall under the 3d January 1693/4 is in order to settle a factory at Spahaune, where they designe if meet with encouragement to drive a considerable trade in broad cloth and stuffs, that can't be mannagd without a Cheif and Councill as is apointed by them, therefore desire youd look upon Mr Benjamin Brangwin as head of their affaires and respect him accordingly.

The Rightt Honourable Company haveing thought fitt to intrust five Armenians viztt. Coja Moratt Surhad, Coja Mercara Surhad, Coja Googas Callendar, Coja Cregory Coldarente and Coja Hoan Colderente, with the whole sale of the woollen manufactury brought in the Nassau and Mary, you are not to intermedle therewith further then our masters have directed; neither to observe what we have wrote said Armenians under the sixth past, if not agreeable thereto, it being out of our power to alter the least tittle therein. Coppys of what is needfull we here with give you viztt their generall to Persia as aforesaid, their generall to the 5 Armenians of the same date, a list of Persia goods to be provided, the Nassau and Mary invoyces, our genrall to the 5 gentlemen under the 6th past that's all we can remember. At your arrivall take the keys of the warehouse in your owne charge, and lett nothing be deliverd out till you have examind the particulars. We are very sorry the Nassau's goods come out soe extraordinary damagd, which the owners must make good to the Rightt Honourable Company, when they have an account thereof. Therefore be sure that each shipp's cargoe be kept apart, otherwise it can never be adjusted. What now we send up is the best, that we doe to save time, tother hope will not be long before it is repackt. We are of the opinion, were it all there together the Armenians would sell the worst first but we can't direct soe must rely upon their judgments to act as they please.

Herewith we deliver you all the phirmaunds that lye by us, except that about the customes in number sixty two, which is very necessary to have interpreted into English, that Mr Bruce says he can doe at Spahaune, therefore pray lett him be interrupted about this business as little as possible, when they are all finisht enquire of the Armenians what course is best to steere, whether to gett a generall phirmaund for all, or inform as these are and what they think the charge will be and advise us.

The Rightt Honourable Company are in hopes this year to gett double the quantity of wooll that has been bought up formerly, which we are confident will never be done by the present broker. Therefore be mindfull not to let these Armenians alone till they have made choise of some able person or persons to go thither and seize upon what they find with his accounts and if they think fitt lett him send the caune and his stewerd a present to the vallue of 14 or 15 tomands. Benwalledass would faine have the credite of giveing it himselfe but since he's not like to continue in his place, and that we look for little if any more of that comodity to come on the last year's investment it's farr better the new broker should carry it because otherwise they'l expect another from him. Now if the sume put downe be not thought sufficient, lett him have what more they shall think in reason convenient.

Coja Auvatick Callander writes that when he went to ask Doud for the rogom[1] he gott to make wine his answer was he had none only pishcasht the Vizier of Shyrash very high for licence. That we intend not to allow, therefore lett not Moola the broker pay him a farthen. If he has it shall be out of his owne pockett. Augau Doud like a rascall advisd he gott a rogom that cost upwards of twenty tomands, which if had been judgd to be worth so much, should have taken it of his hands. By what he has sold and lyes by him he'l gaine vastly more then he has expended, besides what he did was without order. Somebody must be put into his place, which discourse the Armenians about, that no time be lost in our judgments it's farr better in getting a firme rogom then to lye at the Vizier's mercye to abuse our servants and mannage them as he pleases but this with the rest we leave to their discretion.

If at your arivall the five Armenians think it necessary on any account to petition the King and Attamondowlett etc it would be best to have it drawn up in the Agent's name which need not be signd only seald with the Rightt Honourable Company's seal. We hear the King will expect a present and that it is thought the two shipps from England brought one for him which if proves true we can't direct what to doe till you have discoursd the Armenians thereof and given us an account of the value it will amount too.

Wee being advised by Coja Avatick Callander that since the English has bin allways free from paying duttyes it will not be convenient to desire a new phirmaund for carrying gold to Bunder notwithstanding it might be granted, because if should they'l say we never had leave, and that since it was not heretofore allowd what reason was therefore permitting it now, that would give the raddars[2] ocasion to plead as they received pay from the Kink [sic] whatever gold we carry without paying what's customary would be deducted out of their wages. Therefore being duly considerd to request a rogom might perhaps be as bad as allowing the charges. Further he adds it's now 25 years that all other nations have been forct to allow the imposition, but never any thing taken from us. In our judgments what he writes is congruous to reason, however lett the 5 friends know of it that soe we may act secure.

[1] *raqam* (Pers.): royal grant confirming specific trading privilege
[2] *rāhdār* (Pers.): road-guard

190

JOHN GLADMAN, EDWARD OWEN AND THOMAS HARBIN AT GOMBROON
TO THE FIVE ARMENIAN MERCHANTS AT JULFA
20 MARCH 1694/95
E/3/50 FF. 377-378

To   Coja Moratt Surhad
      Coja Mercara Surhad
      Coja Googas Calendar
      Coja Gregory Coldarente
      Coja Hoan Coldarente

Sirs

Haveing wrote you at large soe lately as the 6th past, wherein was incerted all relateing to the sale of the Nassau and Mary's broad cloth, with a list of goods to be brovided [sic] we have only now to add that in a little time one Mr Benjamin Brangwin, who is orderd cheif in Spahaune therefore desire he may be respected accordingly, Mr Thomas Major second, Mr James Bruce third, Mr James Raulins fourth who are his councill, with 2 young writers, will we hope arrive. You'l find them very understanding civill courtious gentlemen that will doe nothing contrary wee realy beleive to the Rightt Honourable Company's orders nor act without your knowledg, the sale of the broad cloth being left wholy at your disposall. However let them have an account of all, for it's they that must countenance the Rightt Honourable Company's affaires, otherwise it may be reported the goods are yours, and soe custome demanded. The writeings that are convenient have delivered them likewise invoyces of both shipps, pray take all the care imaginable to keep the cargoes distinct that so we may know the damage sustaind by each, otherwise it can never be adjusted in England nor demanded by the Rightt Honourable Company from the owners. For 4 or 5 dayes have been hindred by raine, and we fear the river is so high the camells will not be able to pass it, otherwise it had gone sooner. The hundred bales of cloth and ten bales of stuffs orderd for Shyrash shall be sent last of all where pray send a person to receive it. In that caphill we designe to put no wormeaten or rotten goods.

The Rightt Honourable Company expect this year double the quantity of Carmania wooll as formerly, therefore it would be absolutely necessary for you to provide an honest good man to goe downe thither, and turne out Benwalldass, who being put in by Doud, it can never be expected he'l do well, herewith we send you our orders to displace him, that you may translate into Persians and gett Mr Brangwin to put the Company's chop[1] upon it, which when he sees he can't refuse to resigne and deliver all up. It would be convenient he takes the ballance of his account from him if we don't receive it here before. The carrying a present with him to the Caune and steward to the vallue of 14 or 15 tomands is necessary which if you judg too little advise with the chief and councill and give it him. You must be sure to loose no time because the season of the year comes on whereby the Dutch will have an opertunity of getting all up if ther's no body to oppose them. We wrote you in our former as to this affaire soe shall say no more.

The Shawbander has acted very badly in keeping the Rightt Honourable Company's customes from them, their being three years due the tenth of March last. If by any meanes you can find an expedient to gett it will be a very good peice of service don them and what we know they'l acknowledg with thankfullness.

Out of the first money, you receive for the broad cloth lett 700 tomands be paid in part of the 800 Moola took upon the Rightt Honourable Company's account at interest that's gone to the general. He writes us he's to allow 1 per cent per month for it but we desire you not to lett him have more than customary interest which is half or at most per cent. Should he ask why the whole can't be paid, give him smooth words and tell him you have no orders for it therefore as it is but a small matter vastly inferiour to what he had had in his hands, it would be necessary for him to discharge that himselfe otherwise he'l loose his reputation for ever.

Wee are possitive that Doud be not allowd a coz[2] of his charges for makeing wine, he doing it without asking us leave. The gaine he makes thereby is farr greater then that comes to with which he may rest satisfied. Remember to put another in his place that soe we mayn't want a supply for next year. He may act in Doud's station if their be occation for a linguist besides but be sure lett him speak English and Portugeeze otherwise he'l signifie nothing if should have occasion for him here and that we may not lye under the lash of the greedy hungry Vizier of Shyrash to deale with him as he pleases. You may if think fitt gett a new rogom.

All that's here mentiond is in our instructions to the English gentlemen to whome referr you, soe rest

Your very assured friends

and servants

John Gladman
Edward Owen
Thomas Harbin

Gombroone the 20th March 1694/5

What we directed before to pay 700 tomands in part of the 800 taken up at interest we now forbid, and for some reasons we will have noe more then 550 allowd. For the tother 250 Mr Brangwin etc will dispute with the broker concerning it. We are

Idem   J.G.
E.O.
T.H.

¹ *chhāp* (Hind.): official stamp
² *qāz(-beki)* (Pers.): a copper coin, worth variously 5 or 10 dinars

191

INSTRUCTIONS ISSUED BY JOHN GLADMAN, EDWARD OWEN AND THOMAS HARBIN AT GOMBROON TO CAPTAIN BENJAMIN BRANGWIN, THOMAS MAJOR, JAMES BRUCE AND JAMES RAWLINGS
22 MARCH 1694/95
E/3/50 EXTRACT FROM F. 381V

Pray faile not to acquaint the five Armenians with what we have here derected haveing wrote in ours to them as likewise to your selves to pay all that's taken up except one hundred tomands. This we hint to avoid misunderstanding.

Wee have allready signified how earnest we are for you to use your utmost endeavours and likewise to spurr on the 5 Armenians to find out some way to gett the Rightt Honourable Company's customes, which if not to be done without petitioning then to take that course wherby Agent Petitt formerly gott a rogom for the payment of 2 years that the Shawbander was behindhand which was paid imediately.

192

JOHN GLADMAN, EDWARD OWEN AND THOMAS HARBIN AT GOMBROON
TO COMPANY IN LONDON
27 MARCH 1695
E/3/51 EXTRACT FROM FF. 7V-8

Wee shall endeavour to gett this year as much Carmania wooll as possible. The old broker we think not convenient to turne out till the Armenians have made choise of another, who has orders from us to act in that station and displace imediately the other when all Doud's servants are gone. We have hopes your concernes in Persia will goe on currant and well.

Two of the five Armenians Mr Bruce gives but a very slender account of, saying they are gripeing cunning men, and if have an opportunity will not scruple to make use of it to their owne advantage. One is Coja Moratt Surhad 'tother Gregory Colderente.

Our endeavours to gett in the customes has hitherto proved inefectuall for notwithstanding the phirmaund for payment of the same was showne the shawbander's brother moreover an order from court upon agent Pettit's petition for two years errears that was imediately satisfyed, he only replyed he had noe money here, but would write to Congo about it, whose answer might come in 5 dayes, but ther's none appears as yitt, neither do we beleive any will be received without petitioning that we discoursd Captain Brangwin about desireing him to consult the 5 Armenians and take their advise who think can't be against what wee perpose.

It's Aveatik Callandar's advice that since the English has bin allwayes free from paying dutyes the getting a new phirmaund for carrying gold to Bunder is not convenient because by so doing it will be said as we never had leave there's no reason to permitt it now adding thereby the raddars may plead as they receive sallary from the King whatever gold we carry without paying customes must be allowed by them out of their wages, whereby the requesting a rogom might be as bad as allowing the imposition.

193

JOHN GLADMAN, EDWARD OWEN AND THOMAS HARBIN AT GOMBROON
TO ISFAHAN
6 APRIL 1695
E/3/51 EXTRACT FROM F. 19V

By this convayance came two lettrs in Armenians suposed to be from the five gentlemen that wee can't get interpreted excep we trust a fellow that will tell the contents thereof all over the towene. Doubtless when wrote them they apprehended Mr Bruce would not have returned so soon no feare but they have the coppys by them therefore when you arrive order them to be Englished and sent by the first oppertunity.

194

COMPANY IN LONDON TO CAPTAIN WILLIAM BLUNDELL OF THE RUSSELL
9 APRIL 1695
E/3/92 FF. 218-218V

We have laden on board the Russell Frigott one clock and case number G.1 for which your purser has signed 3 bills of lading. This clock and case was intended to have been sent for Surratt on the America, we would therefore have you to deliver the same to Captain Laycock if you meet him at Spithead or elsewhere in the voyage, taking his receipt. But if you should not overtake him before your arrivall at Fort St George, we would then have you deliver the same to our Lieutenant Generall or President and Councill there, to be by them delivered unto Gregory de Cirkis and Stephano de Mercara merchants, or else to our Agent and Councill in the Bay of Bengall to be by them delivered to Coja Surhad Israel and Bauger Aghame or either of them in case you should first touch in the Bay of Bengall before your arrivall at the fort, and for so doing, this together with any of the aforementioned person's receits for the said goods shalbe your discharge.

195

AUGA PERE CALLENDAR AT SURAT [TO JOHN GLADMAN IN GOMBROON]
28 APRIL 1695
E/3/51 F. 38

Worshipfull Sir

I have bought here in Surat sixty six peeces of the Rightt Honourable Company's broad cloath giveing them something more then the market price here, conditionally that they should be delivered to us in Shyraz free of all customs. The above sixty six peces are made into twelve bales six of which contains six peces per bale six ditto five peces per bale marked as per margent from number one to number twelve. Thes are all laden upon shipp Thomas, (Captain Randall Pye commander), by whome your worship will receive a letter from the Rightt Worshipfull Samuel Annesly specifying the totale circumstances thereof. Besides those I have laden upon the same shipp thirty other bales of broad cloth marked as per margent which I desier may be delivered to vakeels Nuree and Jacob in Shyraz free of all customs. For the last thirty bales you are to agree with our abovesaid vakeels hoping that they will content your worship in every respect. And the money (after the delivery of the goods to them in Shyraz) shall readylie be paid to your orders.

I have sent you a small present vizt

one peece silver striped swissea[1]

one peece flowered cuttanee[2] which I desier you would be pleased to accept from him who would count himselfe happy if he could be any wayes serviceable to you.

Haveing nothing more to add then to subscribe myselfe Worshipfull Sir

Your most humble servant to command

Agaperee Callendar

Suratt the 28th Aprill 1695

[1] probably swiss: any of various fine sheer fabrics of cotton made in Switzerland

[2] *kattanee* (Pers.): piece of goods of fine linen or of silk and cotton mixed made in India

196

JOHN GLADMAN, EDWARD OWEN AND THOMAS HARBIN AT GOMBROON
TO ISFAHAN
30 APRIL 1695
E/3/51 EXTRACT FROM F. 47V

For what goods Monsieur Gregory, an Armenian, bought out of the Little Caesar, Captain John Wright Commander, he confest to Mr Owen, four per cent was paid for all: which usage frustrates the Right Honourable Company's expectations quite for a rogom, except it be of use, and taken notice off, is like a man riding in a sedan without a bottom.

197

CAPTAIN BENJAMIN BRANGWIN, THOMAS MAJOR, JAMES BRUCE AND
JAMES RAWLINGS AT ISFAHAN TO JOHN GLADMAN AT GOMBROON
8 MAY 1695
E/3/51 EXTRACT FROM FF. 56, 57

Your worshipfull etc of the 6th as also of the 8th past came safe to our hands the 18th past at Shyraz, but not being able to give any account of the broad cloath deferred answering them untill gott to Spahaune where with god's permission we arrived the 2d instant all in good health only Captain Brangwin who was so ill on the road severall times that wee thought he would scarcely have been able to have gone through and still remains very ill ever since our arrivall.

Wee have waited two or three dayes in hopes of giveing your worship etc some satisfaction about the cloath but none yet appears and wee feare they have mett with much raine as wee did on our journey from Shyraz sometimes 12 houres rainning hard. Wee hope the cloath was then housed and that is the cause of their long stay. This is all wee can say of the cloath.

The two Armenian letters interpreted by Mr Bruce we send inclosed and wounder our five friends should slight so honourable a business of the Rightt Honourable Company as to us they seem to doe by their letters to your worship.

Wee shall acquainte our five friends of Benwallidas his business.

Wee have been perpetually troubled with visitants ever since we came but we hope the heat of it is over. The Dutch came here in grate state. In our next wee hope to give you an account of the state of the house and the constitutions of our five friends unless the cloath come in soon then beleive shall only write to you about that.

198

SIR JOHN GAYER AND GEORGE WELDON AT BOMBAY TO COMPANY IN
LONDON
28 MAY 1695
E/3/51 EXTRACT FROM FF. 70-70V

Mr Bruce is in Persia, and as wee are informed is arrived to great perfection in the Persian and Armenian languages.

Concerning our incouraging the Armenians in their contract, and making their business easy to them, wee have allready wrote your Honours, and shall to the uttmost of our power comply with what wee have promised. They are cleare of their contract by these ships, they coming out beyond the limitted time, and arriving so late, but it's our present thoughts that they will be willing to accept the goods on the termes thereof, if the charges of 50 per cent doth not fright them. But should it so fall out that wee can make more of them then the contract, which it may be wee may (if the charges be not overrated) then wee esteem ourselves also at liberty to serve your Honours by making the most of them. But for a small matter wee will not disoblige the forementioned, though it's probable the brokers will be willing to give beyond what they would at another time in hopes of lessning the Armenians, and greatning themselves, but let it be how it will, wee will to the best of our understanding improve all to your Honours' advantage.

199
CAPTAIN BENJAMIN BRANGWIN, THOMAS MAJOR, JAMES BRUCE AND JAMES RAWLINGS AT ISFAHAN TO GOMBROON
5 JULY 1695
E/3/51 EXTRACT FROM FF. 101-110V

We shall not intermidle with the sale of the broad cloth as wee have acquainted the five Armenians intrusted by our Rightt Honourable Masters in that affair.

Wee doe not find the Armenians forward to dispose of the cloth now itt is here all together. They say itt can never be disposed of all together, it's too great a quantity for their nation or this citty to purchase att once and they find by the Rightt Honourable Company's letters to them, that their desire is that it may be disposed of as soone as arrived here. Wherefore they make this scruple that either your Worshipfull etc (or as they proposed [word obscured]) or wee should give them new orders to sell itt by parcells as soone as they could, (which they say cannot be expected this two yeares) or they must stay for new orders from the Rightt Honourable Company. Now wee have told you that what our Rightt Honourable masters have ordered them wee do not add or diminish the least tittle thereof.

Butt that it's left to them to deale by our masters, as they would were the goods there own, for that they rely wholy on their generosity to deale justly for their advantage and more att present wee could not say, butt acquaint your Worshipfull etc of itt.

Wee have added to the 62 phirmaunds received of your Worshipfull etc a large one, with severall small ones, and att our first conference with the five Armenians, wee desired a person to goe about translating them into Armenian and then Mr Bruce would translate them out of that language into English. They promised itt the first time, in a fewe dayes, they have been reminded as offten as seen but as yett none can be procured. As to what method to take, wether to gett a generall phirmaund or renew the old ones, they say it's out of their way, the linguist must advise us in that pointe.

Wee cannot but be sorry to thinke that our Rightt Honourable masters' hopes should be frustrated in the Carmenia wooll, it was according to your Worshipfull etc instructions proposed to the 5 gentlemen, who promised to looke out for an able man. It has since been frequently urged by sending Mr Bruce to Julpha to desire a dispatch, urgeing the necessity which produced this effect. This day seaven night they sent to our house the person whom they appointed being an Armenian, who they said should depart when wee pleased. Mr Bruce immediatly the same night translated your Worshipfull etc letter and order to Benwallidas into Armenian, and it was sent them to be translated into Persians and the Rightt Honourable Company seale to be putt to itt, but as yett have not got itt done. The present they thinke enough, but the year being so far spent there cannot as they say, be much wooll procured. This year they talk of buying Muskatt wooll which wee understand by others will not be proper for the Rightt Honourable Company. Wherefore itt would not be amiss if this man that goes to Carmenia be informed of what sorts best sutes the Rightt Honourable Company advantage and how picked, which none of us are able to doe. Your Worshipfull etc haveing seen sundry investments made and know best what has been usually sent for England, may the better advise him for though the man may understand the trade of Carmenia as merchants here have drove itt yett wee find he is wholy ignorant in the trade as the Rightt Honourable Company have usually had itt managed for them.

Wee have discoursed Doud who does acknowledg that he told Moola to tell Mr Aveatick Callender that he had never a rogam to make wine, but had been forced to piscash the Vizier otherwise none could have been made. More over he sayes, that he never advised your Worshipfull or any other that he had gott a rogom, for saith he how could itt be when your Worshipfull etc had forbid him spending a farthing att court without order, and noe rogom can be gott here without spending money. Now this is the reason that he gives us that forced him to piscash the Visier of Sciaz otherwise noe wine could have been made, and then the Dutch (who had gott an order from the Attaman Doulett by the intercession of two great eunuchs to whom they had applyed them selves and spent on them no little somm of money) would have laughed to see that wee could not ['have' crossed through] the same privileges as they, which at present in Spahaune wee have not by whot we can see or perceive. Doud confesses that he paid the Vizier twenty odd tomans (besides 150 tomans lent him) out of his own pockett and saith if your Worshipfull etc will not allow itt him the former he must be contented to loose itt.

Wee have not been very pressing on the 5 gentlemen about a man to make wine other things that required more hast haveing [been] much trouble to them allready as appeares by their slow proceeding in all things that wee have desired. Wee find Doud hath cleared the house at Sciraz of all necessarys for the makeing wine and by what wee can perceive he intends to make wine in Sciraz notwithstanding he is out of the Rightt Honourable Company service and this wee gather from his own mouth for said he in discourse I can make wine now, and I know where to send itt to advantage.

Wee acquainted the 5 gentlemen of the shabander's base trick in delaying the payment of the customes and desired them to consider some method of procureing itt. They answered us they were wholy ignorant of what the Rightt Honourable Company dues were in that perticular, and itt was out of their way. The linguist could better informe us, haveing known how wee have proceeded formerly.

That the King must be petitioned about this and all other greivances is certainly highly necessary but if never done untill the 5 gentlemen doe itt wee doe believe wee may suffer sufficiently. By what wee can understand here the Armenians are here very slaves, and have little or noe admittance at court not soe much as with the great omras[1] but stand in feare of every the least officer of the King's or servants of the omras. It's credibly reported that Doud when he used the Court had more liberty and could doe more then any private Persian in Ispahaune or all the Armenians in Julpha.

Wee find the house very bare of necessarys especially in such a citty where some times great men have been treated and must againe if our buisness goeth on and a great quantity of both Arminians and Europe Christians comeing and makeing visitts and some times once in a weeke the king makes a kruik which is the turning of all men out of Julpha some times for one day and a night and some times more. Then sundry of said Armenians and Christians come for lodging and victualls and wee cannot for shame turne them out of doores, when all others as the Dutch and French that live in the citty have their houses full, unless wee will render the English rediculous to the whole town. Now wee know not what necessarys to provide because have no president of what hath been formerly and for feare wee should not be able to answer itt to our masters by providing extravigantly as Captain Brangwin did in his provisions from Surratt to Persia. ... Wee desire the order wee may furnish the house as may be approved off by our masters.

Wee have brought all the phirmaunds safe to Ispahaune and shall not permitt them to goe out of the house, but the man that the 5 gentlemen shall send us shall translate them in our sights.

As to the makeing wine wee shall discourse the 5 gentlemen aboutt itt, when more at leasure. The occasion (by what wee can perceive) for a linguist and that a good one, that hath been brought up in court business some yeares) is soe great that for want of one wee have laien here in ignorance, ever since wee came in all cases and the court officers very angry especially the Attaman Doulett and in a short time, will putt us to many inconveniences, if not exact some summes of money, for he hath begun allready; haveing sent to our house to call our linguist or some Englishman, whereupon wee sent to advise the Callenter who sent us a person, whom he and the rest agreed upon, to be the only person in or about Ispahaune (who has passed between the Attaman Doulett and us wee shall give you a relation after have answered all perticulers of our instructions and letters received) but he neither speakes English, nor Portaguese. They tell us, there is not such a person to be gotton that speaks either language, for when wee first discoursed them alltogether att our house, about getting an other linguist they asked what was the matter Doud could not doe our buisness. Wee answered he had not dealt justly by the Rightt Honourable Company for which he was turned outt. The Kallenter then said itt was well known to all Ispahaune and he believed to all persons that knew any thing of the Company buisness that there was not such an other to be procured in the kingdom of Persia and if he had dealt unjustly by the Rightt Honourable Company itt was to God and his own conscience. They told us allso that the court buisness was trouble some and required one that had been acquainted there with.

The 5 gentlemen wee discoursed, about what they had heard if the King [had] att any time spoken as if he expected a present from the English, by the two Europe ships. They said noe they had never heard any such thing, but they said itt was highly necessary that one was made to him and the Attamma Doulett too. Then we asked their advise of what value itt must be off and in what things itt should be made. They answered itt was out of their way to direct, in such a case wee must govern our selves by our linguist and what wee had done, in such a case and truly wee believe them for the King forceth enough from them, that they have noe reason to piscash them only as the time of yeare is with flowers and fruitt.

Mr Aveatick Callender was much in the right, when he advised itt was not propper or reasonable to petition for the carrying of gold, for it's a thing that never was granted any, wee have offter desired itt as wee understand but itt will never be granted. Some times merchant have a liberty granted for a certaine summe paying such a rate, which wee have never used butt allwayes sent itt privately and if the Attaman Doulett be our friend wee may send att any time, if not, wee shall be soe narrowly watched that 1000 to one if we are not taken and then itt will cost sufficient ere wee gett itt cleare againe.

Wee are and shall be sufficient in his[2] debt, for he hath paid all the chirvadars[3] and the house expences, and must pay the repairing of this house as fast as wee can gett workemen, which at this time are very scarce and deare, the King haveing pulled down his pallace, and inpresseth all men to his service, nay the very Armenians, the great ones not excused and are forced to carry dirt and after his accompts are adjusted to your Worshipfull etc likeing, wee shall judg him a person not fitting to serve the Right Honourable Company longer.

Wee have taken our instructions in hand and acquainted the five Armenians of every particular paragraft according to your directions though at present see but little done by them and shall acquaint them the reason which wee have given why the 800 tomans may be paid.

Wee have given your Worshipfull etc the Armenians' answer about the shawbander and customs, in our answer to the 5th paragraft of our instructions of 20 March past, and tis the opinion of the 5 Armenians that to thinke of petitioning, before our presents be made to the King and Attaman Doulett is to no purpose, without you will have the petition rejected. There is no doubt but wee shall be able to force the shabunder to pay the customs and it may be without petitioning, for he is now in town and under disgrace in much trouble, about the Cong buisness and wee have sent to advise with the Armenians whether it be not best to send an English man and threaten him severely that he doth not give us a possitive order to his janazeen[4] to cleare the accompt in full to your Worshipfull etc satisfaction that presently wee will complain to the King which the 5 friends have approved off and wee shall toomorrow putt it in execution and hope in our next to give your Worshipfull etc great satisfaction therein.

Doud tells us that the present of 5000 shaes was given the Kaune not only for two yeares, which he hath been at Carmenia, but for one yeare and half more, for he was Governour of that place, one yeare and half before he went there to reside, soe that he hath had nothing more these three yeares and a half. However wee have acquainted the Armenians of itt, and the Callenter hath discoursed Doud aboutt itt, before Mr Major and Mr Bruce, who sayes that it is his opinion that Doud did the Company a peice of service in itt, and your bookes may informe you wether the Caune of Carmenia, hath not been formerly piscashed yearly, or your buisness stopped.

Wee acquainted your Worshipfull etc in our letter of the 5 June of the man sent at last to Schiraz by the 5 gentlemen, and wee are now about to dispatch Mr Blower down on bob[5] to take an exact account of the cloth and stuffs in particular as to their numbers. There would have been in our opinion little occasion for this charge, had the accompt of the caphilas been sent with numbers to the bales as your Worshipfull etc writt us and had not the caphilas mixed the two ships' goods, or had they been dispatched according to your Worshipfull etc designe, soe long one before the other that they could not have over taken each other.

Butt wee have found such difference in those goods packed in July that not only the marke and number is lost, but the quality of the goods quite are changed, for instead of the letter Y which is yards and half quarters, wee find marked on the bale S L which is long sayes, and that not in one sort of goods, or one or two bales butt in sundrys. Wee cannot tell how to help itt, but must be content not only to undergoe a vast trouble (if ever to be done which wee question) to make out the just quantity of each sort, but some will be more and some less but allsoe to be at a great charge for 10 hammalls[6] at worke every day in sorting and removing, backward and forward and that which concernes us most is the loss of time, though if the Armenians prove noe forwarder then have done wee may have time enough.

We have furnished the Armenian that is gone to Sciraz with 10 toman to pay the chirwadars, and bear his expences and doe believe wee shall have nothing done by any Armenian with little charges, for though they are naturally saving of their own, they seeme to be very lavish and profuse of other men's ... and shall order Mr Blower to dyett at an Armenian's house but wee suppose both him and the Armenian must be in the Rightt Honourable Company house wee haveing noe body there.

With your Worships etc of the 30 Aprill wee received the charwader's noate for 100 bales of broad cloth and 10 of stuffs with Mr Harbin's perticuler accompt of the markes and numbers of them. Wee could have heartily wished that the goods sent here, had been accompanyed with the like accompt and itt would have saved us trouble and gave your Worshipfull etc satisfaction and put the Rightt Honourable Company to less charge and wee should have been able to distinguish the colours and prices to the great satisfaction of the Armenians which now [is] impossible to doe untill all are opened, and Ispahaun house, tho very large, hath not convenience to doe itt in. And much time must be spent to sort them tho at last hope the Company profitt on them will be satisfaction enough to us for so great a trouble, for hope they will answer the Rightt Honourable Company expectations.

Your Worshipfull etc of the 27 May last came safe to our hands, the 17 June, which shotter wee should not have detained soe long, but the necessity of opening the broad cloth hath taken up our time from morning till night ever since his arrivall, and much more will be spent therein before we shall be able to give the Armenians satisfaction as to the perticuler colours of every peices there being soe many jams[7] which as wee understand this word and allsoe find by opening some of them is all sorts of colours mixed together.

Soone after arrivall wee were visited by all the Europeans of this place and many of the noated Armenians especially the 5 gentlemen intrusted by the Rightt Honourable Company to despose of the broadcloth and to advise us in all things relating to our affaires in this place. The first time they came wee tooke as a visitt but the second which was soone after wee discoursed them of every individall paragraph of our instructions, that required their advise and assistance. They gave us their answers, as wee have before mentioned to each paragraph. The third time the Kalenter with one or two of them came, wee were very pressing for some things to be done which were of most necessity, as the man for Carmenia a linguist and a man for Shiraz and the sale of the cloth, but since that time have not seen them together, but some times there would drop in one of them, and his whole discourse would be for your Worshipfull etc or us to give a new order about the sale of the cloth.

Mr Major and Mr Bruce have waited on them on severall occasions, and in perticuler to forward the man for Carminia. They have promised some time to bring merchants to sell the cloth, but as yett wee have not seen them. Wee find one of them named Hoan Caldarante hath laien down the buisness he being old, and the other four cannot agree, whether they had best sell itt alltogether or by parcells and thus time spends and nothing is done. Wee find some of them drive at perticuler interest in selling itt per parcells for after the first parcell is sold, we may keepe the rest long enough to be sure untill they have sent that to the best marketts, which may be many months if not some yeares, wherefore wee thinke it best they sell it all together but shall leave itt to their prudent management. Wee have opened some part of both ships' cargoe and can now give them some satisfaction as to colours and prizes.

Your Worshipfull etc sent by us, a list of Persian goods to be provided by order of the Rightt Honourable Company but have not mentioned one word whether wee are to provide silk. Wee find by the Armenians none can be procured to come to Bunder time enough to be at Suratt by the 20 January the usuall time of the Europe ships' dispatch, and they say that last yeare's silk was too deare for the Rightt Honourable Company to gett anything by itt. But wee understand that this yeare it will be cheaper if your Worshipfull etc thinke that the same, as Company ordered formerly must now allso be continued, be pleased to advise us that wee may forward itt, and if any other Persian goods be to be provided here, wee desire orders as allso if can instruct us as to price and goodness.

Carmania wooll some times to be procured, as since wee came here wee have been offered two or three parcells, if wee knew but what sorts and prices you have usually from Carmania itt might be worth while to buy itt and encouragement would bring more, and why people should not be willing to bring [itt] and sell itt here for 12 per cent wee cannot understand. It's good profit [words obscured] and no hazard.

[1] also spelled omraues; *omrah* (Ar.), plural of *amīr*: lord or grandee of a Moslem court

[2] refers to Moola

[3] *chārvādār* (Pers.): groom; one who stables and hires out horses

[4] possibly related to *jemadār* (Pers. / Ar.): head of a body of servants; officer of customs or excise

[5] bobtailed horse

[6] *hammāl* (Ar.): a burden bearer in Turkey and other countries of the eastern Mediterranean; a porter

[7] mixed colors

200

JOHN GLADMAN, EDWARD OWEN AND THOMAS HARBIN AT GOMBROON TO COMPANY IN LONDON
5 JULY 1695
E/3/51 EXTRACT FROM FF. 112-113

Hitherto we have had no full account from Captain Brangwin etc gentlemen at Spahaun, the small relation gives but little encouragement that the five Armenians will answer your Honours' expections in the sale of the Nassau, and Mary's, broad cloth etc; whatever there's past from us to the Chief and them accompanys these for your Honours' perusall.

Our request to the Armenians to put in an able honest fellow broker at Carmania they have not complyed with, therefore are forc't to encourage and keep the old one imployed. otherwise there would have bin little probability of buying up any of that commodity this year ... As yitt nobody is entertained by them to make wine, when wee know there's enough would gladly embrace such a good proffer. These persons in our judgements must be interested in the Turkey Company else why should they argue at this juncture of time that woolen cloth etc is not so much in esteeme as formerly whereby the price is fallen, alsoe silk is dearer. Besides to excuse themselves in this nature, one pretending to be decriped, not capable of mannageing business, the rest that they grow old and are forc't to hire others to act in their stid, which is very unworthly done, considering what a great honour is shown them. The like favour certainly was never done to any of their cast. They give no countenance to effect anything that your Honours have ordered, silk that can't be delivered at the factory in truck for broad cloth. Neither is it convenient in their apprehentions for your Honours to send any more tell this be all disposed off, which may lye in the godownes a long time if are no brisker then at present. It's undoubtedly selfe advantage that makes them thus proceed. If have misconstrued things we rely upon your Honours' favour in pardoning us, it's realy out of true zeal for your interest that we thus write; would to God there was no occasion for it.

One Mounser Gregory an Armenian, in very good esteeme amongst Europeans, wareing our habit and breed up in France, gives us to understand, which he declares to have received from two emenent persons, that the Arabs landed at Mangalore where destroyed of Portugeeze inhabitance both man woman, and child, and took tenn Moores' shipps bound to thother coast, and the southward.

201

JOHN GLADMAN, EDWARD OWEN AND THOMAS HARBIN AT GOMBROON
TO BENJAMIN BRANGWIN AND COUNCIL AT ISFAHAN
5 JULY 1695
E/3/51 EXTRACT FROM FF. 114-115V

The two letters interprited by Mr Bruce one from the five Armenians tother from Aveatik Callender wee received. You might have sent the origenalls. In your next pray inclose them to us, for they properly belong to this place. If the gentlemen had a sight thereof sure they never would have presumed to lett them fall into our hands when a cheife and councell was with them to consult what was most conduceing to the Rightt Honourable Company's intrest. They are unreasonable men to press so hard for the agent's going up when it was in a manner impossable for him to undertake such a journey sure they could not imaging him so great a fool as not to have some English men there to countenance thes two cargoes (wee know very well under what curcumstances they ly) the best of them (as wee belive thes persons to be) are but slaves to the world and lyable to all exactions imposed upon them by the Persians we know as they dare not owne two such cargoes as thes are for feare of being fleest besides if they should the government would take it to be theirs and not the Rightt Honourable Company's. It greives us to the very heart that they seemingly refuse to imbrace so great a kindness offered them by our Rightt Honourable masters, one pretending he's decriped and can't stirr in the affaire the rest that they grow aged so are uncapable of manageing theire owne business without the assistance of others, likewise frustrate all the Rightt Honourable Company's designe and don't in the least endeavour to promote the trade of woolen manufactory they declaring it's less in esteeme and price at Spahaun then ever, moreover that the price of silk is much risen we that are in the darke can perceive them faulce and feare they are so farr engaged themselves with the Turkey Company and will not be brought out of that road and have been so much accustomed to it, to advance the Rightt Honourable English East India Company's intrest, they had as good saye they'l serve themselves and no body elce.

It falls out very unfortunately that a new broker upon our advises was not dispacht imediately to Carmenia. If meet with a bad investment this year it will be vastly prejudiciall to the Right Honourable Company and who but the five is to be blamed, know not, in our oppinions it's best to keep this old broker in if one be not gon before this arrives, we wrote him under the 15th past and are in hopes (by faire promises) he'le comply with our desiers.

Concerning Moola broker have wrote you sufficient if he is tardy in sale of the broad cloth it's pity but he should have his reward and severly punisht both in purse and body it will be seen by the sale of thes goods, for Aveatik Callender advises that course cloth will go of at forty shahees a quz shaw[1], that perceive but little probability oft by the disposing of this it will appeare whither Moola be honest or not, God send he may make his woords good, wee don't like any of their procedings hitherto.

Wee are sorry the slothfullness of the gentlemen should add the flux to Captain Brangwin's former distemper. An ample account from you how the brode cloth is like to go off would be very satisfactory to us.

Sure the five Armenians are mad in neglecting to send a person to Shyraz to look after the cloth and stuffs there, the meatherd taken by them can no wayes redowne to their creditt. It's our oppinians they'd rejoyce to see the Rightt Honourable Company's expectations crost. If have not advised the Rightt Honourable Company that the five gentlemen desier they send out no more cloth etc till this be all sold are guillty of a great ommission, and what may be much to their detriment you are nearer them then wee therefore iff anything of moment worth dispacting a packet be not spareing to doe it.

Wee observe what you have deducted out of three hundred and fivety loads first sent which amounts to nine hundred sixty two shahes that's prudently done considering they did not comply with their contract.

Our letters to the five Armenians and Coja Aveatik Callender wee send you open to over look wherein if fiend anything not convenient to lett them know lett Mr Bruce leave it out when have read them put the Rightt Honourable Company's seale thereon.

Wee had rather if possable you disspose of the broad cloth by the gonah or English yeard and not by the quz[2], but this wee must leave to your discretion. Pray don't sell some by one and some by tother becauce it will breed confusion in accounts.

---

[1] gaz-e shāh (Pers.): royal (cloth-)yard, standardized at 90 cm

[2] gaz (Pers.): a measure of length, approximating a yard, but varying regionally; here it may be assumed to be the royal yard

202

JOHN GLADMAN, EDWARD OWEN AND THOMAS HARBIN AT GOMBROON
TO THE FIVE ARMENIAN MERCHANTS AT JULFA
5 JULY 1695
E/3/51 FF. 116-117

To   Coja Morratt Surhad
     Coja Mercara Surhad
     Coja Googas Calender
     Coja Gregory Coldarente
     Coja Hoan Coldarente

Gentlemen

    Yours of the 11th March in Armenians came to our hands after Captain Brangwin etc were in theire way to Spauhaun therefore not thinking it convenient to intrust any persons with the Right Honourable Company's secrets to interprit the same, here sent it after them for Mr Bruce to English it, so understood not the contents thereof till the 29th May which in our oppinions need not have been returned, there being a Chief and Councell to consult with all about mannageing the Right Honourable Company's affairs which wee hope you'l take into your serious consideration they heaving by a perticular favour and confidence in you left all to your discretions. When wrote you under the 6th February the Mary was not arrived, on board whom was two factors ordered up by the Right Honourable Company. Surely you could not immaging that wee intended nobody there but leave all to you, wee read the Company's instructions and know very well their pleasure. What wee desiered was only if a caphila should come before wee could dispatch any body to you that then you'd take the keys of the warehouses from Moola and see them housed. The Company themselves are more mercyful then you, for they never were so cruil to expect their servants should undertake such a journey when had upon them an ague and feaver if the Agent could gain as m[uch] more as the broad cloath was worth it was in a maner impossible for him to goe threw. Doubtless now you are satisfied, and will give us no farther trouble by harping on that string. The Right Honourable Company expected these two ships Nassau and Mary to be at Bunderabasse some months before they appeared which tedious passage is a great dissappointment to them therefore it becoms you to make up this loss by a speedy sale of thes cargoes which wee intreat and begg at your hands. Likewise that you'd dispacth hither what goods is mentioned in their list to be provided the silk suppos is taken care about and a vakeel sent long before this to Gelon. It's a misterey to us, why the woolen manufactery should be in less esteeme now then formerly the 200 bales sent last year could not glut the market, withall though there's a great deal of the Turkey Company's cloath saved and arrived at Smirna it's impossable that can do our masters any damage becaus it must all of necessity receive some wett.

Certainly the Company can be noe gainers by keeping it in the godowne. Avatick Calender wrote us course cloath would go off at 40 shahees per quz but you signifie nothing to us what price it's like to yeald, if may be done would have it sould by the gonah or English yeard reather then the quz but if the marchants will not consent thereto wee must rest satisfied. It was never wrote you the Turkey Company was broke further then they were great sufferers by the storme, which overthrew the whole year's investment which is sufficient to expect the rise of woollen manufactory. For God sake dispatch away these goods that the money may be sent us to forward to Suratt, for they look for great supplyes from hence. Questionless it's as easy to bring silk to Spahaun as carry it to Alleppo and there must needs be as good profitt by exchanging that comodity for broad cloath etc with the Right Honourable Company as with the marchants at Alleppo etc but if the propriaters will not be brought to change the old course for a new one unless they can see some extraordinary proffit, wee can say nothing to that there's in all appeareance as much likelyhood of advantage this way as tother, for undoubtedly the Right Honourable Company if have encouragement would constantly send a certain quantity of cloath stuffs etc to Persia but you don't in the least seeme to countenance it but rather discourrage them all you can by saying the price of woolen falls moreover silks for two years past growes dearer and dearer and that the marchants at Alleppo not understand how silk is risen have under sold (as wee count you mean) their cloath. Wee are apprehensive the Right Honourable Company don't designe to send more goods till they are certain how this that's come goes off however it's nessecary as you hint to us they should be advised thereof that wee wish Captain Brangwin has done who is nearer them then wee. Gentlemen by your writing wee conceive the bent of your inclinations is towards Alleppo and that you have bin accustomed to a trade that way otherwise how can it be for you to decline so great a kindness done you by our Right Honourable masters as to slight what they realy intended out of love in putting so great a confidence in your generosity and fidellity that you seemeingly slight and look upon as a yoke and are uneasy under it by your requesting us to accquaint them that age coming upon you are forced to imploy others to do your business being not able to go through with it your selves. This affaire is not so great when there's such assistance of English as there is. Wee wish it proves not to the Company's deaterement that a person forthwith was not dispatcht to Carmania it's now so late in the year if none be gon that tis better to continue the old broker there, otherwise can't conceive much of that commodity will be forwarded to us. In May he pretended no wool was bought laying the blame upon Doud and Moola for not paying a bill to the amount of with exchange 6628 mamuds $3^{1}/_{2}$ coz. We would have what money he drawes though it be upon Moola should he denye to pay the same that it be not returned for such a thing will spoil all. Wee are informed a person is gon to Shyraz about dispossing of the cloath left there that's very well. Would you had entertained a person to make wine it's a very beneficiall imployment therfore are perswaded hundreds would imbrace it if offered them. Gentlemen if you never intend more to accept of any consignements from the Right Honourable Company lett us beseeach you to act in this under your mannagement that so our masters may have reason to owne your kindness herein whereby your names may be in continuall rememberance both at home and abroad wee have not elce but to wish your prosperity so remain

Your very loving friends to serve you

John Gladman
Edward Owen
Thomas Harbin

Gombroone the 5th July 1695

203

JOHN GLADMAN, EDWARD OWEN AND THOMAS HARBIN AT GOMBROON
TO AVATIK CALLENDAR AT JULFA
5 JULY 1695
E/3/51 FF. 118-118V

Coja Aveatik Callandar

What you wrote under the 11th March in Armenians we received after Captain Brangwin etc gentlemen departed hence so that were forced to send it back for Mr Bruce to interpritt the same which came not to hands till the 29th May. It's strange you should lett such a letter returne when their's a Cheife and Councell at Spahaune which makes your advise of small signification. Certainly you nor the 5 Armenians could imaging but some care would be taken by us to send up persons fitt to receive the broade cloath. All that wee requested at their hands was that if it came before then to take the keys of the warehouses from Moola and see it housed a small curticy considering the favour the Right Honourable Company have done them. We hope now the 5 gentlemen are satisfied without the agent's appearance and that they have taken care about the silk affaire and other matters relateing to the Right Honourable Company's intrest. It's an unresonable thing in you to expect the agent's undertakeing such a journy when ague and feaver upon him and so weake as not able to ride a league. You are sencible ther's no doctors upon the way to cure him therefore what a meserable condition must a man be in when without hope of releife. If this cargo does not goe off according to the Right Honourable Companye's expectation it will reflect very much upon your father for doubtless it was him that advised the Right Honourable Company therein so that it admitts no delayes nor excuses in puting it of. It's strange to us the major part is not sold should there be any coming from Alleppo the keeping it in the godowns will do the Right Honourable Company a great prejudice. Wee are heartily concerned to fiend the five Armenians so indifferent as they seeme to be in theire letters one pretending he's decriped and not fit for anything and the rest complayning they begin to grow old and so necessetate to get others to doe their business for them an abominable shame for so great a favour done them by such honourable persons. Therefore wee beg and intreat you'd bestir your selfe in this affaire and to spur these gentllemen on in disposing of the cloath etc. Our masters realy belive it's all gon before this time and that the goods mentioned in the list with the remaining part of the money is at Surat which will trouble them very much to heare the contrary. Wee sincerly desier the prosperity of your father and selfe and that the name of Callendar may florish both in England and Persia which can never be except a good end be put to this so vast a concerne. We have not elce but rest

Your very loveing freinds

John Gladman
Edward Owen
Thomas Harbin

Gombroon the 5th July 1695

204

JOHN GLADMAN, EDWARD OWEN AND THOMAS HARBIN AT GOMBROON TO COMPANY IN LONDON
24 JULY 1695
E/3/51 EXTRACT FROM FF. 128-129

On the 22d instant arrived here shipp Thomas full freighted from Suratt ... our endeavours shall not be wanting to send this ship full back, but if she returns so soone as to be in India by the 15th October as mentioned in Captain Pye's instructions from the agent and Councill she'l make but a very ordinary freight, no considerable caphilas arriving till the latter end of October or begining of November so that to go halfe full will be no small trouble to us. Our hopes are both goods and money will be dispatcht by Captain Brangwin etc and the five Armenians, but as yet don't understand any of the broad cloth is sold. If the Armenians goe on thus dully it may ly in the ware house a long time undisposed off. We have wrote Captain Brangwin etc to press the Armenians to let's have some of the broad cloth effects downe to goe in this shipp that beleive he will not be wanting to doe. Therefore if it comes not, their can be nobody blame worthy but thes five gentlemen.

To avoid bringing your Honours' affaires under any ill curcumstances at such a time when we are endeavouring to get a new phirmaund from this present King, we ware necesitated upon due consideration to refuse the owning sixty six peces of broad cloth that came in the Thomas as contracted for by the agent and Councill in Suratt, besides which their was on board [gap in text] peces excluded from this contract that Auga Pere Callandar would have had us smothered with the rest, which gaine your Agent nor none in this plase belive does not desier. Their's many here that will be glad with all their hearts nay wacth for an opertunity to bring us into primenirys[1], and thes Armenians if their owne turne be but served care for nothing elce. We should be very sorry if have acted wrong. It would be much better for agent Annesly etc to forbare makeing such contracts were they improper colours at Suratt they might invoyed them here on your Honours' account and not takeing this course. If such a thing should be discovered we should be counted no better than cheats in robing the King and for ought we know your Honours' broad cloth might be thought to be Armenians' goods and to pay custome all for a trifle. When know your Honours' pleasure here-in shall be obedient thereto. The agreement and Agapere Callendar's letter if your Honours pleas to read them may see how it was.

Carmenia wooll we have received not any as yet. The broker their advises the Dutch have sent for their vackeel from thence and intend not to medle this yeare in bying up the comodity moreover that if his bills had been duly paid at Spahaune which we gave particular orders about, he could have had one hundred bales packt up before this and questioned not but in the year's end to have bought up three or four hundred in all. We have soothed him up and wrote to Spahaune about it. Their being no other sent by the Armenians as we know of, have promised to allow him and his consart five per cent provissions which comision Doud took formerly and gave them but three charging eight in the whole; some there is bought but how much am ignorant off, but the picker men understand are not set to worke to cleane it. We hope still they are not now idle. What ever is received your Honours may be sure shall be put on board the Thomas, and we question not but the investment will be pritty considerable.

[1] præmunire: to bring before the courts; to prosecute

205

CAPTAIN BENJAMIN BRANGWIN, THOMAS MAJOR, JAMES BRUCE AND
JAMES RAWLINGS AT ISFAHAN TO COMPANY IN LONDON
6 AUGUST 1695
E/3/51 EXTRACT FROM FF. 137-139V

We departed from Gomroon the 23d March last by order of the Right Worshipfull Agent Gladman etc Councill for Ispahaune where we after a long and teedious journey arrived the 2 of May last finding your honours' house very much run to ruin and the name of the English almost forgotten because no English had inhabited it for some years. Wherefore according to Agent Gladman's etc instructions we began to repair it, which will require some time and we are afraid the charge will be greate, as yett cannot give your honours a satisfactory accompt. Our care shall not be wanting to doe it as cheape as possible.

Soon after our arrival we consulted the five gentlemen appointed to advise us about all things mentioned in our instructions and have given Agent Gladman etc an account at large of their answers and assistance.

The five gentlemen seemed at first not to be willing to accept of that great favour and creditt your honours had been pleased to offer them viz the sale of such a vast concerne as the Nassaw's and Mary's broad cloth as appears by a letter from them to Agent Gladman an coppy of which we suppose the Agent sends your honours by this conveyance. Since which they have acquainted us they will endeavour to serve your honours with all fidelity but at present no cloth is sould they not agreeing amongst themselves whether shall sell all at once or by parsells. We cannot give your honours the reasons at present why the cloth lyes unsould not haveing been much acquainted with these gentlemen's wayes of commerce or long enough in Persia to know whether they act for your honours' interest or theire owne but it seemes strange to us that thay give us no account whether they can sell such a quantity of cloth or the reasons why not. They at first seemed to be of opinion they could not, but some of them contradicting that said they could were it twice as much. Some of them would have had the Agent or us to write your honours not to send more cloth untill this was disposed off which could not be this two yeares, but others of them said that if no more cloth came the people would not alter their course of trade from Aleppa for this quantity but if they once saw that this markett would constantly be supplyed they would leave that trade and then five times as much would not supply the countrey.

We should have acquainted your honours of their opinions in this case sometime since but finding them divided amongst them selves we knew not what to write and we cannot but admire that the five gentlemen themselves were not so civil as to give your honours an answer to the several letters received which we understand by them they have not done to this time. We could wish heartily we could give your honours a more satisfactory account of this affaire then at present are able for want of longer experience but shall endeavour to informe our selves by all imaginable care and diligence that may performe it in our next.

The five gentlemen have told us that they are unwilling to buy silk for your honours' account for that the Turkey marchants will be able to out sell your honours in that commodity. The reasons they aledge are that the silk of the yeare 1693 was bought very cheape and carried to Aleppo and was there ready when the Turkey marchants' cloth came, and the silk of the year 1694 proveing very deare at Gelon and Shambeck from whence it came and the marchants that had carried their silk to Aleppo not knowing it, sold their silk very cheap according to the price they bought it, which is much cheaper then any can be procured now, for though there be plenty of silk this year there are so many byers in hopes of selling to your honours that the price at the places from whence the silk comes is risen very much, every Armenian that had any money by him haveing sent for silk in hope of getting good prices haveing had timely notice of what quantity your honours would want which we think was imprudent of the five gentlemen to lett every body know what your honours had intrusted them with as secrett, for all trade in our opinions ought to managed with secrecy but it's reported to us that nothing writt by your honours to these gentlemen but was talked all over citty and country even by the very shopkeepers some months before our arrival at Ispahaune.

We understand by your honours' generals to Persia that you designe a great trade to these parts with the woollen manufactory of our kingdom. In our weake judgments Ispahaune is the best and nearest mart for and to all places where there is any consumption of that commodity a place of currant trade and vast sums of ready money. It's a magazeenee of trade from whence all the northerne parts as Isbeck Tartaria Casmire Candahan etc all the westerne parts as Armenia Georgia and all along to the Turkes' dominians are supplyed from it, with all Indian commodityes and may be as well with those proper of the kingdom of England. But to carry on this trade as your honours may have designed it we must have better priviledges in Persia then we now have or not be so much imposed upon by the officers of the several places where we reside. Many are the impositions at present that we are lyable to, some for want of better rogoms or phirmaunds others for want of a constant frequenting the court and haveing the Attamon Doulett or Chancelor our freind for without that a rogom is of no signification for any kaun or sharbander will deney the obeying it.

We haveing by the Agent etc orders turned out the linguist Auga Doud, and by the advise of the five gentlemen taken in one of their choosing, but he neither speaks English nor any Europian language neither is he acquainted with one word of our business that hath past in Persia or with anything belonging to the court so that we have no benifitt by him. Neither can we venture upon renewing phirmaunds or getting others when we cannot understand what may be granted us. Auga Doud may be a great rogue for ought we know as most of these easterne linguists are but when necessity requires with humble submition to your honours' better judgment, we are of opinion a rogue may be made use off especially when no other is to be gott that can doe that business as it's your honours' case now in Ispahaune. There is not a man in this citty or Julphai that can speake English nor any person that understands any Europian language that knoweth one word of our business or hath any acquaintance at court whereas Doud can almost say all our phirmaunds by heart and hath more influence on the officers at court then any Christian in all Persia. We speake not this out of any kindness to Doud he being a person we never saw in our lives untill we came to Ispahaune but this is the opinian of the five Armenians and all we have converst with in Persia and we think ourselves bound in duty to acquaint your honours of it that hereafter we may not be blamed. We have met with much trouble since we came here for want of a linguist.

We hope in our next to give your honours a full account of the sale of the broad cloth and what sorts most proper for this place as also an account of silk what sorts best procurable with their prices as also an account of the particular sorts of goods mentioned in your honours' list to be provided by the 5 gentlemen and shall make it our particular business to be skilfull in this trade that no cheats be imposed upon us but that our service may tend to your honours' profitt and interest as in duty bound alwayes to endeavour.

206

John Gladman, Edward Owen and Thomas Harbin at Gombroon to Isfahan
9 August 1695
E/3/51 extract from ff. 141-153

In our opinion the five friends show themselves very weak in thinking we can contredict the Rightt Honourable Company's orders and give others because the cloth can't be disposed of at once. Those that they have is large and ample enough did they designe to goe on briskly in this particular. If the bent of their mind be otherwise the Rightt Honourable Company are like to be finely served we beleive they'd have us desire them to resigne up the consignement. If they won't obay the Rightt Honourable Company how can it be expected we should be observed.

To here the phirmaunds were all interpritted into Armenians for Mr Bruce to English would be good newse. Doud's a rascall to keep those by him that he delivered Mr Bruce, and since given you. The last phirmaund in the late King's time which he charges Mr Petitt to have carryed away would have bin of great use he saying therein was mentioned it was left to the Agent's etc liburty whither to pishcash the Caune or any other officers or not [ ] many more, articles of vallue that might have bin renewed. We wish he has not laid the saddle on the wrong horse and kept it himselfe, his delight being to fling away good lusty summs that are vastly more advantages to him then pedling matters.

Most certaine these Armenians are able to advise you whither it's best to renew the old phirmaund or gett a generall one, herein noe harm in our opinions can come to them. We judge the[re] severall rogoms that must be kept apart as before as about procureing Carmania wooll makeing wine carrying up goods, and many other things that's needless to incert here, because if the Caune or Vizier of any place gives us trouble these smaller matters may be sent to them to peruse, a generall one being of soe great importance as not to be ventured abroad. About this pray press the Armenians to councell you in. The fewer of these small rogoms you gett in our judgments the better but because we can't direct you herein leave it to you to doe what most convenient and for the Rightt Honourable Company's interest.

The perposall made to you by those gentlemen that pretend friendship to medle in buying up Maskatt wooll dos not carry a good face with it except are orderd soe to doe by our Rightt Honourable masters. That from Carmania that's most esteemed in England we judg to be red, pickt as much as they have time to doe in season, some must be unpickt black, mixt, and white. There comes no great quantity of those sorts. If you can't gett a phirmaund to buy as much of this comodity as we can, because of the government then lett it be for as large a quantity as possible with this addition that we mayn't be impeeded by any put in athority as was last year by the Caune's sealing up the warehouses, to the Rightt Honourable Company's disgrace, and damage.

What reason could we have in writeing that Doud paid for a rogom for makeing wine, unless it came from him, know not. Mr Lee was interpreter to the letter that made us signifie to Mr Bruce and Aveatik Callendar if it was worth so many tomands as he gave, then to take it, and pay him. Formerly he was very eger and pressing to give the late Vizier seven years pishcash that came to fourty nine tomands which refuseing to do it pleasd God the Vizier dyed soon after, whereby that charge was clearly saved to the Rightt Honourable Company. It's the nature of these Armenians to engracieate themselves into great men's favours to the Rightt Honourable Company's vast expence and by which means their agents and chiefs are slighted and not lookt upon it being expected what the linguist says must be done wright or wrong.

For the five friends to pretend ignorance about the Rightt Honourable Company customes is not the part of gentlemen. If please they may have admittance at court to preferr a petition to the King as well as Doud only they think this imploye much inferiour to undertake, if can prevaile with them to act, it's well otherwise you must take the wisiest course possible to be thought of. For three years errears to lye dead in the shawbander's hands is what we stomack very much if are like to have no effects for the cloth.

You that are in Spahaune know best whether the Attamondowlett requires a larger pishcash then he ought what's needfull for the Rightt Honourable Company's interest that certainely the five friends won't scruple telling you. Mr Bruce did say it was talkt the Nassau or Mary brought a present for the King, and if noe business can be done without it, you must consider thereof with the Armenians and goe the best and prudentest way to work you can, and if have time lett us understand by an nimble shotter, what to the King, Attamondowlett, with every indevidiall person that we can't name will be expected to which you shall have an answer presently. Otherwise must leave it to your management by all means if to be effected and brought about. Gett the five gentlemen's approbation for thereby we shall act secure. This is our opinion and hope it will be yours, wherein you know we are in the wrong pray desist for this place and Spahaune is at a great distance.

Relateing to Aveatik Callendar's advise not to gett an order to bring gold downe hither, we referr you to the Generall's etc opinion, put down in ours of the 26th past. However if it's to be done with more security by makeing the Attamondowlett our friend, that he must be before can gett a new phirmaund is much better if such a rogom can be procurd. The Armenians will be daily bateing at you to take what chequeens lyes by them in the Right Honourable Company's name, which if they perswaide you to and it be found out, that priviledge will be lost, therefore pray be very cautious how you act and don't preferr a private interest before a generall.

Mr Bruce knows that Moola and Doud hold a consultation togeather, and wrote the broker was wholy swaid by him, adding they mett either at Spahaune or Julpha continually. Therefore for Doud to say he was sick and out of service, thinking thereby to clear himselfe is a flam[1], and truly it was a great creditt to him to make his braggs, when had drawne Moola into his trap that he undersold the cloth eight or tenn shakees in a yard. Moola was orderd to doe nothing without consulting Mr Bruce and he to take Aveatik Callendar's advise, who can write when tis too late it was sold four shakees under price, when might if he knew those merchants carryd them to the factory, and savd the Company so much money wherein he blindly comes of with a flam he did not care to medle least should be counted a buiseybody.

Sure these five Armenians in the sale of this broad cloth will not desire any proffett besides their comission allowd by the Company but as you say it's the nature of them to be lavish of what's none of their owne and you'l find if are necessitated to imploye Doud he'l not be spareing. We could hartily wish the Armenians would doe it themselves without him.

God we hope will restore Captain Brangwin to his former health and use of limbs, doubtless you have all trouble enough and we are very much concerned that Hoan Coldarente under pretence of being old hath laide downe his comission and that the rest cannot agree amongst themselves. We expect they'l all drop and follow his steeps one after another. There's little prospect to the contrary there falling out amongst themselves will bring it to pass for one will plead if you don't engage yourselfe in it I won't. The fire is allready kindled, and wish it mayn't be in a flame by this time, to sell such a quantity of cloth as that is in parcells will take up more then four or five years time, All that you can doe is to give them good words but if they are resolved to lett it lye and rott we must take some other course when once they are for promoteing their owne interest, a thing wee allwayes dreaded, they'l prove themselves greater rogues then Moola that will startle Rightt Honourable Company to here of. If could prevaile with them and that it mayn't prejudice the Rightt Honourable Company in putting of what's not tolerable first whereby to compute the damage of each shipps that none but shopkeepers which make stockings and such little things will buy in our judgments it's best but to sell the good first nobody will meddle with tother allthough pass our sentiments we as well as you must stick to the Rightt Honourable Company's instructions. They are cun-ning fellows therefore be very circomspect for should these prove faulse they'l loose their creditt with the Rightt Honourable Company quite.

A linguist that you understand not nor he you is very insignificent the best of them all can't nor dare nor interpritt what you say we have wrote sufficiently about Doud allready. Necessity has no law therefore leave it to you as before the five Armenians won't demean themselves soe farr as to turne interpreturs therefore can't be angrye at their not officiateing in that station. All us here are as little averst in court affaires as your selves is it brobable [sic] or doe the five friends think a linguist unskild in court business is fitt to be a schoole master. By referring you to such they make themselves rediculous.

By us are not books sufficient to acquaint you what quantitys of broad cloth have been sent on the Rightt Honourable Company's accompt to Persia since this order of allowing noe more then five thousand tomands wherein suppose all other comodityes are excluded. Therefore hope the Attamondowlett will rest satisfid till can gett the perticulars from England that hope you have wrote to the Rightt Honourable Company for gentlemen you have more enemys to deal with then the Attamondowlett. The traders to Aleppo doubtless curse the Company for sending this cloth up therefore it's plaine to us, they'l sett all their wheeles a going to make them suffer sufficiently for this time whereby to prevent their future proceedings and have a care how they come thoart[2] their hasse[3] wherein the five friends if knew their hearts may be deeply engaged with the rest soe that you only strive against wind and tide they vallueing noe interest that crosses their owne. We should be glad if it would prove otherwise. The discoursing them will be to give a knife in their hands to cutt our throats. We are like to see happy dayes when it shall be demanded of Moola to signe a paper to lett the Company sell no cloth without acquainting them thereof, Doud judge is a dealer in that comodity privately. We cannot see that ever this affaire will come to a good issue. Were this Attamondowlett as good as the former there would be no occation of these disputes.

By the Rightt Honourable Company's directions and the list of Persia goods you have you'l see whose orderd to provide them. We very much admire you should write it now, well hopeing some of them were upon the way. As to price and goodness of all goods the Rightt Honourable Company orderd, we can't informe thereof soe pray enquire of the Armenians. This way will prove very tedious, since the shipps arrive so late and that the broad cloth in probability will lye on hand. We think the same instructions about the silk etc may be of force which if you approve of with us, lett be put in execution forthwith.

In all things forgett not to act according to the Rightt Honourable Company's orders and consult the Armenians therein as well as in court affaires if they will give us any advise, and if possible break them of that idle excuse in saying tis out of their way and is the linguist business. Pray wherein your judgments don't correspond with ours, and that it be thought better not to medle therewith lay such clauses a side. The strongest party is at Spahaune there being Captain Brangwin and three of his Councill moreover four Armenians upon the place. Therefore when any matter is debated betwene you and that it be a thing of great importance and will admitt of no delays, endeavour to reconcile it amongst your selves with the Armenians weighing what you doe with due consideration.

[1] falsehood
[2] sic - unidentified
[3] sic - unidentified

207
ARMENIAN MERCHANTS AT JULFA TO COMPANY IN LONDON
12 AUGUST 1695
E/3/51 FF. 155-156v

Your Lordships' most obliging letter written to the meanest of your servants from London January the 5th 1693/4 was presented to us by the illustrious Lord the Agent of Bundar Abassi on the 6th of February of this 1695. We have deferred answering it untill this present, waiting the arrival of the ships with their cargos recommended to us and the discharge of their merchandize here in Ispahaun that we might see their condition and their sorts and their price they were rated at, and that we might be yet better informed of these commodities and your letters before we undertook anything that might redound to the detriment of your most noble and mighty Company and our disgrace. The goods are arrived Ispahaun but being brought mixt and without order we were necessitated to wait until Captain Brangwin (being then indisposed) had recovered his health to put them in order as at present thanks be to God he being better hath done and we have seen them and found them in a good condition except some peices which have suffered damage by the sea.

The great esteem which Coja Panous Callendar had perswaded your honours to have of us we impute it to his goodness more than our deserts and is sufficient to engage us with all our ability to answer it. Moreover we have obligations more pressing us to imploy our utmost endeavours in the service of a Company from whom our nation has always received so great favours and by whom we may promise ourselves great advan-tages for the future. But after haveing well considered the weight of this affair, we find ourselves at last obliged to answer that this charge sur-passeth our ability according as we have already answered the illustrious Agent soon after we had received your letter adviseing him that it behoved him to come up to Ispahaun and take charge of this so great an affair. But Captain Brangwin with his Council being departed Bundar Abbasi afore the arrival of our letter conducting to Ispahaun the said charge of merchandize the illustrious Agent could not understand our letter being writ in Armenians. He sent it by a corset[1] to Captain Brang-win to get it translated by Mr Bruce into English there being a coppy here of the said letter which was translated into English and sent to the illustrious Agent and in the mean time Captain Brangwin haveing left according to your order part of the said goods at Shyraz brought the rest here to Ispahaun contrary to the hope which your lordships gave us, that these cargos might arrive sooner or at least at the same time, with that of the Turkey Company's at Aleppo. The Armenian and Turkish mer-chants had bought the cloth and brought it into Persia before yours arrived, one part of the said cloth haveing suffered damage by the sea. Before any news came of the arrival of your two ships it was sold at Tauveris at 10 abassis and one half and from 10 to 9 per quz shau, and forewith after the news of their arrival the merchants being willing to dispatch their affairs the price fell to 6 abassies. Afterwards came other news that there was also arrived at Aleppo and Smyrna more cloth belonging to the Turkey Company which must likewise be brought to this place. Moreover we have intelligence from Suratt thath the cloth which came from England was sold there at 3 rupees and 2 anas which is one eight part of a rupee. Now considering cloth at that price at Surat what merchants can carry it to India to sell as ordinarily they use to do transporting $1/4$ or $1/5$ part of what usually came from Turkey into Persia, to India from whence it appears that the rate mentioned by your Lordships accouting 22 abassies more or less for a pound sterling campared with the price cloth is at at present there will be found very great difference forasmuch as your Lordships propose that we 5 should take the cargos of these two ships or to distribute them to other customers of our nation upon condition to pay presently $1/5$ part in ready money $1/3$ part after 3 months and $1/3$ part after 6 months, or to pay the two last parts in silk in the term of 8 or 12 months this is an enterprize which truly surpasseth our capacitys as also the abilitys of the rest of the merchants of our nation to whom we have made this proposition and received the same answer according to which we can testify that they are no more capable than we, who are well stricken in age and moreover find ourselves ingaged in another course of negotiation which will be very difficult for us to resign and to embrace this you have proposed to us notwithstanding the advantage which we may obtain, it does not seem convenient that we should be buyers and sellers of one and the same merchandise. Also as touching the sale of it all at once is a bargain we cannot find ever has been made in Persia or Turkey, but it can hardly be done in Surat as it is plain that some time past there came to this place 1200 peices of cloth of the Company's and the undertaker of the selling of this cloth was Moola the Company's broker who delivered it out to the cloth sellers and stockins makers of this place to be paid in 5 months but to abate 1 per cent per month for ready money he received some money in part and advanced the rest hath not reinbursted himself of what he laid down although then it was 2 years that the Turkey Company were not able to bring any cloth and also a great want of the woolen manufacture in these parts so that there is no probability of executing your lordships' orders nor the instance which the Agent gave us to understand by his letter dated the 5th July that his will was that this cloth should be sold immediately and that we should make quick returns in mony and in silk. Behold! that that little portion of cloth which remains at Shyraz as well as the great quantity which remains here although no other cloth should come from any other parts can hardly be turned into money in 4 or 5 years. Moreover this sort of cloth is not at present so much in request as has been formerly and sorts of the woolen manufacture is never sold here in Ispahaun but by little and little and that upon credit and for time there is no place but Tauveris which sometimes sells for ready money and sometimes for exchange of Indian commodities but also by little and little.

These orders therefore of your lordships we cannot put in execution in this place. We beg your pardon for takeing the liberty of telling you that such advices for these parts are an abuse. We are obliged to write without respect or dissimulation fearing lest great damage and detriment may accrew to the Company and to our great shame and confusion. It remains therefore that the Company consider what they have to do with this merchandize and address themselves to some person that has nothing else to do but to sell the said woolen manufacture by little and little and from time to time as he shall meet with chapmen to buy it knowing that it cannot be sold at once but it must be by degrees the which we have not any leisure to perform. As to any other service that is in our power we shall employ ourselves willingly with all imaginable diligence.

As to silk your Lordships desire to know the price. For two years past all sorts of silk have been cheap but since have rose considerablely according as we beleive the illustrious Agent and Captain Brangwin have also advised you it is write to the Agent if he hath authority on the behalf of the Company to impower anyone to sell these effects by little and little that he will depute some person to do it.

We have nothing more, but to pray god for your lordships' health and prosperity we remaine in our weakness

Your Honours' most humble and affectionate servants

Googas Calendar Callentar of Julpha
Mercara de Surhad
Moora de Surhad
Gregory Colderents
Hoan Colderents

Ispahaun the 12 August 1695
I say Julpha [added in different hand]

[1] cossid; *qāsed* (Ar. / Pers.): courier or running messenger

208
COUNCIL AT ISFAHAN TO THE FIVE ARMENIAN MERCHANTS AT JULFA
13 AUGUST 1695
E/3/51 FF. 157-158

To   Coja Murrad Surhad
      Coja Mercara Surhad
      Coja Gogas Calendar
      Coja Gregore Caldarants
      Coja Hoan Caldarants

Gentlemen

Wee can not sitt still and see our masters' designes frustrated and their concernes in eminent danger of sustaining vast detriment and loss with out freely telling you our mind.

As long as your actions seemed to demonstrate your intentions were reall in promoting the Rightt Honourable Company's interest, wee patiently waited to see the effects of your declared promises, but now wee find you are resolved not to concern your selves farther in that affair, but desire some body elce, who has less buisness to doe may be impowered. Wee cannot but acquaint you as in duty bound to our Rightt Honourable masters, that the letter which Coja Googas Coja Mercara, and Coja Gregore Caldarants was pleased to bring us some time since, desireing us to translate into English, that it might be sent to the Rightt Honourable Company which Mr Bruce did, is neither for your creditt nor their satisfaction, but a formall excuse for your delatory proceedings in the sale of the Rightt Honourable Company's broad cloth and give us leave to tell you that itt extreamly contradicts all that you have been hetherto pretending or doeing, for had you designed that the Rightt Honourable Company's affaires should have been managed at this rate, and they have suffered as wee can not perceive but they are like to doe, you confessing soe much in your designed letter to them, why were you not soe kind and just to your esteemed friends, as you acknowledged them to bee, for whose service you say you would venture your lives, as to have acquainted them this upon receit of their first letter that they might have provided speedy remidies in time or have acquainted the Agent etc at Gomroon, who wrote you of the cloth's arrivall time enough, that their sending to Spahaun might have been prevented and some other measures taken, for a better and speedyer markett. But instead of being soe civill or friendly to them, you have been soe unkind and prejudiciall, as not to write them one word of answar, and you have been soe far from satisfieing us of this now your known design, of not your being able to serve the Rightt Honourable Company in this affair, that you have all along flattered us up with the hopes of a good markett ever since our arrivall to this place untill just now.

By desireing to give you the satisfaction of the colours prices and sorts of all the goods, which wee did to your content, and then to encrease our hopes you brought us merchants to see the goods who seemed very well pleased with them, you your selves acknowledging them, to be very good nay better then ever you had seen in Spahaun, and more then all this you acquaint us that you had allotted them into parts, and gott merchants for allmost the whole. All which wee have signified from time to time to the Rightt Worshipfull Agent etc and as he wrote us in his last he has done the same to the Rightt Honourable Company and now when the goods have been 3 months and more here and you pretended soe great a forwardness toward their sale, for you to write the Rightt Honourable Company the burthen is too heavy for you to bear, and that they could not be sold in 4 or 5 yeares, should no more goods come, is a burning shame, and cuts us to the very heart to thinke our Masters should be soe served. Wee are very sorry that the Rightt Honourable Company should be condemned for laying heavyer burdens on the backs of the great and worthy merchants of Julpha then they are able to bear, wee being assured they never designed any such thing. Neither can wee or any persons that know the least of this affair believe itt. Wee have abundance of reason to alledg against your formed letter to the Rightt Honourable Company too long to write now but if you please to come to the English house, or if you should be soe busy that all of you can not, wee then desire that any 3 of you would come, and be better satisfied in what you doe. If Captain Brangwin was able wee would waite on you in Julpha. Wee hope in doeing the Rightt Honourable Company this desired service, you can not prejudice your selves, but give them cause to esteem your friendship, and not only to be kind to you alone, but to all the rest of your people in general which you can not expect, should this affair be slighted by you, and the Rightt Honourable Company's designes and purposes destroyed and tis our opinion nothing can satisfie them in this point but the speedy sale of their woollen manufacture.

Wee write this as particular friends, wishing you all imaginable prosperity and success, adviseing you to consider itt well, wee haveing discharged our duty to God and our masters and friendly part to you and your nation. Wee hope that these our advises may cause you to take such resolutions as may really prove to our masters' interest and wee shall allway be ready to serve you to the utmost of our powers as

Your very loveing friends and humble servants

[unsigned]

Ispahaun the 13th Augustt 1695

209

JOHN GLADMAN, EDWARD OWEN AND THOMAS HARBIN AT GOMBROON
TO COMPANY IN LONDON
16 AND 20 AUGUST 1695
E/3/51 EXTRACT FROM FF. 159-162V

As to transactions in Spahaune we heartily wish they went in a smoother chanell and that the Armenians would act with more life and vigore then they doe.

1st   Our fears are his Excellency etc expectations of large returnes from hence will not arrive soe seasonable as to put on board these shipps which we intend to keep as long as possible to prevent their going without gold or goods.

2dly   From Carmania as yitt no wooll appeares, but we don't despond of receiving some of that commodity the customes we are in some expectations of unless there's a stop put to it on account zadwick[1] for what broad cloth amounts too more then five thousand tomands. Had these Armenians a reall respect for your Honours' interest, when the necessity of selling the broad cloth has bin prest soe hard upon them they would have supplyed your present occasion by the lone of thirty thousand pounds, which compaired with your Honours' kindness is inconsiderable.

3dly   Your Honours' sereene judgements wee know have search't into the deapths of all foren trade. If have presumed to write what's not becomeing us wee humbley begg pardon. That you are served thus by the Armenians, whom your Honours have been pleased to honour with such high favours is to admiration, pray God your estates mayn't suffer. Your Honours will see how strictly they argue in Doud's behalfe, which show they are confrederates and has brought us to the necessity ot a complyance in some measure that we leave to Captain Brangwin etc since are compeld thereto. What business he has done for the Dutch was acted whilst was in your Honours' service, and a great part of the money that Captain Brangwin etc mention was disbursted dureing the embassadores' residence at Spahaune.

4thly   The freights your Honours' shipps makes from hence, a great deale of it is Moores', Persians', and Banyans'. The Armenians some times put on board to a very considerable vallue, which is not out of any respect they have to your Honours more then others, but because they think their goods securer in Europe shipps then countrey vessells, otherwise there would not be such freights made as has been.

5thly   Without these five Armenians' assistance and cordiall proceedings it will be impossible to bring the silk trade drove at Gelon to Spahaune and hither, but if they are no wayes interested therein, in a short time it might put a great damp to the Turkey Company's proceedings, for what can't five such leeding men as they doe with your Honours' assistance, if designe to apply their estates this way, but this in our silley capassitys with submission don't see any probability of bringing it to pass, neither judge it impossible to be effected, your Honours' wisdome and prudence being beyond our apprehentions to perceive. The sale of this broad cloth, which have severall times harpt upon will in some measure be a provth thereof, what we principle desire is to see your Honours' affaires flourish, that shall endeavour to promote, and no wayes think much of any person or persons you shall think fitt to indulge, haveing not to our knowledge been guilty of such unbecomeing crimes.

6thly If your Honours could bring the Armenians to pay Persia consolage for all goods ship't from Bengall, Fort St George, and Fort St Davids, it would amount to a considerable summe, and much rejoyce us to heare they are brought to a complyance.

7thly Of late no English shipps have pretended to goe to Congo, and soe we beleive that contriveance is wholy laide a side.

8thly Hitherto we have endeavourd to make the shawbander understand the customes are due in March, and were it not for Doud there had bin no occasion of those disputes that has risen, and what's more grose, to endeavour the bringing it to be due March following whereby to make your Honours loose a whole year's customes.

9thly What shipp Modena's cloth went of at your Honours have the account as to that of Coja Vossell's how it sold are ignorant; the cheat put upon us by the broker, are endeavouring to finde out and force him to make satisfaction.

10thly Your Agent is very glad that his not landing the Modena's pepper is approved of by your Honours.

11thly All our agreveances in respect to your Honours' affaires shall be laide open, and we doubt not if the Armenians will play the part of men, but to gett such full and ample phirmaunds as shall for the future prevent those impositions as have formerly bin fors't to goe through with paticence.

12thly Shipp Barkley Castle's being taken by the French to our great greife and trouble had notice of long agoe. God we hope will make up that and all other losse to your Honours, which shall allwayes be our hearty payers [sic].

13thly Captain Brangwin etc before this pacquet is dispatch't from Spahaun possible may give your Honours to understand what goods and money is upon the way hither or in a readyness to dispatch. By his last there's little or noe encouragement of receiving either.

14thly Of late two unhappy accidents falling out in freight money put on board shipp Quedah Merchant and Nassau, which the comanders of both shipps declares Sychan wronged them of, whereby his Excellency etc is displeased with our keeping him in service ... but as it is can't be without him. We have wrote to the five Armenians to send us a person to overlook his actions, which expect they will comply with but nevertheless untill he's instructed in these matters, will be of little use. In Bunder, they are all of Sychan's cast. Therefore it's in vaine to look out for a supply.

15thly Except the noise of the French and pyrates upon this coast scares the merchants, we can't perceive but the Thomas and Mocha Friggatt will goe full freighted for Bombay and Suratt.

Your Honours' most devoted humble servants

John Gladman
Edward Owen
Thomas Harbin

Gombroone the 16th August 1695

Upon clouser of the foregoing came a Carmania cossett who brought us a letter from the new broker, sent thither by the Armenians dated the 8th instant, whom we should be glad may doe well. By what he writes his predecessour would have played the rogue and made excuses for his not buying up wooll as he has done hitherto, notwithstanding all the arguments that has bin used in our advices to him. There's in the warehouses if Coja Fannuse dos not mistake, three thousand seven hundred sixty eight maund that hope he'l make up a considerable quantity more, and send seasonable to be put on board the Thomas and Mocho Friggatt.

Your Honours' most devoted humble servants

John Gladman
Edward Owen
Thomas Harbin

Gombroone the 20th August 1695

[1] also spelled zadiack; *sad-yak* (Pers.): one per cent, one of the customs dues on imported goods

210
JOHN GLADMAN, EDWARD OWEN AND THOMAS HARBIN AT GOMBROON TO ISFAHAN
20 AUGUST 1695
E/3/51 EXTRACT FROM FF. 163-164

On the 12th instant came into this roade the Mocho Friggatt Captain Lenard Edgcombe Comander who was dispatched from Bombay the 29th of May which being very late in the yeare came empty, the Generall etc's designe in sending her being cheifly for the security of the Rightt Honourable Company's estate that he thinks we have receved from you on account sale of the broad cloth and does realy expect that both she and the Thomas will goe full shipps from hence in company because of the rumor of French, one pyrate and Arrabs that are cruseing up and downe, his Excellency etc being jealous these marchants if are possest feare will heardly be perswaded to lade their goods upon a single bottom. We are not limitated now to time therefore if ther's any prospect of sending us any of the Rightt Honourable Company's effects, either in goods or money early enough for the shipps to depart hence soe as to be dispatcht for Europe in January, we will detaine them as long as possable we dare but this you must imediately advise us about, although are at the charge of hireing a cossett on purpose; consider demorage runs high and you'l fiend by the clause in the Company's letter that's hereinclosed they have sent out no more by the Benjamin Mocho Friggatt and Tonqueen being possest of large supplyes from us. They all three arrived Bombay the 15th May. Pray urge and press the Armenians to do something. Surely they [words obscured] but may be prevailed with by perswading arguments. If can get any thing from them that's considerable lett Mr Bruce and who elce you think fitt, see it out of danger.

By the Mocho Friggatt came three of the Rightt Honourable Company's servants, vizt Mr William Topham factor Mr William Hicks writer and Walter Evans an apprentice, the first left to our disposall as we shall thinck convenient the two latter ordered to be sent to Augau Peree's family to learne the Persian and Armenian languages. We intend to send them all three togather please God they live, judging Mr Topham may be serviceable to you in case Mr Bruce and Mr Rawlins' distemper should continue.

Pray remind the Armenians to supply us with an able honest fellow to inspect into Sychan's actions in makeing freight and contracts with camell men and disposeing of cargos, to prevent his putting cheats upon the Rightt Honourable Company and others.

211
CAPTAIN BENJAMIN BRANGWIN, THOMAS MAJOR, JAMES BRUCE
AND JAMES RAWLINGS AT ISFAHAN TO THE FIVE ARMENIAN MERCHANTS
8 SEPTEMBER 1695
E/3/51 F. 173

To   Coja Morah Surhad
     Coja Mercara Surhad
     Coja Gogas Calendar
     Coja Gregory Colderents
     and Coja Hoan Colderents

Gentlemen

We come now after so many perswasions used to beg that you will no longer disagree among yourselves and be of two different opinions but give your final answer of what you design to do in that great concerne of our Right Honourable masters' broad cloth.

We talking yesterday with Coja Gregory Colderents found him to have seemingly left of the business. The same day some short time after we had the honour to discourse the Calentar Coja Gogas Calendar upon the same subject who we find wholy inclined as he hath been all along to promote the Right Honourable Company's interest by the speedy disposal of their cloth now in your hands, and he hath not only spoke this but manifested it, by divideing the whole into six parts, and offering to take one fifth or 1500 peices, which if the rest of the gentlemen (who we cannot suppose but knew as well how to dispose of it as the Calentar) would have performed their parts five sixts of the cloth would have been sold and the other sixt Captain Brangwin does now engage to take.

This we desire you will consider and do the Company a peice of service that may be both to your future honour and interest. We desire it may be thus concluded or your answer to the contrary in the behalf of the Company.

212
AGREEMENT BETWEEN BOMBAY COUNCIL AND ARMENIAN MERCHANTS
9 SEPTEMBER 1695
E/3/51 FF. 174-176

Articles of agreement indented, had, made, concluded and agreed upon this ninth day of September Anno Domini sixteen hundred ninety five, between the Honourable Sir John Gayer Knight General of India, Persia and Arabia for affaires of the Right Honourable English East India Company etc Council of the one part and Callendar d'Callendar of Surat merchant of the other part. Whereas the Governor and Comittee for affaires of the abovesaid Company did some time since lade on board the good ships Mocho Friggat, Benjamin and Tonqueen Merchant (through God's permission now arrived in the East Indies) the severall goods and merchandizes herein particularly mentioned vizt eight hundred and four bales qt. two thousand four hundred thirty seven broad cloths, thirty eight bales qt. seven hundred seventy peices stuffs, twenty four bales of cloth rashes qt. one hundred twenty rashes, Rushia hides seventeen bales qt. one hundred thirty seven bundles, clocks cases six qt. thirty three, sword blades nine chests qt. four hundred dozen, being of the vallue of thirty one thousand eight hundred ninety three pounds eleven shillings one penny prime cost and charges included also four thousand forty three small and two hundred eighteen great piggs[1] qt. five thousand four hundred twenty three hundred weightt seven pound of lead, also iron ordinance severally two peices qt. five hundred fifty eigh hundred weightt one quarter twenty three pound the first charge and cost thereof amount likewise to the summ of three thousand two hundred eighty five pound eleven pence, and did by bills of lading consign them to their Leiutenant Generall President and Councill at Surat. Now these presents witness that the said Sir John Gayer etc Councill have for divers good and valluable considerations thought fitt to make the following agreement with the said Callender d' Callandarr for and on the behalf of the said Right Honourable Company. That is to say first that within three dayes after landing the said goods and merchandizes into the said Company's godowns or warehouses at Surat and arrival of our advices concerning this contract the President and Councill there shall and will deliver unto the said Callendar d' Callendarr, Augau Peeree Callendar or their assignes all the said cloth, cloth rashes, stuffs, Rushia hides, clocks, sword blades, lead and iron ordnance, except such part thereof as is hereafter mentioned to be remaining on this island, and on board the Mocho Friggatt, all which goods remaining on this island are to be esteemed as delivered at the same time that the said Callendar d' Callandar Aga Peeree Callendar or their assignes shall receive the other goods by the Benjamin, he allowing the said Generall and Councill for the said cloth, cloth rashes, stuffs, Rushia hides, clocks and sword blades the summ of thirty one thousand eight hundred ninety three pounds eleven shillings and one peny and thirty per cent advance thereupon and also the summ of three thousand two hundred eighty five pound eleven pence for the lead and iron ordnance and fifty per cent advance thereupon, as also the summ of three thousand rupees advance upon the whole cargoes, besides the custom and charges that shall be disbursed and paid upon the landing and houseing the said goods at Surat.

Secondly That what sea damage shall have hapned to the aforesaid goods and merchandizes in the voyage, such allowance shall be made to the said Callendar d' Callendarr Auga Peeree Callendarr or their assignes for the same, as the above Generall or President and Councill at Surat shall judge reasonable, which if he thinks not fitt to accept of he is at liberty to leave the said damaged goods on the hands of the said Generall and Councill, and that the said Callendar d' Callendar Aga Peeree Callendarr or their assignes, shall after the said goods are landed and housed have the key of the warehouse where the same shall be put, security being first given by Aga Peree Callendar and the said Callendarr d' Callendarr and such other as shall be to the sattisfaction of the Generall, President and Councill for the payment and sattisfaction for the said goods according to agreement and in case the security they offer shall not be approved of, that then the said Callendarr d' Callendar Auga Peree Callendarr or their assignes are to have the goods delivered to them as they shall pay for them allowing discount for what money shall be paid before the time herein after agreed on or goods to that vallue, and shall have the use of the Right Honourable Company's godowns wherein the said goods shall be lodged for any convenient time not exceeding six months without payment of any rent for the same, the said Callendar d' Callendarr Auga Peeree Callendarr or their assignes bearing the risque of the said goods during that time. Item the said Callendar d' Callendarr doth for himself his executors and administrators covenant and agree to and with the said Generall and Councill by these presents that the said Callendarr d' Callendar Aga Peree Callendar or their assignes shall and will within three dayes after the landing and houseing of the said goods at Surat, and Augau Peeree Callendarr's receipt of the forementioned advices accept and receive the same and pay and allow for the same the said severall summs before mentioned and agreed to be by him paid, which said payment is to be made in money at the rate of eight rupees and a half per pound sterling in manner and forme following, that is to say one third part of the whole vallue of the goods within two months after landing the same at Surat, one other third part within two months then next ensueing, and the other third part within two months next following. And in case the Generall President and Councill shall judge it more for the Right Honourable Company's advantage to accept of indico, callicoes, druggs or other goods instead of money in sattisfaction for the whole or any part of the said goods, then the said Callendarr d' Callendar Agau Peree Callendarr or their assignes shall deliver such goods at the prime cost they stand them in, time enough to lade them upon the Right Honourable Company's first returning shipping for England and that the said goods shall be as cheap or cheaper, and better in their kind then any other goods of the same sort, which the said Company's servants can purchase or buy of any other person or persons whatsoever. Provided always that if it shall happen that the ship Benjamin shall not arrive at Surat and deliver her goods on shoar before the last day of October next, then it is agreed that the said Callendarr d' Callendar Aga Peeree Callendarr or their assignes shall be at liberty to accept or refuse the said goods as shall seem best to them, any thing herein contained to the contrary notwithstanding. And further 'tis agreed by the parties to these presents that if shall happen that the ship Mocho Friggat gone to Persia, on board which are one thousand six hundred sixty five small piggs of lead part of the forementioned goods and merchandizes shall not arrive at Surat river's mouth before the said Callendarr d' Callendar shall have sold all the other lead which came by ships Thomas Benjamin and Tonqueen and that any ships shall in the mean time arrive from England with any quantity of lead, that then the said Callender d' Callendarr,

Auga Peree Callandar or assignes shall be at liberty to accept or refuse the abovesaid one thousand six hundred sixty five piggs of lead and in case they shall accept them them they shall be allowed such longer time for the payment of the money for the same as shall intervene between the last sale thereof which he or they shall have made, and the arrivall of the said ship Mocho Friggat over and above the time herein before limmitted and agreed upon by the said Generall and Councill and Callendar d' Callendarr. And whereas there is now remaining in this fort two thousand twenty five piggs of lead and twenty one bales of cloth and stuffs and nine chests of sword blades part of the goods before mentioned, the said Generall and Councill do covenant and promise to deliver the same to the said Callendarr d' Callendar, Aga Peree Callendar or assignes upon demand, and further if the said Callendar d' Callendar Auga Peree Callendar or assignes shall have occasion to transport the same to Surat that then the said goods shall be transported thither at the sole rescoe and charge of the said Right Honourable Company provided also that if the Generall and Councill shall have occasion for or think fitt to reserve any small quantity of the forementioned goods for presents on the Right Honourable Company's account that then it shall and may be lawfull to and for the said Generall and Councill to reserve three or four bales thereof as they shall think fitt, onely allowing to the said Callender d' Callendar Aga Peeree Callendar or their assignes the same price which he has agreed to pay for the same. And lastly 'tis agreed that although the President and Council at Surat shall not approve of such security as Aga Peree Callendarr shall offer, nevertheless the said Aga Peree Callendarr shall (as soone as he has received the said goods) have the keys of the godowns or warehouses (where the same shall be lodged) delivered into his hands and custody, any thing before specifyed to the contrary in anywise notwithstanding. In wittness etc

Signed sealed and delivered in the presence of
[No names appear on the copy agreement]

[1] pig: oblong mass of iron from the smelting-furnace

213

Be it known unto the Calendar Goodas Mooratt Marcar Gregore and Hoan that whereas you understand the meaning of the Right Honourable Company's letter so concering these stuffs and cloth which they have sent you to sell that they must be sold all together it is not so. The Company's orders is so that you can sell it all together and if you will you can sell it by lettle and lettle to as many chapmen as comes and that where as the Company writt that it should be presently sold the meaning of that is that if it may be presently sold it's so much the better but if not you may be as long a selling it as you pleas till it may be all sold. When you come you are to make up the price but as for gathering together and receiving the mony that's none of your buysness that our broker knows best how most proffitable and when to receive the money all your buysness is to sett the price.

Ispahaun September 9th 1695

214
CAPTAIN BENJAMIN BRANGWIN, THOMAS MAJOR, JAMES BRUCE AND JAMES RAWLINGS AT ISFAHAN TO ARMENIAN MERCHANTS
9 SEPTEMBER 1695
E/3/51 FF. 179-180

Whereas you delivered us a paper without date or your signing but sufficient testimony present as the reverend father Ely that it was writt by Coja Mercara Surhad and read to Coja Gogas Calentar and Coja Gregory Coldedente who agreeing to it the contents whereof are not conformable to the Right Honourable Company's desire to you in their's of the 3d January 1693/4 and 30th March 1694 according to the best of our understanding where they not only desire but endeavour to perswade a speedy sale of the woolen manufacture consigned you per the ships Nassau and Mary but because we cannot comply with that your paper for our Right Honourable masters' interest we have given you an other paper with this our opinion of the Right Honourable intent and meaning in their's of the 3d January 1693/4 which we hope will perswade you to a speedy sale of the Right Honourable Company's cloth now in your power to sell and we shall esteem ourselves

Your humble servants

B Brangwin
T Major
J Bruce
J Raulins

To   Coja Moratt Surad
      Coja Mercara Surad
      Coja Cogar Calender
      Coja Gregory Coldarent
      Coja Hoan Coldarent

Dated Ispahaun September 9th 1695

    We the subscribers do declare according to the best of our knowledge
and judgement, that the true intent and meaning of that paragraph (of the
Right Honourable Company's letter to the 5 Armenian gentlemen bearing date
the 3d January 1693/4,) which says that we desire that this cloth may be sold
immediately, as soon as comes to Ispahaun, the words imply or mean, that
they desire you to sell it speedily, and not to lett it lye in their warehouses and
rot, which will cause them to be great loosers by it, and do not confine you to
sell it all at one time, or in one bargain, or to one man, but so as your
discretion shall direct you, provided that the sale of one part, be not an
hindrance to the speedy sale of the rest, and that you leave it not unsold so
long in their warehouses, to become rotten, to their great detriment. Witness
our hands dated in Ispahaun
September the 9th 1695

[unsigned]

215

COMPANY IN LONDON TO SURAT
13 SEPTEMBER 1695
E/3/92 EXTRACT FROM FF. 220V-221, 222V-223, 223V

    As to a settlement in the Naigue of Moodera country, you do well
enough to propose it, but we will not run upon it hastily. All such new
proposalls at first appear with fair faces, and sometimes serve our servants turn
for a trip or two at first, but end with the Companye's great loss. Multan and
Scindy are brave provinces for many sorts of extraordinary good and cheap
commodities, but whenever the Company shalbe induced to settle factoryes
in those provinces, or any other way to arrive at a trade in them, otherwise
then by the Armenians, they shall infallibly come off with great loss. And
upon this occasion, we must repeat our former injunction to you, never to
attempt to make any new settlement, without our positive order. Patta or
Tatty in Scindy we know is a great place of trade, but there is not water enough
for our Europe ships, and to keep small ships in the country we have too
much experienced, doth but devour our stock, and wast our stores, by the
extream profuseness and neglect of your East India management.
    We cannot at all understand, nor Coja Panous himself, what you mean
by your following words vizt. you wish it had been incerted in the contract

they were to be at all charges, untill the goods were in our warehouses, and such the contract is, and the meaning thereof so acknowledged to by Coja Panous himselfe, so that if Aga Perir hath not paid you all he should according to such a meaning, you must demand it of him, and he will pay you by his father's order.

We would have you not to fail at any time of keeping one of our youths in Aga Perir's house to learn the Armenian and Persian languages, as Mr Bruce and with greater speed and effect, then we can hope any other will, by whom we find by his knowledge in the tongues, very good effects in our affairs in Persia already.

Coja Panous Calendar informing us by his enclosed representacion that in the year 1694, he having bought the ship Thomas's goods according to contract it was therein specifyed, that if his son Aga Perir Calendar should deliver any goods proper for England, our factors should allow him the same price they gave to others, but when he had loaden a quantity of coffee and pepper on our ships, President Annesley would allow him but 5 rupees for his pepper and 12 rupees for his coffee, though he gave the Banians 6 rupees $^3/_4$ for the pepper and 12 rupees $^5/_8$ for the coffee they sold, we would therefore have our Generall Sir John Gayer upon a strict inquiry into the truth of the matter of fact to do Aga Perir justice, giving us an account of the whole transaction.

We have reposed a great trust in our Armenian friends at Ispahaun, and have reason to believe, we shall find them very faithfull to our interest, as we hope you will also experience Aga Perir Calendar to be in those severall agreements made here with his father relating to his management at Surratt of which we have had some account already and hope to hear more particularly by our next shipping from our good Generall, that he has approved himself firm to our interest, which if our Generall shall find, we would have him make the said Aga Perir such a small handsom present, as he shall think fitt, and therewith the four cheeses you will receive on the Scepter.

216

CAPTAIN BENJAMIN BRANGWIN, THOMAS MAJOR, JAMES BRUCE AND JAMES RAWLINGS AT ISFAHAN TO COMPANY IN LONDON
14 SEPTEMBER 1695
E/3/51 FF. 187-190V

Our last to your Honours was of the 6th August per via Alepo in which wee gave butt an imperfect account of your Honours' affaires in these parts begging your Honours' patience untill our next for a full and ample satisfaction therein and now are forced to desire the same because of the necessity of a quick dispatch to acquaint your Honours of the unhappy misfortune your Honours have mett with in employing such of the Armenian nation who have proved ungratefull and att last after long and tedious consultations with them and all the arguments and perswasions that wee could use, they have layd down and denyed acting any further in that great affair comitted by your Honours to their management, the sale of woolen manufactory which came per ships Nassaw and Mary as your Honours will perceive by their letter signed by four of them inclosed, and a coppy that wee now send your Honours of whatt they intended to have sent some dayes past.

2 This letter that they intended to have sent had gone butt upon our seeing of itt we argued as well the incivillity as the unreasonableness of it as allso the severall contradictions and barefaced untruths that were there laid down whereby they endeavoured to perswade your Honours into a false opinion not only of their abilityes but of all the kingdom of Persia for that those 5 persons to whom this merchandize was consigned are able to buy three times as much with their own ready mony is apparent to all Julpha. And that the kingdom of Persia is able to consume twice as much per annum is allowed by all Persians on the place. Wee told them by way of perswasion that it was uncivill to treat our Right Honourable Masters with such rough language as the words of their intended letter whereas your Honours' letter was with so much civility and true friendship.

That it was unreasonable for them to lay down and desist acting in an affair of so great concerne when they had so long with fair pretences endeavoured to perswade us that they would with all fidelity care and diligence performe our masters' business and especially when they knew that none of us nor any in Persia had power to dispose of it if they denyed acting therein and that it must lye unsold as they well knew and by their letter prove untill the Right Honourable Company should be acquainted with itt and that trust reposed in them be put into the hands of others.

That it was a contradiction to say it could not be sold in less than 4 or 5 yeares and presently after in the same letter to tell your Honours that when that letter was gone they would doe their utmost for a speedy sale thereof, first declaring itt an imposibillity and yett say they will endeavour to performe that which they allow to be impossible.

That itt was notoriously false to say that these goods were not in as much request as formerly and that such a quantity could not be sold in this place and that they could not be turned into mony in less than four or five yeares and bringing that instance of Moola our broker's not having received the money for the Modena's cloth to this day, who might have had the mony the same hour he sold the cloth allowing the abatement mentioned by them, but then having more mony than he knew how to employ lett itt remain in the buyer's hand att an extraordinary interest which he could gett no where else, part of itt remaines to this day to his great satisfaction and profitt. Thatt was the cause he advanced the money presently, could he have gained nothing by laing down the mony he would have been hanged ere he would have disbursed six pence.

3 These reasons being given they tooke back the letter and carried it to a Carmellitan fryar a perticular friend of the family of the Surhads and gott it by

him putt into the method and language as they have now sent it your Honours and brought it to us a second time but then sealed not letting us see what allterations or additions they had made but our friendly correspondence with the said padree privately procured us a coppy of itt and we find little difference in the substance only in the modelling and civill language which now it hath and before it had not. After wee had received this letter sealed to forward to your Honours and found they were resolved to lay down this business wee were very much concerned to see all your Honours' expectations crossed, and kept the letter some few dayes and were resolved to try once more if by our endeavours and sollicitations we could perswade them to an allteration of their mind wherefore wee alleadged to them the great loss and dettriment that would accrue to your Honours under these following heads.

1st That if this cloth were not soon disposed of by them but must continue the whole or any part of 4 or 5 years in your Honours' goedownes it would be all rotten or if should remaine untill your Honours were acquainted with it and another order come to them or any person else for the disposall of itt, it might reasonably be expected that a great part of it must of necessity perish and be worth little or nothing, they knowing how it was not only touched with the worm but a great deale of itt damged by the sea and how great a loss this would be to your Honours they could easily judge.

2d The disapointment your Honours would meet with in the great designe your Honours have of continueing a considerable trade to these parts by annually sending ships from Europe with more of the same manufacture and how Panous Callendar assured your Honours it would sell now, and if more should come on the back of this before sold how great damage it would be to your Honours.

3d Your Honours' disapointment of your affaires att Suratt having long expected the returnes there and to thatt intent the Generall had dispatched the Mocha Frigatt from Bombay for the better securing the concernes which ship arrived Gomroone about the 12 of August last.

4th The considerable loss that attended your Honours being out of your mony so long and such a quantity of cloth to lye dead.

5th The necessity wee had here in Ispahawn for mony to carry on our business your Honours supposing the cloth would have been quickly sold.

4 These heads were laid down plainly unto them as your Honours' perticular friends and in whom your Honours had confided as wee find by your generall by the Mocha Frigott for the withdrawing the cloth and silk trade from Alepo to these parts and so to Europe by the long seas, though of that wee mentioned nothing to them not knowing whether your Honours were willing they should know it. Wee enlarged on these head with all inducing and perswasive arguments that our weak capacityes could furnish us with but found it was impossible to wash the blackmore white for they told us in sundry discourses and att sundry times, that it was against their interest, and as they have plainly told your Honours in their letter that they are aged and ingaged in

another course of trade which no benefitt your Honours can propose or have proposed can induce them to forsake.

5 We not being satisfyed but continually tormented to think that this cloth of so vast a concerne must remaine here in the warehouses and suffer great and unavoidable damage by these gentlemen's desisting to endeavour to sell it and that wee should be on the place and see it and have no power to dispose of it or skill to allter these gentlemen's resolutions taken to your Honours' great loss and disapointement, your Honours being positive in your 6th paragraph of your generall to Persia of the 3d of January 1693/4 that this cloth be not disposed of to any but these 5 gentlemen or whom they should sell it to and the Agent of Gomroon more restrictive in the 1st paragraff of our instructions dated the 23d of March 1694/5 forbidding us to intermeddle with the sale thereof.

6 We thought of another expedient to try if these gentlemen would lend their assistance to the speedy sale of these goods and flattered ourselves if any thing would ingage them this would to the speedy sale of the whole att once. Wee writt them another letter Captain Brangwin being ill of a fever ague and flux and that which induced us to write rather than discourse them longer on this subject, was that wee might have an answer in writing for wee had perceived they had not only equivocated in their words but sometimes seem to deny that ever they said so.

The letter wee have here inclosed. Now wee had perswaded the Calentar Coja Googas Callendar to this designe and Captain Brangwin engaged himself in it for no other intent or interest but that a finall end might be putt to this business and all the cloth disposed of att once butt it tooke no more effect than the rest of our prementioned arguments though a very easy and probable way for the accomplishing our desire. For they would give us no answer in writing but came and discoursed us telling us that the Callentar and the Captain were great merchants and could take so much but for their parts they were poor and unable to undertake so heavy a burden though they knew and we told them that both the family of the Surhads and Coldarents were able to buy twice as much as the whole with their own proper estates and that wee would take either of their single words for the whole. To which they would give us no answer but told us they could not doe this business according to the Right Honourable Company's orders who had declared to them in their letter that they must dispose of this cloth all att once which they had writt your Honours was impossible but if wee would give them under our hands that the true intent and meaning of the words of your Honours' letter to them of the 3d of January 1693/4 were according to a note which they would write for us to sign that then they would still endeavour to sell it as chapmen came to buy it. Coja Mercara Surhad immediately writt the note in Armenians and we gott it translated into English which wee have allso herewith sent which when wee saw was not according to the true intent and meaning of your Honours' letter to them in which you press them to a speedy sale immediately as soon as the cloth came to Spahawn, and in your generall prementioned to Persia in the 3d paragraph urge the necessity of a quick sale here for that your Honours have been forced to sell part of what you usually sent to India gave away the rest or permitt it to be eat up with the white ants or other insects and in the 6th paragraph that wee should observe your design was to make a cleare and quick dispatch of the sale of these goods. Now considering these your orders wee thought it not in our power to give them under our hands that they might sell these goods in as long time as they pleased when wee knew they had declared to your Honours that they could not be turned into mony in 4 or 5 yeares and by that time wee knew many of them would be perished by the worm etc damages.

Moreover we haveing some intimation of these gentlemen's design to ask us whither we could give them any new orders sometime before, wee wrote to Agent Gladman etc to know how they would direct in itt who in their answer to us of the 9th of August past in the 2d paragraph say these words.

In our opinion the 5 friends show themselves very weak in thinking we can contradict the Right Honourable Company's orders and give others because the cloth cannot be disposed of att once. Those that they have are large and ample enough did they design to goe on briskly in this perticular. If the bent of their minds be otherwise the Right Honourable Company are like to be finely served. Wee beleive they have a desire to resign up the consignment. If they won't obey the Right Honourable Company how can it be expected wee should be observed.

Wherefore we gave them a note under our hands as wee understood your Honours' meaning the which they acquainted us the next day they liked not or was not sufficient for unless we could give them a note according to what they writt they continued of the same mind and desired their letter might be sent and they would concern themselves no farther in thatt affair. Wherefore wee dispatch these by express with a packet from India which came by the Mocha Frigott to acquaint your Honours of these their resolutions notwithstanding all our endeavours if our lives had laid att stake and hope your Honours will beleive that wee have used our uttmost skill and judgement for the better carrying on your Honours' designs, and excuse us if have acted anything amiss. We shall forward this relation to the Agent and Generall and if have any further orders from either shall act according to them, otherwise we must of necessity waite your Honours' which we hope will be as speedy as possible. Wee can only att present farther advise your Honours that the Armenian nation or merchants of Julpha were able to give a greate stroake to the withdrawing the trade from Alepo as your Honours intimate in yours per the Mocha Frigatt were itt their interest or were they willing especially such persons as are the Right Honourable Company's friends and would resolutely sett about itt with hopes of a future benefitt, one of which we have found Coja Googas Calendar, butt the family of the Surhads and Coldarents your Honours' enemyes in this affair being the most concerned in the Europe trade by way of Alepo of any merchants in Julpha and are leading men very rich especially the Surhads but the most positive perverse and crossgraind gentlemen in any thing they are sett against which we find they are against your Honours' furnishing this markett with the woolen manufacture, they having sold much of their own cloth since the arrivall of your Honours' which they bought or trucked for Indian commodityes att Tavris. The common saying in Julpha is that Mercara Surhad seldom or never setts his hand to any business with design to doe good to any body but himself, but if he can to confound it, and we cannot give your Honours the satisfaction who of the Armenians are here that are willing to undertake this greate affair. Wee shall name one whom wee know to be as able and knowing as any man in Julpha and very willing who is not engaged in the Turky trade which is Auga Doud whom with Agent Gladman's leave wee have readmitted to your Honours' service because wee could doe nothing in Spahawn without him and the 5 Armenians gave it their opinion that had Auga Doud been our linguist all the while wee have been in Spahaun the cloth would have been in a much more readyness and nearer if not alltogether sold ere now. But your Honours have no good opinion of him. 'Tis true he may be one who aimes att getting mony, itt may be more than he ought, in your Honours' service but your Honours may be assured no person in Persia is able to performe your business like him and wee are really perswaded by what we have discoused him he values not all Julpha provided he can effect anything which may oblige your Honours he being very much dissatisfyed about what Agent Gladman hath writt against him and as he saith without ever giving him any reason or proving anything against him to any other person. Wee know butt [?one] more who is Hoannes Jamallents who is old but hath an ingenious son who is brisk in his trade. We would give your Honours an account of the disinterest the Armenians think the subversion of the Turky trade will bring upon them butt must referre untill send the coppys of this per Suratt ships with thatt addition and whatt else wee can prepare for your Honours' perusall.

217

CAPTAIN BENJAMIN BRANGWIN, THOMAS MAJOR, JAMES BRUCE AND JAMES RAWLINGS AT ISFAHAN TO COMPANY IN LONDON
30 SEPTEMBER 1695
E/3/51 EXTRACT FROM FF. 200V-201

The phirmaunds translated into English but the Persian language is so criticall that wee cannot find a man that can put them into true Armenians as yett. Coja Panous Callandar's son was about some of them but could not performe it to purpose since could not find a man that was capable but are looking out for a good scrivan the Dutch having gott our old one which was turned away when we had little business such another not to be found.

We shall consult the Armenians in all wee doe because it is your Honours' order as have done nothing hitherto without their advice. A new broker is gone to Carmania by their orders and we hope he will make a good investment. He never could have a better opportunity for the Dutch have nobody there which they will next yeare we understand.

218

SIR JOHN GAYER AT BOMBAY TO SURAT
29 OCTOBER 1695
E/3/51 EXTRACT FROM F. 232V

By our contract with Callender de Callender wee were to deliver him the goods by the last of October, or elce he was at libertye to refuse his bargain. This time through what is fallen out, in probabillity will be elapsed ere they can be delivered, therefore you must imediately know of Augau Peere whether he will stand to his bargain or no, that you may be at a certainty, for wee know not how soon our expected shipping may fall in with goods of the same kind.

It's not our opinion that he will have any thoughts of refusing, seeing none of our ships are arrived, but should he do so, advise us by the Munchua.

219

SAMUEL ANNESLEY AND EPHRAIM BENDALL AT SURAT TO BOMBAY
12 NOVEMBER 1695
E/3/51 EXTRACT FROM FF. 246-248

Augau Peree has consented to stand by his bargain for the three ships' cargoes though the time for the delivery thereof to him be elapsed and notwithstanding the goods should be hindered from being landed or afterwards be detained by the Governor till our trobles are cleared and though in the interim other ships should come from Europe with the same goods and when he has any of the goods delivered into his possession that may inable him to send your Excellency rupees 20000 he will doe it.

Since you have received no letters from Court we [give] your Excellency the following account ... which we turned into English as we could from the Persian etc as follows.

The Siddee's vukkel at Court to his vukkell at Surat

"The letters from the port of Surat arrived that the English had robbed the ship Gunsway from which news the King was very angry. An order was issued out that a phirman should be sent Siddee Yacood Caune to take Bombay and put the English in Surat in irons and what money was plundered from the ship to be taken from them and restored to the owners. In the juncture of which time the English vukkell was there and petitioned the King that if it was his command, the Generall would come to court and the Chief of Surat would come before him and that the English for 100 years had drove a trade in his country and never did any such thing."

The combinacion against us is very strong so that none of these countrey people dare appear in our cause though they know our innocence. Hodeje Zaied confest he desired to come to us a seldome as possible because of the rabble and discontenting thereby the merchants. Augau Peree is shy of our servants comeing nere his house, and sending to him for a copy of Issa Cooley's letter by one of them almost scard him out of his wits, being afraid we designed as he said to bring him into the same condition with our selves.

We desire what letters your Excellency shall hereafter send us be under Hodje Zaied's covert, Augau Peree being very timerous and that you would be pleased to write him a complemental letter to be our vukkeel, being a person most fitted for it.

220
COUNCIL AT ISFAHAN TO THE FIVE ARMENIAN MERCHANTS AT JULFA
23 NOVEMBER 1695
E/3/51 FF. 261-262

To   Coja Morad Surhad
      Coja Mercara Surhad
      Coja Gogas Calendar
      Coja Gregore Colderents
      Coja Hoan Colderents

Gentlemen

Our Right Honourable masters the East India Company were pleased out of a candid opinion they had of your integrity to honour you with the consignment of that great quantity of broad cloth and stuffs which is in our factories here at Ispahaun and Shyraz the which you were pleased to refuse, as appears by your letter of the 12th of August to our Right Honourable masters confirmed by your answer sent us by Gregore Colderente by word of mouth the 10th September viz that unless we would sign the note writt the day before by Coja Mercara Surhad you could not further concern yourselves in this business. We not mention how unkind you were in so doing haveing alledged it often to your faces, to which you could give us no reasonable answer.

What we come now to desire is that though you would do the Right Honourable Company no good (as you were pleased to say if the cloth must rot let it rot in the Company house) that you will do them no harm, for seeing we have ventured to run the hazard of breaking our masters' orders rather than lett the cloth lye and rott, about to dispose of it we may in justice and honesty expect you will not go about to hinder them that are willing to buy it.

Some intimations we have had of your proceedings, how you have been buzzing strange stories in the ears of the buyers, of what black mountains will fall upon them and theire children if they buy any part of this cloth of us, and that you wonder we shauld pretend to sell it now, when we should not do it when we would not do it when you advised us to it, and that how we can suppose to send (what we cannot sell here) to Tabries Erivan Arzaroon etc places of the kingdom of Persia where cloth usually sells. We cannot sit still here in Ispahaun and hear these things and be silent, our duty to God and our masters obligeth us to acquaint you of these things to disswade you from proceeding further in such base actions, as you are Christians be not so shamelessly unjust, as to prejudice them that have dealt so kindly by you and your nation in general, and make not them just enemies, which have and are so willing to be serviceable to you.

Have they never done you nor yours no kindness, should you deny it you would deny your own handwriteing or do you not value their friendship that you should endeavour to oppose their interest and designs. We stand amazed to see you go on and persist in such most abominable courses of ingratitude. Have you no consideration of the future, what do you think the Right Honourable Company will think of you whom they have been pleased to term the great and worthy mer-chants of Julpha. They cannot but alter their opinion when they have those things in their answers to ours, who must of necessity acquaint them of it stile you the most pernicious enemies of the English nation.

We could heartily wish you would give us something in an answer to this. If you do not this will demonstrate to our Right Honourable masters and the whole world, that we have discharged our dutys and your silence will give us to understand that you are guilty.

Pray take it not amiss for we do this by way of advice as friends and as one Christian ought to admonish another when seeth his neighbour commit errors worthy of admonition as we should be willing to receive the same from you who are

Your loving friends to serve you what lyes in our powers
[unsigned]

Ispahaun 23d November 1695

221

SIR JOHN GAYER, WILLIAM AISLABIE AND BENJAMIN STACEY AT BOMBAY
TO GOMBROON
4 DECEMBER 1695
E/3/51 EXTRACT FROM FF. 274-275

Mulcand the broker that Aveatick Callendar mentions in his letter will as he writes lett you have to the amount of 5 or 6000 tomands. At this distance wee can see no reason why you should not take it of him before any other, seeing he offers it, and is a person recommended by said Callendar so duely quallified to serve the Right Honourable Company as a broker, neither can wee see any reason why you should not entertain him in the Company's service, for by what we can perceive by what Aveatick Callendar writes in his letter to the Agent, he doth sincerely endeavour to promote the Company's interest and wee have not found but that all of the family do so, and it's certainly their interest so to do, but you and Captain Brangwin being on the place, if you find Mulcand not duly quallified, must make choice of such a one as is.

The 5 Armenians whome our Right Honourable masters intrusted with the sale of the cargoes of the Nassau and Mary wee would not have you be rash in censuring of them. They will undoubtedly preferr their owne interest to any other, and it's highly probable that their having long used the Alleppo trade do think themselves at present injured by our masters sending out such quantity of woollen maunfactory, fearing it will spoile their old beloved merchandize at the forementioned place, as it certainly will. This is one reason that at present makes them cold in the Company's business, and it may be puts them on doing that which may obstruct it. A 2d reason is the largness of the quantity of the cloth which hitherto they have not been accustomed to, and so feare they shall miscarry in the sale thereof. A 3d reason is the greatness of the price the cloth is invoiced at probably had not been so high had our masters thought the ships would not have had so long a passage ere any could have come there by way of Alleppo. A 4th thing these persons stumble at is the dearness of silk. All these put together they find themselves under such discouragement as they desier nothing more than to slip their neks out of the colar. Now for the 1st of these when the Armenians find, (notwithstanding the discouragment our masters meet with) that they will continue trade in Persia as they must do, being obliged to send out so much of the maunfacture of the nacion yearly, they will be past all hopes of maintaining their Alleppo trade which will make them resigne it, as Aveatick Callendar observes they have in a great measure already done and will consequently put them on embracing this of our masters and a little time will innure them to the sale of so large a quantity of goods, especially if the consumption is so great as Captain Brangwing writes. For the third our masters must sell at that price the markett will afford, and not lett their cloth lye and rot in warehouse and for the fourth which is the dearness of silk they must also buy at the markett price if they will trade in that commodity, and we cannot well conceive how the cloth and silk trade can be seperated, and the silk we suppose will be carryed much cheaper to Bunder than to Alleppo though the frieght to England will be much dearer from India than from Alleppo. Wherefore we would not have you neglect or desert the above persons but make what use of them you can, or such of them as will concerne themselves in the Company's affairs. Especially considering Captain Brangwing writes in his to them that Coja Gogas Callendar is wholly inclined and hath been all along to promote the Company's interest, but if any of these gentlemen or all of them should refuse to be concerned in the sale of the cloth, you must not therefore lett it lye and rott, but endeavour to sell all as soon as possibly at the best rate you can, and for a broker to assist you herein we cannot (as before observed) at this distance think of a better that him nominated by Aveatick Callendar.

Wee cannot give any advice about the price of silk at what rates you should take it at, but seeing as Aveatick Callendar writes the Agent that the merchants have ordered their silk should not be carried to Alleppo, we hope it will not prove so dear as expected, but should it prove as dear as at Alleppo twil be better if necessity requires, to take at that price than to lett the cloth be spoilt for want of a markett, but in this we would have you advise with the above or such of them as will concerne themselves according to our masters' orders and with Aveatick Callendar to whome we have caused his brother now with us to write to encourage him to your assistance.

222

CAPTAIN BENJAMIN BRANGWIN, THOMAS MAJOR, JAMES BRUCE AND
JAMES RAWLINGS AT ISFAHAN TO COMPANY IN LONDON
18 DECEMBER 1695
E/3/51 EXTRACT FROM FF. 288-290V

Four of the five gentlemen that your Honours were pleased to intrust with sundry others that are the great traders to Europe by way of Aleppo combined together by all means immaginable to hinder us, both from selling here and sending to other places which your Honours will plainly perceive by a letter which we thought fitt to send the 5 gentlemen in which we declared them guilty of what therein was alledged against them unless they answered itt and vindicated themselves which they did not and so were condemned by their own silence copy of which letter is herewith.

Wee could write your Honours many things relateing to their bace actions and of the many tricks and unjust means they have used to oppose your Honours' designes but must att present only name four of them, our diary being full with descriptions of the dayly prejudices they have done to your Honours in this affair.

1st Their designing never to permitt this cloth to be sold if they could help it which plainly appeares by a strategem Coja Mercara invented when the newes of the cloth's arrivall att Gomroon first came to this place. Vizt for as soon as the 5 gentlemen received your Honours' letter per ship Mary and Nassau together with Agent Gladman's of the arrivall of the broad cloth and stuffs and that the Agent would send it up speedily to this place, Coja Mercara declares to all people both in Spahawn and Julpha that as soon as the cloth etc came here it should be disposed of lett the price be never so low which put the merchants of Julpha into such a consternation that they knew not what to doe, wherefore they all immediately dispatched away shotters to their vackeells or factors that were att Aleppo Tavris etc places with orders very strict that upon no account whatsomeever they should buy any cloth and in case they had before these orders came, to dispose of it again att any rate and return their money to Spahawn in chequeens, for that they should never be able to sell a piece cloth after the arrivall of such a quantity as belonged to your Honours. When Coja Mercara was sattisfyed thatt all the principall merchants had given the above orders and saw his project take he immediately wrote to all his own vackeels att Aleppo Tavris etc giving them orders to buy whatever cloth they could gett and bring it into the kingdom of Persia and dispose of it to the severall places that could vend it and bring a good quantity to Ispahaun assureing them that none of the English cloth should be sold in 4 or 5 yeares if ever, by which it is reported he got considerable a great quantity of his cloth was brought to Ispahaun and which all sold and severall others upon his doing of it did the same.

2 If ever they permitted this cloth to be sold it should be in so long time as that your Honours' design of sending more should be frustrated to prove which we think there needs no more than what they have given your Honours under their own hands in saying it could not be sold under four or five yeares.

3 That when they did dispose of it it should be att such a low rate whither to others or by taking it themselves that your Honours should never be encouraged to send more and that plainly appears by the plott that Coja Gregore Coldarents laid in the beginning vizt

When it was proposed by some of the 5 gentlemen that it was highly necessary to answer your Honours' first letter and give a plain answer that they could not serve your Honours in this affair, Coja Gregore Coldarents said no first lett the cloth come and if your Honours' orders would not permitt them to take the cloth att 20 shahees per yard or so cheap as that they could gett considerable att least 50 per cent then said he lett itt lye unsold butt in case we can make, said he, such a benefitt why should we refuse it. To confirm and prove the whole we cannot but give your Honours the following relation of a hott dispute that hapned on the 29th November last att the reading the inclosed letter which wee sent to the 5 Armenians between the 2 Surhads and

Coldarents of the one party and Mr Aveatik Callendar on the other party, vizt Coja Moratt Surhad and Coja Gregore Coldarents being assembled att the Calentar's house with Coja Mercara Surhad and Mr Aveatik Callendar they opened our foresaid letter which as soon as they had read Coja Gregore Coldarents began to quarrell with Mr Aveatik Callendar saying thatt he had gone to the English house and informed the English Captain etc that they had been endeavouring to hinder the sale of the broad cloth and stuffs after which they said that his father was worse than a devill for that the devill would not lay so heavy a burden on men's shoulders as he had done. To which Aveatik answered that though they thought it so heavy a burthen to sell the Right Honourable Company's cloth they had sold no small quantity of their owne since that came there haveing come into the citty 3000 pieces of broadcloth and all sold and 2000 pieces more would be sold this winter in Spahawn alone and if 5000 pieces could be expended in Spahawn three times as much might be sold to people that carried it to all other parts of the country. To which they all answered they were much obliged to his father and him for holding their hands before the sun that nobody might see any light but the Company and they allso said that Mr Aveatik had made storye of his own invention and told the English Captain etc that they had divided the cloth into 32 parts and that he knew people that would take off $^{24}/_{32}$th parts of the whole, the which Aveatik owned, he had told the English so and seeing they forced him to it he would gett the merchants which would have taken so much of itt to wittness itt under their hands, att which they were angry and quarrellsome words arose they saying that now his father had advised the Company to send so much cloth and now the English Captain etc could not sell it endeavoured to lay the blame on them to which Aveatik answered that it was to no purpose for them to goe about and lay the blame on others as if they were blameless for that neither he nor his father nor the English Captain etc had ever done anything in this business butt what they could vindicate and thatt his father in adviseing the Company to send so much cloth here yearly had proposed a very beneficiall trade for that so much cloth and more might be vended here yearly and in what the Captain or he himself had said that this cloth might all have been sold before now they had spoke the truth and could prove it.

Wee meeting with such obstructions and impediments from those that your Honours have relyed on as trusty friends wee cannot but give your Honours such true accounts thereof as the foregoing and hope by that meanes shall remain blameless. We have spent some time in preparing our cloth for sight having according to the shopkeepers' desires divided the fine cloth into head, belly, and foot and auroras[1] the same which they have seen and desired we would doe the same by the reds, greens and jams. Which accordingly wee did and on the 28th they saw all and were satisfyed teling us that they would call a consultation of their brethren and in a day or two treat about a price.

On the 3d instant about 14 of them came and said they were resolved to treate for the whole but desired longer time. We told them to talk of the time would be of no consequence untill came somewhat near a price or saw that there was a likelyhood of agreement. Wherefore we discoursed about the price and soon found that they had received instructions from the great Armenians of Julpha the traders to Aleppo for the most they offered was very little above prime cost in England and they required 3 years time to pay the mony in deducting 1 per cent per mensem for whatever mony they should pay in before the 3 years were expired which was 36 per cent to be abated for present mony. The which wee nott agreeing to they departed and said they would consider of itt and in two dayes give their finall answer which we waited but they not coming according to promis we sent them word we would not loose more time. Upon which they would have made other propositions to have held us farther in suspense untill they had disposed of whatt cloth they had by them which they had bought of Coja Mercara Surhad etc and untill the best time of sale was past which we perceiving endeavoured to prevent and to their great damage we found out a means to hinder them from selling so spedily as they expected. Viztt on the 11 instant we with the advice and assistance of Coja Aveatik Callandar procured one Coja Nooree a vackeell of Coja Panous Callenderr who hath been in England and speakes good English and wee think understands cloth well. Wee intrusted him with 65 pieces of cloth and 47 pieces of stuffs and ordered him to sett up a shop in the caravansera and undersell all the shopkeepers which he hath begun though not without a great deale of trouble all Julpha allmost opposing it especially the traders to Alepo and all the Armenian shopkeepers butt wee having ordered him to tell them that in case they hindered him in the least measure we would complain to the government for seeing we had sold so much cloth to him we could not expect our mony unless he disposed of it and that he was as free an Armenian and had as great a liberty to trade as any of them and that we would vindicate him.

He hath disposed of some small matter to advantage and hope not only by his meanes to dispose of a greater quantity this winter but to know the reall value of all sorts of cloth whereby to govern our selves in the sale of the rest to merchants that carry itt from hence to severall parts of Persia.

Wee have treated with severall merchants for small parcells but have not disposed of any yett they not coming to our price one of which we are bound to mention. Viztt the 27th November we sent for Coja Gregore Coldarents one of the 5 gentlemen who coming we acquainted him that we had adventured to breake our Right Honourable masters' orders and were endeavouring to dispose of the cloth rather than see them suffer such an unaccountable loss seing they were pleased to refuse doing our masters such a kindness and because we were formerly desirous of buying those hundred bales which were att Shiraz and the other gentlemen would not sell him them we thought fitt to make him the first profer of them before we sent any body to dispose of them. To which he answered that he had severall reasons for buying them att that time which would not be of validitty now.

1st That then it was the best of the yeare for buying and selling of broadcloth and if he had bought it then, he might have had the product of it in cash long before now.

2dly That then there had little or no cloth come whereas now the markett was satisfyed in all parts and there was no necessity nor occasion for any more.

3dly The time was now past for making that use of itt which he then designed because he then intended if he had bought it to have sent $1/2$ of itt away to Muskatt to be there disposed of and one quarter he would have brought to Ispahawn and left the other quarter att Shiraz none of which could be effected now when all parts were filled with cloth and the season of the yeare past and so upon the whole matter told us it was not his interest to buy it.

Wherefore we dispatched away Mr Blower to Shiraz with orders to Amir Joan an Armenian who lives in your Honours' house att Shiraz and makes our wine to expose to sale what cloth and stuffs were there and Mr Blower would inform him of the differences of the prices to whom we gave an invoyce with instructions how to act. We hope shall dispose of some small part thereof before the winter is over both att Shiraz and here though att a low price. Could we have begun when first we came we are really perswaded very little cloth had now remained and your Honours' expectations as to price fullfilled and the sole reason why the Armenians would not comply with your Honours' desires (though they were very well sattisfyed they should have gott mony by itt att least 20 per cent and have satisfyed your Honours in all particulers) was because they would not forgoe their beloved Aleppo trade and that we can never propose to sell such a quantity now nor att such prices as they or we might have done att first is demonstrated by Coja Gregore Coldarents his reasons why he would not now buy the 100 bales of cloth and stuffs att Sciraz wherefore shall not enlarge on this subject, butt beg your Honours' patience some few dayes when we shall dispatch other advices of the whole state of your affaires as found them att the death of the late Agent.

We have notice by Coja Panous Callendar's son that another ship will be speedily att Gomroon with more cloth. Wee could have wished our advices could have been with your Honours before she came out not that we think your Honours have or will send out more cloth than the kingdom of Persia is able to vend had we your Honours' order to settle att Tavris Shambackee and Muskatt and disperse cloth to these parts but we must acquaint your Honours that the sortement of cloth by the Mary and Nassaw was not proper for these parts, both as to price and collours for 1st very little fine cloth will sell here and none so fine as the scarletts and crimson we have by us for itt is not a thin cloth the Persians want but a very thick cloth and well glossed because a thin cloth will not bear their linenings of heavy furrs nor keep out the sharp peircing air of this climate. Wherefore a thick sortt of cloth which comes from Holland by way of Muscovy overland is much admired here and though we

can nott beleive itt costs so much as your Honours' crimsons and scarletts you
will sell for considerable more. 2dly no auroras of above 20 li per peece will
sell for profit the Persians not understanding the value of cloth that exceeds
20 li butt auroras very course of 12 or 13 pounds and so to 15 li att most are
very proper. Jams the same from 9 pound to 12 none to exceed 13. Redds but
a few, popinjayes[2] double the quantity of reds att least.

The collours most proper for the jams are our cloth collours of all sorts
coffee collour, nuttmeg, cinnamon, copper, worme wood, purple some few
and yellows but not light ones, French greens, olive, murrey[3], white, a bale or
two of black and these full of collours not slightly dyed.

Blews, flesh naked salmon deroy nor any fading collour is no wayes
propper. Wee mention this imperfect account of collours and prices for fear
a shipp may be coming out as this arrives but in our next wee shall be very
exact and send the collours painted on papers and whatt quantity of each and
send musters of said cloth per first ship.

[1] aurora: rich orange hue
[2] popinjay: bright shade of green
[3] purple-red color

223

COMPANY IN LONDON TO PERSIA
15 JANUARY 1695/96
E/3/92 EXTRACT FROM FF. 224-225

It seems to us that all the advise you have had from Amatike Calendar
is very honest, wise and disinterested, and that you can never have a faithfuller
or wiser counceller in that country, and therefore we would have you make
him a present in our name of 3 or 4 peices of cloth of such colours and finess
as you shall think fit, not as a reward, for we know he expects none from us,
but as an acknowledgment of our gratitude for the service he has done us, and
may further do us, in recommending to you a right honest man to supply the
place of Doud, whose advice therein we would have you exactly persue as well
as in the case of your broaker, except he prove honester, then he hath hither
to by the accompt you have often given us of him.

Mr Bruse by the language he hath attained, is not only serviceable but
necessary to us, and therefore we would by all means have him encouraged and
raised immediately, if he be capable of it, to be second or third of our factory
of Ispahan, as our Agent shall think fitt, and the party, who is in that
employment at present, must be content to give way to Mr Bruse as his senior
in India what ever he may be in age.

We do not this to discourage him or any others, but we must prefer one that we believe is honest, and has attained to perfection of the two languages of Pertian and Armenian, especially, while we have no other in either of our Councills besides him, that understands either of those languages which are so necessary to our affairs there.

Upon this occasion we must likewise inculcate to you the absolute necessity we have, that you should always keep two of our English boys in some Armenian houses in Julpha, always separated from their acquaintance in conversation of English, untill they have arrived to the full knowledge of writing and reading these two languages.

By the invoice of Charles the Second, you will find what cargo we have sent you for the carrying on of our commerce at Ispahan and Shyraz in the English manufacture, concerning which we can give you no further advise then we did by the Nassau and Mary. You must proceed in the disposall and return of this cargo, as you did in those, and with all the expedicion possible you can, considering the great loss we have sustained, as you may observe by the inclosed copy of the letters to Surratt, but besides the silk we expect in return, you may likewise send us the value of ten thousand pounds in Ispahan chints, some whereof are painted upon karibauds[1] fifteen yards long and near three quarters broad, others upon finer and thicker cloth of yard broad, and five yards long, the works and colours are narrow, and the more variety of works, and colours of all sorts stripes flowers or otherwise the better, provided, there be not less twenty peices of one sort, that if they should be wanted, for furnishing of a roome and bed, there may be enough of one sort to serve such an occasion. We suppose you may have these goods immediately in truck for cloth, being informed, there are vast quantityes and great variety to be had at all times in Ispahan, in which particular, you may take the advise of our five Armenian friends, as well as of Avalike Callendar. The finer the paintings are for workmanship and colours, the better account they will turn to here.

We think fit to acquaint you, that you will find our cloth and stuffs this year much dearer then formerly, all woollen manufactures being risen within this two years 40 per cent, as our Armenian friends will understand as well from Mr Calendar as from their correspondence at Aleppo, and therefore we hope and conclude they will accordingly advance those goods in price there.

Charles the Second being discharged of her outward bound cargoe, we would have you send immediately to Surratt with such a freight as you can procure for her, which ought to be more then in former times of peace, we now paying double freight, these four ships having thirty four pounds per ton, and the four we have ready to follow these forty pounds per ton. We do not mention our own silk and other goods to be laden upon her, because we take it for granted, you will not forget doing of that in the first place with what money you can get in readyness, and we hope likewise with the chints we have now writt for, which Coja Panous tells us we may have great quantity of in Ispahan at any time.

We would have our foresaid cargoe by the Charles the Second as we have before wrote you disposed of in the same manner as we directed the former cargoes by the Nassau and Mary, and that therein you do all things that may be agreable to the inclination of our five great Armenian friends at Julpha whom we have trusted and must trust, if ever we intend to make a considerable cloth trade in Persia.

One of our letters to them we send you open, the other sealed with the Company seal which is of the same contents you are to send to them with what speed you can and to pursue such advices as you shall receive from them but least by sending up to Ispahan, and staying for advices from thence, some may be lost, we would have you immediately upon the landing our goods, send up half our woollen manufactures to our Chief and Councill at Ispahan, ordering them, as we do you to follow such directions in the delivery or sale of our goods as they shall receive from our friends Coja Moratt Surratt, Coja Marcara Surhad, Coja Gogas Calendar, Coja Gregory Coldarente and Coja Hoan Coldarente or any three of them.

---

[1] cummerbund; *kamar-band* (Pers.): waist-belt

224

COMPANY IN LONDON TO THE FIVE ARMENIAN MERCHANTS AT JULFA
15 JANUARY 1695/96
E/3/92 FF. 226V-227

Wee send you with this a copy of our last letter with an invoice of the goods, we have consigned to our Agent and Councill in Persia by this ship Charles the Second, whereof Captain John Dorrill is commander. You best know how many of these goods would be proper for us to send to Shyraz, and how many and what sorts to send Ispahaun. We rely upon your wisdom and fidelity in the disposall of these goods in the same manner as we did of those we sent last year by the ships Nassau and Mary and have therefore given order to our Agent and Councill at Gombroon and our Chief and Councill at Ispahaun to deliver them to you for sales or otherwise as you shall direct and as they did proceed with those cargoes we sent you by the before named ships.

We have no more to intimate to you at present but that you wilbe certifyed by Coja Panous Calendar and will perceive by our invoice that all woollen goods here are risen about thirty per cent above the price they were at, when the Nassau and Mary sailed from England, which we hope you will have a regard to in the disposall of these, because we intend you a yearly supply, we desire that the sales may be perfect, and the accounts yearly adjusted with as much expedition as conveniently may be.

225

COMPANY IN LONDON TO FORT ST GEORGE
20 FEBRUARY 1695/96
E/3/92 EXTRACT FROM FF. 232, 233

You let the Armenian Merchant for China abundantly too cheap, considering the vast charge our ships now sail at, we giving to this ship Sampson by charter party 40 li per ton and 12d per diem demorage.

We must continue to advise you to indulge the Armenians, who you say had been usefull to you in procuring the hushbull huccum from the Mogol to confirm all our priviledges in all parts of India. And we must do them the right to acknowledge, they have been very usefull to us by their advice in the sale of a vast quantity of the English manufacture in Persia which we could never have effected to advantage without their assistance. They are certainly the most knowing men in all the inland parts of the East Indies than the Dutch or any other nation on the face of the earth and being a frugall people not delighting in pomp vanity ease or luxury you may have the service often of them at a less charge to us than of one of our prodigall luxurious servants, and one or two of them in the inlands parts of India can do you more service in finding out new goods buying and providing them and drawing new inhabitants to your place than ten of your raw unexperienced men, which want not only language but too often want temperance and solidity, and must of necessity be fooled and bafled by the cheating dubashes or interpreters, which you are necessitated to send along with them, and which underhand will take off the sellers dustores[1] of all the goods you buy at any great distance from the Fort whatever you can say or do to the contrary.

[1] dustoor; *dastūr* (Pers.): customary commission payable on cash transactions

226

SIR JOHN GAYER, JOHN BURNISTON, THOMAS PATTLE, WILLIAM AISLABIE
AND BENJAMIN STACEY AT BOMBAY TO COMPANY IN LONDON
18 MARCH 1695/96
E/3/51 EXTRACT FROM FF. 379v-381

Had it not been for those imbroilments wee have been under with the government by reason of the pyrat wee should have had goods enough ready to have laden hom the Benjamin, Mocho Friggat and Tonqueen, but wee question whether the stock that the America had brought would have procured liberty for their exportacion, for our creditors have been so many times promised large supplys and we have so often failed them that now they will beleive nothing more they say of that kind till they see it. However our utmost endeavours shall not be wanting to make what provission we can possible of goods according to your Honours' list, and that we may the better performe this business it's our present thoughts to joyne Auga Peree and Benwallidas together, for that the former will want the latter's credit, but wee can't promise that they will provide to any considerable amount ere money arrives. The General had already wrote to Auga Peree, but has not received his answer. Wee will give them the encouragement your Honours has ordered us of leting them remayne in warehouse till money arrives to pay for them, without which it's impossible to have any provided, and interest for their money they must be allowed. The America arriving so late little or no goods can be got before the raines for that season is past, and the time at hand for giving out money to provide goods for the next yeare. The General wrote to Augau Peree to provide a quantity of cotton before the America arrived, but he delayed by reason of our troubles and want of money, but whether he has bought any of late he has not yet wrote him. If he has not, wee beleive wee shall not be able to get any large quantity of that commodity this yeare, for that by this time it's all or near all bought up, and the next crop will not be till February next wee are very sencible of the great demorage your Honours pay and wish it were in our power to give the ships quick dispatches to ease your Honours of that burden.

Your honours will observe by our letter overland of the 12th October 1695, the coppy of our contract with Callendar the Callendar enclosed, and by coppies of other letters, that wee have not been wanting in our endeavours after a speedy sale of the woollen manufactory of the cargoes of the three last shipps, but the troubles of the government has hindred their delivery, as your honours will perceive by the coppies of our letters to and from Surat. How the sayes will take wee do not yet know but feare not well.

Your honours' contract with the Armenians for the cargoe of the America shall be duely complyed with on our side as soon as our present troubles will permit, and wee will not faile to do our utmost to encourage Auga Peree to the provission of Sindy and Multan goods, and shall receive them from him on the termes your honours have agreed with Coja Panous Callendar. The Generall has twice wrote to him since the arrivall of the America, but the days of mourning for his brother Callendar the Callendar lately deceased not being over, no answer is yet returned; the loss of this brother is great to Auga Peree, and not very small to your honours. He was on this island about 5 months, and designed to live here to negotiate matters between the Generall and Councill and his brother, for that circumstances would not permit the Generall going to Surat, but being seized of a violent feaver, as soon as he was a little recovered he went to Surat where he dyed about three months after his arrivall there.

227

ARMENIAN MERCHANTS AT JULFA TO COMPANY IN LONDON
UNDATED, RECEIVED OVERLAND VIA LEGHORN AND AMSTERDAM 10
APRIL 1696[1]
E/3/51 FF. 399-400V

1 These are to informe your Honours that the letter your Honours wrote us under date 1694 the Agent sent us from Gomroon we received it and haveing read it we wrote to the Worshipfull Agent that this was a heavy burthen that it could not be done by us but that he should come to Spahaune. In the meantime that our letter was on the way going to Bunder Captain Brangwin with those of his Councill were on the way with the broad cloth coming to Spahaune butt our letter being written in Armenians the Worshipfull Agent sent a shotter to Captain Brangwin that Mr Bruce should translate that Armenian letter and send it him in English that he might understand it. We had the coppy of it at Spahaune so Mr Bruce translated it and sent it to the Worshipfull Agent.

2 According to your Honours' orders Captain Brangwin left the goods that were for Shiraz to come thither and brought the rest for Spahaune. As for what your Honours wrote concerning the cloth that comes to Turkey that the Turkey Company could not send any cloth before your Honours' was arrived.

3 The Turkey Companyes' cloth came to Allepo and Smerna and the Turkish and Armenian merchants bought it and brought it to Persia. Of this cloth some was damaged before the news of your Honours' two shipps arrived came they sold it at Tavris from $10^1/_2$ to 9 abasses per guz (which is 2 inches more than the English yard). When they heard of the arrivall of these two English shipps the marchants was in such haste to sell that though sold it for 6 abasses and now of late againe there is news come that more of the Turkey Company cloth is come to Allepo and Smirna which is to come to this country. Further the Right Worshipfull Agent wrote your Honours' servants a letter dated [gap in text] 1695 that the Right Honourable Company had done us and our people so great a favour in consigning these goods to us and that it will be more proffittable for us to bring silke to Spahaune and there receive broad cloth for it and so likewise your Honours write, but we must informe your Honours that marchants who have formerly traded in one way will very difficultly turn out of it. He further writes that it is your Honours' will that this woollen manufactury may be imediately sold that the silk and money for it may be returned. Your Honours likewise write the same that your desire is so in this countrey it is very hard to doe so it will be a long time ere sold.

4 As for that your Honours have ordered for Shiraz though there should goe no more cloth there from any parts that cloth will scarce turn to mony there in 4 or 5 yeares. As for the goods which are come hither to Spahaune if there come neither cloth nor stuffs from any other parts this will

hardly turn all to money here in 4 or 5 years. Heretofore what cloth came from Turkey to Persia $1/4$ or $1/5$ of it went to India but now we have news from Suratt that the English cloth which came last is sold there for $3^1/8$ rupes per yard and now how can marchants carry cloth to India. Lett this likewise be known to your Honours that this sort of cloth is but little expended and little in request now in comparison of what it was formerly and againe to informe your Honours why we have been so slow of writeing it is because wee were desireous first to have these goods come to Spahaune and se every sort by it selfe and understand the pices of them severally as your Honours have wrote them that neither the Right Honourable Company might suffer any wayes nor we have any reason to be ashamed afterwards. It came but was mixted and Captain Brangwin not well. As soon as it pleased God he grew better they sorted it and wee saw it. As for that price your Honours has pleased to sett on it viz 22 abassies per pound leaveing it to us to sell for more or less if compared with the price that cloth was sold for at Tavris there will be found a great deale of differance and more it appeares by your Honours' letters that your willing that either we these five of us should take of all this cloth for money to pay $1/3$ present $1/3$ at 3 months and $1/3$ at 6 months or else to lett our people have it at the same rate or to lett marchants have it to bring in silke for it from within the space of 6 months to 9 months. As for the first that wee should take it off we have not abillity to doe it, it is a very heavy burthen to us partly because we are now grown old and likewise that we should be both the buyers and sellers is not a fitt method. As for our country men's takeing it off, whomever of them we have spoke to as yett have answered us that it was a very heavy burthen more then thay can bear and they knew it was soe to us. That which your Honours write that this woollen manufactorie should be sold all at once such a sale can neither be in Turkey nor in Persia, though we have heard that in Suratt the Right Honourable Company's goods have been sold alltogeather formerly. When there was here but 1200 pieces of cloth your Honours' broker Moola had the sale of it. He sold it to the shopkeepers and stockin makers to receive the money in five months. He abated them 1 per cent per month to receive some before due and the rest he made up himselfe that he might received it by little and little but to this day he has not received it all especially at such a time when for two yeares the Turkey Company had not been able to bring any of theire cloth heither and when such sort of cloth was much wanted in this country and further we must informe your Honours that here in Spahaune woollen manyfactures sell by little and little. It happens indeed that sometimes at Tavris a quantity may be sold for ready money and sometimes a quantity may be bartered for Indian goods. Again as for this order your Honours give concerning these goods such an order and such a country cannot agree. In respect of this country such an order is a mistake, we are so rude as to write this plaine because we are desireous that neither the Company should suffer any loss nor wee have reason afterwards to being ashamed. After this letter is gone wee shall mind the business and see if possible whether or noe there be any will buy it all together wee shall be very ready to serve your Honours. Your Honours must take care and thoroughly consider this affair and order it to some other person who has no other business but the sale of the cloth for this is not in our power to doe. If it were in our power wee'd serve your Honours with our live and to informe your Honours of the condition of silke indeed 2 years agoe all sorts of silke were cheape but have grown dearer and dearer these two years which wee suppose the Worshipfull Agent and Captain Brangwin have informed your Honours of.

Your Honours' most humble servants

> Morad Surad
> Mercara Surad
> Gogas Callenter
> Gregore Caldarence
> Hoan Coldarence

[1] This letter may be the "uncivil" version of Doc. 207 which is mentioned in Doc. 216, and, if so, probably dates from early August 1695. Both documents 216 and 227 were received in London via Leghorn and Vienna on 10 April 1696. A problem with this identification is that Doc. 216 speaks of forwarding a letter signed by four Armenians, whereas both documents 207 and 227 are signed by all five merchants.

228

CAPTAIN BENJAMIN BRANGWIN, JAMES BRUCE AND JAMES RAWLINGS AT
ISFAHAN TO COMPANY IN LONDON
16 APRIL 1696
E/3/52 EXTRACT FROM FF. 50V-51V

And now we should give your honours an account at large of the unkind usage we hear and Mr Major at Tabris hath met with from the Armenians that are deeply engaged in the Aleppo trade, but shall only name one, which is that some of them (as Mr Major acquaints us) acquainted the king's vizir or deputy of that place, that if he permitted the English to carry their cloth without paying customes, in a short time none would be able to trade but the English, and then no customes would be received, and how did he expect the king's souldiers would be paid of or maintained, which usually received their pay out of that revenue. And how pressing an argument that was to the Deputy Governour to prove unkind and damage your honours' affairs, we leave to your honours to judge.

We find by a generall to Persia from his Excellency of the 29th December past received the 9th March last, that Auga Perey Kalentar hath

informed strange stories concerning our actions here, the which we suppose
may have been sent your honours, wherefore we have here inclosed sent the
coppy of our answer to the General etc, to vindicate ourselves and prove how
unjust the accusations are and though when had answered the General etc we
had not had oportunity to discourse the 5 Armenians about it, we have since,
who declare it to be all false, and so far from haveing the least appearance of
truth, that they declare they cannot say, that ever we gave them the least angry
word, or shewed them the least incivility or disobliged them in anything. Had
your honours been here in their places, we could not have been more
circumspect in how we treated them, useing all imaginable civility beyond
expression, waiting on them to their own houses, to our great shame as the
people of this place have upbraided us with since; and as Agent Gladman writt
us never were the Armenians so waited on by a Chief and Council and that
Agent Gladman approved of what Captain Brangwin etc had done. We have
here inclosed a clause of his last perticular letter to Captain Brangwin, and
therefore hope your honours will not entertain the false information of a
person, that we know not upon what account or for what reason but pure
invention, hath gone about to stain our reputations. We should send your
honours attestations under all sorts of people, as well Christians as heathens,
of the notorious falsity of we are accused of, but think it in its self so
ridiculous, that it would be needless.

229
COMPANY IN LONDON TO GOMBROON
4 MAY 1696
E/3/92 FF. 236-236V

By the inclosed to our Chief and Councill at Ispahan, you will see what
resentment we have made of their unhappy delay in the disposall of our cloth,
which whether to impute to the too great relyance we had on the Armenians,
or to ill conduct of our Councill there, we shall not now determine, but we
have reason to complaine, and shall expect that our Agent doth hereafter shew
us why, he did not at the receipt of our letters by the Nassau and Mary
immediately repair to Ispahan, according to our positive orders, by whose
advise and assistance this, this great affair might have been brought to a happy
issue.

We are very unwilling to entertaine any hard thoughts of one, whom we
have reason to believe hath hitherto been ready, willing and able to serve our
interest in all respects, and we shall forbear therefore to make any reflection
thereon, or on the great miscarriage at Ispahan till such time we have the naked
truth of this matter explained to us.

You will see by the inclosed, what we have now resolved on in order to the speediest and best dispatch of our cloth, and for the future carrying on of this trade in such a currant, as may not easily be interrupted.

To this end we rely that our Agent, (leaving his busyness at Gombroone under the best care) will with utmost speed and diligence repair to Ispahan there to consult such of the Armenian nation, as he shall find are inclined to our service, and with the help and assistance of our Councill there, to fall heartily to work in the disposall of our cloth in such manner and at such prices as best he can, regarding not so much the proffit as the dispatch thereof.

And we would have you know that nothing can oblige us more to think well of your service and integrity towards us then your zeal and diligence in this great affair.

You know already the necessity we are under of forceing this trade, and this we apprehend you will find no great difficulty to effect. The Julfaleens will soon be weary of bringing cloth from Turky, when they see you undersell them, which be sure to doe, and when once you are in condition to pay them half money, and half cloth for their silk, that commodity will of course be brought to you, and in order to this, you must make it their interest by the encouragement which you give them.

We are not a little surprized that our Councill at Ispahan should think Doude the onely fit man to serve us, and more to see, that our Agent should on any termes, or upon the greatest necessity, conceede to his admission to our service, certainly you must have forgot the character you have all along given of him, and the rogueries, wherewith you have impeached him, how this matter was brought about, we shall expect to know.

We are yet in hopes our Councill at Ispahan will have made some considerable progress at least, in the dispatch of our cloth before this comes to your hand, and should it be otherwise we must condemn you all of infatuation to let such a commodity lye so long for new orders.

We have now a large parcell of cloth comeing forward to you, and therefore, however the success may be in the dispatch of the former parcells, we require you to use your best judgement and diligence in setling this trade at Ispahan, which being well managed by you and our Councill there, may become a noble mark to your honour and our advantage. And the better to effect this, be sure no opportunity be lost in the dispatch of any of our cloth either for mony at any price, which the market will afford, or in barter for commodityes proper for Europe, a list whereof you have already had or in any other such way as may encrease the consumption and tend to a speedy dispatch thereof.

If there should be occasion of trusting any the Julfareens or any other of the Armenian nation, you may take opportunity privately of informing your selves their ability or honesty by the Callendars on whose integrity we believe you may relye.

We must recommend to you to hasten what effects possibly you can to Surratt, where our concernes we doubt will have suffered very much for want of those supplyes, which we depended on from your sale.

As to other matters we refer you to our next letters, and you will supply what may be now wanting by your care and diligence in all our affaires and that you will answer that good character, we have entertained of you, that no private interest or particular friendship will make you admit of any practice, that may not be for our service.

We cannot but observe to you, that the Dutch have letters from Persia 3 months fresher then any we have from you, whereby they have opportunity of giving necessary directions for managing their affairs, that we are uncapable of doing for want of the like care and diligence in our servants, which we the more wonder at, at this time, when we have had so unfortunate an account of our affaires at Ispahan. However that we may not suffer again by such carelessness, we order and direct, that for the time to come you give us at least once every month or six weeks a particular account of the state of our affaires under your care, what are the prices of all European goods in Persia, and of all Persian goods proper for our markets, and which sorts are in greatest plenty, and in every thing else to give us the best information you can if occurences in all other of our factoryes and places in India.

We leave it to our Agent's discretion when he arrives at Ispahan to send down Captain Brangwin to remain at Gombroon in his absence, if he sees it best for our service so to doe.

Send copyes of our letters to you and Ispahan to our Generall at Bombay.

230
COMPANY IN LONDON TO ISFAHAN
4 MAY 1696
E/3/92 FF. 237-237v

Your letters of the 6th August and 14th September last, we have very lately received, forwarded to us via Aleppo, together with Agent Gladman's pacquet of the 20th August, whereby we are not a little surprised to see, that in all that time, there had been no beginning made in the sale of our cloth by the Nassau and Mary.

You must needs think we cannot but make a severe reflection of the miscarriage of so important an affair, and your own reasons must tell you (that however we had given our instructions in order to the promoting and continueing so great a trade) that such a commodity must not lye by in our warehouses to perish, nor so great an affair stand still, for want of what you call sufficient orders.

Tis true, that we had a great relyance on the ability and inclination of the Armenians to serve us, and possibly had they been fairly treated by you, they might herein have given you and us such an assistance in this affair, as might have inabled us to have diverted the course of their former way of trade, and this was the great inducement, that led us to so intire a confidence in them promising our selves, that hereby they would find an interest at least equivolent to their travelling trade.

But if we have been mistaken herein, yet nothing that we can see by our own orders or the circumstance of this affair can justify your sitting still and waiting fresh orders from us, for the dispatch of our cloth, which you very well know, besides the disappointment we shall have of the effects thereof, must (in such a tract of time, as an answer to your letters require) be in great measure consumed with the worme.

You seem to be apprehensive hereof, and therefore acquaint us the severall advances you had made to see to bring the Armenians to some termes for disposall of the cloth, wherein if you have been sincere with them and us we think you have done well.

But in the papers relating to the constructions of the orders which we have given them for disposall thereof, we see so little difference in those which they offered to you to signe, and which you offer to signe to them, that we cannot but entertaine a suspicion of your integrity to our service or your friendship to them, for you must needs conclude that if they had any desire to serve us in this affair, they would dispatch it as fast as they could, notwithstanding this nicety in what they would have had understood by our orders that they should sell the whole parcell by little and little, if they could not sell it all at once.

And we would appeal even to your selves, if under such a dilemma you should not have chosen to comply with their scrupulous humour, rather then have crampt them with such a clause as you put in your own paper which you propose to them vizt: that they should sell a part provided it would not hinder the sale of the rest.

This we are affraid discouraged their attempt to serve us, though it may be true as you say, that this trade doth at present cross their interests, yet we have reason to think that nothing could have contri-buted more to our inlargeing and continuing this trade than a friendly correspondence and assistance from those Armenians.

And though the family of the Surrads seem to you to be averse to the encouraging hereof, yet we have good assurance to believe, and you seem to own as much, that the Callendars were free to give us their assistance.

What then could induce you to think Doude a fitt man to serve us? One that your selves think a self ended coveteous griping and tricking courtier and our Agent hath always represented to us as trecherous base and an enemy to us, certainly this betrayes your discretions if not your candour, and give us violent suspicion, that there hath been underhand dealing with him, and that you have imposed upon our Agent in getting his concesison (under such necessity) to the admittance of so experienced a knave.

We are very unwilling to pass any censure, till we have this matter more explained to us, and we yet hope you will have tryed all wayes to bring the sale of our cloth to an issue, and that you have made investments thereof according to the orders given you.

But since we have reason to fear the worst, and that we have now another large parcell of cloth comeing towards you by the Charles the 2d, we have ordered our Agent Gladman immediately upon receipt of our letters, that he repair to Ispahan, and there by the most friendly endeavours to prevail with the Armenians (such of them as incline) to give them assistance as well in disposall of what cloth may remaine as what is now comeing towards you.

But in case after all they should decline acting therein, our order is that you assist him with your advice and councill in order to agree on such method as may with most facility be taken for the readiest sale of our remaining cloth, and for the making investments according to the orders already sent you.

You are then also to consult, either with the Callendars, if they incline to assist you, what wilbe the most likely way to bring the silk merchants to Ispahan, or if they decline this to find out such of the Julfareens or Armenians as you see are best able and most ready to give you assistance herein.

And we would have you know, that our aime is not to make a large profitt on our cloth, but to make a large vend, and this cannot be done any other way, but by selling cheap, which will not only increase the consumption, but discourage their fetching cloth from Turky.

We would therefore recommend your selling to the Julfareens in parcells at lower rates then what you sell for consumption of Persia, for their encouragement of comeing to your market with their silk and for your cloth and that hereafter, there may be room for no more excuses, we recommend it in especiall to you to loose no time but with your utmost skill and diligence to fall heartily to work in the disposall of our cloth in such manner as our Agent shall direct, and that the same care may be taken in making returnes to Surrat in such commodityes as we have recommended to you, where we fear our affairs have suffered very much by this unhappy delay.

231

AUGA PERE CALLENDAR AT SURAT TO SIR JOHN GAYER AT BOMBAY
7 MAY 1696
E/3/52 FF. 56-59v

[Translation into English from Portuguese]

I have received from your Excellency 5 letters, one of the 26th February, two of the 10th March, one in Persia, and another in Guzuratt of the 14th and 15th of the last month in all which take notice of what your Excellency hath wrote mee, and your Excellency's complaint that in all this time I have not wrote you, howbeit that failure was not for want of will, but that rather from that time to this day the many disgusts and troubles I have had and continue so, that I could wish God would take mee away that I may not see greater, and so many are they that I may compare them with those of the prophet Isaias Chapter 3rd: verse 18 or as Joseph in condition, my brother whom God was pleased to take unto himself, and that which continues my grief is what I foresee, my old father will also have, who hearing thereof will receive thereby a deep wound, when hee comes to know for what I sent him to Bombay I know not what to say. Albeit I give thanks to God for thus disposing of him and conforming myself to his divine will.

1 That I have not wrote all this time to your Excellency was by reason of my mourning, as also because Mr Bendall sent mee not your Excellency's letters as he was ordered, but now I answer. Your Excellency wrote of 3 ships of the Company's that were coming, that if I and Benwallidass could buy the merchandizes required you would send a list of them to bee done accordingly.

2 That when there should bee a joint consent your Excellency would remitt me orders to bee put in exicution.

3 That I should send my answer about making of (chellas) chints at Scindy and Multan according to what my father had agreed in England.

4 That the bill of 7500 rupees received from Ramagee Commatee is for to buy goods for China.

5 About a sending a ship for Bengall.

6 About sending gunnys[1] and ropes for embayling and package of 100 candys[2] of cotten.

7 That I should pay for your Excellency's account to Mr Robbinson rupees $848^1/_2$ and to Mr Bendall what hee should require for your Excellency's account and what was necessary.

8 The price of ellephants' teeth which if would turne to account at this port you would remit mee.

Great is my fortune with respect to the great important affairs your Excellency imploies mee about, as to the which (as I have said before) all are troubles and disappointments for that I want arms and strength in so much that for my owne self I have no will or minde, earnestly desiring rather to dispose of what I have, and to depart from this countrey, for the troubles I have for my deceased brother.

I discoursed about the first with Benwallidass, and told him it was necessary wee engaged in this particular unto which hee answered mee that I saw how difficult the times were to performe such a business, to which I replyed that hee would shew himself serviceable, it must bee on this occasion, and hee being a broaker to the Company and of your Excellency's would not now medle therein, but when the troubles were over many would do it. I had severall dayes debate with him about the same, there were severall of his friends (merchants) discoursed about this affaire in private the result of which was as followeth.

1 That they would take an investment of 5 leck of rupees for the Company they giving aforehand 1 leck, and the remainder to bee paid when the goods were shipt on the ships, then wee should bee paid with those goods that goe into the countrey commission according to the Company's rules, and when the goods arrived at this port they were for the Company's account according to former custome, and as for all goods to bee dispatched in my name because they cannot bee done in the English and in the severall places where it was necessary I will send Armenians to assist at for the right chusing of good goods, according to the abovesaid the aforesaid persons do require to whom I told them I would advise your Excellency that I might have your consent and order.

2 I begg of your Excellency a satisfactory order in case you grant what I have wrote as above and that I should make the investment, that any accident should happen (which God forbid) that it should come to the Governor's ears by so envious persons that wee assist the English in the investment giving in the name of Armenians, the charges thereof should then bee on the Company's account.

3 In case there should not bee a ready dispatch for the goods (which God forbid) the intrest of that time delayed (according to custome) shall bee on the Company's account as to what money the goods shall amount unto.

4 Your Excellency knowes that in these affairs there will not want those that will envy mee, and seek to do mee hurt, so that when it shall happen that any writes to your Excellency about the goods being good or badd, it may bee of dammage to mee, if your Excellency should hearken thereunto, to certifye my faithfullness I would desire your Excellency to send a person that hath knowledge of said goods to see them and examine them that they bee according to the invoyce I shall send your Excellency distinctly.

5 Benwallidass and Saneardass his brother desire that they bee made the Company's broakers and that no other may bee joyned with them as was done to his father, and to have the honour hee received in Councill, vzt neither his uncles nor other enemies disaffected persons may come into your factory that

may create them trouble or loss in the Company's affairs. What they alledge herein seems to mee very reasonable, and I have both their promises that they will write to your Excellency as to the abovesaid, and that your Excellency agreeing hereunto would bee pleased in answer to send them an order sealed with the Company's seale that they may bee the Company's broakers after these troubles are over, under which they are now labouring under, and that afterwards they may take the charge of the Company's service, and act as their father Binjee Parrack had done before them, and till these things are ended there ought to bee great silence and secrecy, as to what is wrote your Excellency, the aforesaid paper or order I am as it were assured your Excellency will send them to confirme them as to your affection and good will towards them as also the Company's and whereas your Excellency would have the Company's affairs forwarded with all expedition, I thought it convenient on considerations of the foregoing particulars, to write to your Excellency when you would bee pleased to order mee to settle the affairs of the within land places, this monsoon being almost ended and winter approaching.

About the leck of rupees for the buying of the goods or the 5 of what your Excellency orders, if the same cannot bee procured without difficulty from the factory, I have spoaken to the aforesaid Benwallidass to favour in a bill as to which particular hee will not bee wanting.

And as to what may concern my parte I ask not, nor doe not desire of your Excellency nor of the Company anything of commission, having this affaire in the same account as if my father had wrote mee, earnestly desiring to serve the Company to my utmost in all things that your Excellency may have intire satisfaction from the Company to the conferring yet of greater posts on you.

As to the particulars your Excellency writes off, I shall readily performe your Excellency's commands.

To make an investment at Sindy and Multan I shall bee very ready, but in order thereunto tis necessary that your Excellency send a vessell because it cannot bee effected by land and from Multan I will order to come by land.

I have prepared two Armenians to goe within land to buy the goods that when it shall bee necessary that they depart for the account of your Excellency bee pleased to send mee an order that I may also give them.

The Company's letter mentions to send to order about allass[3] from Ahmadavad, I do not know whether they are to have flowers with gold, or without them, according to my father's letter it seems to bee without them, as to the which I desire your Excellency to advise mee.

As to the buying of goods for China and as to the bill Ramjee Comattee sent, I am very well contented to doe it, but now the monsoone is gone, and no libertie of trade, this occasion is past.

As to the sending of ships for Bengall wee have not the order of the Anibob, and the monsoon is past, and about the Carwarr Merchant the President may have wrote your Excellency.

The delay of the gunny and ropes hitherto was occasioned for want of being chopt, and dispatched from the custome house and likewise of a boat, but now may goe within 2 or 3 dayes.

By your Excellency's order I paid Mr Bendall rupees 848$^{1}/_{2}$ to pay unto Mr Robbinson, which have charged to your Excellency's account, and to said Mr Bendall I paid by order of your Excellency rupees 4065, and what for the future hee shall ask I shall not bee wanting to deliver it him for your Excellency's service, unto which shall bee ready.

As to the elephants' teeth bee pleased not to send them, because whatsoever comes is deposited by the Moores.

The letter which your Excellency sent to Issa Gully I remitted forthwith to the camp, and at present I have no newse worth your Excellency's notice to write of the which having I shall imediately impart the same to your Excellency.

Your Excellency wrote mee about buying whatever bales of indigo procureable this winter, hitherto I have not met with more than 100 to 150. The caphila Jamadarised is coming, when that arrives the price will bee cheaper, and about the Benjamin's goods I doubt not but that the President may have this day wrote your Excellency touching which particular I have not been wanting to use my utmost dilligence to procure a grant from the Governor about them which hee hath given and I have brought home to my house part of the goods and I hope to doe so by the remainder in a few dayes that I may prevent the objictions of any to the Governor about that affaire.

The present broakers of the Company have given mee sufficient trouble and loss about my business, of which I am very silent, and take all with great patience, representing or committing all unto God who will reward them according to their deserts, however I ought not to have omitted giving your Excellency notice and also the President and Councill.

About the goods of the ship America I had taken a resolution of ordering them to Daman to sell them there, but by your Excellency and other considerations doe adjudge the price there will bee low, I have deferred the same, requesting your Excellency that care may bee taken about them, that they may bee left in some good place.

The President informed mee about some cochaneale at Bombay. I have agreed with some merchants for the double seer of 40 pice weighte rupees 45 the seer being good, and pickt and wee sifted, not having dust, your Excellency may send to Daman about the quantity of 8 maunds for so much I have agreed with the merchants for, it may bee sent securely in some boate, and then the merchants may goe there. Your Excellency may send it to Havidass Tapidass which may serve for an advertisement.

The accounts which I have with Mr Welden I have hitherto been waiting that hee should have finished them with your Excellency of which I have no notice. I begg the favour there may bee no further delayes therein, and when your Excellency shall bee pleased to give answer to what I now write as above

I desire it may bee in Portugueze that I may understand it, and give mee no more trouble, but as to other particulars it may bee wrote in Guzzurat.

I have notice of your Excellency's sending the America home for Europe, being so, I have with this accompanied a letter for my father, which request your Excellency to forward and shall account my self much oblieged to your Excellency, for which I shall remaine oblieged as your humble servant, God preserve your Excellency many years.

Your Excellency's most humble servant

Agapery Callendar

Surat May the 7th 1696

Translated out of the Portugueze language by Ephraim Bendall
May the 22d 1696

¹ *gōnī* (Hind.): sack made of coarse material
² *kanti* (Malay.): weight used in India, averaging 500 lbs.
³ *atlas* (Ar.): silk-satin manufactured in the East

232
COMPANY IN LONDON TO BENGAL
4 JULY 1696
E/3/92 EXTRACT FROM F. 247

We can now give the good news of the safe arrivall at Plymouth of the Armenian Merchant, London Frigott and Amity all from the Fort, the Nassau also from Bombay is come into the River and almost unladen for which mercy we desire to be truly thankfull to almighty God.

Herewith you will receive Coja Panous Calendar's contract for 2 chests of glass Venice beads or necklaces valued at 224 li sent down to Portsmouth designed to go on the Sidney, by which you will observe that he is to advance 40 per cent thereon. He has already paid the 112 li into our cash which is to be deducted out of the totall amount of the invoice, but in regard we have not examined the two chests, neither know whether the same are truly valued, or what other sorts of commodityes are contained therein, we would have you on their arrivall, make a particular inspection into them, and give us an account of their content and value upon their sale with you together with a sample of them that we may supply you therewith hereafter, or with anything else of that nature if you give us encouragement.

233

NATHANIEL HIGGINSON, JOHN STYLEMAN, WILLIAM FRASER, FRANCIS
ELLIS, ROGER BRADDYLL, CHARLES BARWELL AND MATTHEW EMPSON
AT FORT ST GEORGE TO COMPANY IN LONDON
30 SEPTEMBER 1696
E/3/52 EXTRACT FROM F. 156

Neither Armenians nor other merchants can be prevailed with to contract for the provision of painted callicoes and other fine goods (not made in these parts) upon their own stock and risgoe at 15 or 20 per cent advance on the prime cost, nor can it be expected till the warrs between the Mogull and Morattas are finished, and the land passage rendred more free and safe. Till when there cannot be an inland vend of Europe goods proportionable to the quantity yearly received, nor can wee procure any quantity of overland pepper or sticklack, nor make considerable investments of callicoes in such parts as are the seat of warr, robbed and plundred both by Moors and Moratta armys in turnes.

234

JAMES BRUCE AND JAMES RAWLINGS AT ISFAHAN TO COMPANY IN
LONDON
1 OCTOBER 1696
E/3/52 EXTRACT FROM FF. 175-178

Itt haveing pleased Allmighty God to take from us Captain Benjamin Brangwin late Chief for your Honours' affaires in Persia we presume hereby to give your Honours advice thereof as allso an accountt of all such passages both before and since his death as are of any moment and we have not hitherto informed your Honours of vizt

Our concludeing to send some of your Honours' broad cloth and stuffs to Muskatt upon the following considerations 1st that we knew the great quantity of reds and auroras we had in the house would be very long ere disposed of in Ispahaun and they together with light green being the properest and allmost only collours that were sent thither to be carried into the north of India we thought itt might be a great help towards the sale of them.

2d We were advised by Mr Thomas Major from Tavris that upon the arrivall of your Honours' cloth there the Armenians who had brought cloth from Allepo dispairing of ever selling itt in Ispahaun had resolved to send itt without passing through Ispahaun the nearest way to Muskatt. Therefore we concluded that if we could gett some of your Honours' cloth there as soon or sooner then theirs and so spoyle their markett by underselling them we might att last make them weary of their cloth trade and untill we did so we could not expect vent for so much cloth as your Honours designed to send here yearly.

Haveing thus concluded of the necessity of sending cloth thither we dispatched Mr William Lee (there being nobody else we could spare that understood the Persian language) on the 6th of July past with 150 bales broadcloth viztt 40 bales of reds 40 ditto popinjays 40 ditto auroras 10 ditto yellow 15 ditto jams and 5 ditto fine crimsons and scarletts with 15 bales stuffs of all sorts and haveing advice from Mr Thomas Major of the sale of most part of that cloth we had sent by him in January last to Tavries we dispatched likewise on the 14 July 150 bales more for that place to be conducted thither by one Monsieur Isaack De Lestoille a Frenchman whom for want of Englishmen we entertained in your Honours' service ... this Monsieur Isaack spoke sundry languages very well as Portugueze, French, Itallian, Armenians, Perians, Turkish, and Indostans.

The Dutch who have allwayes manifested themselves to be your Honours' utter enimyes are att present watching an oppertunity and we beleive will assist the King of Persia against Muscatt designing thereby to gett over our heads and make themselves masters of the Gulph of Persia and whereas your Honours have expected assistance of the Armenians in your business with the goverment yett being bound both by our duty to God and your Honours to speake the truth of what we have sene and know we must say that little assistance is to be expected from them who are not able to defend themselves against such monstrous impositions as the King's sending twice or thrice every yeare for all their wives and daughters and keeping so many of them as he pleases generally 8 or 10 sometimes 100 whom he distributes to his slaves att pleasure and further if the Armenians had had any power in Persia your Honours' affaires would have felt itt ere now and plainely perceived that they are not such friends as persons ought to be who could entertain any gratefull sence of those high and long continued favours your Honours hitherto have confered upon them.

We have been busy these few dayes past in giveing notice to Gomroon and other parts of Persia of Captain Brangwin's death.

235

JAMES BRUCE AT ISFAHAN TO EDWARD OWEN AT GOMBROON
11 OCTOBER 1696
E/3/52 EXTRACT FROM FF. 182-182V

Mr Aveatik Callendar who is going hence for Suratt being desirous to carry some goods with him, proposed to buy the 28 bales of ruinas and 18 bales of Bulgar hides that (as formerly advised) are gone towards you offering to give a bill of exchange for payment of the mony in Suratt but I refusing that he said he would pay the mony in Gomroon upon delivery of the goods. Wherefore I came to a bargain with him att shakees 88 per pair for the Bulgar hides and shakees 340 wz per bale for the ruinas garbled and skinned over to be delivered him aboard ship but I have not made any positive aggreement with him butt conditionall as that itt should be a bargain if you approved of and consented to itt and if that the goods were nott sold before he arrived Gomroon. Wherefore if you can think of a more beneficiall method of disposing of them ere he arrives itt will be better for perhaps after all he does not intend to pay for them in Gomroon but thinks perhaps to gett you to take his note or bill for the amount of them which I suppose you will not willingly doe. He is a proud man carrying itt very high and often talking of the Right Honourable Company and the Generall's favour to their family and oftner of how much they had enriched the Right Honourable Company of late, talking among the Persians that his father is one of our Right Honourable Masters. He showed me a letter one day from his brother Augapery wherein he had writt that the Generall was so ready in granting whatever they desired that he beleived if they should ask Bombay Castle he would give itt them. He told me likewise that he had a letter from his Excellency but did not show me thatt and a contract under his Excellency's hand and seall that all the Right Honourable Company servants in Persia should be under him and that such persons as either he or his brother should pitch upon and approve of should be brokers and linguists in all parts of Persia. I can not immagine what should prompt them to desire such a priviledge. I daresay itt is not for any burning zeall that Mr Aveatik has for the Right Honourable Company's interest, itt may be he designes considerable proffitt to himself thereby. I was affraid to write this to his Excellency though I beleive his Excellency would not take itt ill to be informed of such scandalous affronts as they putt upon him in talking of giving Bombay to an Armenian but I discharge my duty in acquainting any of my superiors.

236

SAMUEL ANNESLEY AND EPHRAIM BENDALL AT SURAT TO COMPANY IN
LONDON
15 DECEMBER 1696
E/3/52 EXTRACT FROM FF. 270V-271

The Ahmadavad broker's accounts not being concluded (who stands charged with sundry frauds committed in the severall investments he hath made for your Honours) we were forced to substitute an Armenian Mirza Caune to buy what goods your Honours had ordered from that place, and in the time of our late imprisonment, by some means or other the goods were discovered to be ours, and were seized on by that Governor's duwan (son in law to the Governor of this place) upon which the Armenian procured a purwauna[1] from this Governor to him to clear them, and sometime after that (the former being ineffectual) we dispatcht a duplicate order with an officer, notwithstanding which our last advices are that he detains a bil for 1500 rupees and hath stopt browne goods, narrow baftas and birampauts[2] etc to the value of 14000 rupees, our broker tells us they perceive his intentions are to keep that 1500 rupees. They say also they have advices the other goods are making ready and may be down time enough for this year's shipping, if we send up money to release them till which they cannot be removed.

[1] *parvāna* (Pers.): written order, pass, license or permit
[2] plain white and dyed cotton cloth

237
EDWARD OWEN AND THOMAS HARBIN AT GOMBROON TO COMPANY IN LONDON
16 JANUARY 1696/97
E/3/52 EXTRACT FROM FF. 296-296V

Coja Aveatick Callendar ... is gone to Congo to take his passage on the Portugueeze armada which is just upon its departure for Buss.

As to the sale of the woollen manufacture they were in great hopes of selling all this winter but unexpectedly there came news of near three thousand peices comeing to Spahaune by the way of Muscovy and above one thousand peices is octually come thither so that they are a little fearfull of accomplishing it now.

238
EXTRACT FROM SURAT GENERAL LETTER TO BOMBAY
14 APRIL 1697
E/3/53 F. 22

The President enquired of Augau Peeree about his complaint to the Rightt Honourable Company of injustice to him in the price of his coffee and pepper, and he denys he did any such thing but lay it on his father. However it be the accusation is false; for his pepper he is allowed $5^1/_2$ rupees per the maund and the freightt not paid which is $^3/_4$ rupee more and custome time and brokerage saved is seaven per cent which is $^1/_2$ rupee more so that altogether he was allowed 6³/₄ rupees for if Mahmud Zaied who owned the other pepper paid ³/₄ rupee per maund freightt and designed not to bring it to Suratt but to send it to Bengall besides he paid part of the custome which Augau Peeree did not. Next he paid the Parracks and his own broker 3 per cent brokerage and Augau Peeree paid none. Next he sold on trust on an interest bill which the other did not but for ready money and lastly the President entreated Mahmud Zaied to let him have it but Augau Peeree entreated the President to take his. Augau Peeree being left to his liberty might have sold it in town if he had pleased and certainly would have done it had it been to his advantage. As to the coffee the banians were allowed for theirs no more then 11³/₄ rupees the maund all charges included and not 12⁵/₈. We refer to the clauses of the President's letters to the Right Honourable Company and his Excellency and Councill on this subject herewith sent by which appears Augau Peeree is allowed for his coffee ¹/₈ in each maund more then the Darians and that in 906 maunds (as his came to) amount to rupees 113¹/₄ which we hope Your Excellency etc will order him to repay.

239
COMPANY IN LONDON TO FORT ST GEORGE
16 APRIL 1697
E/3/92 EXTRACT FROM F. 271

We observe what you write touching the Armenians' application to the Nabob's camp for redressing an injury offered one of their nation by the Moors Juncanners and commend your way of proceedings therein, and resenting such particular applications, which we will by no means allow for the reasons you mention as well as many others, that may be very easily given. And to the end that an effectuall stop may be put to any future attempts of the like kind, we would have you procure satisfaction to such of your inhabitants as shall hereafter receive abuses from the Moors or Gentue officers or people of any kind, and not to suffer any inhabitants under your Government to make particular applications for any injury put on them by the Moors, but what shalbe done by from you on their behalfs.

You write the Armenians refuse to provide us painted callicoes at 15 per cent advance on the prime cost pretending the unsettled condition of the country governments, and the fear of being robbed, or rather, that they think the proffitt too small sea voyages being more gainfull. To which we answer, that those whether pretented or reall reasons, we think should the rather encourage and prompt you to be getting all the painters and other handicrafts people you can from the inland towns to settle at Madrass or Fort St Davids, by which means, we may in some measure repair the want of a currant trade for paintings and chay¹ goods during the wars in the country, and that you may have no reason to complain for want of those goods, we dare venture to give you our present Lieutenant Generall and Councill liberty to use your discretions in encouraging the Armenians or others to bring you large quantities thereof though it be at something above 15 per cent advance on prime cost not doubting, but you will take care so to manage this our permission, as that we may be encouraged to continue it hereafter on other occasions.

We shall be glad to hear that Coja Gregorye's invitation to his poor countrey men at Julpha to repair to and reside at Madrass has mett with a good effect esteeming it our advantage to have Madrass as populous especially with Christians as possible, which we would have you use all possible wayes and means to encourage and if you could get some Armenians to serve in our garrison as we formerly ordered, we should think it an acceptable service.

[1] deep red dye made from root of an Indian plant

240

COMPANY IN LONDON TO BOMBAY
16 APRIL 1697
E/3/92 EXTRACT FROM FF. 282-282V, 284

We are to answer one of yours of the 19th and two of the 18th March 1695/6. Your intention of joyning Aga Pera and Ben Walidas we very much approve of, hoping they wilbe obedient to all your orders, and not hold correspondence with our back friends, which we have reason to doubt the Parrocks are and countenanced too much for secrett private ends by some of our own people at Surratt of which the vast damage allowed upon the Thomas her cloth gives us a further suspicion, and the rather because Captain Pye affirmes some of the Armenians to whom the whole damage was due, told him, they were allowed but one eighth part thereof pray enquire stricktly, and with your utmost skill, who had the rest, and for what cause, and whether the owners were not greatly wronged in that adjustment or computation, and recover what they were wronged of from the partyes, which clandestinely got possession of it.

We are sorry the troubles at Surratt or anything else should hinder your sending us a just accompt of all our debt and creditts at Surratt, believing our estate is not so bad in that place, as we and you have been informed. And therefore pray make it Mr Bendall's particular charge or some other person in whom you can confide to see that busyness effectually done, and if there be any East India goods in store or upon the road or bespeak for which money hath been given out, such goods must be brought to the Companye's creditt for we know the Parrocks make a debt of it at interest, as soon as they have order to buy goods, pretending they must immediately send or remit money into the country, whereas we have reason to think that pautkaes, and all such ordinary goods are bought at long time.

We intend by the Bedford to send you Silvester Venturo as a writer a boy who served old Mr Calendar and speaks the Armenian language well, who you may keep at Bombay as an interpreter, or otherwise dispose of him as you shall think best for our service.

We are sorry the Armenians are like to be such loosers by the unsaleable limon coloured cloth of the Benjamin and Mocha's cargoes, and that we may hereafter avoid the like evill in any other, as we shall in that colour, do you by every conveyance send us an accompt of the sorts quantityes qualityes and colours of cloth vendible at Surratt with as particular directions as possible and the prices of all sorts of woollen goods at that markett as you see in our Persia letter we have ordered to be done there.

241
COMPANY IN LONDON TO GENERAL AND COUNCIL OF INDIA
12 MAY 1697
E/3/92 F. 293V

Since closing our larger pacquett by the Bedford and Dorothy we have made another contract with Persia De Marketon for the 4 chests of glass ware on board the Dorothy marked P321, 322, 333, 334. amounting to £156:16s:6d for which he is to advance 50 per cent as by his contract sent on that ship appears. But in regard his and Zachary D'Avatick's money fell short instead of the one third part mention'd in their severall contracts enclosed in our pacquetts to be received here they two have paid only the summes following vizt: Persia De Marketon but 950 li instead of 1259 li.1s.9d in his cloth contract, and 52 li:5s:6d in his glass contract, and Zachary D'Avatick but 574 li:17s:10d instead of 591 li:12s:7d which is his true proportion to have been paid hereby contract, wherein you will find a small mistake vizt: his 156 cloths doe amount unto £1774:17s:10d whereas in his contract it is said to amount to 1773 li:17s:10d which summes so paid short vizt: £361:7s:3d by Persia and 16 li:14s:9d by Zachary you are to receive on delivery of their goods at 8½ rupees per £ sterling.

You are like wise to take up our cashire's receipt from the said persons, and the other two Armenians Eager de Mezer and Gogebeck de Aviett and Sir John Chardin when you allow them in account the moneyes they have paid here our cashire Mr Portmans having given each 2 receipts of one date and tenour.

242

COMPANY IN LONDON TO GENERAL AND COUNCIL OF INDIA
18 MAY 1697
E/3/92 F. 294v

You will find by our letters and invoices by the Bedford and Dorothy that we have agreed with the Armenians for severall parcells of cloth and other goods on board those ships according to their contracts enclosed in these pacquets and that there might be no misunderstanding between the Armenians and you touching the delivery of those goods and the commission due on that account unto you, we have at their request told them, it shalbe the same and no more than what was formerly allowed by Coja Panous Calendar vizt: one per cent according to what we wrote to Surratt the 29th February 1691 by some Armenians who tooke passage on the Modena which order we now confirm.

243

JAMES BRUCE AND JAMES RAWLINGS AT ISFAHAN TO COMPANY IN
LONDON
11 JUNE 1697
E/3/53 EXTRACT FROM FF. 69, 77-77v

On the 2nd instant allso came to our hands a parcell of letters from Aleppo every one torn open by the Arabbs and most of them lost there comeing to our hands only a letter to Aveatick Callendar adviseing of his father's death with 2 or 3 scraps of newspapers etc. If there was any thing from your Honours itt is lost.

On the 5th currant we received letters from Tavris adviseing us of the arrivall of the 2 Armenians we sent to take charge of your Honours' affairs in that place. Mr Major writes there is a pacquet come to Erivan from your Honours which he dayly expected to arrive in Tavris and if there was no particular orders from your Honours therein he wold come away for Ispahaun in 14 or 15 dayes though at the writing of that letter had not delivered any thing to the Armenians sent by us and that besides the 620 pieces of your Honours' cloth which he sold in February last to Coja Mercara's vackeel att so intollerable a rate as 18 shakees per guz of Tavris which is larger than Ispahaun with 6 months vadaw[1] 20 pieces abated for damage, auroras, jams, redds, and greens pickt out of the whole. He hath now allso thrown away 300 pieces more att a more intollerable a rate then the above mentioned. We can't immagine what should be the meaning of such actions after he had received our letter not aproving of the sale of the first parcell and when att the same time he wrote us that there was no cloth in town but your Honours' nor any news of more a comeing from any parts and if we would send 900 pieces more itt would doe very well.

We hear the Queda Merchant a particular ship being hired by Auga Pery in Suratt was sent to Bengall where she took a lading for Persia and in her way to Gomroon put in att Muscatt where the Arabs have stopt her demanding all goods that belong to Armenians or other the king of Persia's subject aboard of her.

[1] *vādā* (Pers.): giving back, returning; contract for fixed term, or agreement especially for the payment of money at a stipulated period

244

EDWARD OWEN, JAMES BRUCE AND JAMES RAWLINGS AT ISFAHAN
TO COMPANY IN LONDON
15 JULY 1697
E/3/53 EXTRACT FROM FF. 90-92V

By this ship Charles we shall send to Bombay all the aurora and fine cloth received per ships Nassau and Mary, it being altogether improper for this market, for the doing whereof we have his Excellency etc's order.

No endeavours shall be wanting to dispose of ship Charles the 2d's cargoe, and that remaines of the Maries and Nassau's cloth, but we are very doubtfull of effecting it this winter, because this kingdom is full of cloth, and we have news dayly of more comeing in via Muscovia, and the way to Cabul and the northern parts of India is stoped up by the Osbeag war, which hinders the sale of great quantityes. And your honours must not expect so quick a sale of cloth for a year or two more, as may be afterwards found, for now both the Turkey Company and the Armenians in general, (who are equal enemies to your honours' designed trade in this kingdom,) endeavour what they can to discourage your honours by the daily importing great quantities of cloth on the latter their account, but if your honours continue to send that commodity yearly they will be discouraged, as severall of them are already, by giveing positive orders to their vakeels in Europe, not to buy any more cloth. The Turkey merchants at Aleppo, (as Coja Mercara one of the five intrusted gentlemen, and others have told us), have by them two year's cloth, which they could not sell because of that great quantity of your honours' cloth in Persia, so that the Armenians have carried their silk themselves to Europe. The Turkey merchants finding your trade likely to be ruined, all of them drew up a paper and signed it, and sent it to the grand seigneur at Constantinople, acquainting him that great number of the king of Persia's subjects, brought yearly vast quantities of silk into his dominions, and exported most gold and silver, which was vastly detrimental to him, and much enriched Persia, and so requested he would forbid it, which he did. At which the gentlemen at Aleppo were not a little glad, supposeing that now per force, the Armenians must take their cloth, but this order occasioning diverse disturbances, it is again countermaunded, and instead thereof diverse mints are set up, on the borders of his kingdom, vizt at Aleppo and Erzeroom, and no gold or silver is to be exported, unless it has his stamp upon it, the charge whereof is so great, that no gain is made thereon, and so things lye at present. He sayes further, that the Turkey merchants have wrote to their principals to send no more cloth, for if things be thus, they must rise and leave the place. The truth of this last, your honours are able to judge. Cloth will be a dull commodity for a year or two more, till some Company be weary and give out. There is a great deal on the properness of the colours, and among the Charles's cloth are a great many improper ones. If we can sell her cargoe, your honours will send out no more improper colours, because some of the samples of cloth sent over land must, (we hope) arrive safe. As to trucking cloth for silk, if it can be effected, it will be certainly a means, to vend a good quantity yearly and speedily, but to bring that about are many hindrances.

1 Nobody is allowed to export raw silk by sea. except the Dutch, who are forced to take their quota yearly, if silk be cheap, but being this year dear, the king will give them none. To get a rogom from the king to give us leave to export yearly one or two hundred loads of silk free of duties will be very difficult. For besides the great loss to the king, being four toman per load, we shall have the Dutch, the Armenians, and the Governor of Gelawn our enemies. The latter will be so, because a great part of his income is from duties on the silk; yet if your honours think it necessary to be got, if a present be made the king and his Ahtimadoulet, and your honours are willing to be at the expence of two or three thousand toman presents included, it may be got in all likelihood, especialy if the Ahtimadoulet be alive, who is a man of 90 years of age, and very covetous, and the king very simple: without a present to the king Aga Doud sayes it will not be accomplished. An embassadore is much expected, and if one came, it would be a great help to the obtaining this grant, or any other your honours should desire.

2d The Armenians would all be against it, because if the English should get leave to go to Gelawn, and buy silk free of duty, they will loose the profit of the silk trade, and that will be the greatest, if not only means to turn the Aleppo trade, for they will then consider, that it is better for them, to bring silk to Taveris or Ispahan and truck it for some cloth and some money, whereby they shall be gainers, than to let the English run away with the profit and unless your honours send to Gelawn and buy silk, the Armenians will never bring it to Ispahan, for a reason which your honours will see, that Coja Mercara, Coja Gogas Callendar, and Coja Gregore Colderent gave us on the 6th instant. The whole discourse that passed between us, was in substance this, that your honours in a letter of a later date, then that by the Charles reccommending the sale of her cargoe to them, (meaning that of the 4th May as we suppose), had cleared them of intermedling in your honours' affairs. We told them there was no such contained in that letter. They said they understood it so. However from the first said Coja Mercara I have declared, I could not meddle with the Company's business. The Callentar said he had no time to concern himself with it. And Coja Gregore said, perhaps others might be more holy, but for his part, he always looked on his own interest in the first place, and said he we can't take of all the cloth on our own accounts, for every place is full of it, except Heaven and Hell, so we should loose by it, and if we should sell it for the Company, it would not be sold in some years, and to sell it by little and little, that your honours' servants can do as well. If we designed to take silk for it, we must agree with the merchant before he went to Gelawn to buy it for so much profit, and then to tell him what cloth we would give him, and agree the price. To this we answered, that we were not to dispute how to dispose of it, that was left to them, what we desired was to have your positive answer, whither they would accept the consignment or no? But instead of a direct answer, Coja Mercara begun to reflect on the miscarriage at Taveris, out of spite to that trade, saying, I told you all along that would not turn to account, see what good comes of it, some of the cloth lies and rots, other is sold for loss. And as for bringing silk to Ispahan said they, that is but wind, for no body will be so mad, when we carry it to Aleppo. We have more ways then one to dispose it; for there are English, French, Venetians and Dutch, and if we can't sell it them for ready money, part money, cloth, cocheneal, amber, coral, or false pearl, then we can carry it to Europe our selves, but if we bring it to Ispahan there is only you to buy it, and if you won't give us a price, than we must let you have it, as you will, and take cloth at what price you will, for you won't let us put it on board your ships for England. To this we answered, that they could not fear that, for the Company had desired them, to take the cloth and dispose of it themselves, and to themselves if they pleased, and to give them silk at their own price. They said what good has the Company's cloth done here, it has ruined abundance of people. But being still prest to give a direct and positive answer, Coja Mercara said he was no cloth merchant, and could not meddle with it, and the Callentar said he could not meddle with it, and Coja Gregore said nor he neither, for he was so old, that he feign to trust his own business to the management of others, and how then could he do another man's, and they said they would give their answer in writeing to your honours, which is here inclosed. Herementioning the Armenians, we take the oportunity to acquaint your honours, of two things lately done by Coja Gogas Callendar to your honours' prejudice, the one is publick and known to every body, and the other not so publick. That, that is well known, is that he sent the king of Persia a present of four or five hundred toman in China ware and other Indian rarities, and made friends at court, so that at last he got the king's order for the writeing a letter to the king of England, desireing that as he had freed his subjects from paying custome in his countrey, so he would free the vakeels of Coja Gogas

Callender in England of it, and order that whatever his vakeels should have a mind to lade on the Company's ships for any port in India should be taken on board, as likewise the same from India to England. This comeing to the Armenians' knowledge, they seeing that he alone would drive all the trade, and being at difference with him at the same time, they went in a body to the king, and showed him, how detrimental it would be for him to do so, and got the order revoked. Another thing is, and as is pretended, was done only against the Ahtimadoulet, who endeavoured what he could to hinder the king's letter on the king of England, that the Callendar goes early in the morning to the Nazar (our great enemy) and tells him, if the king should grant the English a rogom clearing them of zadiack over all Persia, whereas before they were clear only for 5000 tomans in Ispahan, that they would ruin the king's revenues, bringing all merchants' goods under their name, and that for to bring this about, the English had given the Ahtimadoulet and his people two thousand tomans. Whereupon the Nazir goes to the king, and tells him this before the Ahtimadoulet, and getting the omraues on his side, prevailed with the king to revoke his order for the rogom, and this was the first hinderance in our business, which thank God is with much trouble at last happily ended, the afnama being brought us the 14th instant will [sic] the king's seal, and all the old rogoms renewed, and new ones granted, and we must say that Aga Doud has from beginning to the end of this business has been very diligent and stirring.

245
COMPANY IN LONDON TO ISFAHAN
1 SEPTEMBER 1697
E/3/92 EXTRACT FROM FF. 304V-305

The account you give us in yours of the 1st October of the slavery the Armenians live in under the Persians is no news to us, and the same, such of their nation as has been here, have alwayes informed us, and advised us themselves for that reason not to make publick use of Armenians in Persia, which was the reason, we formerly recommended Coja Gregorio, who goes for an European and a Frenchman, but is in truth a Christian. He lived many years in Bengall did great busyness for the French and sometimes for the English, and no doubt, but he has the same estimation in the place where he now lives, knowing the condition of the Armenians and the disposition of the Persian court, we were not so weak to think the Armenians could serve us with their power or interest at court, but that they might and would have been of great assistance to us in the sale of our cloth, and all other points in trade, and secretly could and would have given you the truest, frugallest and certainest directions how to proceed in all our affairs at court, although they durst not appear personally themselves to act in it. But some may think it improbable they should ever depart so much from their own interest, as to advise us how to deprive themselves of the Aleppo cloth trade. To which we reply, it's true, that it is not reasonable to expect it, it is against nature and reason to expect that such wise men should further our trade to the ruine of their own, which per adventure, they have been possessed of ever since any cloth was made in the world, for most certainly they are the most ancient merchants of the world, and therefore, as we put the matter upon them it was not intended to doe them an injury but a benefit to them, and all their countrymen, that they might have the cloth cheaper at Ispahan than at Aleppo, and that themselves might have the further trade of it to Tefflies, Tabris, the borders of Tartaria, and all other marketts, where they used to carry cloth for sale from Alepo and what else is it they do now. They are the generall buyers of cloth at Alepo and have the further trade of it to other places, and if they can buy the cloth at their own homes as cheap as at Alepo it would be to the advantage and not the loss of their nation, which we have been the larger upon, that our Agent may be the better able to declare and explain our meaning to those people, whereas on the contrary upon Captain Brangwin's pretended hypothesis in scattering our estate in severall parts of those vast and wide countryes, we cannot in common prudence or according to the principles of humane nature expect other than that the Armenians in all such places should by all the civill arts they can use without force be opposites to our trade in cloth, and we cannot think the worse of any of the Armenians for being against that, which is directly against their interest.

Upon the whole matter we shall expect the account we writt for from you of all that is past, that we may know where we are, and what is become of our scattered estate, and for the future, we desire our Agent and Councill to keep our estate close about them, and make their sales only in Ispahan as the English do at Aleppo. Let the Armenians have our cloth at Ispahan as cheap as they can possibly buy it at Alepo or rather cheaper, and then you may expect their friendly and honest advice, which we would alwayes have you, have a great regard to, though we do not confine you to follow it, when you do not think it for our interest.

246

SIR JOHN GAYER, JOHN BURNISTON, ENOCH WALSH, WILLIAM AISLABIE AND BENJAMIN STACEY AT BOMBAY TO COMPANY IN LONDON
18 DECEMBER 1697
E/3/53 EXTRACT FROM FF. 207-207V

Wee wish wee could give your Honours as good a character of the Armenians as you desire.

They are a people not guilty of those open debaucheryes and extravagencies that Europeans are but they are like all other of these Eastern nations in designing, and cheating if they can.

When the President and Councill was to adjust the damages of the 3 ships' cargoes sold Agapery and his brother, because the Bulgar hides perpetuanas and stuffs were the worst part of his bargaine and such a drugg that hee should lose by them though the damage of the former was computed to bee but 88 rupees, and the latter which was 8 bales to bee but 166 rupees, there being as they wrote us 49 pieces not at all the worse, Agapery by the benifitt of his contract to refuse damaged goods when adjusted threw the whole on your Honours' hands, though the President and Councill offerd to allow him more than the reale damage as your Honours may see in the letter to us of the 17th May 97, which is in letter booke no.Z. Agapery would also have put goods on the President and Councill's hands that hee had provided ere his contract for Ahmadavad etc goods arrived that were wholly impropper for the markett of Europe, and others that was fitt to bee sent home hee rated them higher as they write us than they could provide them by the broakers. Hee did a long time refuse to provide any goods according to his father's last contract, but at last hee has consented to provide some, but to what amount we don't yet know. Wee are very sencible that the Parracks and perhaps some others doe endeavour to represent them as ill as possible to us for that they are much offended with the method your Honours have taken in imploying them; therefore wee are very cautious in crediting reports concerning them. In the detecting the cheat of the Mint Shrofes at Suratt that wee advised of in our last the chief instrument was Agapery; but wee doe think the chief motive that induced him to it was his hatred to Vittule Parrack, who is his enemye as much as possible hee can bee on all occasions.

247
COMPANY IN LONDON TO BENGAL
26 JANUARY 1697/98
E/3/93 EXTRACT FROM FF. 13V-14

Your building a double brick godown, we don't think much of considering the necessity you were then under, and the hazard of fire, we think you did well enough to appease the merchants by the method you took, after so severe a loss, and in making Coja Panous Calendar's factors easy in adjusting the damaged broad cloth to their satisfaction. We likewise approve of your orders for providing some luckhowries[1] et cetera Pattana goods, whereby you may the better distinguish how well the Armenians deal with you in the goods, they are by contract to provide for our account.

[1] lacowrie: plain white cotton textile from Bengal

248
THOMAS MAJOR AT TABRIZ TO COMPANY IN LONDON
12 FEBRUARY 1697/98
E/3/53 EXTRACT FROM F. 354

On the 14 past arrived an other carravan from Spahaun with 900 pieces broad cloth and 100 stuffs the which hope may all be sold before Nourouze[1] though att present cloth yeilds a miserable price by reason of the great quantitys that come from Turkey there haveing arrived here upwards of 8000$^{1}/_{2}$ pieces since my departure from Spahaun reds and greens att 17$^{1}/_{2}$ to 18 shakees per orchum[2], jams 23 to 24 shakees, auroras 30 shakees per ditto fine cloth none sels besides 5 to 6 months payment the which the Armenians sell att and I am forced to doe the same, or elce could not be able to procure customers, though I thanke God have sold more then any two persons of them, and on the 7th instantt have disposed of 600$^{1}/_{2}$ pieces broad cloth to Coja Caleust vakeell to Coja Mercar Surhad att 18 shakees per who designes to send itt over land to India.

[1] *Nawruz* (Pers.): New Year's Day in Persia (March 21); first day of solar year
[2] sic - unidentified [?corrupt form of *okka* (measure of weight)]

249
COMPANY IN LONDON TO BOMBAY
10 MARCH 1697/98
E/3/93 EXTRACT FROM F. 28V

By the enclosed contracts you will see our agreement with the Armenians for the cloth on board the Thomas, whereof Eager D'Meazer and Pocra D'Petrus have paid their full fifth part of the money as therein mentioned. But Persia D'Marketom has paid but 483 li: 17s: 1d which you must take notice of, the rest being to be made good to you in Surratt.

250
COMPANY IN LONDON TO SURAT
10 MARCH 1697/98
E/3/93 EXTRACT FROM F. 30

We take notice of the account you give us of the goods left upon your hands by Auga Peree, and the low price you are bid for them, but not one word can we read, whether or for what they are disposed of. If it be not done already, take it for a constant rule, always to sell our cloth and other perishable goods as well as you can at invoice price or under, rather than keep them in your warehouse which your discretion must tell you is the ready way to encrease our loss. If Auga Peree designed the yellow cloth for Persia as you intimate we hope you have been so prudent as to send it thither, if you could not get it off at Surratt.

251
COURT MINUTES
29 APRIL 1698
B/41 P. 278B

The Court demanding an account, what forwardness the Com-pany's letters and advices for India, were in, for dispatch of the Mary, and Russell, now at Gravesend, were made acquainted, that the invoices, and contract for the glass, and cutlary ware laden on those ships, could not be perfected, untill the advance money, which was to be paid by the Armenians, on delivery of their goods at Surrat, were adjusted. On serious debate whereof had, the Court were pleased to order, that twenty five per cent, be taken of them over and above the prime cost and charges, on the said goods, which is to be inserted, in the invoices, and contracts accordingly. And forasmuch, as by a previous contract, the said Armenians agreed, to pay down here one fifth part of the value of the goods, which are to be delivered them, at Surrat, which they cannot fully answer the Court thought fit to direct, that the three Armenians be obliged, by contract, joyntly, and severally, to take off, and receive from the Company at Surrat, the whole quantity of goods invoiced, and laden on the said ships Mary, and Russell, according to their respective agreements.

252
SAMUEL ANNESLEY, STEPHEN COLT AND EPHRAIM BENDALL AT SURAT
TO COMPANY IN LONDON
6 MAY 1698
E/3/54 EXTRACT FROM FF. 35V-38V

The Armenians from Persia have brought 700 double peices of fine broad-cloth, and have sold the scarlets by themselves at 6 rupees the yard, and greens at $4^1/_2$, and both in equal parts for $5^9/_{16}$ deducting $5^1/_4$ per cent for time and brokerage. What wee have sold of your Honnours' woolen manufacture wee have obliged the merchants not to carry to Persia til the limited time of the factors' contract there is expired.

Some Armenian merchants in a Dutch ship lately arrived from Persia brought 400 pieces of broadcloth sold them by your factors there. So that Augau Peeree bought some of the aurora cloth at rupees $4^1/_2$ per yard deducting $5^1/_4$ per cent. The French sold their cloth lately at 2 rupees the yard that the Pontchartrain brought out.

Augau Peeree sent an express to the Armenian gone to court who was nocqueda of the Queda Merchant to disswade him and the rest of his company from complaining or to lay the capture of the ship Queda Merchant upon al Europeans in general, but this day he came and told us another Armenian here had received advice that Mooculleescennie had presented them al before the King, and laid it to our charge alone, requesting a goozbundar or messenger to carry orders to this Governour to force us to make sattisfaction for their loss, or bring Samuel Annesley and the chief broker to court to answer the charge before the King. Which 'tis said is granted. Wee hope this may be some way or other diverted ... Wee apprehend much trouble and expence from this covetous oppressive Governour, but wee think he'le not fal upon us before the Moco fleet is imported, least he endangers it thereby; after which 'tis probable our trade wil be stopt, and our persons confined, if he proceeds not to more violent courses.

253

COURT MINUTES
7 SEPTEMBER 1698
B/41 PP. 308B-309A

A Court of Committees holden the 7th September 1698

On reading a report from the Committee for Buying of Goods, touching a contract, by them made with Mr Ongley, on behalf of Persia De Marketom, and other Armenians, which follows in haec verba:

By the Committee of Buying Goods, the 6 September 1698.

Present

Sir William Gore, Sir Rowland Aynsworth, Mr Cock.

This Court having, on the 31th of August last, referred to us, the proposall made on account of the Armenians, for their taking off the Company's hands at Surrat, to the value of twenty five, of thirty thousand pounds, in cloth, and other goods; wee have accordingly discoursed with Mr

Ongley, on behalf of Persia De Marketom, and other Armenians, and do find, that they are ready to contract, for twenty five thousand pounds value, in cloth, and other woollen manufactures, and for five thousand pounds value, in the goods following, or some of them vizt. lead, corrall, cocheneal, false pearl, looking-glasses, amber, iron, cordage, assidue[1], and glass ware, to be delivered to their order, at Surrat, allowing the Company twenty five per cent profit, on the prime cost, and charges of the said goods, to pay down one third of the money here, as the Company pays it, and two thirds at Surrat, within six months, after the arrivall of the said goods; or to be allowed discount, according to former contracts, for what paid sooner; to have a servant, or merchant, go on the ship, wherein the goods are, free of charge; to allow the like, and no greater charges, on the landing of the goods, at Surrat, than the Company themselves pay, as mentioned in former contracts, and the Company to be obliged, to send no more cloth to Surrat, this season.

Whereupon, having further debated the matter, with Mr Ongley, and the said Persia De Marketom, wee have agreed with them for twenty six thousand pounds value in woollen manufactures, and four thousand pounds value, in the forementioned commoditys or any of them, on the conditions aforesaid, excepting onely, that the merchant, who is to accompany the goods, pay the usuall charges.

That the adjustment of all manner of sea damages, that may happen, in the voyage for which onely, an allowance is to be made, be left to the President of Surrat, for the time being, and a person chosen by the Armenians, and in case they do not agree, then to Sir John Gayer's single determination.

That if the Company's officers, at Surrat, shall take any of the glass ware, or other goods to the value of a chest, two, or three, in proportion of sorts, they shall pay for the same according to the invoice price, with a proportionable allowance for damages, on the other goods, of the like sort, in the voyage.

That the time, for paying the two thirds of the money at Surrat, be only four months.

The value of the rupee, and other matters, not before particularly mentioned, to be the same as in the last contract.

All which is submitted, to the further determination of this Court.

The Court approved thereof, and ordered, that it be left, to the said Committees, to cause a contract to be drawn up, pursuant to the agreement, mentioned in the said report.

---

[1] arsedine: gold colored alloy of copper and zinc rolled into thin leaf and used to ornament toys, etc.

254
COMPANY IN LONDON TO BENGAL
28 OCTOBER 1698
E/3/93 EXTRACT FROM FF. 60V, 61

We are informed by Mr Bowridge that doreas[1] mulmulls[2] and cossaes[3] may be bought 40 per cent cheaper at Baharro beyound Pattana than at Culcutta and if that should be soe, we think it may not be amiss for you to send Mr Ralph Sheldon or an Armenian merchant thither to buy up the value of fifteen or twenty thousand pounds in those commodityes at that place, which may help to bring your engrossers, such as Muttradas, Golollchund, Mannickchund and Nehallchund to more reasonable rates, but whatever you do with those men, it would be best to do it at first assoon as you receive our letters, and receive their goods which are ready into your godowns, and pay them in Rs 8/8 because if the New Company should send out ships, as it's likely, and we believe they will, all goods that are ready wilbe raised in price upon the arrivall of a ship or two from the New Company.

There are admirable and great variety of silks and silver and gold stuffs at Banharas, to which place, we once sent a factor whose name, as we remember, was Mr Dod, and he did send us some few variety of very fine silks and silver stuffs, but he was so unfaithfull in his whole pro-ceedings buying and charges, that it did not only cause us to repent that experiment but beat us off from ever attempting it again, but now we are of opinion, that if you could gett Cojah Surhaud, or any honest Armen-ian, that we could trust with two thousand pounds value, to invest at Benharres, allowing him only commission for what he so invests and brings down to you, we think it might be worth our while to renew that experiment which providing successfull might prove a means much to enlarge our trades in those parts, but you must by all means direct, that the gold and silver in any such silks for England, be not beaten or pressed down as the former Benharres stuffs were, because such beating or flat-ting down of the gold or silver, broke the plate to such a degree, that in wearing the plate soon shattered out, let all the Benharres goods be packt up in good dry chests by themselves and invoiced by themselves, that we may the better observe, how we are dealt with by the party you intrust.

[1] doria; doriyā (Hind.): striped Indian muslin
[2] malmal (Hind.): thin variety of plain white muslin
[3] plain white muslin

255

NEGOTIATIONS BETWEEN COMPANY SERVANTS AND ARMENIAN
SHOPKEEPERS AT ISFAHAN
21 DECEMBER 1698
E/3/54 FF. 100-101V

Wednesday the 21st December 1698

The Armenian shopkeepers haveing been here severall times, to see the stuffs and at last came to 95 mamoodies per piece for the Charles the 2d's perpetuanoes and 15 months vaddaw, to abate 1 per cent per month. Wee had often aquainted them that wee could not sell those perpetuanoes unless they would take all the sayes in the house with them and now also desired Auga Doud to use all the endeavours he could to get them to take the says and in such case wee would agree with them for the perpetuanoes. Hereupon they offered 40 mamoodies per piece for them and at last after much ado came to 50 as the same vaddaw as aforesaid; so for 2 or 3 days have left off talking with them till 1 day Auga Doud went to the caravansaroy and calling them together aquainted them had brought yaupungees[1] and were a goeing pack up all the stuffs and send em away and further that he had no designe upon them that he was not broker and should gett nor loose anything whither they bought them or let them alone but that as he was their friend and countryman he had been endeavouring to do them a kindness and had been laying downe before the English the trouble and loss of sending away the stuffs, shewing them how much their charges would amount to with freight and danger of the seas and dammage both by land and sea with abundance of other arguments he had been at them severall days and brought em down to 80 mamoodies per piece for the says, and therefore in one word if they would take em at that price they might bargaine for them and perpetuanoes together but if not he desired their final answer for he could not offer to mention a lower price then that. He discovered to them that upon the lowness of the price that nothing could be cheaper and that they cost twice as much in England. To all which they replyed that if they were worth never so much or cost what they will what should they do with things that they could not turn into money and what should they gett by them if they bought them for 10 mamoodies per piece and kept them till they rotted, that they had sold but 3 or 4 boats of them to Persians and some had brought them back again, after cut to pieces curseing and drubbing them because they durst sell them such stuff, and that nevertheless they came the next day again to see them and seperated all the dammaged from the good ones, and this day had a long conference about them and the utmost they would come to after all was that for the says they will have 100 pieces allowed for dammage to make the whole good they will give 70 mamoodies per piece on 15 months vaddaw to abate one per cent per month for what they pay beforehand and that means they take the says they will give but ninety mamodies per piece for the perpetuanoes with the same vaddaw and interest at the same rate.

---

[1] probably pongee; *pŭn-chī* (Chin.): soft unbleached kind of Chinese silk

256

JAMES BRUCE, JAMES RAWLINGS AND JOSEPH HARRIS AT ISFAHAN TO GOMBROON
30 DECEMBER 1698
E/3/54 EXTRACT FROM FF. 104-105

On the 23d currant wee came to an agreement with the Armenian shopkeepers for the Charles the 2d perpetuanoes and all the sayes jams both new and old at 190 shakes per piece for the Charles' perpetuanoes long ells and Colechester ells being 1500 pieces 140 shakes per piece for all the sayes on which wee were to allow 60 pieces for damages, the vadaw to nixt nouroose come 12 months being $14^1/_2$ months time from this time to abate one per cent on what payd beforehand and to pay 1 per cent per month for what [should remain?] after the time was out, but the bargain is come to nothing at last for they would give no manner of security for the payment of the money not so much as to be bound for one another, as they did agree for the Charles' cloth sould them nor to pay for them as they carryed them out, nor to make over their money to their brokers to pay it on the expiration of the time but to trust barely to their honesty whither they will pay us or no and Moola would not inshure any thing upon those termes. They owe him still 3500 tomans on account of the Charles the 2d's cloth sold them last year which he has payed the Company long agoe and the most substantialest of them has broke three times in Spahaune and sometimes payd 50 shakes per tomand in composition and as Moola would not trust them, wee could not think it secure to trust them and so broke off the bargain again though wee don't question to find out some other way to dispose of them ere this winter be over.

257
SURAT CONSULTATIONS
28 JANUARY - 19 FEBRUARY 1698/99
E/3/54 EXTRACT FROM FF. 143V-148

[28 January]

Last night many Turks and Arrabs gathered about Auga Peeree's house in a tumultuous manner and threatned his life because they said he had composed the difference between the Governor and us in such a manner, that they were excluded from receiving any of the 1400000 rupees the King ordered them for their losses in Hasson Ammedon's ship. Auga Peeree sending us word thereof, wee immediately ordered Venwallidas to go and complain of it to the Governor and desire him to discountenance such proceedings in the beginning, least they proceed to a greater height.

[4 February]

Some Armenians in towne after a freight of about 25000 rupees for the Mary to Persia and will oblige themselves to lade her in twenty dayes time. Wee told them wee would make no agreement for her but would recommend it to the Generall and Councill.

[7 February]

Auga Peeree Callendar offers us for the tarr pitch and iron on board the Mary, Thomas and Russell 30 per cent and for the gunns 50 per cent upon the invoyce all charges to be his making only the allowance of usual time. Wee would have perswaded him to buy the cordage and anchors, but he declines medling with them. Wee told him wee would write to his Excellency Sir John Gayer about it.

[9 February]

Being ordered to press the Armenians to give 4 corge per ox bale freight upon the Mary to Persia, wee have been endeavouring to do so some dayes past, but this day they brought us their determinate answer that they will not give it.

[18 February]

Offering to clear the Armenians' cloth that they bought of our Right Honourable Masters in England, that came out in the Thomas Mary and

Russell; Bhidas refused to let it pass in our name but wil have it entered as their owne. The Armenians that bought goods of the interlopers in the same manner, having done so, rather then submitt to this, wee resolved to let it lye and ordered Venwallidas to employ his interest to remove this interruption.

[19 February]

The Armenians that owne the cloth in the customehouse consent that wee shall give the Governor etc 3000 rupees to let it pass as English and pay custome accordingly, so wee gave Venwallidas order to offer the summ, for which he tels us as he can accommodate the matter.

258

COMPANY IN LONDON TO BOMBAY
6 APRIL 1699
E/3/93 EXTRACT FROM F. 88

Enclosed comes the Armenians' contract for one hundred eighty seven cloths, on which they have paid one thousand thirty five pounds, eleven shillings and eight pence here which is to be deducted out of the totall amount. You have a contract made with Captain Heath for sixteen iron guns, and a bill of exchange for our generrall or Mr Bendalls paying rupees 1335 into our cash at Bombay or Surratt inpursuance of the said contract.

259

SIR JOHN GAYER, JOHN BURNISTON, ENOCH WALSH, WILLIAM AISLABIE
AND BENJAMIN STACEY AT BOMBAY TO COMPANY IN LONDON
8 APRIL 1699
E/3/55 F. 22

This is at the request of Agapery Callendar to recomend to your Honours' favour two Armenians (the bearers hereof) who we presume he hath intrusted to negotiate his affaires with his father's trustees. We think it unnecessary to give you any character of them for that they are strangers to us, and knowing your Honours' inclinations to encourage them, it's needless for us to request it. Agapery has promised to pay, and we have wrote to the President and Councile to receive, their permission money. They have some diamonds laden on the Thomas on which ship they take their passage, they have also a small box of goods which they say is for presents therefore we told

Captain Pye that we would advise you thereof that he might come to no damage by receiving of it seeing we could not diswade them from carrying it with them.

260
COMPANY IN LONDON TO BENGAL
20 DECEMBER 1699
E/3/93 EXTRACT FROM F. 125V

Since Coja Surhad Israel was so serviceable to you in his negotiations at the Prince's court, you will do well to confer upon him the needfull marks of our favour to encourage his past and future behaviour.

261
CONTRACTS BETWEEN COMPANY IN LONDON AND ARMENIAN MERCHANTS
APRIL 1700
E/1/196 PP. 43-46

To all people to whom these presents shall come Gregorio de Stephanes merchant stranger sendeth greeting whereas the Governor and Company of Merchants of London tradeing into the East Indies have laden on board ship Tavistock whereof Captain Mathew Martyn is Commander, the severall goods and merchandizes and of the respective values hereundermenconed the perticulars whereof are more fully enumerated in the invoice of the said ship Tavistock amounting in the whole to the sume of nine thousand foure hundred twenty eight pounds five shillings and eight pence marked and numbered as hereundermenconed and consigned the same unto their Generall and Councill of Bombay or President and Councill of Suratt. Now know yee that the said Gregorio De Stephanes doth for himself his executors administrators and assignes covenant promise and grant to and with the said Governor and Company and their successors by these presents that he the said Gregorio de Stephanes or his correspondences Joseph De Stephanes and Aved Auga or his factor or their or either of their assignes shall upon the said goods' arrivall att Suratt or within three dayes after their landing and houseing in the Company's warehouses there receive and pay for the same the said summes of nine thousand four hundred twenty eight pounds five shillings and eight pence and eighteen per cent advance thereon makeing in the whole eleaven thousand one hundred twenty five pounds seaven shillings and six pence according to the covenant aftermencioned and shall and will allso pay the custome and charges that shall be paid on landing and houseing the said goods as aforesaid. And whereas the said Gregorio De Stephanes hath paid into the Company's treasury here the summe of foure thousand seaven hundred and fourteen pounds two shillings and ten pence which is hereby declared and agreed to be accepted for the first payment in part of the prime cost and charges of the said goods, he the said Gregorio de Stephanes doth for himself his executors administrators and assignes covenant promise and grant to and with the said Governor and Company, that he or his said correspondents shall and will pay or cause to be paid unto the said Generall or the said Company's President and Councill the summe of four thousand seaven hundred and fourteen pounds two shillings and tenn pence being the residue of the prime cost and charges of the said goods together with eighteen per cent advance on the whole within six months after the arrivall of the said goods att Suratt as aforesaid the said Gregorio De Stephanes or his assignes being allowed the usuall discount in case of payment before the end of the said six months Provided always and it is hereby expressly declared and agreed that in case the said goods should happen to be lost or micarry in the voyage (which God forbid) so as they shall not come to the hands of the said Company's Generall or their President and Councill at Suratt, then and in such case the said Governor and Company and their successors shall well and truely pay or cause to be paid unto the said Gregorio de Stephanes or his assignes the said summe of four thousand seaven hundred and fourteen pounds two shillings and ten pence received as is before mencioned with interest after the rate of six per cent per annum from the date of these presents. Item it is agreed that if any sea damage shall happen to the said goods in their voyage reasonable allowance shall be made for the same as the Generall or President and Councill shall think fitt and that for each pound sterling to be paid on the goods aforemencioned att Suratt the said Generall or President and Councill there are to receive eight rupees and a half. But before any of the said goods shall be delivered into his or his correspondents' custody he or his correspondents shall give security by bond to the said Generall or President and Councill's satisfaction for makeing due payment for the said goods according to the agreement aforemencioned. And in case the security offered should not be approved of then he the said Gregorio de Stephanes or his correspondents shall have the said goods delivered unto them as they pay for the same allowing discount. In wittness whereof to the one part of these presents the said Governor and Company have caused their common seale to be affixed and to the other part thereof the said Gregorio De Stephanes hath sett his hand and seale this six and twentyeth day of Aprill 1700

The goods abovemencioned are as followeth vizt

Two hundred eighty one bales of broad cloth containing 843 Value £9428:5:8

Gregorio de Stephano

G:S

Sealed and delivered in the presence of
Robert Blackborne Secretary William Blackborne

	£	s	d
The like contract with Ariton de Shaudiback for goods to the value of	2332	18	4
The like contract with Johannes de Mirzo for goods to the value of	677	11	8
Ditto with Johannes De Avid for	1295	4	1
Ditto with Boydasar De Gorgorio	2022	8	7
Ditto with Asander De Mardirote for	1327	18	1
Ditto Grigrio De Stephanes for white lead for	104	11	10

Received the 26 Aprill 1700 of Mr Ariton De Shaudiback the summe of eleven hundred and sixty six pounds nine shillings and two pence in part of payment for broad cloath shipt on board the Tavistock for Surat Captain Martyn Commander I say received for the Honourable East India Company £1166: 9: 2 John Du Bois

Received 26th Aprill 1700 of Johannes De Merza the summe of three hundred thirty eight pounds fifteen shillings and ten pence in part of payment for broad cloath shipt on board the Tavistock for Surratt Captain Martyn Commander I say received for the Honourable East India Company £338:15:10 Per me John Du Bois

Received 26th Aprill 1700 of Johannes De Avid the summe of six hundred forty seaven pounds twelve shillings in part of payment for broad cloath shipt on board the Tavistock for Surratt Captain Mathew Martyn Commander I say received for the Honourable East India Company £647:12: - Per me John Du Bois

Received 26th Aprill 1700 of Gregorio De Stephanes the summe of foure thousand seaven hundred and foureteen pounds two shillings and ten pence in part of payment for broad cloth shipt on board the Tavistock for Surratt

Captain Mathew Martyn Commander I say received for the Honourable East India Company
£4714: 2s:10d Per me John Du Bois

Received 26th Aprill 1700 of Mr Bogdasar De Gregorio the summe of one thousand and eleaven pounds foure shillings and foure pence in part of payment for broad cloth shipt on board the Tavistock for Suratt Captain Martyn Commander I say received for the Honourable East India Company
£1011: 4s: 4d John Du Bois

Received the 26th Aprill 1700 of Mr Ascandar De Mardiros six hundred and sixty three pounds nineteen shillings in part of payment for broad cloth shipt on board the Tavistock for Surratt Captain Martyn Commander I say received for the Honourable East India Company
£663:19: - John Du Bois

Received 28th Aprill 1700 of Grigrio De Stephanes fifty two pounds five shillings and eleven pence in part of payment for white lead shipt on board the Tavistock for Surratt Captain Martyn Commander I say received for the Honourable East India Company
£52: 5s:11d John Du Bois

262

CONTRACTS BETWEEN COMPANY IN LONDON AND ARMENIAN
MERCHANTS
MAY 1700
E/1/196 PP. 51-54

Contract with Baubar De Sultanum on behalfe of Arutyn De Shaudiback for 4 bales of broad cloth contayning 12 cloths 4 chests of glass ware 2 chests of wrought iron and looking glasses one box of corrall beads amounting in the whole to 710 li:01s:11d. Dated 7th May 1700. Correspondents or order.

Contract with Grigrio De Stephanes on behalfe of Bogdasar De Gorgorio for 47 broad cloth containing 147 cloths amounting to 1006 li: 3s: 9d. Dated 7 May 1700. Correspondents Gregorio Dea Agob John Agnozar de Bogdasar.

Contract with Bauber de Sultanum on behalfe of Ovanes de Meazer for three chests of broad cloth containing 22 cloths, one chest of wrought iron cutlers ware etc amounting in the whole to 338:18: 6. Dated the 7th May 1700.

Contract with Grigrio De Stephanes for 94 bales of broad cloth containing 282 cloths 5 barrells of rough amber 4 chests of cutlers ware telescopes musquets etc amounting in the whole to 4083 li:11s: 8d. Dated 7 May 1700.

Contract with Arutyn George on behalfe of Ascondur De Mardirose for 43 bales of broad cloth containing 69 cloths amounting to the value of 797 li:02s: 4d. Dated 7th May 1700. Corespondent Ohon De Marcar Holder.

Contract with Arutyn George on behalfe of Johannes de Avid for 20 bales of broad cloth containing 60 cloths amounting to 656 li:10s:01d: dated 7th May 1700. Corespondent Menas De Panow or his factor.

Additionall contract with Grigrio De Stephane on behalfe of Bogozas de Gorgorio for 9 bales of broad cloth containing 27 cloths amounting to 258 li:03s: 4d. Dated 9th May 1700. Corespondents Gregorio de Agob John and Agdozar de Bogdazar.

Additionall contract with Arutyn George on behalfe of Johannes De Avid for one bale of broad cloth amounting to 44 li:07s:10d. Dated 9th May 1700. Correspondent Menas de Panous or his factor.

Additionall contract with Ascondar De Mardirose for 4 bales of cloth shipt on the Tavistock amounting to 148 li:02s: 0d. Dated 9th May 1700. Correspondent Ohon de Marcar Holder.

Additionall contract with Grigrio De Stephanes for 3 bales of cloth amounting to 110 li:03s:01d on the Tavistock. Dated 9 May 1700. Corespondents Joseph De Stephanes and Avid Auga or his factor.

Received 10 May 1700 of Gregorio de Stephanes merchant stranger fifty five pounds one shilling six pence in full of what he was by contract to pay downe on account of cloth shipt on board the Tavistock for Surratt for which I have given three receipts of this tenour and date one of which being taken up the other to be voyd for the East India Company.
£55: 1: 6 John Du Bois

Received the 10th of May 1700 of Ascander de Mardirose merchant stranger per Arutyn George merchant stranger seventy four pounds one shilling in full for what he was by contract to pay downe on account of cloth shipt on board the Tavistock for which I have given three receipts of this tenour and date one of which being taken up the others to be void for the East India Company.
£74: 1: - John Du Bois

Received the 10th May 1700 of Johannes De Aved merchant stranger per Arutin George merchant stranger twenty two pounds three shillings and eleven pence in full for what he was by contract to pay down on account of cloath shipt on board the Tavistock for which I have given three receipts of this tenour and date one of which being taken up the others to be voyd for the East India Company.

£22: 3:11 John Du Bois

Received 10th May 1700 of Bogdasar de Grigorio per Gregorio De Stephanes merchant stranger one hundred twenty nine pounds two shillings eight pence in full of what he was by contract to pay downe on account of cloth shipt on board the Tavistock for Surratt for which I have given three receipts of this tenour and date one of which being taken up the other to be voyd for the East India Company.

£129: 2: 8 John Du Bois

Received 10th May 1700 of Gregorio de Stephanes merchant stranger two thousand and forty one pounds fifteen shillings ten pence in full of what he was by contract to pay downe on account of cloth shipt on board the Martha for which I have given three receipts of this tenour and date one of which being taken up the other to be voyd for the East India Company.

£2041:15:10 John Du Bois

Received the 10th of May 1700 of Arutun De Shaudeback merchant stranger three hundred fifty five pounds one shilling in full of what he was by contract to pay downe on account of cloth shipt on board the Martha for which I have given three receipts of this tenour and date one of which being taken up the others to be voyd for the East India Company.

£355: 1: 0 John Du Bois

Received the 10th May 1700 of Ovanes De Mirza merchant stranger one hundred sixty nine pounds nine shillings and three pence in full for what he was by contract to pay downe on account of cloth shipt on board the Martha for which I have given three receipts of this tenour and date one of which being taken up the others to be voyd for the East India Company.

£169: 9: 3 John Du Bois

Received 10th May 1700 of Ascander De Mardirose per Arutin George merchant stranger three hundred ninety eight pounds eleaven shillings and two pence in full of what he was by contract to pay downe on account of cloth shipt on board the Martha for which I have given three receipts of this tenour and date one of which being taken up the others to be voyd for the East India Company.

£398:11: 2 John Du Bois

Received the 10th of May 1700 of Johannes de Aved by Aratin George merchant stranger three hundred twenty eight pounds five shillings in full of what he was by contract to pay downe on account of cloth shipt on board the Martha for which I have given three receipts of this tenour and date one of which being taken up the others to be voyd for the East India Company.
£328:05:00 John Du Bois

Received the 10th May 1700 of Bogdasar de Gregorio merchant stranger per Gregorio de Stephanes merchant stranger eight hundred and three pounds one shilling and tenn pence in full of what he was by contract to pay downe on account of cloth shipt on board the Martha for which I have given three receipts of this tenour and date one of which being taken up the others to be voyd for the East India Company.
£803:01:10 John Du Bois

263
COURT MINUTES
22 JANUARY 1702/03
B/44, PP. 65B-66A

The Court takeing into consideration, the report from the Committee thereunto appointed, touching two Bills of Exchange drawn on the Company from the President and Councill of Bengall, at Fort William, in Culcutta, the one without date, for three thousand eight hundred seaventy five pounds, payable within thirty dayes, after the arrivall of ship Sidney, in the River of Thames, unto Nathaniel Higginson Esquire and Coja Malleer Auwannoes, Armenian, the bill importing, that it was, for twenty thousand rupees at two shillings six pence, with fifty five per cent bottomree advance; the other dated at said Fort William, the 19th January 1701/2, for four thousand two hundred sixty two pounds ten shillings, payable within thirty dayes after the arrivall of ships Josia, in the River of Thames, unto Nathaniell Higginson Esquire and Coja Malleer Auwannoes, Armenian, the bill importing, that it was for twenty two thousand rupees worth of Patana goods, received there of Coja Surhad Israel, valuing the rupee at two shillings six pence, with fifty five per cent bottomree advance. And it being pretended, that the reason for drawing those bills arose, from a contract made here with Coja Panous Calender, dated the 21th January 1695, which imports that the said Panous covenanted, that he, or his assignes, should by their factors in Bengall, provide for the Company, at Patana, and parts adjacent, luckhowries printed and white, and any other sorts of measured goods, and commodityes, with their own money, to be delivered the Company's agents, and factors at Hughly, or Chuttanuttee, according to the Company's order, for which they were to be allowed fifteen per cent on the prime cost of the said goods, and all other necessary charges, which should arise upon the same, till they arrive at Hughly, or Chuttanuttee. And if the said Panous or his factors, should be willing to insure the adventure of the said goods for England, on the Company's shipping, the Company's factors, should give them bills of bottomree on the Company, for the value of such goods, as they should so insure, with fifty five per cent advance on the said one hundred fifteen pounds, which should be paid here to the said Panous, or order, within thirty dayes after the arrivall of the said goods, in the River of Thames, reckoning eight rupees in such case for one pound sterling. And forasmuch, as it does not appear by the invoices, come home by the said ships Sidney, and Josia, nor by any letters, or other advices, received from the said President and Councill, that the goods, for which the bills were drawn, were sent home by the said ships, although by the contract, the bills of bottomree of fifty five per cent were to be given, payable thirty dayes after the arivall of the goods, so insured, in the River of Thames, this Court cannot conceive the Company obliged, to pay the said two bills of exchange. However the Court do hereby declare, and order, that if on the arrivall of the next ships, from the Bay, it shall be made appear to them, that twenty thousand rupees worth and twenty two thousand rupees worth, of Patana goods, were received by the said President and Councill, of Coja Surhad Israel, as is mentioned in the said bills, pursuant to the conditions of the contract before mentioned, and that the said goods were provided by the Armenians, with their own money, at Patana, and parts adjacent, and for their own accompt singly, and no others, and were laden on the said ships Sidney, and Josia, by the said President and Councill, on the said Armenians' risco, this Court will pay the said two bills of exchange, with interest, from the times they became due.

264
FORT ST GEORGE CONSULTATIONS
28 SEPTEMBER 1708
P/239/84 EXTRACT FROM P. 96

There wanting a Portugueez and Arminian Alderman in the Mayors Court tis agreed that we recommend Francisco Cordoza and Auga Pera to the Mayor and Aldermen to be elected as such.

265
FORT ST GEORGE CONSULTATIONS
8 JANUARY 1708/09
P/239/84 EXTRACT FROM PP. 159-160

This day the Armenians, Moores, and Jentues inhabitants of this place hearing that the Governor[1] designed home upon the Litchfield delivered in a petition (as entered after this Consultation) requesting that he would stay till the business of the phirmaund was negotiated with the Grand Mogull, and all the Councill urged the same, which the Governor could nor would not promise to comply therewith, but take some days to consider thereof, having disposed all his affairs for going home on the Litchfield.

Wee this day sommoned Mr Lewis, Auga Peere, Narrain and Surapau to be with us in Councill to consider of this weighty affair negotiating with the King, who approved of the answer to the letter and what had been done in the preparation of a present to be sent him on his arrivall at Golcundah.

[1] governor was Thomas Pitt

GLOSSARY

The vocabulary words are in the form in which they appear in their respective documents. The numbers in parentheses refer to the documents.

abassees	*abbāsi* (Pers.): silver coin worth 200 dinars (166)
allass	*atlas* (Ar.): silk-satin manufactured in the East (231)
ardass	Persian silk, coarser in quality and cheaper than legee (161)
assidue	arsedine: gold colored alloy of copper and zinc rolled into thin leaf and used to ornament toys, etc. (253)
auroras	aurora: rich orange hue (222)
baftas	*bāfta* (Pers.): woven; coarse to fine quality calico (127)
bancksall	bankshall: warehouse; office of a harbor master or other port authority (178)
birampauts	plain white and dyed cotton cloth (236)
bob	bobtailed horse (199)
bottomaree	bottomry: contract whereby owner or master of a ship borrows money for a voyage at interest or premium, pledging the ship as security (if the ship is lost, the lender loses the money)(181)
brawles	brawl: blue and white striped cloth from Gujarat (162)
buckshaw	probably some kind of container (25)
callenter	*kalāntar* (Pers.): elder or alderman; city official appointed by central government, with functions like those of a mayor in western Europe (177)
candys	*kanti* (Malay.): weight used in India, averaging 500 lbs. (231)
caphilas	*qāfela* (Ar. / Pers.): caravan (30)
carravanseroys	caravansary: an inn in eastern countries where caravans rest at night (129)
carwarr	*kharvār* (Pers.): ass load, about 700 lbs. (54)
cavidall	possibly distortion of caveat: warning, admonition (20)
chapmen	chapman: merchant, trader (168)
chay	deep red dye made from root of an Indian plant (239)
chequeens	also spelled sequins; *zecchini* (It.): gold coin current on the shores of India (177)
chirvadars	*chārvādār* (Pers.): groom; one who stables and hires out horses (199)
chop	*chhāp* (Hind.): official stamp (190)

271

chuppar   *chāpār* (Turk.): mounted messenger or courier (187)

cogiah   also spelled coja and cojah; *khwāja* or *khvāja* (Pers.): a title of
                   respect given in Muslim lands to wealthy merchants (7)

consulage   duties on goods (174)

corset   cossid; *qāsed* (Ar. / Pers.): courier or running messenger (207)

cossaes   plain white muslin (254)

covets   covid: measure of length; its length varied at different places
                   and times, from 36 to 14 inches (36)

coz   *qāz (-beki)* (Pers.): a copper coin, worth variously 5 or 10 dinars
                   (190)

cozzy   *khāss* (Pers.): select, eminent, noble; applied to chief officers of
                   state and the nobles of the court (107)

cuttanee   *kattanee* (Pers.): piece of goods of fine linen or of silk and cotton
                   mixed made in India (195)

demorages   demurrage: a charge for detaining a ship beyond the agreed
                   period of time (112)

doreas   doria; *doriyā* (Hind.): striped Indian muslin (254)

drugg   drug: commodity no longer in demand and thus very difficult to
                   sell (181)

dubashes   *dōbāshī* (Hind.): literally, "man of two languages"; interpreter or
                   commissionaire, employed in transacting business with
                   natives (142)

dullbarre   dalbehera: officer in charge of subordinate collectors of revenue
                   (43)

dustores   dustoor; *dastūr* (Pers.): customary commission payable on cash
                   transactions (225)

eight   silver coin, piece of eight (4)

Ettamen Dowlett   *E'temādu'd-dawleh* (Pers.): chief minister (37)

fardles   fardel: bundle or small pack (16)

fatts   fat: cask, barrel; measure of capacity (65)

fine   end (30)

firmaens   *farmān* (Pers.): royal decree, grant, licence, permit (5)

flam   falsehood (206)

godownes   godown: a warehouse or store for goods in Asian countries
                   (perhaps a metathesis of *dukkān* (Ar.), meaning store) (138)

Gombroone   also known as Bandar Abbas, a port on the Persian Gulf (6)

gruff   coarse-grained (145)

gunnys   *gōnī* (Hind.): sack made of coarse material (231)

hammalls   *hammāl* (Ar.): a burden bearer in Turkey and other countries of
                   the eastern Mediterranean; a porter (199)

husball huccum   *hasbu'l-hukm* (Ar.): literally, "in accordance with the decree"; a
                   phrase used in documents issued by officers of state on
                   royal authority (72)

hypothecation   pledging as security (112)

jams   mixed colors (199)

janazeen	possibly related to *jemadār* (Pers. / Ar.): head of a body of servants; officer of customs or excise (199)
karibauds	cummerbund; *kamar-band* (Pers.): waist-belt (223)
kintlage	kentledge: pig-iron used as permanent ballast (117)
lacres	lac; *lākh* (Hind.): one hundred thousand (134)
lapis lutia	also spelled lapistutia: mineral used pharmacologically and for finishing of copper and zinc (179)
liggee	legee; fine quality Persian silk (161)
lignum	lignea; cassia lignea: an inferior kind of cinnamon (158)
luckhowries	lacowrie: plain white cotton textile from Bengal (247)
magazenes	magazine: warehouse, depot (18)
mammodies	also spelled mamuds; *mahmūdi* (Pers.): Persian silver coin (worth 25 tomans) and money of account (181)
mand	*mān* (Pers.): weight used in India and Western Asia, varying in value; in Safavid Iran, the Tabriz *mān* weighed about $6\,^1/2$ lbs., the Royal *mān* twice as much, i.e., about 13 lbs. (4)
meggardone	possibly distortion of *moqaddam* (Ar.): a headman, leader and, by extension, representative of a community (40)
moody	modi: steward, chandler (106)
mounzells	*manzel* (Ar. / Pers.): a halting place, stage of a journey, a day's ride (26)
mulmulls	*malmal* (Hind.): thin variety of plain white muslin (254)
murrey	purple-red color (222)
musters	muster: sample (4)
necquedah	*nākhudā* (Pers.): ship's master (104)
niccanees	niccanee: medium to coarse quality striped cotton cloth from western India (162)
Nourouze	*Nawruz* (Pers.): New Year's Day in Persia (March 21); first day of solar year (248)
olibanum	aromatic gum resin in the form of yellowish lumps, formerly used as medicine (138)
omras	also spelled omraues; *omrah* (Ar.), plural of *amīr*: lord or grandee of a Moslem court (199)
oppoponga	opopanax: fetid gum resin obtained from the root of a yellow flowered plant, formerly of repute in medicine (133)
paladkeen	palanquin: covered litter borne by means of poles resting on men's shoulders (188)
pautkaes	white and dyed coarse cotton cloth from western India (162)
perpetuanoes	perpetuana: durable English woollen cloth (81)
piggs	pig: oblong mass of iron from the smelting-furnace (212)
pishcashes	*pishkash* (Pers.): present, offering (53)
popinjayes	popinjay: bright shade of green (222)
poze	weighing (4)
primenirys	præmunire: to bring before the courts; to prosecute (204)
purwauna	*parvāna* (Pers.): written order, pass, license or permit (236)
qtg	also spelled qt: containing; amounting to (179)
quz	*gaz* (Pers.): a measure of length, approximating a yard, but varying regionally; here it may be assumed to be the royal

yard (201)

quz shaw   *gaz-e shāh* (Pers.): royal (cloth-)yard, standardized at 90 cm (201)

raddars   *rāhdār* (Pers.): road-guard (189)

rashes   rash: a smooth textile fabric made of silk or wool (87)

ratteens   ratteen: thick twilled woollen cloth (179)

refuge   variant of refuse: dross; worthless but still saleable (62)

rogom   *raqam* (Pers.): royal grant confirming specific trading privilege
                  (189)

ruinass   *rūnās* (Pers.): madder; dyestuff, red root from Ardabīl area (183)

sal armoniac   sal-ammoniac: ammonium chloride (138)

samanaes   shamiana; *shāmiyāna* (Pers.): striped calico, possibly used for
                  awning or canopy (5)

sapan wood   wood yielding a red dye; also known as brazilwood (97)

sapetto   *sabad* (Ar. / Pers.): basket (25)

sayes   say: woollen cloth of fine texture (179)

seare   also spelled seer; *sir* (Pers.): weight varying in different parts of
                  India or a measure of capacity (35)

shabandar   *shāh-bandar* (Pers.): literally, harbor-king; port officer, often also
                  head of customs (18)

shahees   *shāhī* (Pers.): a small silver coin (4)

shaloones   shalloon: closely woven woollen material (179)

shatir   also spelled shoter and shotter; *shāter* (Ar. / Pers.): a running
                  footman, courier, runner (7)

shellack   shellac: purified lac resin with dye extracted, chiefly used in
                  varnishes, polishing and sealing waxes (117)

sheraffs   *sarrāf* (Ar. / Pers.): money-changer, moneylender, or expert
                  employed to detect bad coins (15)

sovaguzzes   medium quality white cotton cloth from Gujarat and Broach
                  (162)

Spahan   also spelled Spahaune, Spahawn, Aspahaune, Ispahaune,
                  Ispahan; modern spelling, Isfahan: the then capital of Persia
                  (7)

stamel   stammel: coarse woollen cloth, usually dyed red (36)

sticklack   sticklac: crude form of resin, a substance secreted by a scale
                  insect and used chiefly in the form of shellac (117)

Swakin   possibly port of Suakin on the Red Sea (94)

swissea   probably swiss: any of various fine sheer fabrics of cotton made
                  in Switzerland (195)

tapseils   tapsail: medium quality striped cotton cloth from Gujarat (162)

teeth   (slang) ivory (68)

tillett   tillet: coarse cloth used for wrapping textile fabric and garments
                  (81)

tokassy   probably related to *takāzā* (Ar. / Pers.): demand, requisition;
                  process of debt collecting (149)

tomands   *tumān*   (Pers.): a sum of 10,000 dinars (4)

trankey   *trānkeh* (Pers.): small vessel used in pearl-fishery in the Persian
                  Gulf (176)

vackelles   also spelled vukkel, vuckell, vuckeelle; *vakil* (Pers.): an agent or

	representative especially of a person of political importance; a minister, envoy, or ambassador (47)
vadaw	*vādā* (Pers.): giving back, returning; contract for fixed term, or agreement especially for the payment of money at a stipulated period (243)
virine	probably riverine (10)
woormeseede	wormseed: various plants, or their dried flower heads, used to treat intestinal worms (47)
yaupungees	probably pongee; *pŭn-chī* (Chin.): soft unbleached kind of Chinese silk (255)
zadwick	also spelled zadiack; *sad-yak* (Pers.): one per cent, one of the customs dues on imported goods (209)
zerbasses	also spelled zerboff; *zarbāf* (Pers.): gold weave, i.e., brocade silk or gold brocade (25)

APPENDIX

1. Select quotations from European travellers' accounts

Cited from

de Bruyn, Cornelis, *Travels into Muscovy, Persia and Part of the East Indies*, London, 1737.

Chardin, Sir John, *The Travels of Sir John Chardin into Persia and the East Indies*, London, 1686. Argonaut Press edition, 1927; with an introduction by Sir P. Sykes. Dover edition, 1988.

Fryer, John, *A New Account of East-India and Persia, in Eight Letters ... Being Nine Years Travels, Begun 1672 and Finished 1681*, London, 1698.

Herbert, Sir Thomas, *Some Yeares Travels into Africa and Asia the Great*, London, 1677.

Tavernier, Jean Baptiste, *The Six Voyages ... through Turkey, into Persia and the East Indies, for the Space of Forty Years*, London, 1677.

de Thévenot, Jean, *The Travels of M. de Thévenot into the Levant*, London, 1687. Gregg edition, 1971.

de Tournefort, Joseph Pitton, *A Voyage into the Levant*, London, 1718.

On New Julfa

The City of *Ispahan* hath also great Suburbs, where many Persons of Quality live. The best built, most beautiful and richest of all, is the Suburbs of *Giolfa* [Julfa], that lies beyond the River of *Senderu*, and the Walls of its Gardens being near that River; in this Burrough or Suburbs live the *Armenians*, whom *Schah Abbas* the first, transplanted thither, after he had ruined a Town of that Name in the Upper *Armenia*; And they thought fit to give this new Habitation the Name of their ancient Town and Countrey, to preserve the memory of it ... [de Thévenot, Part II, p. 79].

* * *

Zulpha [Julfa] ... is so much encreas'd for some years since, that it may now pass for a large City, being almost a League and a half long, and near upon half as much broad. There are two principal Streets which contain near upon the whole length, one whereof has on each side a row of *Tchinars*, the roots whereof are refresh'd by a small Channel of Water, which by a particular order the *Armenians* bring to the City, to water their Gardens. The most part of the other Streets have also a row of Trees, and a Channel. And for their Houses, they are generally better built, and more chearful than those of *Ispahan* [Tavernier, Bk. IV, Ch. VI, pp. 157-8].

* * *

Old *Julfa* [old section of New Julfa] is much larger than all the other districts put together, and contains near two thousand families, of which are those of some of the most wealthy, and most considerable merchants ... [de Bruyn, Vol. I, Ch. XLVI, p. 225].

On Armenian Merchants and Foreign Trade

Trading is a very honourable Profession in the *East*, as being the best of those that have any Stability, and are not so liable to change. ... The Name of Merchant, is a Name much respected in the *East*, and is not allowed to Shop-keepers or Dealers in trifling Goods; nor to those who Trade not in foreign Countries: 'Tis allow'd only to such as employ Deputies or Factors in the remotest Countries: And those Men are sometimes rais'd to the highest Ranks, and are usually employed in Embassies [Chardin, p. 279].

* * *

... He [Shah Abbas I] brought into the Capital City a Colony of *Armenians*, who were a Laborious and Industrious People, and had nothing in the World when they came there; but in the space of thirty Years they grew so exceeding Rich, that there were above threescore Merchants among them, who, one with another, were worth from an hundred thousand Crowns, to two Millions, in Money and Merchandize [Chardin, p. 139].

* * *

... [T]he *Mahometans* are not the greatest Traders in Asia, tho' they be dispers'd almost in every Part of it ... Wherefore in *Turky*, the *Christians* and *Jews* carry on the main foreign Trade: And in *Persia* the *Christians* and *Indian Gentiles*. As to the *Persians* they Trade with their own Countrymen, one Province with another, and most of them Trade with the *Indians*. The *Armenians* manage alone the whole European Trade ... [Chardin, pp. 280-1].

* * *

The *Armenians* at this day are the greatest travellers East and West of any *Asiaticks*: desire of gain and affectation after novelties inducing them: Albeit indeed the advantage they have in their scituation, so near neighbouring the Seas *Caspian, Euxine, Mediterranean* and the *Palus Meotis* [Sea of Azov], give them more than ordinary encouragement; and whence it comes, that at this day the generality more incline to Merchandize than *Mars*, notwithstanding that the *Turk, Tartar* and *Persian* are oft causlesly quarrelling with them; and that the *Turk* and *Persian* by turns domineer over them [Herbert, pp. 158-9].

* * *

The Commerce of *Persia*, as in all other Kingdoms, consists of the Country and Forraign Traffick. Only with difference, that the Country Trade is in the hands of the *Persians* and *Jews*, the forraign Traffic in the hands of the *Armenians* only ... [Tavernier, Bk. V, Ch. XII, p. 229].

* * *

... [T]he Armenians trouble themselves with nothing but Trade, which they follow with the utmost Attention and Application. They are not only Masters of the Trade in the Levant, but have a large Share in that of the most considerable Places in Europe. They come from the farthest Parts of Persia to Leghorn. Not long since they settled at Marseilles. There are many in Holland and England. They travel into the Dominions of the Mogul, to Siam, Java, the Philippine Islands, and throughout all the East ... [de Tournefort, Vol. II, p. 291].

* * *

... [T]he *Armenians* being skill'd in all the Intricacies and Subtilties of Trade at home, and travelling with these [goods] into the remotest Kingdoms, become by their own Industry, and by being Factors of their own Kindreds Honesty, the Wealthiest Men, being expert at Bargains wherever they come, evading thereby Brokeridge ... [Fryer, p. 263].

* * *

At length those *Armenians* became so exquisite in Trade, that several of them have left Estates of two, some twenty thousand Tomans. But the richest among them was *Cotgia*, or Monsieur *Petrus*, who left forty thousand *Tomans* in coyn'd Money, besides his Horses, Furniture, and Lands in the Country, his Jewels and Plate; all which are never reckon'd a Merchant's Estate, but only the ready Cash with which he trades. *Cotgia Petrus* was very much esteem'd for his Charity, and the great Church which he built, which is a kind

of Co[n]vent, with a Bishop and Monks. Nor is the fair Market-place, all
environ'd with Shops, a little beholding to his Generosity [Tavernier, Bk. IV,
Ch. VI, p. 159].

On Armenian Language and Interpreters

The Language of the *Armenians* is either vulgar or learned: the learned
is only us'd by the Ecclesiasticks, in reference to their Religion. They write like
us, from the left to the right, having found out peculiar Characters about four
[sic] years since. They have three Languages very natural to them, which
however are very different: the *Armenian*, which is their ancient Country-
speech, which they have preserv'd from Father to Son; the *Persian*, which is the
Language of the Country where they live; and the *Turkish* of which they make
very much use in course of Trade. ... There are some *Armenians* speak *Italian*
and *French*, as having learnt it in Europe ... [Tavernier, Bk. IV, Ch. VI, pp. 159-
60].

* * *

They [the Armenians] have sumptuous Houses, Enriched either by
being Merchants, or Interpreters to Foreign Ministers, they being addicted to
Learn Languages ... [Fryer, p. 269].

2. Facsimile of a letter written by an Armenian merchant[s?] in the vernacular to the directors of the English East India

Company

(Only the opening and closing portions of the four-page letter are shown here. E/3/53 ff. 393-394v.)

INDEX

1. NAMES OF ARMENIAN MERCHANTS (KHOJAS)

Given the many difficulties in transliterating the corrupt version of Armenian merchants' names into English, we present them here as they appear in the documents.

A

Bauger Aghame 194
Coja Ahmud 178
Coja Arabett 39
Aved Auga (or Avid) 261, 262
Coja Auvaite (later Mahmoud Osaine) 177
Coja Malleer Auwannoes 263
Zachary D'Avatick 241
Johannes De Avid (or de Aved) 261, 262
Gogebeck de Aviett 241

B

Cogee Auga Beague 47
John Bell (or Jonne Belly) 67, 71
William Bell 60
Agnozar De Bogdasar (or Agdozar de
    Bogdazar) 262

C

Calendar family 161, 229, 230
Calendar de Calendar (or Callendar) 212,
    218, 226
Coja Auga Pere Calendar (or Callendar,
    Aga Perir Calendar, Age Pere
    Calender, Aga Pere Callender, Aga
    Pera Callendar, Aga Pirir, Augau
    Peree, Augau Peerce, Aga Peeree,
    Auga Perir, Auga Peere, Auga Perey
    Kalentar, Agapery Callendar,
    Augapery, Aga Pera, Auga Pery, Auga
    Pera) 134, 135, 146, 151, 152, 156,
    167, 168, 173, 175, 176, 181, 182, 186,
    195, 204, 210, 212, 215, 217, 218, 219,
    226, 228, 231, 235, 238, 240, 243, 246,
    250, 252, 257, 259, 264, 265
Coja Aveatick Calendar (or Callender,
    Avetick, Avadcik, Avedick, Auvatick,
    Amatike, Avalike, Avatick Callendar,
    Aveatik Callandar) 62, 74, 77, 153,
    179, 180, 183, 188, 189, 192, 199,
201, 202, 203, 204, 206, 221, 222,
    223, 235, 237, 243, 246
Coja Coha Geogas Calendar (or
    Callendar, Coja Googas Calendar or
    Callendar, Gogas Callenter, Gogas
    Callendar) 165, 166, 171, 174, 179,
    180, 183, 187, 188, 189, 190, 191,
    192, 193, 197, 199, 200, 201, 202,
    203, 204, 205, 206, 207, 208,   209,
    210, 211, 213, 214, 215, 216, 217, 220,
    221, 222, 223, 224, 227, 228, 229, 230,
    244
Jaco Jacob Calendar (or Callender) 62,
    65, 67, 71
Coja Panous Calendar (or Calender,
    Callendar, Coja Panous Kalendar,
    Cojee Panure Callendar, Coja Fanos
    Callender, Coja Panous Callender,
Coja Fannusc, Auga Pa Panous Callender)
    111, 112, 115, 116, 118, 122, 126,
    133, 134, 136, 145, 149, 152, 157,
    165, 166, 167, 168, 170, 171, 173,
    174, 175, 179, 182, 203, 207, 209,
    215, 216, 217, 222, 223, 224, 226,
    231, 232, 235, 238, 240, 242, 243,
    246, 247, 263
Coja Caleust   248
Carrabett   28
Mirza Caune   236
Chiragos   68
John Christian   52
Gregory de Cirkis   194
Coldarente family   216
Coja Gregorio   245
Coja Gregory Coldarente (or Caldarentes,
    Gregore Caldarence   165, 166, 171,
    174, 179, 180, 183, 187, 188, 189,
    190, 191, 192, 193, 197, 199, 200,
    201, 202, 203, 204, 205, 206, 207,
    208, 209, 210, 211, 213, 214, 215,
    216, 217, 220, 221, 222, 223, 224, 227,
    228, 229, 230, 244
Coja Hoan Coldarente (or Caldarentes,
    Coldarence) 165, 166, 171, 174, 179,

281

2. Statements made about Armenians and Armenian merchants by the English East India Company and its factors

5, 10, 14, 23, 31, 34, 45, 48, 49, 54, 79, 107, 116, 121, 122, 127, 131, 136, 140, 146, 148, 151, 184, 192, 199, 204, 206, 209, 220, 225, 235, 244, 245, 246

3. Capacities in which some Armenians assisted the English East India Company

Contractors for silk 22, 109, 110
Interpreters 60, 133, 161, 166, 190, 205
Shipowners 163
Settlers and workers in English East India Company towns, e.g.,
Fort St George, Bombay 112, 126, 139, 143, 163, 184, 239
Soldiers (to be offered employment as) 143, 239
Trading partners 112, 115, 116, 117, 118, 120, 121, 123, 124, 125,

4. References to rival trading European nations

5. Place Names

6. *Names of English East India Company officials, factors, and representatives*

7. Exports to Asia

8. Imports to England

9. Ships

10. Currencies, weights, and other measurements

www.ingramcontent.com/pod-product-compliance
Lightning Source LLC
Chambersburg PA
CBHW080925050426

42334CB00045B/1